CELESTIAL NAVIGATION

IN THE GPS AGE

REVISED AND EXPANDED

John Karl

Cover design by Rob Johnson, www.johnsondesign.org
Editing and book design by Linda Morehouse, www.webuildbooks.com
Revised edition editing by Rebecca S. Bender
Painting on inside front cover, oil on canvas,
    "Captain Sumner Discovers the Celestial Line of Position"
    by John H. Karl

Printed in the United States of America
First Edition, Third Printing
ISBN 978-0-939837-75-7

Published jointly by

Paradise Cay Publications, Inc.
P. O. Box 29
Arcata, CA 95518-0029
+1-707-822-9063
+1-707-822-9163 (Fax)
www.paracay.com
info@paracay.com

Celestaire, Inc.
4609 E. Kellogg Drive
Wichita, KS 67218
+1-316-686-9785
+1-316-686-8926 (Fax)
www.celestaire.com
info@celestaire.com

To Karen, shipmate in life

FOREWORD

Celestial navigation is seen today in a different light than before GPS became affordable and ubiquitous. Yes, it is the only manual way to navigate at sea (and one needs a manual way to do anything important at sea). But when celestial navigation was required, it seemed like work. Now it can be fun. It frees us from keys and menus that only serve to summon the expertise of some programmer and lets us do something by ourselves—with our own two hands.

Today's navigator needs not be an expert anymore, but should know enough to use celestial fixes as a backup. Of course he may take the study further, and therein lies the enticement. Celestial navigation is easy to start, but can take time and study to master. Activities like this have always held lasting fascination (some would say addiction) for us.

John Karl's book lets the reader proceed in this way. A line of position is put on a chart after only 40 pages. But then he will take you further in understanding the science and art of celestial navigation than any other book I have seen. *Celestial Navigation in the GPS Age* is a mixture of history, math, and rational explanations that the reader may sample as desired.

This may not be the only book to which you are exposed in learning celestial navigation, but it certainly should be one of them.

—Kenneth Gebhart

Kenneth Gebhart is the author of the Celestaire Navigation Catalog. He is well known for his celestial navigation seminars given at most sailboat shows.

PREFACE

Browsing in a bookstore when I was about nine, I bought a book called *American Practical Navigator* by someone I had never heard of—Nathaniel Bowditch. I guess it caught my eye because I was interested in boating and sailing. Wading through Bowditch was tough going at that age. I had never heard of logarithms or haversines. But I did learn something about navigation and astronomy, which, looking back, I think was responsible for leading me into science.

After this encounter, Bowditch sat on my bookshelf for many years. Then while studying physics at The Massachusetts Institute of Technology, I stumbled upon a sextant in a pawn shop, bought it, and dragged out Bowditch again. This time I understood a whole lot more about astronomy and mathematics. Living in Marblehead made practice sights easy from the top of a hill near Red's Pond where I could view the sea horizon. At that time, I practiced sight reductions using the log-haversine method taught in Bowditch.

Much later during my sporadic 60-year sailing experience, and after retiring from a physics career, I left Hawaii headed for San Francisco on a 34-foot cutter. Having not sailed blue waters for some years, I discovered how very simple sight reduction has become with a scientific hand calculator. Moreover, I realized that all modern sight reductions are based on just one math formula, expressed in two ways. How very simple modern methods have become. Nonetheless, the practice of celestial navigation has changed little over two hundred years, for navigators still use ancient tables of logarithms or trig functions. Yet today, I can't imagine a scientist or engineer who, faced with evaluating a simple trig expression, would reach for a set of tables rather than a hand calculator. After all, handheld scientific calculators have been available for over three decades and now cost under $10.

Recently I had the opportunity to teach celestial navigation aboard the three-masted S/V *Denis Sullivan* on a leg from Milwaukee to Montreal. That experience inspired me to write this book. My goal as a scientist and teacher is to explain away the mystery of the subject in a simple fashion while covering the fundamental concepts better than ever before. My goal as a sailor is to provide the simplest possible sight reduction procedure that can be reliably and comfortably used at sea, using either calculators or tables—that's a personal choice. My tenet is that modern developments can be used to provide deeper understanding and much broader applications of celestial navigation than the old ways.

You and I will take a navigator's celestial journey that integrates the old with the new, tables with calculators, celestial navigation with GPS. We'll assume no mathematical sophistication. Rather, we'll first explain how anyone can easily do the math as a series of instructions, perfunctorily punching designated calculator buttons. Then we'll explain how the math relates to sight reduction tables, how to use the tables, and their advantages and disadvantages. We'll not develop the math; we'll explain it. It tells us everything. Listening to its simple story, we'll gain deep insight that will stick with us long after the celestial voyage ends with the rattle of the anchor chain. By understanding the mysteries of the heavens, we'll rapidly arrive at a simple, cheap, memorable, and reliable sight reduction procedure.

Please read with care, interest, and pleasure, and come away with a useful, if unusual, skill.

— John Karl, February 2007

Preface to the 2nd Printing

In addition to making minor corrections and improvements from the first printing, I've adopted a more conventional notation for the azimuth angle from true north, changing it from Az to Zn. Also, beyond these slight improvements, the section on Polaris sights has been revised, and the sextant arc error tables in Appendix G have been made more convenient.

— John Karl, February 2009

Preface to the Revised and Expanded Edition

My goal in writing this book has been to present an accurate, clear, and comprehensive treatment of celestial navigation, while simultaneously enabling the reader to work a sight reduction after reading only a few pages. This edition now provides an even shorter and easier path to useful celestial navigation by introducing simple tabular methods first. Then optional calculator methods follow for those wishing to take full advantage of their flexibility.

The section on stars has been expanded to include a more complete treatment of using H.O. 249 (UK's NP 303) for stars, which then leads into planning sights of stars and planets, along with details on star-planet identification and viewing. The chapter on special sights has been expanded to treat three different Polaris sight reductions, speed corrections for meridian shots, and even obtaining LOPs without a sextant. Chapter 10 now includes more discussions on constructing plotting sheets; using universal plotting sheets; making three different kinds of running fixes; performing compass deviation checks at sea; and using ocean pilot charts for planning voyages.

Finally, in several places it was possible to improve the discussion by making minor changes, adding more detail, and more figures.

— John Karl, October 2010

ABOUT THE AUTHOR

John Karl is a physicist, artist, pilot, writer, and sailor. He learned celestial navigation 50 years ago and has been sailing for 60 years. Karl has sailed the Pacific Ocean, East Coast, Great Lakes, Florida Keys, and the Bahamas. He has taught celestial navigation workshops at the University of Wisconsin and aboard the 3-masted S/V *Denis Sullivan*. He has also conducted marine research in the Great Lakes on the R/V *Salmo* and in the Gulf of California aboard the R/V *Melville*.

ACKNOWLEDGMENTS

It's a pleasure to gratefully thank my son, John, for his critique of early versions of the manuscript; Michael Briley for providing proper-motion star data; James McKee for his helpful and productive review of the manuscript; and my two publishers for their commitment to celestial navigation.

I'm also very appreciative of the time and effort of Stan Klein, Geoffrey Kolbe, and Steve Whiteside in reviewing the book and suggesting valuable changes and corrections for the 2nd printing. George Huxtable not only was very helpful suggesting corrections, but also helped me improve the way stellar aberrations are handled in Appendix G.

CONTENTS

1

INTRODUCTION

The Heroic Era

Nearly 500 years ago an adventurous fleet of five ships sailed from Spain to explore the world, searching for a western route to the Spice Islands. Three years later, after losing one ship to the rocks, one to a storm while at anchor, one to desertion, one to fire, and losing the fleet commander, Ferdinand Magellan, to death at the hands of Philippine natives, the ship *Victoria* returned home, having completed the first circumnavigation of the world.

This was the heroic era of discovery, and with the advent of the mariner's quadrant and primitive declination tables, it was the dawn of a new age of celestial navigation. From the ancient Babylonians and Greeks through all the centuries of exploration and discovery, studies of the heavens have been awe-inspiring, satisfying, and useful. Early transatlantic explorers such as Eric the Red and Leif Ericson must certainly have navigated by the heavens.

Improvements in celestial navigation aided great sea expeditions to follow, such as those of Vasco de Gama and Sir Francis Drake. By the time Captain James Cook commanded the *Resolution* on his 1772–75 around-the-world expedition (aided by his infamous first mate, Mr. William Bligh), John Harrison had developed his H-4 chronometer, Hadley had designed the modern sextant, and the *Nautical Almanac* had been published for six straight years. The era of modern celestial navigation had begun.

One heroic example of celestial navigation in the twentieth century is the open-ocean voyage made by Ernest Shackleton during his 1915 Antarctic expedition. After the *Endurance* was crushed by pack ice in the Weddell Sea, Shackleton and his company of 28 men and three lifeboats drifted on Antarctic ice floes for well over a year. When they finally reached open water, they navigated to Elephant Island near the northern tip of the Antarctic Peninsula. After setting up camp there, Shackleton selected a four-man crew—which of course included his navigator, Frank Worsley—and set out in a jury-rigged 22-foot lifeboat for the whaling station on South Georgia Island, a speck in the mid South Atlantic some 800 miles away. Fighting ice and bad weather all the way, they used infrequent breaks in overcast skies to navigate safely to help in just twelve days. Shackleton saved his entire exploration party—by using celestial navigation.

For many centuries scores of similar episodes dramatized the role of reliable and practical methods of celestial navigation. The sailors who risked their lives at sea not only found adventure for themselves and inspired the stories we now enjoy, but they also discovered new worlds and new trading partners that changed cultures, governments, and economic conditions for everyone—forever.

The Story Retold

Today we study celestial navigation because of a romantic attachment to world history and to those who went to sea before us. We learn celestial navigation because it's a universal icon of the sea, because it's as interesting as the heavens are, because we love the independence it provides, and because we'll need it when our GPS fails. It's soul food, practical soul food. When we practice the noble shipboard ritual of the sextant, we join a bit of the lives of the seafaring heroes that have gone before us. We live the heritage.

Why do we still find our place on earth by searching the stars? Because a good sea story is always retold. Celestial navigation has served adventurous mariners from before Cook's time; it continues to serve today's commercial, military, and blue-water pleasure sailors.

Yet much of celestial navigation has changed little over the past 200 years—for instance, tabular methods are still used—but there have also been modern developments: Inexpensive and portable computer technology has given us PCs, laptops, handheld calculators, and the Internet. The quartz digital watch and the GPS have changed the practice of celestial navigation at home and at sea.

We'll explain all of this, the old and the new, the simple and the more advanced, beginning . . . well, at the beginning.

The Fundamental Idea

An Ancient Observation

In 150 B.C. the Greek astronomer and mathematician Eratosthenes observed that at noon, near the time of the summer solstice, vertical posts at Alexandria cast the sun's shadow on the ground, whereas at Syene (now called Aswan) in southern Egypt, it was reported that posts there cast no shadows at that time, and that the sun illuminated the entire bottom of a well, the sun being directly overhead at that time and place. Eratosthenes's belief that the earth is spherical, and that the sun's rays are essentially parallel to one another, enabled him to make inferences and calculations that were truly elegant in their simplicity and great power—the power to offer proof that the earth is spherical and, moreover, to measure its circumference.

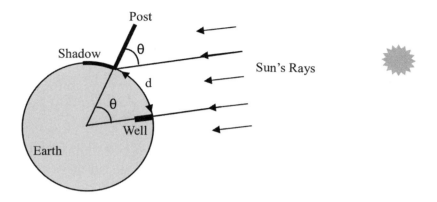

Figure 1.1 The sun casts a shadow of the post at Alexandria, but the sun is directly overhead the well at Syene. The arc distance d along the surface of the earth, between the post and the well, is proportional to the angle θ, the angle between the sun's rays and the post.

Eratosthenes's ideas are shown in Figure 1.1, where we see the spherical earth, the well at Syene, the post with its shadow at Alexandria, and the parallel rays of the sun. We label the angle between the sun's rays and the vertical post θ (the Greek letter theta that Eratosthenes might have used and that is still widely used for angles today). In the figure we draw the radial line that extends from the center of the earth through the post at Alexandria. The sun's rays make the same angle θ with this radial line, both at the center of the earth and at its surface. The arc distance d is the distance along the earth's curved surface from Alexandria to Syene. We see that it's a fraction of the earth's circumference.

Now, looking at the angle θ at the center of the earth, we discover a fact of central importance to celestial navigation: the arc distance d is proportional to the angle θ. For example, if θ is halved, d is halved also. This means that d equals some constant times θ. Or we say in equation form that d = constant x θ. In fact we can see, as Eratosthenes did, that when θ goes all the way around the earth (that is, when θ = 360°), d must equal the circumference of the earth. Therefore, the constant must be equal to the circumference of the earth divided by 360°. We can see this by writing this statement in the language of equations. It then becomes

$$d = (\text{circumference} / 360°) \times \theta \qquad (1.1)$$

Now when we substitute 360° for θ, the equation says that d equals the circumference, confirming that the equation must be right.

Eratosthenes determined θ from the ratio of the post's height to its shadow. Then using the known distance from Alexandria to Syene for d (about 500 miles), he solved Equation 1.1 to calculate the earth's circumference. He got 25,500 miles. That's within 2.5 percent of today's value of 24,874 miles, not bad for over two millennia ago.

The Key Concept

Eratosthenes's observation in the form of Equation 1.1 leads to the kernel of celestial navigation. It tells how far an observer is from the spot directly under the sun by measuring the angle θ. Substituting $2\pi R$ for the circumference, and using for the earth's radius today's mean value of 3440 nautical miles (nm) gives

$$d = (2 \pi\, 3440 / 360°)\, \theta = 60.04\, \theta$$

or, rounding off we get

$$d = 60 \text{ nm} \times \theta \qquad (1.2)$$

Equation 1.2 is *the guts of celestial navigation.* It shows that by measuring the sun's angle from the vertical we can determine our distance from the spot directly under the sun. Moreover, each degree simply represents 60 nm, or *each minute of angle is one nautical mile.* (Because of geodetic complications, the nautical mile is not defined exactly equal to 60 per degree. However, rounding it off to 60 nm is sufficiently accurate for most purposes.) The spot "directly under the sun" is called the sun's *geographical position,* its GP. If your shadow falls completely within your feet, you're standing at a unique spot on earth, the sun's GP. Of course this unique spot is constantly moving because of the earth's rotation. But that inconvenience is handled by the *Nautical Almanac*, which lists the sun's GP for every second of universal time, UT. (UT used to be called GMT, Greenwich Mean Time.) So by measuring the angle θ, you can determine your distance from the GP, and the almanac tells you where the GP is located.

The Mariner's Angle

At sea, because of a ship's motion, it's difficult to measure the angle from the vertical that Eratosthenes used. Instead, navigators use a marine sextant to measure the angle from horizontal, as shown in Figure 1.2. This angle of the sun's rays from the horizontal is called the sun's *altitude* (H). It's just 90° minus the angle of Eratosthenes. In celestial navigation, we call the Eratosthenes angle the *co-altitude* (coH).

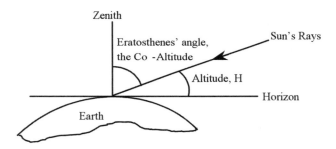

Figure 1.2 The sextant measures the sun's altitude H, which is the angle the sun's rays make with the horizon at the observer's location.

The two angles are just complements of each other, meaning simply that their sum is 90°.

We've focused on the sun because of its role in the history of navigation, and because the sun is the most available and easiest body to shoot. We'll delay the treatment of the moon, planets, and stars until we have a practical, understandable, and reliable sun-sight reduction procedure. Then with only a few perfunctory modifications we'll be able to handle the other bodies. (Actually, potential celestial navigators who are only interested in the bare-bones fundamentals couldn't be faulted too much for limiting their skills to sun sights.)

So far we've been able to visualize the problem in two dimensions because Alexandria is almost due north of Syene, with the plane of Figure 1.1 containing the earth's center (that is, Alexandria, Syene, and the earth's center all lie in a plane). For more general cases, we need to extend our thinking to three dimensions.

The Equal-Altitude Line of Position

The 3-D Picture

For a complete understanding of navigational astronomy we must picture the sun's rays in relationship to the spherical earth as shown in Figure 1.3. By neglecting tiny geometrical considerations (as Eratosthenes did), we can consider the sun's rays coming from a point on the sun's disk to be parallel to one another. The altitude and co-altitude of a sun's ray at one observer's location are shown at the top of the figure. And all the other observers shown in the figure are located where they see identical altitudes. With a little 3-D perception, we can see

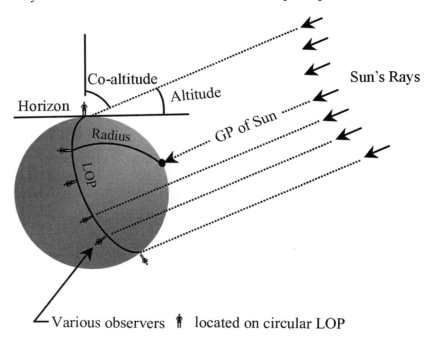

Figure 1.3 All the equal-altitude points lie on a circular LOP with radius equal to the co-altitude, centered on the geographical position of the sun.

that these equal-altitude locations must lie on a circle centered on the GP, with a radius equal to the observer-GP distance, as shown in Figure 1.3. This radius is the same distance d as in the example of Eratosthenes, and as we have just seen in Equation 1.2, its length is just 60 nm times the co-altitude. This equal-altitude circle is called a line-of-position, or LOP, determined by the measured sextant altitude.

One way to visualize the geometry of this circular LOP is to imagine a cylinder (sailors might imagine a beer can) open on both ends. The parallel line elements of the cylinder represent the parallel rays of the sun. Now visualize a sphere, such as a tennis ball, fitted to the end of the cylinder to represent the earth. The circle where the can's rim contacts the tennis ball is the equal-altitude LOP on earth.

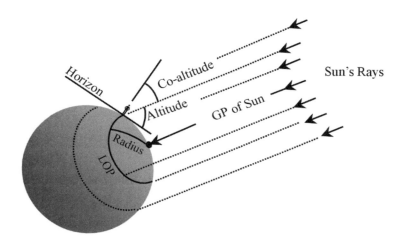

Figure 1.4 This observer sees a higher altitude than the observer does in Figure 1.3. Therefore this observer is closer to the sun's GP, and consequently the radius of his LOP is smaller.

The altitude measured by each observer depends on his distance from the sun's GP. Figure 1.4 shows an observer who sees the sun's altitude higher than do the observers in Figure 1.3. The closer the observer is to the GP, the greater the observed altitude, and conversely, the farther away the observer is, the less the altitude. If you're at the sun's GP, it's directly overhead, and therefore its altitude would be 90°.

If you're a quarter of the earth's circumference away from the sun's GP, its altitude is zero, and you're seeing a sunrise or sunset. Furthermore, since all observers who are the same distance from the GP will measure the same altitude, a single altitude measurement doesn't tell them where they are. Rather, it tells them that they're somewhere on this line of *equal-altitudes*—that is, on the sun's LOP.

It's important to emphasize that the radius of this circular LOP is the *great-circle* distance from the GP, while the LOP itself is a *small circle*. The plane of a great circle passes through the center of the earth, whereas the plane of a small circle does not. The meridians and the equator are examples of great circles; parallels of latitude are examples of small circles.

Since one sextant observation just tells us we're somewhere on the LOP, we need more information to fix our location on this circle. This information can take on many different forms, such as a bottom

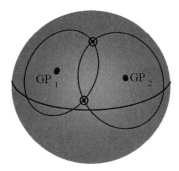

Figure 1.5 When plotted on the earth's surface, two celestial LOPs usually intersect at two locations so widely separated that selecting the right one is not a problem.

sounding, a radar bearing from shore, or even another celestial LOP. In the latter case, shown in Figure 1.5, these two circular LOPs would usually intersect in two places, leaving an ambiguity between two possible observer locations. However, as we'll see later, these locations are almost always so far apart that ambiguity is not an issue. The intersection of two LOPs of any kind is called a *fix*, as discussed later in

Chapter 10. Determining fixes is a simple matter of plotting intersecting LOPs, for now our emphasis will be on determining celestial LOPs.

And determining a celestial LOP is simple—conceptually, at least. Here's a summary of what we'd think of doing: (1) We measure the sun's altitude with a sextant and subtract it from 90° to get the co-altitude, (2) then we get the sun's GP from the *Nautical Almanac* using the time of the sight, and (3) finally, we plot a segment of the circular LOP with its center at the GP and its radius equal to one nautical mile per minute of co-altitude. So we're done; our ship is somewhere on that LOP. This process of converting our celestial observations into latitude and longitude (or other information) useful to the navigator is called *sight reduction*.

We've now described our first sight reduction procedure, but there's a catch. The LOP's small circle with its corresponding great-circle radius forms a 3-D figure in space, as you remember from Figure 1.3. And we do know everything there is to know: the location of the LOP and its radius. The question becomes, exactly how do we use this knowledge of the 3-D figure to plot the LOP on a flat chart?

To clearly and correctly explain the resolution of this question, we approach it in stages. First we show the limitations of mechanical methods; then in Chapter 2, after some preliminaries, we discuss methods that lead to understanding the fundamental nature of the solution (they're also useful computer techniques). Following that, Chapter 3 explains the St. Hilaire method, the standard method of sight reduction used in celestial navigation since 1875.

The Limitations of Mechanical Methods

Since the small-circle LOP and its great-circle radius occupy three dimensions, they could be properly represented mechanically, on a globe. By measuring the circle's radius along a meridian (using the fact that each minute of latitude is one nautical mile), then using the sun's GP (which we get from the sight's time and the almanac) as the center of the circle, we strike an arc of the LOP in the geographical region of interest. The result is exact, in principle. But to read off the resulting ship's position to the same accuracy as the common 1:1,000,000 marine chart, we would need a rather large navigator's station—it would have to house a 42-foot globe.

Since a globe of this size is pretty unreasonable, why not use a flat chart? Because flat charts present two problems. First, just as with the globe, the chart would have to be unreasonably large. For example, an observed altitude of 20° would have a co-altitude of 70°. Multiplying the 70° by the 60 nm per degree gives 4,200 nautical miles for the observer-GP distance. The smallest scale charts (i.e., ones that cover the largest area) used in marine navigation cover about 600 miles. So our GP is way off the chart.

We might propose charts of much smaller scale, say ten times smaller covering ten times the distance. They would cover some 6,000 miles. But that produces another problem. The plotting resolution and the associated accuracy of locating the LOP would drop tenfold. So the chart size is a problem, *but it's not the fundamental problem.*

The second limitation of the mechanical method is more severe—it is fundamental: Even with an unreasonably large chart, it's impossible to accurately plot the large great-circle radius of the LOP on a flat surface to the accuracy required in marine navigation. The small-circle LOP with its great-circle radius is a 3-D figure in space that cannot be directly transferred to a flat surface. A spherical orange skin cannot be pressed flat without breaking it.

It is true, however, that for sufficiently high altitude sights we can stretch the orange's skin, i.e., plot the LOP approximately. With an altitude greater than 80°, and its co-altitude less than ten degrees, the GP-LOP distance becomes a manageable 600 miles or less. Then in this case of smaller GP-LOP distances, the error of measuring and plotting the great-circle distance on a flat chart starts to become acceptable. But the great majority of sights have lower observed altitudes whose larger GP-LOP distances can't be accommodated. So we're forced to conclude that, except for very high altitudes, using mechanical methods with flat charts, regardless of size or scale, will not work.

The Only Solution

Since mechanical methods will not work, we'll have to use mathematical ones—we'll have to use our heads rather than our hands. We needn't delve into the development of this mathematics, known for over 1,000 years, but we will use it. By doing so, we can correctly transfer the known 3-D information into coordinates that can be plotted on a flat chart. We rightfully expect that we can *calculate* any point we wish on the LOP because we know everything there is to know: its radius, the location of its center, and the necessary mathematics. Therefore we can use this information to plot the points of the all-important equal-altitude LOP. The next chapter explains how we can plot these LOPs.

2

PLOTTING THE
CELESTIAL NAVIGATION LOP

If the mathematical formula $d = 60\,nm \times \theta$ is the guts of celestial navigation, then geometry is its heart and soul. In this chapter we'll discuss the geometry necessary to describe the locations of the observer and the celestial body, both relative to the North Pole. These three locations form corners of a very important triangle, called the navigation triangle. We'll see that understanding the geometry of this triangle enables us to do everything, such as plotting the coordinates of the all-important celestial LOP, computing fixes from two altitude observations, and finding time from lunar-distance sights. We first describe the coordinates used to define this triangle. Then, without delving into any math, we explain how knowledge of this triangle is used to plot celestial LOPs, enabling us to fully appreciate subsequent discussions of modern methods.

Coordinates

Latitude and Longitude

Navigational astronomy uses the familiar spherical coordinates of latitude and longitude, with some minor name differences for celestial bodies. Furthermore, navigational astronomy takes the view that all celestial bodies rotate around the earth, a view expressed by Pope Urban VIII during the 1633 Roman inquisition. Galileo was forced to accept this same view under the threat of a heresy conviction—and possible death. We use the earth-centric view, not because of a death threat, but because it gives a useful, simplified description of celestial astronomy that's necessary for practical navigation. We're not astronomers—we're navigators.

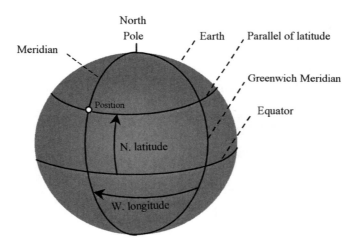

Figure 2.1 Latitude is reckoned north or south of the equator. Longitude is reckoned east or west of the Greenwich meridian.

The coordinates of a point on earth are given by the familiar latitude and longitude as shown in Figure 2.1. Latitude is designated north or south of the equator. To distinguish between these two in the equations that follow, we'll use a positive sign for northern latitudes and a negative sign for southern latitudes. For longitude, measured east or west from the Greenwich prime meridian, we'll designate east as positive and west as negative.

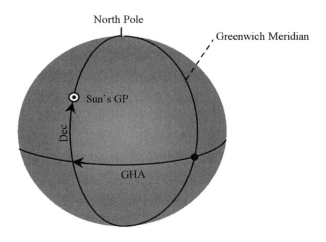

Figure 2.2 Declination is analogous to latitude, and Greenwich Hour Angle is analogous to longitude.

Greenwich Hour Angle and Declination

The coordinates used to describe the location of celestial GPs are analogous to latitude and longitude. But now they're called *Declination* (d, or Dec) and *Greenwich Hour Angle* (GHA) respectively. See Figure 2.2. Declination, like latitude, is reckoned from the equator, positive north and negative south. Greenwich Hour Angle is the same as longitude, but it's reckoned from the Greenwich meridian *westward* from 0° to 360°. It's called an hour angle because it also can be measured in hours, according to the earth's rotation of 360° per day, or 15° per hour. We can either say, for example, that Papeete is 150° west of Greenwich or that its GHA is 10 hours. Thus it's easy to convert from degrees and minutes of arc to hours, minutes, and seconds of time (or the reverse). But we must be careful to distinguish between minutes of time and minutes of arc, and likewise between seconds of time and seconds of arc. (For example, four seconds of time equal one minute of arc.) Declination and GHA are tabulated for every second of Universal Time (UT) in the *Nautical Almanac* for all the bodies used in celestial navigation. The almanac solves the problem of using celestial bodies while they're moving.

The Navigation Triangle

Sun and Earth

Now that we can locate the ship and the sun by their coordinates, we'll see how these coordinates relate to each other. Since both sets are described relative to the earth, we can place them on the same drawing, as shown in Figure 2.3a. Next, to make explanations efficient, we need to introduce some terminology. The first new term, discussed at greater length below, is the *local hour angle*, labeled LHA in the figure. It's the polar angle between the ship's meridian and the sun's meridian. Next, recall that the angle from directly overhead of the observer to the sun's GP is the co-altitude (coalt, or coH). So we draw this co-altitude, in Figure 2.3b, by connecting the ship's location and the sun's GP with a great-circle arc. Now just as the co-altitude is the complement of the altitude (remember, that's 90° minus the altitude), we introduce the *co-declination* (codec) as the complement of the declination and the *co-latitude* (colat) as the complement of the latitude. Thus the co-declination is the great-circle arc from the sun to the North Pole, and

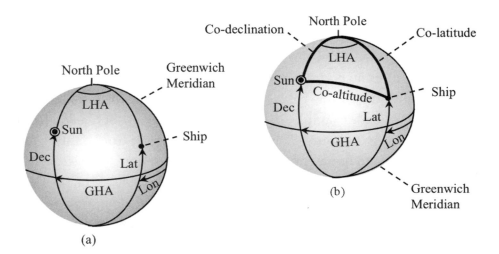

Figure 2.3 (a) Coordinates of the sun and of the ship superimposed. **(b)** Connecting the ship and sun locations with the co-altitude completes the navigation triangle, shown in heavy line. The co-declination and the co-latitude are the other two sides. The LHA is one of the three included angles in the navigation triangle.

the co-latitude is the great-circle arc from the ship to the North Pole, as shown in Figure 2.3b.

Next we see, as shown in Figure 2.3b with a heavy line, that these three coordinates—the co-altitude, the co-declination, and the co-latitude—describe a triangle on the earth. These three lines form the *navigation triangle*, which is of primary importance to sight reduction. Since this is a triangle on the surface of a sphere, understandably it's called a *spherical triangle*. And just like a triangle in plane geometry, it has three sides, three apexes, and three included angles. But that's about where its similarity ends, for spherical triangles have very different properties than the more familiar plane triangles. Not surprisingly, *the navigation triangle is the road map to most sight reductions*. After all, it relates everything of interest: the ship and sun locations, their coordinates, and the all-important co-altitude, which is the radius of the celestial LOP.

We now have two sets of terms that describe the navigation triangle. First we have the familiar altitude, latitude, and declination, used when talking about navigation in general. Second, we have their complements, the co-altitude, co-latitude, and co-declination, which are necessary when talking about the actual sides of the triangle. One is just 90° minus the other, so we can easily switch from one coordinate to the other. Furthermore, for our convenience, this switch is automatically included in the sight reductions themselves.

In the following, it's important to know a few things about the navigation triangle. It has six parameters: three included angles and three sides. The sides are all great circles. *If any three of these six parameters are known, the other three can be calculated.* Knowledge of either the LHA or the longitude is equivalent, because they're simply related via the GHA of the sun, which we know from the almanac. All the relationships among the angles and sides of the triangle are well known to mathematicians; the ones relevant to celestial navigation are given in Appendix A, where they're formulated in terms of the more familiar variables: declination, latitude, and altitude. It might be of interest to the curious, and a relief to the timid, to know that in this book *we will use just one of these equations*, in only two different ways, for all of our sight reductions. This one equation, discussed first in Chapter 5 (also see Appendix A), correctly gives us everything we need. We needn't worry about how it's derived, we just need to use it, and Chapter 5 will show how.

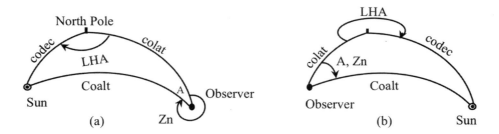

Figure 2.4 The three sides of the navigation triangle are the great circle arcs, the colat, the codec, and the coalt. Two of the three angles are the LHA, and the azimuth angle A. In (a), the GP is west of the observer, and Zn = 360 – A. In (b), the GP is east of the observer, and Zn = A.

The Local Hour Angle

In addition to the three sides of the navigation triangle, we'll now discuss some details of three angles that are also major players in the game. These angles, shown in Figure 2.4, are the LHA, introduced earlier; the *azimuth angle* (A); and the *azimuth* (Zn). By convention the LHA, the polar angle between the sun's meridian and the observer's meridian, is measured westward from the observer's meridian, ranging from 0° to 360°. The LHA gets its name because it's an hour angle of the sun, but it's reckoned from the observer rather than from Greenwich. A schematic diagram, viewed looking at the North Pole in Figure 2.5, shows how the LHA is related to the observer's longitude and the sun's GHA. By inspecting the figure, we see that west longitudes are subtracted from the GHA to get the LHA, and east longitudes are added to the GHA to get the LHA. Therefore, by using the convention that east longitudes are positive and west longitudes are negative, we can cover both cases by simply writing

LHA = GHA + longitude (2.1)

When needed, 360° is added to or subtracted from the result of Equation 2.1 to bring the LHA into the 0° to 360° range. This is the convention used in sight reduction tables, but we'll see later that the sign of the LHA and multiples of 360° are irrelevant in computer calculations. As an exercise in applying the 360°, you might redraw

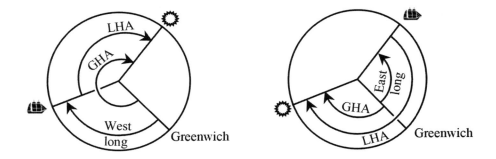

Figure 2.5 Diagrams, looking at the North Pole, show how to combine GHA with either west longitudes or east longitudes. Both cases are covered by using LHA = GHA + long, with the convention that west longitudes are negative, and east longitudes are positive.

Figure 2.5 (left) with the west longitude greater than the GHA, and Figure 2.5 (right) with the sum of the east longitude and the GHA greater than 360°. Then you can see how Equation 2.1 also correctly gives the LHA because it's always measured westward toward the sun. Drawing these will increase your understanding and confidence.

Azimuth Angle and Azimuth

The other two angles are also shown in Figure 2.4. The azimuth angle A is the angle between the co-latitude and the co-altitude. Since it's an included angle, it's always less than 180°. The mariner's azimuth, Zn in the figure, is quite different. It's also an angle between the co-latitude and the co-altitude, but it starts at 0° at true north and ranges clockwise around to the co-altitude. So its range is 0° to 360°. It's the familiar angle that compasses use, but in celestial navigation Zn is always reckoned from true north, not magnetic north. The relationship to the angle A can be seen in each case in Figure 2.4. When the sun is west of the observer as in (a), the LHA is less than 180° and Zn = 360° − A. When the sun is east of the observer as in (b), the LHA is greater than 180° and Zn = A. Sight reduction tables use a different azimuth angle, called Z, which is also simply related to Zn. More detail is given in Chapters 5 and 12.

Three Plotting Methods

The Concept

In preparation for understanding all of our following discussions, and without actually using the mathematical relations for the navigation triangle, we'll take a verbal walk through three different approaches to plotting LOPs. This vicarious stroll through direct ways of plotting the equal-altitude LOP will enable us to better appreciate the standard, although seemingly indirect, method of sight reduction of the next chapter.

The whole purpose of sight reduction is to determine the latitude and longitude of some points on the all-important equal-altitude LOP. And we observed above that it takes three known parameters of the navigation triangle to solve for any of the other three parameters. But after taking a celestial observation, we only know two pieces of information: the sun's altitude and its declination. (We don't know the LHA because that requires knowledge of the ship's longitude.) Thus we're stumped; we are short one piece of information.

However, if we use these two known sides of the triangle (the co-altitude and co-declination) and *assume* a value for a *third* parameter, we can solve for the latitude and longitude of an LOP point that has that third parameter's value. Thus by varying this third parameter and keeping the co-declination and co-altitude constant, we can trace out the latitude and longitude coordinates of points on the LOP, plotting them on a chart. This is how we use the navigation triangle to solve the 3-D geometry problem that cannot be solved using a flat chart.

Plotting Variables

Since the third navigation-triangle parameter suggested above varies along the LOP, giving us sequential points on the LOP, we'll call it a *plotting variable*. Any third variable will work. We could, for example, pick the longitude as the plotting variable. Then using three known quantities, LHA (from this assumed longitude and the sun's GHA), observed altitude, and declination, we could calculate the latitude of that point on the LOP (Equation A.9 of Appendix A). Repeating this process for selected longitudes traces out the LOP by its latitude and longitude coordinates; that's just what we want.

Also we could do the reverse: we could pick the latitude as the plotting variable. Then we would calculate the longitude of a point on the LOP from this latitude, declination, and observed altitude. (The resulting longitude comes from calculating the LHA, and using the known GHA of the sun, see Equation A.10 of Appendix A.) This is exactly what Captain Thomas H. Sumner did while commanding the *Cabot* off the coast of Ireland on 18 December 1837. He was bound ENE up St. George's Channel, closed-hauled with a SE wind making Ireland's coast

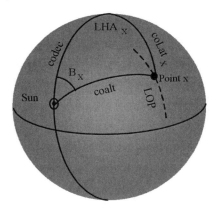

Figure 2.6 The location of any point x on the LOP is calculated from the sun's declination, observed altitude, and the bearing from the sun to that point.

a lee shore. By calculating the longitude for three separate latitudes, he unwittingly demonstrated that it's possible to compute, and hence to plot, the location of any number of points on the LOP. Fortunately, the plotted LOP fell right in line with his course, which safely guided him to Small's Light (off the coast of Wales) for his landfall.

A third plotting variable (which is particularly convenient for computer use) is the bearing angle B_x between the sun's meridian and the co-altitude arc. As shown in Figure 2.6, it's the bearing from the sun to a variable point x on the LOP. By incrementing B_x, we can conveniently sweep out any desired arc of the LOP. Now, the three known quantities are the co-altitude, the co-declination and the variable angle B_x. So we increment B_x, computing the latitude and longitude of points that trace out the LOP. For interested readers, Exercise 1.22 shows how the equations are developed for this method.

It's significant to point out that all of these methods produce the same exact LOP (i.e., within the accuracy of the almanac and the altitude measurement). There are no assumptions—no assumed position, no dead reckoning. Using any of these three methods, we can *easily and exactly* plot the latitude and longitude coordinates of the LOP on any map projection. To emphasize this point, Figure 2.7 shows the result of using the B_x method to map out a portion of an equal-altitude LOP in the region of the Great Bahama Banks with the sun's GP located at a declination of N17.8° and a GHA of 82°. In this example, the observed altitude was a rather high 83°, demonstrating the curvature of the circular LOP.

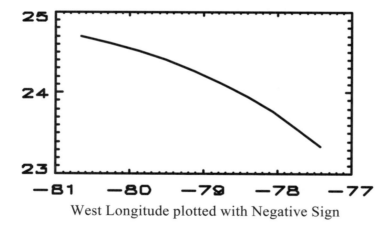

West Longitude plotted with Negative Sign

Figure 2.7 An 83-degree equal-altitude plot, using the bearing Variable B_x to calculate points that trace out the LOP in the region of the Great Bahama Banks.

This discussion shows that there is no problem calculating the points on an equal-altitude LOP directly and accurately. But now the question becomes, what is the best approach, given limited computational facilities at sea? What is the minimum number of points needed: ten, three, or even two? Ten points, such as we used in Figure 2.7, can be easily plotted using a computer. But if we wanted to trade off accuracy for less computation, what would be the absolute fewest number of points? Clearly one point won't do, but two points do determine a straight line.

That's the concept behind the sight reduction method universally used today to reduce the computation so it can be done by hand: Use the known mathematics of the navigation triangle to solve the great-circle problem, then reduce the calculation load by using a straight-line approximation to the LOP.

3

THE ST. HILAIRE METHOD

The Captain's Idea

The adoption of the above ideas to the simplest straight-line LOP approximation has two requirements. First, the calculation of the straight line's position should be as simple as possible. And second, we want a convenient way to specify the geographical region where we wish to plot a segment of the LOP.

The method published by Captain Marq de Saint Hilaire in 1875 meets both of these requirements simultaneously. It finds the bearing and distance from *any* preselected point, defining the region of interest, to the nearest point on the LOP. It then uses that result to simply draw the straight-line approximation tangent to the LOP at that point. It's appropriate to call this preselected point a reference point, because it refers to the geographical area where we want to plot the LOP. This point can be anywhere, such as near a ship or sometimes elsewhere. Traditionally this point has been called the *assumed position*, the AP of the ship. But that's misleading; we are not assuming the ship is there—to the contrary, we usually expect it is not. In fact, Chapter 10 discusses the desirability of plotting special LOPs that are far away from any ship. Specifying the AP simply says that we want the portion of the

LOP that is nearest to this location.

For continuity with the rest of the celestial navigation world, as a concession to history, and against all sensibility, we'll continue to call this point the AP. But please remember, in spite of using this misnomer, we are making no assumptions.

Specifying this AP by its latitude and longitude gives three known quantities in the navigation triangle: the LHA (from the AP's longitude and the sun's GHA), the latitude of the AP, and the declination of the sun. As Figure 3.1 illustrates, we use these three known quantities to solve two navigation triangle equations, one for the *azimuth angle* A (the bearing to the GP), and the other for the altitude that would be observed at the AP, called the *calculated altitude*, H_C.

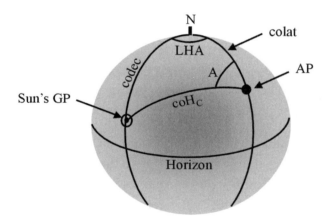

Figure 3.1 The St. Hilaire method uses the navigation triangle to calculate the altitude at AP from the LHA, latitude, and declination. (The equivalent variables coH_C, codec, and colat identify the triangle in the drawing.)

At first this may seem like a strange approach, but we can see its advantage by imagining the equal-altitude contours in the vicinity of the AP, as shown in Figure 3.2. Because we calculate the altitude at the AP, by definition the H_C contour passes through this AP. But the actual *observed altitude* (H_O) is on the LOP of our ship, labeled the H_O contour. The contours increase in altitude toward the GP and decrease away from it, as we saw earlier. The great-circle distance *along the azimuth line* between these two contours is just their altitude difference in minutes of arc, or equivalently, in nautical miles. If we step off the difference $H_O - H_C$ (measured in one nautical mile per minute of arc) along the azimuth line from AP, we arrive at point A shown in Figure 3.2. This distance is called the *intercept distance*. In this example, A is toward the GP, which means that the observed H_O must have been greater than H_C. Of course, with a different AP, the intercept might be away from the GP.

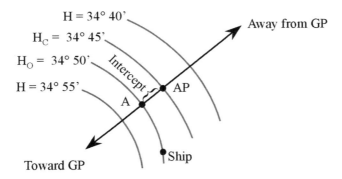

Figure 3.2 Equal altitude contours. The AP is on the calculated contour, H_C. Both point A and the ship are on the observed altitude contour, H_O.

So now we have calculated one point on the LOP. And there is no approximation; point A is, for all practical purposes, exactly on the LOP. We could call this point a "PLOP," that is, a point on the LOP. Therefore, as in the tracing methods discussed in the previous chapter, we could repeat this process with as many different APs as we wish, finding other PLOPs all along the LOP, as shown in Figure 3.3. This shows that specifying the AP contains no assumptions; rather, it functions exactly like the plotting variable we discussed in the previous chapter. That is, it specifies where we wish to calculate a PLOP. It specifies our area of interest. Recall that Sumner took a different approach: he specified a latitude of interest, then asked what longitude his LOP crosses that given latitude. The St. Hilaire approach asks for the location of that unique PLOP which is closest to the AP. This is very handy because this one special PLOP allows a very convenient approximation to the LOP without further computation.

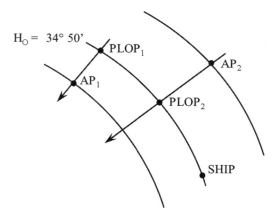

Figure 3.3 Any AP, such as AP_1 and AP_2, will lead to intercepts that give points exactly on the ship's LOP, such as $PLOP_1$ and $PLOP_2$. Selecting more APs and calculating more PLOPs will trace out the LOP exactly.

The Straight-Line Approximation

We know the straight-line LOP that is nearest to the AP must pass through point A. And we know the LOP must be perpendicular to the azimuth because the azimuth is directed toward the sun's GP, in the direction of the greatest rate of change of altitude. So the direction of the least rate of change of altitude, i.e., constant altitude, is perpendicular to the azimuth line. Thus without further calculation, the straight-line LOP is drawn at right angles to the azimuth at point A, as shown in Figure 3.4, as an approximation to the true LOP. That's it. That is the St. Hilaire method (sometimes called the *intercept method*).

The Error

The St. Hilaire method uses mathematical spherical geometry to cover the great majority of the GP-AP distance; this permits mechanical plotting to cover the remaining small intercept distance. The accuracy of locating point A in the above figures is dependent only on the tiny error in approximating the great-circle intercept distance as a rhumb line (i.e., a straight line on a Mercator map) over small distances. In practice this error is always negligible, as demonstrated in Exercise 3.5 in Chapter 13.

Another error arises from the divergence of the straight-line LOP from the true curved LOP. This depends on the distance along the LOP from the tangent point, A, compared to the curvature of the LOP. For altitudes less than about 75°, the curvature of the LOP is small enough that this discrepancy is acceptable. And the curvature of the LOP is even less for lesser altitudes. For example, with a 80° altitude, a point along the straight-line LOP 60 nm from the point of tangency lies 3.0 nm from the true LOP. But if the altitude is reduced to 75°, and the distance along the LOP reduced to 15 nm, the error drops to only 0.1 nm. This is the justification of the straight-line approximation for altitudes that aren't too great.

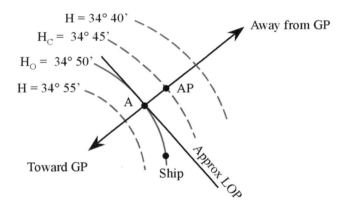

Figure 3.4 The straight-line approximation to the true LOP. The ship lies near, but not exactly on the approximate LOP.

We can see from Figure 3.4 that this error in the straight-line approximation lessens as the AP approaches the ship's actual position. So it's natural to use the ship's estimated position for the AP, as is usually done in direct calculation methods. Many tabular methods use whole degrees of latitude and LHA in order to permit tables of reasonable size. This whole-degree limitation can increase the intercept distance by as much as 40 miles. Even so, the error in approximating this larger intercept distance by a rhumb line is still quite small.

We'll make different choices for the AP, depending on circumstances.

For example, using estimates of factors such as speed, course, and drift to plot our current position is called *dead reckoning,* DR. We might select an AP latitude and longitude in whole degrees nearest to our DR position in order to make calculations easier, plotting easier, or less confusing (as in a two- or three-body fix). Or, as we'll see in Chapter 10, we can have an occasion to use an AP that is completely unrelated to our current DR position. In all cases it's important to remember the distinction between the DR position and the AP. The DR position is an estimate of our current location. The AP is a reference point of our choice, specifying where we want to compute a section of the celestial LOP. In selecting the AP, we assume nothing.

When Captain Sumner first plotted his three points from three different assumed latitudes, he seemed to be surprised that they fell on a straight line. That revelation is curious because it should have been obvious to contemporary mathematicians, such as Nathaniel Bowditch, that over short distances the small-circle LOP would plot as a straight line at any reasonable scale. Nevertheless, because Captain Sumner seems to have been the first to realize this fact, the straight-line LOP approximation is sometimes called the *Sumner line.* He published his result in 1843, six years after his discovery. Eight years later he was committed to an insane asylum, where he spent his remaining 26 years. It's never been reported that his mental state was due to practicing celestial navigation.

Why St. Hilaire?

We have seen that chart size, chart scale, and large GP-observer distances are not the problem in plotting celestial LOPs. Using a plotting variable and sufficient calculations, an LOP can easily be plotted exactly— with no assumptions and no approximations. Sumner's use of three latitudes to calculate three points on the LOP is an example. Indeed, we could use Sumner's method to compute just two points and connect them with a straight line to get an approximate LOP. That's exactly the same amount of work as calculating the two equations in the St. Hilaire method.

So then, why St. Hilaire? *The answer is, the St. Hilaire method is insensitive to problems that plague other methods that use only two solutions to the navigation triangle.* The Sumner method runs into problems with LOPs of certain orientations. For example, a selected parallel of latitude might not even intersect the LOP, giving no solution at all. See Exercise 1.24. On the other hand, the B_X plotting method is robust, but it requires solving at least five equations, two for each of two points' latitude and longitude for the straight-line LOP, plus a fifth to specify where to start the plot. St. Hilaire accomplishes all we need with just two solutions.

In Summary

The St. Hilaire method selects a reference point, the AP, in the area of interest, usually near the ship and the true LOP. It combines this point's longitude with the sun's GHA to get the LHA. Then it takes this LHA, the sun's declination, and the AP's latitude to calculate H_C and Zn. The difference between H_C and the observed sextant altitude H_O measured in minutes of arc becomes the intercept distance in nautical miles. Finally, the bearing to the sun is plotted on a chart at the AP position, and the intercept distance is stepped off either toward or away from the GP, depending on whether H_O is greater or less than H_C. At that point, the LOP is drawn at right angles to the azimuth. This short paragraph states the entire St. Hilaire sight reduction method. The remainder is details: looking up altitude corrections and the GP in the almanac, and solving the navigation triangle.

4

The Nautical Almanac—An Overview

The Daily Pages
The Altitude Corrections

Before we can actually work up a St. Hilaire sight, we'll take a (perhaps welcomed) interlude from the intricacies of the navigation triangle. We need to familiarize ourselves with the *Nautical Almanac* in order to locate the body's GP, which is in constant motion while we're trying to get a bead on it. Published annually since 1767, the almanac tabulates the GHA and declination of all the celestial navigation bodies, as well as the necessary altitude corrections to be applied to sextant readings. It is published by the U.S. Government Printing Office, and jointly by Paradise Cay, Inc. and Celestaire, Inc. It's widely available directly from these publishers and from marine supply stores.

The Daily Pages

We'll be using the excerpts from the almanac in Appendix C. Most of the almanac consists of daily pages, as they are called (three days per page). For a sight reduction of the sun, we simply look on the daily pages for the sun's declination and GHA at the date and UT hour *before* the sight, and then add an increment to the GHA for the sight's extra minutes past the tabulated hour. This increment simply accounts for the earth's rotation of one degree in four minutes (360° in 24 hours). A convenient table at the back of the almanac, called *Increments and*

Corrections, gives these additional degrees and minutes to add to the GHA.

Later on, we'll use these pages for the moon, Venus, Mars, Jupiter, Saturn, and the first point of Aries (a reference point discussed later), used to determine the GHA of stars. In some cases, we'll need an interpolation factor, called *v*, used for interpolating the GHA for the moon and planets. Similarly, another factor, called *d*, is used for interpolating the declination of the sun, moon, and planets. All together, these tables give the GHA and declination for every second of UT to the nearest 0.1' of arc. The extraction of the declination and GHA data from the almanac will be discussed in more detail in the individual sight reductions that follow.

Of less interest, the daily pages also list supplemental data, such as the Local Mean Times (LMT) of sunrise, sunset, twilight, moonrise, and moonset *at the Greenwich meridian* for various latitudes. The sun's equation of time, the time of meridian passage of the sun and moon, and their semidiameters are also included.

The Altitude Corrections

Three altitude corrections must be applied to the sextant altitude to get the *observed altitude* (H_O). These are discussed in more detail in Chapter 9. The first correction, the *index correction*, is not listed in the almanac because it depends on the individual sextant whose arc normally doesn't read exactly zero at zero altitude. The next two corrections are listed in the beginning of the almanac on page A2, and on a special tear-out card that can be used as a handy bookmark. The first of these is the *dip correction*, which is due to looking past the true horizon because the observer's eye is above sea level. This means the sextant altitude is always too great, so this correction is always subtracted. The index and dip corrections are applied to the *sextant altitude* (H_S) to give the *apparent altitude* (H_A).

The correction applied to H_A to give H_O is the *altitude correction* (sometimes called the main correction). For the sun and the moon, it consists of two parts: the effect of refracting (bending) light in the atmosphere and the body's semidiameter. The almanac conveniently combines these two effects into just one correction. The sun's altitude correction is listed on the left side of the almanac's page A2. The stars and planets are listed separately because their semidiameter is not needed in the altitude correction, which in their case only includes the effects of refraction. Additional tables, for correcting H_A to H_O for altitudes below 10° for the sun, stars, and planets, are on page A3. Because the moon is so close to the earth, a separate table, on page xxxiv, must be used to correct lunar altitudes to get H_O.

We'll see how to use this almanac data as we discuss the individual sight reductions; further description of the tables and their use is given in the almanac. The almanac is also very handy for learning about navigational astronomy from a careful study of its data, as we encourage you to do via the exercise set in Chapter 13. For now, we'll concentrate on the essentials of sight reduction.

5

Sun Sight Reductions

We're now equipped to work up sights. First we'll address sun sights, then we'll explain the slight modifications required to treat all the other navigational bodies. A sight reduction has four distinct components: (1) applying altitude corrections, (2) obtaining the declination and GHA from the almanac, and finding the LHA from the AP longitude, (3) solving the navigation triangle for H_C and Zn, and (4) plotting the LOP from the intercept distance and azimuth. Since the last step is rather perfunctory, we'll concentrate on the first three. And of the first three tasks, computing H_C and Zn contains the biggest mystery for most beginners. So we'll treat it in detail using two different methods: first by looking up H_C and Zn in *sight reduction tables*, then by *direct computation* using a handheld calculator.

In either case, the St. Hilaire method requires obtaining the altitude and azimuth of a celestial body from the body's declination and GHA, using the AP's latitude and longitude. The longitude is added (observing its sign) to the GHA, yielding the LHA. Thus the three inputs to the triangle problem are the latitude, declination, and LHA. Whether from tables or by direct calculation, the solutions originate from the same relatively simple equations. Using tables, we look up somebody else's solutions; using the calculator, we calculate them ourselves. First we'll discuss using H.O. 249 tables, then the H.O. 229 tables, and finally the calculator. The United Kingdom's version of H.O. 249 is Nautical Publication NP 303 (also called Air Publication AP 3270), and the equivalent to H. O. 229 is their Nautical Publication NP 401.

Using Inspection Tables

The sight reduction tables list solutions (for altitude and azimuth), with H.O. 249 and H.O. 229 functioning nearly the same. Both tables tabulate all three inputs (latitude, declination, and LHA) to whole degrees; this limits the otherwise unfeasible number of entries to a useable size. This works perfectly with the St. Hilaire method, which allows flexibility in selecting the AP: The AP latitude can be selected in whole degrees, and the AP longitude can be selected to make the LHA whole degrees. But there's no such freedom for the declination, so we're left with the necessity of interpolating the tabulated altitude and azimuth for the declination minutes between its tabulated whole degrees. In practice, the major difference in the two tables is that H.O. 249 was developed for air navigation, tabulating to 1.0′, while H.O. 229 was developed for marine navigation, tabulating to 0.1′ of arc. Sight Reduction Tables H.O. 249 are published in three volumes. Volume I is for the major navigation stars, while volumes II and III are for the solar system bodies, the sun, moon, and planets. This means that volumes II and III only include declinations up to 29°. So they can't be used for stars with larger declinations. For our sun-sight examples we'll use Volume II (see Appendix D), which covers latitudes 0° to 40°. There's more discussion on the tables in Chapters 11 and 12.

The Worksheet

Introducing a worksheet to formally organize our work will aid the explanation, and help avoid mistakes. Some navigators view them with a condescending eye, but I see them as a neat solution to the organization task. They remind us of the required steps, allowing us to focus on the more interesting aspects of navigation. In practical experience, many navigators jot down data as if they were using a worksheet when they are not. They probably learned by using worksheets—and they benefited from it.

Sun Worksheet for H.O. 249	
Body	H_s
Date	index
UT	Dip _____
	H_A
DR Lat	Alt _____
DR Lon	H_O
AP Lat	
AP Lon	GHA
	m s _____
Dec	GHA
	AP Lon _____ (E+, W−)
H_{TAB}	LHA
Corr _____ d	
H_C	
H_O	
	Zn

Figure 5.1 A sun sight reduction worksheet using direct calculation.

We'll start with a simple worksheet that is limited to sun sights, and then in the next chapter introduce a universal worksheet, good for all sights. Blank copies of these worksheets are available in Appendix E. Figure 5.1 shows a blank worksheet for a sun shot to be worked up with sight reduction tables (either H.O. 249 or H.O. 229). Reducing a sight is as easy as filling in this simple worksheet. The worksheet is partitioned off to reflect the three tasks mentioned above: The top-right block contains the three sextant corrections discussed in the previous chapter. The left and right blocks second from the bottom contain the almanac declination and GHA data along with the LHA calculation. And the bottom two blocks contain the solution of the navigation triangle, the H_C and intercept calculation being on the left, the azimuth calculation on the right.

Sun Worksheet for H.O. 249		
Body *Sun's Lower*	H_S *59° 33.1'*	
Date *10 May 05*	index *– 1.5'*	
UT *19ʰ 18ᵐ 39ˢ*	dip *– 2.8'*	
	H_A *59° 28.8'*	
DR Lat *N24° 17'*	alt *+ 15 .4'*	
DR Lon *W78° 29'*	H_O *59° 44.2'*	
AP Lat *N24°*		
AP Lon *W78° 34.3'*	GHA *105° 54.5'*	
	m s *4° 39.8'*	
Dec *N17° 48'*	GHA *110° 34.3'*	
	AP Lon *–78° 34.3'* (E+, W–)	
H_{TAB} *59° 18'*	LHA *32°*	
H_C *59° 32'*	*+18' X 48' / 60' = 14'*	
H_O *59° 44'*		
12 Toward	Zn = 360° – 95° = *265°*	

Figure 5.2 The sun sight reduction using H.O. 249.

Now we'll fill in this worksheet with an example of an afternoon sun sight on the Great Bahama Banks, just west of Andros Island. On 10 May 2005, at DR position N24° 17′, W78° 29′, we observed the sun's lower limb to the west at an altitude of 59° 33.1′ at 19:18:39 UT. The eye height above sea level was 8.5 feet. The sextant index correction is –1.5′.

The completed worksheet is shown in Figure 5.2. The top three shaded items indicate the data used to enter the reduction tables. The bottom two shaded values are our final result, the intercept and azimuth. The worksheet is not completed in a sequential left-to-right, top-down fashion, as we would read. Rather, it's filled in as we collect the various required items, letting the worksheet provide the organization. First, in the upper left-hand block of the worksheet, we enter the lower limb of the sun, the time and date. At the same time, we write in the DR latitude and longitude in the next block below.

Altitude Corrections

Since the altitude corrections are completely independent of the rest of the sight reduction, they can be done at any time. I usually do them next. Looking at the almanac excerpts in Appendix C, you can verify the dip and altitude corrections shown in the upper right-hand corner of the worksheet. (For the altitude corrections, we'll maintain the 0.1′ precision that's listed in the almanac and provided on many sextants.)

The GHA and Declination

Now with the almanac still in hand, turning to the daily pages for 10 May 2005 (see Appendix C again), looking down the left-hand column (of the right-hand page) for the sun at 19 hours, and finding GHA = 105° 54.5′, enter that in the middle right-hand block of the worksheet.

And while your finger is still on the 19-hour row, read off the declination of N17° 47.9′, which we mentally interpolate for the 18 min 39 sec past the hour. Since we're now only working to one minute of arc, we'll interpolate the almanac's tabulated declination to the nearest whole minute: The hourly declination change, listed at the bottom of the sun's column (appearing as *d* 0.6′), is used to decide between rounding the 47.9′ portion of the tabulated declination down to 47′ or up to 48′. In the present case, 18 minutes past the hour is roughly one-third of an hour, so the declination changes roughly a third of the hourly 0.6′ increment, or 0.2′. Thus 48′ is the closest whole minute of declination. So we enter N17° 48′ on the worksheet.

Before putting down the almanac, turn to the 18-minute page of the Increments and Correction table in the back (Appendix C). This table gives the adjustment to the GHA for the minutes and seconds past the hour ("m s" on the worksheet). Then, looking down the left-hand column for the extra 39 seconds, find 4° 39.8´ in the column labeled Sun and Planets. Write this 4° 39.8´ in the middle right-hand block on the worksheet right under the GHA. Now close the almanac and set it aside—we're finished with it.

Next, from the DR latitude of N24° 17´ in our example, we pick an AP latitude of N24° for the nearest whole-degree to the DR's latitude, and enter it in the left-hand side of the worksheet.

The LHA

Next, add the tabulated GHA to its minute and seconds adjustment, then combine the GHA and the DR longitude to get the LHA. As we saw in Equation 2.1, add east longitudes to the GHA and subtract west longitudes from the GHA to get the LHA, as the E+ and W– on the worksheet remind us. If the sum exceeds 360°, subtract 360° from it. If the difference is negative, add 360° to it.

The Sketch

At this point, to keep the big picture in mind, I highly recommend making a sketch of the navigation triangle, scaled to the particular sight. In Figure 5.3 you see such a sketch drawn appropriate to this sight. The DR is roughly at the right place with a latitude 24° north of the equator; the sun is drawn in a bit lower, representing its 17° declination. Likewise, the DR's longitude and the sun's GHA are drawn in proper relationship with the sun west of the DR (because its GHA is 110° while the DR's longitude is only W78°) with a LHA that looks like 32°. The sketch immediately shows that the DR longitude should be subtracted from the sun's GHA to get the LHA, agreeing with the (E+, W–) reminder on the worksheet. Also, we verify that the azimuth is to the west, which surely the navigator would be aware of when the shot was taken. These sketches keep the big picture in mind and help us to avoid catastrophic mistakes.

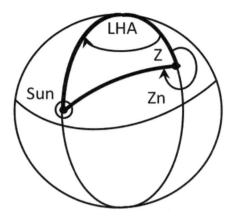

Figure 5.3 A sketch of the sun sight, drawn roughly to scale. With the LHA less than 180°, the GP lies west of the AP, and Zn = 360° − Z.

Using H.O. 249 Tables

Now we're ready for H.O. 249. Since the computed altitude is going to be interpolated for declination, the declination is *always* entered in the tables as the *whole degree part* of the actual declination found in the almanac. So instead of entering the table with N17° 48′ for declination, we enter with N17°.

Thus we enter H.O. 249 (see Appendix D) with the arguments Lat = N24°, Dec = N17°, and LHA = 32°. Being careful to look in the Latitude-Same-Name-as-Declination section (because both are north in our example), we find H_C = 59° 18′, d = +18′, and Z = 97°. On the worksheet we enter the altitude of 59° 18′ as H_{TAB}, the *tabulated* value, because it's not yet the calculated value corresponding to our declination.

Consequently, H_{TAB} is next interpolated to the actual value of declination. Interpolation tables are provided (see H.O. 249, Table 5, Appendix D), but I think it's just as easy to do it yourself (well, only if you have a calculator handy). The *d*-interpolation factor is just the difference between tabulated altitude for 17° declination and for 18° declination. (You can verify this by inspecting the table.) So we add to H_{TAB} the fraction that it changes as the declination increases from 17° to 17° 48′. Thus the correction is +18′ x (48′/60′) = +14′, as shown in Figure 5.2, where we've used the bottom right-hand block as a workspace. Then we carry the +14′ correction to the bottom-left block for addition to H_{TAB}, giving $H_C = 59°\ 32´$. Since H_O is greater than H_C, the intercept is *toward*.

Although the *d*-correction is positive in this example, it can be negative. That is, increasing declination produces a decreasing H_C. The sign of *d* is indicated in the tables, which you can also tell by inspecting the values of H_{TAB} versus declination.

In the bottom-right corner is the azimuth treatment. The *azimuth angle* Z in the tables is not the azimuth from true north, but simple rules for converting Z to Zn are conveniently given at the top and bottom of the left-hand side of each page in the tables. In this case, you find in the tables that $Zn = 360° - Z$ because the LHA is less than 180° and the latitude is north. This azimuth angle Z is an auxiliary angle used to simplify the inspection tables. (We'll see later that direct computation uses a *different* auxiliary angle, called A. Both are simply related to Zn, the azimuth from true north, but by different rules. For interested readers, more detail is also given in Chapter 12.)

Just as with the tabulated altitude, we must also interpolate the tabulated azimuth angle Z for declination. But because we only determine Z to one degree, we can interpolate mentally: The table shows that as the declination increases from 17° to 18°, Z drops two degrees from 97° to 96° to 95°. The middle value of 96° corresponds to a 17° 30´ declination. But our 17° 48´ declination is closer to 18°, so we pick its corresponding Z of 95°. It might seem that we're being too picky by interpolating the azimuth. But at times the difference in azimuth between consecutive declination entries can be ten degrees, leading to appreciable error in the LOP if this interpolation is omitted. Always check the Z tabulated at the next higher degree of declination.

It just remains to plot the intercept toward the sun in the Zn direction and draw the LOP at that point, at right angles to the intercept, as shown in Figure 5.4. If you know your position at the time of the sight, you can compare the two by plotting them on a chart to see how well they agree. However, when using direct computation, to simplify practice you can use the known position (from the GPS, for example) as the AP position, avoiding the extra plotting step. Then the intercept distance would ideally be zero. Any departure from zero is a measure of the sight quality. Under *ideal* conditions, an experienced navigator will usually agree with the known position to within one nautical mile. Under average conditions, expect differences of one to three miles. However, this GPS comparison can't be done with tables because they restrict the AP latitude and longitude to integer degrees. In that case, you need to plot the AP and LOP on a chart and then compare the LOP to your GPS position.

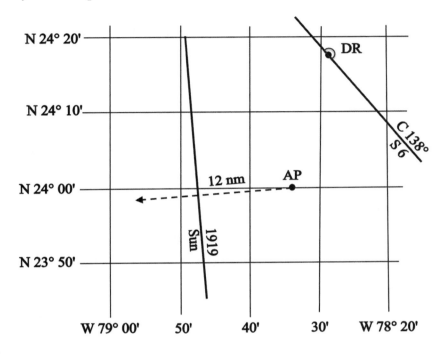

Figure 5.4 A plot of the azimuth and intercept for our sun sight example.

Using H.O. 229 Tables

Sight Reduction Tables H.O. 229 are published in six volumes, each covering 15° of latitude. We use Volume II, covering 15° to 30° latitude, in our examples (excerpts are in Appendix D). Because H.O. 249 was designed for air navigation, it's tabulated to only one minute, implying it's accurate to the nearest minute (an accuracy of ±0.5′). Similarly, with its values tabulated to 0.1′, H.O. 229 seems to imply ten times the accuracy, i.e., to the nearest 0.1′ (or ±0.05′). Unfortunately, that's not the case at all. The best H.O. 229 can do is ±0.2′, which, compared to

H.O. 249's ±0.5´ accuracy, is only marginally better. The price paid for higher accuracy is twofold: First we have to interpolate the almanac's data for the hourly change in the body's declination. And second, fortunately only in some cases, we must use a double interpolation to achieve the full accuracy of the tables.

The declination interpolation is rather easy: While looking at the almanac's daily page for 10 May 2005, at the bottom of the almanac's sun column you'll find the hourly change in declination where it says d 0.6´. Write the 0.6´ increment next to the declination on the worksheet (as shown in Figure 5.5), observing that it's positive because the sun is increasing toward the summer solstice, which can be verified by observing the increasing declinations in the almanac.

Then while you're looking at the 18-minute page of the Increments and Correction table in the back (Appendix C) to get the adjustment for the 39 seconds, look across to the right in the column labeled *v/d corr*^{n}. There you'll find that our *d*-value of 0.6 indicates a declination correction of 0.2´. This correction is written on the worksheet as +0.2 because the declination is increasing. So add this 0.2 to the 17° 47.9´ declination to get the 17° 48.1´ shown on the left side of the worksheet.

The second-order interpolation of H.O. 229, called a double second difference (DSD) is more complicated: but it's only necessary in some cases at high altitudes (above about 60°). When the DSD correction is required, the tables show a dot next to the *d*-interpolation factor. You will find this dot by scanning the H_C column in the tables under the high altitude conditions, such as at small LHAs and nearly equal latitudes and declinations. The introduction to H.O. 229 gives instructions for applying the DSD correction using interpolation tables provided. Even when the indicated DSD corrections are made, the accuracy can drop to ±0.3´. For practicing sight reduction, you might simply avoid this complication by checking the table before the observation at the expected altitude to see if the DSD interpolation will be required. Or you can just accept the loss of accuracy in these rare cases. The DSD corrected altitude is always better than the 1.0´ accuracy of H.O. 249.

Without the second-order interpolation, the two tables function practically the same, but they have their arguments ordered differently: H.O. 229 has LHA page headings, declination in rows, and latitude in columns; H.O. 249 has latitude page headings, LHA in rows, and declaration in columns. (See Appendix D for the H.O. 229 excerpt.) This arrangement means that for the azimuth interpolation you look in the row below, whereas in H.O. 249 we looked in the column to the right of the table entry. Figure 5.5 shows that the sight reduction is nearly identical to the reduction of Figure 5.2, which used H.O. 249. The only difference is the declination interpolation and all work carried out to tenths of minutes.

Body	*Sun's L L*	H_S	*59° 33.1'*	
Date	*10 May 05*	index	*– 1.5'*	
UT	*19^h 18^m 39^s*	dip	*+ 2.8'*	
DR Lat	*N24° 17'*	H_A	*59° 17.8'*	
DR Lon	*W78° 29'*	alt	*+ 15.4'*	
AP Lat	*N24°*	H_O	*59° 44.2'*	
Dec	*N17° 47.9'*	GHA	*105° 54.5'*	
d +0.6	*+0.2'*	m s	*4° 39.8'*	
Dec	*N17° 48.1'*	GHA	*110° 34.3'*	
		AP Lon	*W78° 34.3'*	*(E+, W–)*
H_{TAB}	*59° 17.6'*	LHA	*32°*	
corr	*14.7'*			
H_C	*59° 32.3'*	$+18.3' X 48.1' / 60' = 14.7'$		
H_O	*59° 44.2'*			
	11.9 Toward	$Zn = 360° – 95° = 265°$		

Figure 5.5 Sun sight reduction with H.O. 229.

Using Direct Computation

With the advent of the first digital computers in 1936, the U.S. Hydrographic Office published the first precomputed sight reduction tables, H.O. 214. These were called inspection tables because one simply looks up the altitude and azimuth for a given latitude, declination, and LHA (as opposed to dealing with logarithms). Later H.O. 249 followed in 1947 for air navigation, and the more precise H.O. 229 was produced for marine use.

Now in this GPS age, with the widespread use of handheld

calculators, programmable calculators, computers, and spread sheets, many navigators are abandoning these tables in favor of doing their own calculations. There are advantages and disadvantages to each approach, as discussed in Chapter 11. It's a personal choice. But it's nice to learn and practice both methods, preferably never settling for just one. Advantages of direct computation include better accuracy, no required interpolation, and the freedom to use your DR position as the AP. And this comes about with relatively simple equations. Writing L for latitude and d for declination, the equations giving H_c and Zn are:

$$\sin H_c = \sin L \sin d + \cos L \cos d \cos LHA \tag{5.1a}$$

$$\cos A = (\sin d - \sin L \sin H_c) / (\cos L \cos H_c) \tag{5.1b}$$

where A is an azimuth angle playing the role of the Z azimuth angle used in tables. But although A and Z are the same in the northern hemisphere, they are different in the southern hemisphere, see Chapter 12 for details. The rules to get Zn from A are simple:

if the LHA is greater than 180°, Zn = A,
if the LHA is less than 180°,   Zn = 360° – A.

Readers not familiar with trig functions shouldn't be scared off by these equations. (They are really applications of the same triangle relationship. The second equation is just a relabeling of the triangle sides and angles, now solved for cos A. See Appendix A.) We'll discuss the use of the simplest handheld scientific (meaning they have trig functions) calculator. Those not familiar with calculators will want to look at the detailed discussion in Appendix B on using handheld scientific calculators for direct computation. There we show how to use a calculator at a purely mechanical level, reading our equations as a series of instructions, simply telling us which buttons to press on a calculator. Viewed in this way, using equations is as simple as looking up numbers in tables. Anyone can do it.

Our approach is to store L, *d*, and LHA in memory locations, numbered one though three respectively, immediately after the required conversion from degrees and minutes to decimal degrees. By using this storage sequence we look upon Equation 5.1a as a set of keystroke instructions by writing it in the form

$$\sin H_C = \sin [1] \sin [2] + \cos [1] \cos [2] \cos [3] \qquad (5.2a)$$

where [1] means to recall memory number one, where the latitude is stored; [2] means to recall memory number two, where the declination is stored; and [3] means to recall memory number three, where the LHA is stored. Then after multiplying out and adding the sines and cosines on the right-hand side, the inverse-sine button gives H_C. After we calculate H_C, we immediately store it in location [3], reusing that location in preparation for the azimuth equation, which now reads

$$\cos A = (\sin[2] - \sin[1] \sin[3]) / (\cos[1] \cos[3]) \qquad (5.2b)$$

Sun Worksheet for Calculators			
Body *Sun's Lower Limb*		H_S	*59° 22.1'*
Date *10 May 05*		index	*– 1.5'*
UT *19:18:39*		dip	*– 2.8'*
Lat *N24° 17'*		H_A	*59° 17.8'*
= +24.28333° STO[1]		alt	*+ 15.4'*
		H_O	*59° 33.2'*
Dec *N17° 47.9'* *d = +0.6'*		GHA	*105° 54.5'*
d corr *+0.2'*		m s	*4° 39.8'*
Dec *N17° 48.1'*		GHA	*110° 34.3'*
= +17.80167° STO[2]		Lon	*W78° 29.0'* *(E+, W–)*
		LHA	*32° 5.3'*
Sin H_C = sin[1]sin[2] + cos[1]cos[2]cos[3]		= 32.08833° STO[3]	
		Cos A = (sin[2] – sin[1] sin[3]) / (cos[1] cos[3])	
H_C	*59.43155°*		
	59° 25.9'	*LHA GT 180°, Zn = A =*	
H_O	*59° 33.2'*	*LHA LT 180°, Zn = 360° – A =*	
	7.3 Toward		*264°*

Figure 5.6 The sun sight reduction worksheet using direct calculation.

Then similarly using this form as another keystroke reminder, we compute A, and then find Zn from azimuth rules given along with Equation 5.1b. Using the three memory locations saves reentering L, d, and H_C multiple times (and most inexpensive calculators only have three memory locations). We'll see more details and nuances of the method as we present actual examples of sight reductions.

Figure 5.6 shows our previous sun shot worked up with a worksheet designed for calculator use, having reminders of the equations and their use. Blank copies of this worksheet are available in Appendix E. Of course, the only departure from our worksheet for tables is obtaining H_C and Zn from the latitude, declination and LHA. All the other blocks in the worksheet are the same.

First note the icons STO[1], STO[2], and STO[3] that remind us to store the preceding values into memories [1] through [3] for subsequent calculation of H_C and azimuth angle A. At the top of the bottom two blocks we find the altitude and azimuth angle equations in calculator format telling what buttons to press (you don't need to know more than that).

Calculator Details

Taking the calculator in hand and looking at the worksheet, convert the latitude, declination, and LHA from degrees and minutes to decimal degrees before storing each one of them into memory. (The calculator function that converts degrees-minutes-seconds to decimal-degrees, the DMS→DD key, isn't useful because celestial navigation uses decimal fractions of minutes, not seconds. So do the conversion yourself, which is really no more work for our application.) The first conversion is for the N24° 17′ latitude. Enter the 24° into the calculator, press +, enter the 17′, press ÷, enter 60, press =, and you have added 24° to 17′/60 to get decimal 24.283333°. Next immediately store this decimal latitude in location [1] by pressing the store key followed by the number 1. The STO[1] icon in the latitude line of the worksheet is a reminder. In principle there is no reason to write down the decimal value as shown on the worksheet, except for checking possible errors later on. Next convert the declination and the LHA, storing them in memories [2] and [3] respectively. Notice that this procedure avoids entering long decimal values, which are susceptible to data-entry errors. Remember to negate southern latitudes and declinations using the +/− key, just before the store operation.

Next, using the reminder equations on the worksheet, execute the keystrokes we discussed (also see Appendix B) to compute H_C *followed immediately by storing* H_C *into memory [3].* Then convert H_C back to degrees and tenths of minutes. Do this by subtracting the 59° from the 59.43155 appearing in the display, and then multiplying by 60 to get minutes, rounding it off to the nearest tenth-minute when you write H_C on the worksheet. Then compute the angle A (again see Appendix B if necessary), and using the azimuth rules on the worksheet write down Zn. Since H_O is greater than H_C, the difference gives an intercept distance of 7.3 nm *toward* the sun's GP. (Notice that the intercept is different than in the same previous sight example because we are now using a different AP.)

This completes the sight reduction. It might seem complicated at first because we've given a lot of details, including calculator nuances, that will soon become second nature. With a little practice it will become infinitely simpler than it first appears. In fact, it's so simple, it will fit on a 4x6 card and take less than ten minutes.

There's a whole spectrum of computers that can be used to solve Equations 5.1 for altitude and azimuth, from calculators, to PCs, to the Internet. In fact, at first you might prefer to use the NGA website's celestial navigation computer (see the bibliography in Appendix K) for armchair introductory practice. That way you can learn different components of sight reduction separately, concentrating first on the big picture.

Four Examples of Sun Sights

Now you're ready to practice sun-sights. Here are four examples you can work with the almanac excerpts in Appendix C. Calculate the intercept distance (toward or away) and the true azimuth. You can work them using tables H.O. 249, H.O. 229, or a calculator, or for an easy start you might even use the online calculators at the government websites listed in Appendix K. If you use direct computation, still take the AP latitude and the LHA to be the nearest whole degree so that you can compare your results with our discussion in the following pages where you'll find workups of these four sights, using all three methods. If all these numbers make you uncomfortable, read the beginning of Chapter 13 for a recommended easy entry into practicing celestial navigation. When you've mastered these exercises, you'll be well on your way to being a celestial navigator.

Northwest of Hawaii your DR position on 11 May 2005, UT 00^h $19^m 39^s$, was estimated to be N24° 13´, W153° 21´. An observation of the sun's lower limb, bearing westward, gave 59° 26.9´ with an index correction of – 3.2´. Your eye height above sea level was 10.3 ft.

Northwest of Brisbane on 12 May 2005, UT $03^h 18^m 13^s$, your DR position was S24° 15´, E161° 42´. Looking to the northwest, you observed an altitude of 37° 45.3´ for the sun's lower limb. The index correction was – 1.3´ and eye height 8.5 ft.

Southeast of the Canary Islands at UT $11^h 18^m 03^s$ on 10 May 2005, with an estimated DR position of N23° 41´, W22° 54´, an index correction of + 2.4´, and an eye height of 21.3 feet, you observed the sun bearing eastward with an upper limb altitude of 59° 40.5´.

About 200 miles west of West Australia on 11 May 2005 at UT 02^h $19^m 55^s$ your first mate estimated the ship's DR position at S23° 44´, E111° 51´. The sun's lower limb altitude was 37° 41.5´ to the northeast, with an index correction of –2.9´ and a height of eye at 15.2 feet.

Listed below are the workups of the above four practice sun-sights. The workups are shown in the H.O. 249 format, but results are given for all three methods. The associated recommended sketches for the sights are shown in Figure 5.7, where we've labeled the LHA and the azimuth Zn. Remember that the calculator azimuth rules are different than the ones listed in the tables, because the azimuth angles A and Z are different. In each method we've rounded off Zn to the nearest degree, the practical limit of plotting precision. Note in each sketch that the altitude and the actual azimuth seen by the navigator agree, giving some assurance that a huge goof hasn't occurred. These

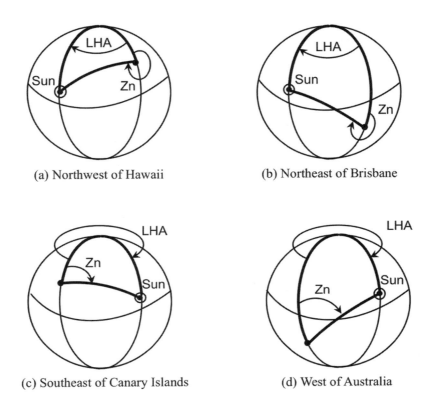

(a) Northwest of Hawaii   (b) Northeast of Brisbane

(c) Southeast of Canary Islands   (d) West of Australia

Figure 5.7 Sketches of the four sun-sight examples.

sketches help to keep the big picture in mind as opposed to just following rote instructions. We've used the same AP position for all three methods so that their results can be compared. But of course, in actual practice, the direct calculation method normally uses the DR position for the AP. Some advantages and disadvantages of each method are discussed in Chapter 11.

<u>Northwest of Hawaii</u>: The workup of this sight, shown below, with H.O. 249 gives H_C = 59° 33´ and Zn = 265°. Using interpolated declination of N17° 51.3´, H.O. 229 gives H_C = 59° 33.2´ and Zn = 265°. Direct computation gives H_C = 59° 33.4´ and Zn = 265°. They all agree within the expected accuracies. The difference between the exact calculated altitude (using eight decimal digits) and H.O. 229 (the 33.2´ compared to the 33.4´) demonstrates the ±0.2´ limitation of H.O. 229 when using simple first-order interpolation, even though DSD interpolation isn't indicated in this case.

Body	Sun's Lower	H_S	59° 26.9'	
Date	11 May 05	index	– 3.2'	
UT	00:19:39	dip	– 3.1'	
		H_A	59° 20.6'	
DR Lat	N24° 13'	alt	+ 15.4'	
DR Lon	W153° 21'	H_O	59° 36'	
AP Lat	N24°			
AP Lon	W153° 49.4'	GHA	180° 54.6'	
		m s	4° 54.8'	
Dec	N17° 51'	GHA	185° 49.4'	
		AP Lon	–153° 49.4' (E+, W–)	
H_{TAB}	59° 18'	LHA	32°	
corr	+15'			
H_C	59° 33'	+18' X 51' / 60' = +15'		
H_O	59° 36'			
	3 NM	Zn = 360° – 95° = 265°		

Northeast of Brisbane: Entering H.O. 229 with an interpolated declination of 18° 8.5′ gives H_C = 37° 33.5′ with Zn = 321°. Direct computation also gives H_C = 37° 33.5′ and Zn = 321°. Note that the east AP longitude adds to the GHA to run over 360°, but is reduced by that amount to the integer 32° for use in the tables.

Body	Sun's Lower	H_S	37° 45.3′
Date	12 May 05	index	– 1.3′
UT	03 18 13	dip	– 2.8′
		H_A	37° 41.2′
DR Lat	S 24° 15′	alt	+ 14.8′
DR Lon	E 161° 42′	H_O	37° 56.0′
AP Lat	S 24°		
AP Lon	E 161° 31.7′	GHA	225° 55.0′
		m s	4° 33.3′
Dec	N 18° 8′	GHA	230° 28.3′
		AP Lon	+161° 31.7′ (E+, W–)
H_{TAB}	37° 40′		– 360°
corr	– 6′	LHA	32°
H_C	37° 34′		
H_O	37° 56′	$-47′ \times 8′ / 60′ = -6′$	
	22 NM	Zn = 180° +141° = 321°	

Southeast of the Canary Islands: Interpolated declination from the almanac is 17° 42.9′. Using H.O. 229 gives $H_C = 59° 30.7′$ with Zn = 96°. Direct calculation gives $H_C = 59° 30.9′$ and Zn = 96°. Here again, H.O. 229 demonstrates its lack of 0.1′ accuracy when using the simple first-order interpolation. This verifies that H.O. 229 using only first order interpolation at ±0.2′ accuracy is not really much better than H.O. 249 with its ±0.5′ accuracy.

Body	*Sun's Upper*	H_S		*59° 40.5′*
Date	*10 May 05*	index		*+ 2.4′*
UT	*11 18 03*	dip		*– 4.5′*
		H_A		*59° 38.4′*
DR Lat	*N23° 41′*	alt UL		*– 16.4′*
DR Lon	*W22° 54′*	H_O		*59° 22′*
AP Lat	*N24°*			
AP Lon	*W22° 25.2′*	GHA		*345° 54.4′*
		m s		*4° 30.8′*
Dec	*N17° 43′*	GHA		*350° 25.2′*
		AP Lon		*–22° 25.2′(E+, W–)*
H_{TAB}	*59° 18′*	LHA		*328°*
corr	*+13′*			
H_C	*59° 31′*	*+18′ X 43′ / 60′ = +13′*		
H_O	*59° 22′*			
	9 NM Away	*Zn = Z = 96°*		

<u>West of Australia</u>: Declination interpolated from the almanac for this UT is 17° 52.6′. Here H.O. 229 gives $H_C = 37° 46.0′$ and $Zn = 40°$. Direct calculation shows $H_C = 37° 46.1′$ and $Zn = 40°$.

Body	Sun's Lower	H_S		37° 41.5′
Date	11 May 05	index		– 2.9′
UT	02 19 55	dip		– 3.8′
		H_A		37° 34.8′
DR Lat	S23° 44′	alt	LL	+ 14.8′
DR Lon	E111° 51′	H_O		37° 50′
AP Lat	S24°			
AP Lon	E112° 6.5′	GHA		210° 54.7′
		m s		4° 58.8′
Dec	N17° 53′	GHA		215° 53.5′
		AP Lon	+112° 6.5′ (E+, W–)
H_{TAB}	38° 28′	LHA		328°
corr	–42′			
H_C	37° 46′	$–48′ \times 53′ / 60′ = –42′$
H_O	37° 50′			
	4 NM	$Zn = 180° – 141° = 39°$

Why all the fuss about precision? Yes, you can have a lot of fun with celestial navigation, and even rely on it in certain emergency situations, without thinking much about accuracy. But accuracy is important for selecting the sight reduction method appropriate to individual needs and circumstances, for evaluating a navigator's skill, and for cross-checking the GPS. We have discussed precision because it's an important distinction among the three methods, varying from 1.0′ to 0.1′. If a cavalier one-minute precision were used for all seven additions and subtractions in a sight reduction, and ±0.5′ errors all accumulated in the same direction, the result would suffer a 3.5-mile error. Even when the navigator is being careful, almanac data, altitude corrections, sextant calibration, and timing can easily contribute a 0.2′ error each. (Although the almanac is tabulated to 0.1′, it's only accurate to from 0.2′ to 0.3′.) Thus the accumulation of these uncertainties, exclusive of the sight reduction itself, can well exceed one mile. See

Chapter 10 for more detail. It's the individual navigator's decision whether to compound these errors with unnecessary error from the sight reduction. Many navigators find an immense satisfaction from learning and practicing celestial navigation that transcends open-water requirements. One doesn't shoot at a target without aiming for the bull's-eye.

We've discussed these three methods for both comparison and completeness, believing it's best to get the details straight in the beginning. These sun-sight reductions form the basis for all the sight reductions that follow. Once you thoroughly understand these examples, you have a couple of options. You can read on through the following chapters learning more sight reductions.

Or since you now fully understand sun sights, you might prefer to pause and practice your own sun shots, gaining confidence and satisfaction. Of course, you'll need a sextant, current almanac, watch, and calculator or tables. Armed with these essentials of celestial navigation, first read the section in Chapter 9 on Sextant Checks and Adjustments and the following one on Sextant Observations. Next read the beginning of Chapter 13 for ideas on starting practice. Then go to the nearest horizon (natural or artificial) where you know the exact latitude and longitude for checking your results, and begin your life anew—life as a celestial navigator.

6

Sights of Other Celestial Bodies

Appropriately, we've used the sun for our model celestial sight. And now, with just minor modifications, we can treat all the other navigational bodies: four planets, 173 stars, and the moon. Given the vicissitudes of conditions at sea, the complete celestial navigator wants to take advantage of these additional opportunities.

Availability

The moon has unique availability. For more than half of its 28-day lunar cycle the moon is available over large portions of the daytime or nighttime. The planets and stars suffer from limited availability. A major problem is the visibility not of these bodies themselves, but of the horizon. Usually, it's only during the hours of twilight, just before sunrise or just after sunset, that they are both simultaneously visible. Venus (with a magnitude of –3.8) is the third brightest object in the sky after the sun and the moon, so it's the easiest to see during twilight, and can be even seen in broad daylight if you know where to look (hint: precompute its expected altitude). Morning star and planet sights are easier than evening ones. In the morning you can take all the time you need to locate the objects before the horizon becomes visible. In the evening, by the time you get familiar with all the celestial landmarks, the horizon might be dark. The actual prime viewing time can be quite limited, depending on latitude—as short as 20 minutes at low latitudes to 24 hours near the Antarctic and Arctic Circles during their seasons of long twilight.

Obviously, for celestial bodies to be seen, their GHA can't be too close to the sun's. A graph in the beginning of the Nautical Almanac shows the position of the planets relative to the sun. That is, it plots the difference between the planet's GHA and the sun's, and adds 12 hours to give the local mean time of meridian passage. The almanac also lists the universal times of sunrise, sunset, and twilight so the navigator can compute which stars and planets will be simultaneously observable with the horizon.

Star charts are readily available form a variety of sources, including the Nautical Almanac and the back inside cover of this book. Later we'll discuss identifying and viewing stars and planets. And we'll see shortly that H.O. 249, Volume I, makes a very effective star finder, but only for seven stars at any one time. One might think that all this fuss is contrary to one of the splendors of celestial navigation, which is learning and absorbing nature's wonders. Just gather the necessary stargazing items: a good viewing location away from cultural lighting, a couple of good star charts, a blanket, a bottle of wine, and a soul mate. The rest is easy. Then with just a minimal effort in the first couple of days at sea, or preferably the first couple of weeks before putting to sea, one can learn the position of all the important planets and stars that will be available during your upcoming voyage. And of course, the more one is familiar with the night sky the easier each of these "relearning" sessions will be. Isn't that a far better approach to appreciating the world around us than studying a bunch of tables? Why go to sea without already knowing the whereabouts of the beacons that nature has provided for the ship's safe journey? However, even with this intimate knowledge of the sky, under some conditions, such as haze or breaks in clouds, star and planet identification can be difficult. In those cases, by all means, precalculate the expected altitudes and azimuths from your estimated position so that you can readily spot the right ones in the available time.

The Planets

The four navigation planets are Venus, Mars, Jupiter, and Saturn. Because each of these executes rather different motion compared to each other and to the sun, their GPs are tabulated individually in the Nautical Almanac. This means that their sight reduction is practically the same as for the sun. A sample planet sight reduction is shown in Figure 6.1, where we introduce our universal worksheet, accommodating all the navigation celestial bodies (a blank copy is in Appendix E). The left middle side of this worksheet has free space where we can sketch the navigation triangle for the sight.

Our planet example is from the Pacific: While eight days southwest of Hawaii and about 700 nm northwest of Christmas Island, Jupiter was observed to the east at an altitude of 39° 15.4′ in the early morning twilight of 11 May 2005 at 05^h 19^m 44^s UT. The vessel's estimated position was N5° 16′ W168° 58′. The eye height was 9.5 feet and the index correction was +0.5′.

The sight reduction shown in Figure 6.1 uses a whole-degree AP derived from the DR position so that it can be followed using either direct computation or sight reduction tables. There are two very minor differences from a sun sight: First, the refraction altitude correction is taken from a different table in the almanac, the one right next to the sun's altitude correction table. This table differs from the sun's because it doesn't include the sun's semidiameter and parallax correction. Also, because of the variation in earth-planet distances during the year, there is a slight additional altitude correction (never exceeding 0.5′) for Venus and Mars.

The other difference from a sun sight is a small adjustment to the planet's GHA. This adjustment, called the *v-correction*, is handled similarly to the d-correction for the sun. The value of *v, with its sign*, is taken from the bottom of the planet's GHA-declination column in the daily pages. Then entering the *v-or-d* section of the Increments and Corrections Table at the back of the almanac, the amount to be applied to the planet's declination, *honoring the sign of v*, is found for that particular value of *v*, exactly as is done for the *d*-correction. The general-purpose sight reduction worksheet has a line in the GHA calculation to remind us to enter these *v* corrections for planets.

Universal Worksheet for Calculators			
Body *Jupiter*		H_s	39° 15.4'
Date *11 May 2005*		*index*	+0.5'
UT *05^h 19^M 44^s*		*dip*	−3.0'
DR Lat *N5° 16'*		H_A	39° 12.9'
DR Lon *W168° 58'*		Alt	−1.2'
AP Lat *N5.0°*	STO[1]	U/L	HP
AP Lon *W169° 22.1'*		*Temp, P*	_____
		H_O	39° 11.7'

DEC *52° 30.6* *d* −0.1		GHA *114° 25.3'*	(Aries for star)
d-corr *0.0'* (Not stars)		*m s* *4° 56.0'*	
DEC *52° 30.6'*		*v* +2.6 *+0.8'*	(Moon, planets)
− 2.51° STO[2]		GHA *118° 82.1'*	
		SHA _____	(Of Star)
310°		GHA *119° 22.1'*	
		LON *−169° 22.1'*	(E+, W−)
Zn		*+360°*	
Jupiter		LHA *310°*	STO [3]

$$\text{Sin } H_C = \sin[1] \sin[2] + \cos[1] \cos[2] \cos[3]$$

$$\text{Cos } A = (\sin[2] - \sin[1] \sin[3]) / (\cos[1] \cos[3])$$

$H_C =$ *39.487539°* STO [3]	
= *39° 29.3'*	
$H_O =$ *39° 11.7'*	*LHA GT 180°, Zn = A* = *97°*
17.6 Away	*LHA LT 180°, Zn = 360° − A =*

Figure 6.1 Jupiter Sight Reduction using the universal worksheet with an AP for use with either a calculator or tables.

After we've found the LHA, we sketch the sight's navigation

triangle to help us better understand nautical astronomy and to help us avoid huge goofs. Note how the co-altitude seems to be about 50°, and hence the altitude is about 40°. The azimuth seems right also, somewhere around 90°. So everything makes sense, giving us confidence in our work.

The Moon

The moon's orbit about the earth gives it several unique properties relevant for navigation. First, a full moon is seen for only about six days during the lunar month, while a partial disk is seen in one of its phases for the remaining 12 useable days (or so). So the observer must select the upper or lower limb to make sure that the full radius of the disk is used for the sight. Second, on those beautiful moon-lit nights the moon's bright reflections from water-surface wavelets can fade out short of the natural horizon, giving a depressed false horizon. While these two considerations require some caution, they introduce only limited possible error, and in known directions. Thus coupled with its unique day/night availability, and the excellent LOP crossing angles the moon frequently has with the sun and stars, the navigator shouldn't neglect or demean moon shots.

Because of the moon's close proximity to the earth, we can no longer use the approximation that the observer is effectively at the earth's center. The error in this approximation is called *parallax*, which is based on its maximum value, called horizontal parallax (HP), as discussed in Chapter 9. At the back of the almanac there is a special two-part altitude table for the moon that combines all three corrections: refraction, parallax, and semidiameter (including *augmentation*, see Chapter 8 and Exercise 4.7). The top table is entered with apparent altitude and gives the main correction. Then the bottom table is entered with the HP and the second parallax correction is extracted. (There's a separate column for the upper and lower limb.) Both corrections are always added, and 30′ is subtracted from these two if it's an upper limb sight.

Figure 6.2 shows an example of the universal sight reduction worksheet of Appendix E filled in with a moon sight from the Tasman Sea. The DR position was S34° 13′, E161° 43′ at 02:19:14, on 11 May 2005, when an observation of the moon bearing northeast gave a sextant altitude of 25° 21.6´. Eye height was nine feet and the sextant index correction was –3.3´.

The moon's motion relative to the earth is quite different than either the sun or the stars and therefore requires its own listing in the almanac's daily pages. And because of this more variable motion, both *d* and *v*

Universal Worksheet for Calculators	
Body *Moon's Lower Limb* Date *11 May 2005* UT *02ʰ 19ᵐ 14ˢ*	H_S *25° 21.6'* *index* *–3.3'* *dip* *–2.9'* H_A *25° 15.4'*
DR Lat *S34° 13'* DR Lon *E161° 43.0'* AP Lat *S34.21667°* STO[1] AP Lon *E161° 43.0'*	Alt *60.7'* U/L *2.0' LL HP 55.1* Temp, P _____ H_O *26° 18.1'*
DEC *N27° 41.8'* *d* +3.2 *1.0'* (Not stars) DEC *N27° 42.8'* *+27.71333°* STO[2] 	GHA *177° 47.1'* (Aries for stars) *m s* *4° 35.4'* *v* +9.0 *+2.9'* (Moon & planets) GHA *181° 85.4'* SHA _____ (Of Star) GHA LON *E161° 43.0'* (E+, W–) *342° 128.4'* LHA *344° 8.4'* *344.14000°* STO [3]
Sin H_C = sin[1] sin[2] + cos[1] cos[2] cos[3] Cos A = (sin[2] – sin[1] sin[3]) / cos[1] cos[3]	
H_C *26.27514°* STO[3] *26° 16.5'* H_O *26° 18.1'* intercept *1.6 Toward*	LHA GT 180°, Zn = A = *16°* LHA LT 180°, Zn = 360° – A =

Figure 6.2 A lunar sight reduction using the universal form with a calculator.

corrections are given for each hour. When entering the almanac's daily pages for the moon, simply read across the five columns, and copy onto the sight reduction worksheet the GHA, v, the declination, d, and HP. Give d a sign corresponding to whether the declination is increasing or decreasing. Then using the Increments and Corrections Table at the back of the almanac, treat the v and d corrections just as for the planets, except note that there is a separate column for the moon's increments because its apparent daily rotation around the earth is less than the sun's. The corrections are a bit more complicated than for the other bodies, resulting in almanac errors that can reach 0.3´. You can confirm the whole sight reduction in Figure 6.2 by looking in Appendices C and D, paying particular attention to corrections for d and v, and for the moon's altitude.

Our favorite sketch for this sight is shown on the worksheet. As in the previous example, we have a case where the LHA is greater than 180°, making it exterior to the navigation triangle. (The interior angle, 360° − LHA, called the *meridian angle*, is conventionally labeled t.) In direct calculation it doesn't matter which angle is used: The cosine function in the calculation of H_c is insensitive to adding or subtracting 360° and even to positive or negative LHAs (see the cosine plot in Appendix F). So it wouldn't matter if the GHA and east longitude added up to more than 360°. We could use that number as is. That's why the calculator rule for finding the LHA is so simple: *Add east longitudes to the GHA, and subtract west longitudes from the GHA.* These nuances can save a few calculator operations, but remember that the precomputed sight reduction tables require the conventional LHA ranging westward from 0° to 360°.

The Stars

The sextant altitude corrections are the same for the stars as for the planets, but with no additional corrections, such as for Mars and Venus. But their GHA is treated differently than all the other celestial bodies. Because of their vast distance from our solar system, they have very little apparent motion among themselves, their daily motion being entirely due to the earth's rotation about its axis. Their GHA changes by the second because of the earth's rotation, but the hour angles among themselves and their declinations are constant over periods of many days. Therefore, a huge amount of almanac space can be saved by listing the GHA of a single point among the stars, and referencing the star's hour angles to that point, rather than to Greenwich. The vernal equinox (the point where the sun's path crosses the equator in the spring) is chosen for that reference point, and is called the *first point of Aries* because it lies in the constellation of Aries. Frequently we just call it Aries. Sometimes the symbol γ is used for Aries.

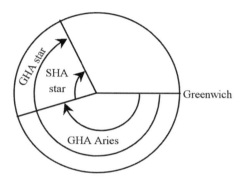

Figure 6.3 The GHA of a star is the GHA of Aries plus the SHA of the star.

So the hour angle of a star is reckoned from Aries instead of from Greenwich. This hour angle from Aries is called the *sidereal hour angle* SHA of the star. The GHA of the star is obtained by adding its SHA to the GHA of Aries, as shown in Figure 6.3. If the sum exceeds 360°, then 360° is subtracted from the sum. Notice that both the SHA and the GHA of Aries are measured westward from zero to 360°.

Since both the SHA and the declination change only slowly, they are listed only once on the daily pages for the 57 common navigation stars. (And even that is far more often than needed, but is tabulated on each page for convenience.) The GHA of Aries is then listed by the UT hour, and adjusted to the second with the Increments and Correction Table at the back of the almanac. Aries has its own column in the increments table because the table is now interpolating sidereal time rather than solar time. Because the celestial position of the stars is so stable, there are no *d*- or *v*-interpolation corrections for them.

Star Sights by Tables or Calculator

We'll take an example of a star sight while approaching Rio de Janeiro from the south. On 12 May 2005 Sirius was observed to the west at $20^h 18^m 44^s$ UT at an altitude of 54° 48.0´. The DR position was S23° 44´, W37° 23´.

Universal Worksheet for Calculators	
Body *Sirius* Date *12 May 2005* UT *20: 18: 44*	H_S *54° 48.0'* index *−4.1'* dip *−3.4'* H_A *54° 41.5'*
DR Lat *S23° 44'* DR Lon *W37° 23'* AP Lat *S24°* AP Lon *W37° 2.5'*	Alt *−0.7'* U/L HP Temp, P _____ H_O *54° 39.8'*
DEC *S16° 43.4'* d-corr _____ (Not stars) DEC *−16° 43.4'* *−16.7233333°* STO[2] 	GHA *170° 41.1'* (Aries for stars) m s *4° 41.8'* v _____ (Moon, planets) GHA *175° 22.9'* SHA *258° 39.6'* (Of Stars) GHA *74° 2.5'* LON *−37° 2.5'* (E+, W−) LHA *37°* STO [3]

$$\text{Sin } H_C = \sin[1]\sin[2] + \cos[1]\cos[2]\cos[3]$$

$$\text{Cos } A = (\sin[2] - \sin[1]\sin[3]) / (\cos[1]\cos[3])$$

H_C *54.663650°* STO[3] H_C *54° 39.8'* (Calculator) H_C *54° 40'* (Tables) H_O *54° 39.8'* intercept *0.0'*	19 x 43.4 / 60 = +14' Z = 95° Zn = 180° + 95° = 275° *LHA GT 180°,* Zn = A *LHA LT 180°,* Zn = 360° − 85° = 275°

Figure 6.4 A star sight reduction using the universal worksheet with either a calculator or H. O. 249.

The sextant index correction was –4.1' and the eye height was twelve feet.

The sight reduction is shown in Figure 6.4, using the universal worksheet of Appendix E. The AP was selected to make both the latitude and LHA integer degrees so that the example can be worked with either tables (Appendix D) or a calculator. As shown on the right-hand side, the major distinguishing feature of the star reduction is the extra step of adding the GHA of Aries to the star's SHA to get the star's GHA. Minor differences are the absence of d and v corrections, and the altitude correction taken from the star-and-planets table on page A2 of the almanac. The sketch of the star sight (which I always recommend) is shown on the worksheet.

The calculated altitudes are shown in the lower left-hand block for both the calculator results and the tabular results. The table's H_c of 54° 40´, comes from the tabulated value of 54° 26´ plus the altitude's declination interpolation of 14´, as shown at the top of the lower right-hand block. The 0.0´ intercept has no special significance—it's just another intercept, dependant on the AP selected. Also notice the different azimuth angles, Z from the tables, and A from the calculator, and how they're converted to true azimuth Zn differently. You can follow this workup using the almanac excerpts from Appendix C, and tables from H.O. 229 or H.O. 249, Vol. II, in Appendix D. Or you can use a calculator. However, since H.O. 249 Volumes II and III only cover the solar body declinations from zero to 29°, they are not intended for star sights. But H.O. 229 does cover all declinations, and H.O. 249, Vol. I, has a simplified, although restricted, method of treating star sights.

Star Sights by H.O. 249, Volume I

Because a star's declination is essentially constant throughout the year, the solution of the navigation triangle for a particular star depends on only two variables (rather than the normal three): the observer's latitude and the LHA of Aries. This makes it feasible to precompute the altitude and azimuth for a few selected stars and list the results in one volume under the observer's latitude and the LHA of Aries. Volume I of H.O. 249 does just that (see Appendix D, H.O. 249, Volume I). It lists seven stars selected for observability and for good LOP crossing angles, given the latitude and LHA of Aries. The three stars labeled with the diamond symbol have the best crossing angles for a fix. Stars in all capital letters are the brightest (magnitude 1.5 or brighter). Because a star's availability depends on the LHA of Aries and the observer's latitude, the selection of the seven stars changes as the LHA and latitude change throughout the volume.

This simplification is readily apparent by using Volume I of H.O. 249 in the above example. We simply compute the LHA of Aries as follows:

GHA of Aries   170° 41.1' from almanac: 2000 hrs 12 May 2005
time adjustment   4° 41.8' for 18 min and 44 sec
GHA of Aries   175° 22.9'
AP longitude   −37° 22.9' makes Aries LHA integer degrees
LHA of Aries   138°

Then turning to Appendix D, H.O. 249, Volume I, on the Latitude-24°-South page of Volume I under LHAΥ = 138°, we find under *Sirius* that H_C = 54° 58' and Zn = 275°. That's it—simple, a major advantage of star sights with H.O. 249. The resulting H_C is slightly different than in the above H.O. 229 example because it's reckoned from a slightly different AP longitude.

This simplification of Volume I allows many star sights to be worked up on one worksheet. Figure 6.5 shows an example of five star sights worked up using the worksheet from Appendix E. It uses the same example from our approach to Rio de Janeiro on 12 May 2005 at DR position S23° 44´, W37° 23´. The sextants altitudes shown were shot with an index correction of − 4.1. The height of eye was 9 ft on the leeward side of the boat, and 12 ft on the windward side.

Note that, while the AP latitude is the same for each star, the different GHA of Aries forces a different AP longitude for plotting their intercepts. Additionally, the resulting LHA of Aries is not always the same for each star as you look up their H_C and Zn in Volume I.

Another attractive feature of H.O. 249, Volume I, is star selection and identification. It's pretty easy to compute the LHA of Aries for an anticipated round of stars: Look in H.O. 249 for the best ones for a fix, and then go on deck to look for them at their listed altitude and azimuth. So Volume I offers some unique advantages, but as usual, there are compromises. It's another book added to the celestial navigation kit, one that covers only seven stars for each LHA and one that goes out of date. The volume is published every five years and is useable for nine years with special corrections for the earth's precession and nutation.

Star Worksheet for H.O. 249, Vol. I				
Date *12 May 2005* DR Position *S23° 44' W37° 23'* AP Lat *S24°*				

	◆ *Spica*	◆ *Canopus*	*Sirius*	*Betelgeuse*	◆ *Pollux*
UT	*20:18:44*	*20:19:16*	*20:19:43*	*20:20:17*	*20:20:31*
1 May	*219° 01'*	*219° 01'*	*219° 01'*	*219° 01'*	*219° 01'*
12ᵈ 2000ʰ	*311° 40'*	*311° 40'*	*311° 40'*	*311° 40'*	*311° 40'*
m s	*4° 42'*	*4° 50'*	*4° 57'*	*5° 05'*	*5° 09'*
GHAΥ	*175° 23'*	*175° 31'*	*175° 38'*	*175° 46'*	*175° 50'*
AP Lon	*37° 23'*	*37° 31'*	*37° 38'*	*37° 46'*	*36° 50'*
LHAΥ	*138°*	*138°*	*138°*	*138°*	*139°*
H_C	*28° 44'*	*47° 19'*	*54° 58'*	*32° 42'*	*33° 37'*
Zn	*90°*	*217°*	*275°*	*297°*	*336°*
H_S	*28° 59.5'*	*46° 55.4'*	*54° 47.8'*	*32° 38.0'*	*34° 20.4'*
index	*−4.1'*	*−4.1'*	*−4.1'*	*−4.1'*	*−4.1'*
dip	*−2.9'*	*−3.4'*	*−3.4'*	*−3.4'*	*−3.4'*
H_A	*28° 52.5'*	*46° 47.9'*	*32° 30.5'*	*32° 30.5'*	*34° 12.9'*
alt	*−1.8'*	*−0.9'*	*−1.5'*	*−1.5'*	*−1.4'*
H_O	*28° 50.7'*	*46° 47'*	*54° 40'*	*32° 29'*	*34° 11.5'*
intercept	*7 toward*	*32 away*	*18 away*	*13 toward*	*35 toward*

Figure 6.5 The workup of five stars using the worksheet in Appendix E for H.O. 249, Vol. I.

Viewing Stars and Planets

As noted in the beginning of this chapter, the stars and planets have the advantage of providing a true fix (essentially) among several bodies. We say "essentially" because unless the vessel is dead in the water, small running fixes actually connect the several sights. (See Chapter 10 for a discussion on the short-run fix.) However, many navigators neglect this complication on vessels running under ten knots, or so.

The trade-off for this multi-body fix, selected among the navigation stars, the four planets, and the moon, is the time window where the bodies and the horizon are simultaneously visible. In addition to this viewing window, which can vary from just a few minutes up to hours at extreme polar latitudes, is the problem of identifying the various stars and planets. In this GPS age of celestial navigation we can easily take the "earthy" approach discussed earlier, perhaps taking a few star shots as the occasion conveniently arises. But for the navigator who wishes to conquer difficult shots, such as through broken clouds, or wishes to pass certification exams, a more methodical approach is called for.

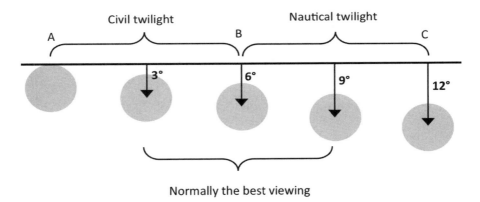

Figure 6.6 Twilight locations of the sun. The almanac gives times of (A) sunrise, sunset, (B) the darkest civil twilight, and (C) the darkest nautical twilight. These times are the UT on the Greenwich meridian and are also the approximate Local Mean Times (LMT) on other meridians.

The nautical almanac lists twilight, rising, and setting times in the daily pages for predicting the best viewing window. Figure 6.6 shows the definitions of sunrise/sunset, civil twilight, and nautical twilight. While the visibility of the stars, planets, and horizon can vary considerably, depending on sky conditions, generally the time of best viewing is centered on the darkest civil twilight, labeled B in the figure. At the sunset or sunrise it's generally too bright to see the bodies, and at the darkest nautical twilight (C in figure), it's generally too dark to see the horizon.

The times tabulated in the almanac can be used directly as the approximate LMT (local mean time) on your meridian. Thus a quick look at the Civil Twilight Time column gives the center of the best viewing at your latitude, mentally interpolating for latitude if you wish.

Or if more accuracy is desired, these times can be adjusted for your DR longitude, converted to time. Alternatively, the almanac times can be interpolated for latitude and longitude using somewhat tedious Tables I and II on page xxxii of the almanac (not shown in our appendices).

As an example of a detailed estimate of best viewing time, we'll consider our position southwest of Rio de Janeiro is expected to be near S23° 44′, W37° 23′ when evening twilight approaches on 12 May 2005. In preparation for a round of star shots, we wish to know the UT of the best viewing conditions. First we convert our W37° 23′ longitude to time from Greenwich. We can use the almanac Arc-to-Time table, or a calculator which gives (recalling earth motion is 15°/hr):

Longitude to time conversion $(37° + 23′/60′) / 15 = 2.4922 = 2{:}30$

Then we interpolate each of the times for our latitude south of the tabulated 20° in the almanac: First we round off our 23° 44′ latitude to 24°. This places our latitude the fraction 4°/10° of the interval between the tabulated times of 20° and 30°. We multiply this fraction of 0.4 by the time interval between the 20° and 30° latitudes. For example, the sunset time interval is $33 - 17 = 16$ min, giving $16 \times .4$ min past the 20° tabulated time of 17 hr 33 min. So the three times are:

Sunset: $17 + (33 - 16 \times 0.4) = 17{:}27$
Civil twilight: $17 + (56 - 14 \times 0.4) = 17{:}50$
Nautical twilight: $18 + (23 - 12 \times 0.4) = 18{:}18$

Each of these three events occurs 2:30 later at our longitude. In particular, the middle of the good viewing window is at: 17:50 UT at Greenwich, plus the 2:30 later, gives 20:20 UT at our DR longitude.

Identifying Stars and Planets

You can learn to identify stars using any of a wide variety star charts, such as the simple one inside the back cover of this book, to sophisticated devices that are almost home planetariums. One extreme example is a hand-held telescope called the *Sky Scout*, which uses an internal GPS receiver, magnetic compass, and gravity sensor to tell where it's pointed and therefore what star you're looking at (and it even talks to you).

One simple approach starts with the handy diagram from the Nautical Almanac on its page 9, which for a given date, shows the Local Mean Time (LMT) of meridian passage of the sun and five planets (See Figure 6.7). The straight dashed diagonal lines, sloping downward to the right across the diagram, show the Sidereal Hour Angle (SHA) on the meridian at the selected date and time. Note that the sun line (solid line near 1200 LMT), which represents actual solar time, is always near local noon, but at times can lead or lag LMT by about 15 minutes, representing difference between mean solar time and actual solar time (called the equation of time). The shaded band,

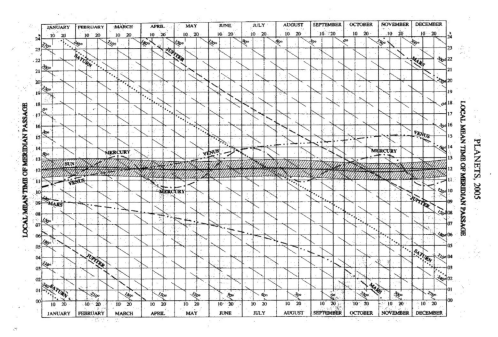

Figure 6.7 The planet diagram from the almanac, showing times of meridian crossings (shown also in Appendix C).

centered on the sun line, represents the time that planets are too near the sun for observation. A lot can be learned and appreciated from this diagram. For example, checking the slope of the SHA lines over one month shows that a given SHA occurs on the same meridian two hours earlier, making up 24 hours per year. That is, the stars rise one day earlier over a year's time, because the sidereal year is one day shorter than the solar year see (Exercise 2.2).

The SHA information from this planet diagram can make the star chart inside the back cover more useful. First look at the almanac's diagram for the date and time of interest to find the SHA on your meridian. Then look at our back-cover star chart keeping in mind which point is directly overhead (on your zenith) at that time: the SHA from the almanac's chart is on your meridian, and the declination of the overhead point is equal to your latitude. Now the portion of the sky that is within your field of view is a hemisphere, centered on your zenith (on a clear unobstructed night). This gives a good idea of what to expect when you start sky gazing.

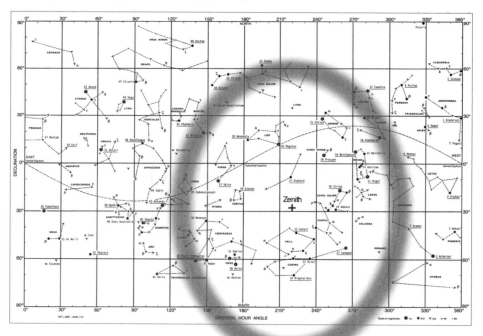

Figure 6.8 The star chart showing our expected hemispherical view of the night sky centered on our zenith at S24° and SHA 220°. The horizontal and vertical scales differ. The view is to the south, making the east to the left and the west to the right.

And an even better picture emerges when we consider where the horizon will be. Consider for example, that when we were southwest of Rio de Janeiro 12 May 2005, at position S24° W37°, we found that our best viewing was centered around 1748 LMT, call it 1800. Entering our almanac's 2005 planet chart with this date and time, we locate our zenith's SHA at 220°. Then moving to the star chart we plot our zenith at SHA 220° and declination S24°, corresponding to our latitude. Mark this zenith (with a pencil) as shown in Figure 6.8. Then sketch in a 180° by 180° ellipse, representing the visible hemisphere, by measuring off the star chart, using the scales appropriate for each axis. Now the zenith with its horizon, shown in the figure as a thick hazy ellipse, gives us a pretty fair picture of what to expect at viewing time.

Viewing the chart as shown in the figure, we're looking south with east to our left and west to our right. North is at the top. To coordinate this sky chart with the vast hemisphere of outside open sky, turn the chart so that the direction you're facing is at its bottom: facing east, the left-hand side goes to the bottom, facing north, hold it upside down, facing west, hold the chart's right-hand side to the bottom.

For example, we see Alphard nearly overhead, due north just a bit (about 15°). On our meridian about 35° to the north, we see Leo, with its navigation stars Denebola, and Regulus just slightly east of north. And about 50° to the southeast lies the Southern Cross, Crux. To the northwest at 50° (about 40° altitude) we see Orion with its easily identifiable stars. The great arc of Capella, Pollux, Procyon, and Sirius (the brightest star in the sky) lies just to the east of Orion. But judging from the arc distance on the chart, it looks like Cappella is very near the horizon.

On the opposite end of the big picture scale is the tiny picture of precomputing individual star altitudes and azimuths. This is particularly easy with H.O. 249, Volume I. Again using our Rio de Janeiro example, we expect to be at approximate DR coordinates S24°, W37° at the center of the best viewing time, the end of civil twilight, at 20:18 UT.

So using an abbreviated form of our H.O. 249 star worksheet, in Figure 6.9, we compute the GHA of Aries at 12 May 20:18 and use an AP longitude of 37° 11´ to get a LHA of Aries of 138° for all seven stars listed in the tables. The simple computation is shown in Figure 6.9, listing the expected altitudes and azimuths for all seven stars. With the

2° to 4° field of view of most sextant scopes, the one-degree precision is plenty good for locating stars. Sweeping the horizon about 30°, or so, on each side of the precomputed azimuth, with the sextant set to the star's altitude, should easily locate the desired star for a shot—even through broken clouds.

Star Worksheet for H.O. 249, Vol. I							
Date *12 May 2005* DR Position *S23° 44' W37° 23'* AP Lat *S24°*							
	Regulus	♦*Spica*	*Acrux*	♦*Canopus*	*Sirius*	*Betelgeuse*	♦*Pollux*
UT	*20:18:44*						
1 May	*219° 01'*						
12^d 2000^h	*311° 40'*						
m s	*4° 30'*						
GHAϒ	*175° 11'*						
AP Lon	*37° 11'*						
LHAϒ	*138°*						
H$_c$	*51°*	*29°*	*39°*	*47°*	*55°*	*33°*	*34°*
Zn	*23°*	*90°*	*154°*	*217°*	*275°*	*297°*	*337°*

Figure 6.9 An abbreviated version of our star worksheet showing the pre-sight computation of the seven stars in H.O. 249, Vol. I.

We've made good use of the almanac's planet diagram for stars, but it's called a "planet diagram" for good reason. Its principal purpose is to give a quick insight into the location of the four navigation planets relative to the sun and the backdrop of the stars. Being members of our solar system, the planets are very, very, close to us compared to the stars. The closest navigation star, Sirius is 8.6 light-years away, and the Polaris you see is back in history by 650 light-years. Because the stars are so far away, their motion among themselves (called their *proper motion*) appears very small compared to the planets which circle our sun as shown in Figure 6.10, just as our Earth does. It's the planet's motion in front of the star field that gives them their name from ancient Greek, *asteres planetai*, meaning wandering stars.

The almanac's planet diagram (Figure 6.7 again) shows the LMT of meridian crossing of five planets for each day of the year. (For some reason Mercury is shown, even though it's too close to the sun for observation.) First, notice the difference in the behavior of planets whose obits lie outside of the earth's orbit, Mars, Jupiter, and Saturn (called outer planets) and the paths of the inner planes, Mercury and Venus. The outer planets, particularly Jupiter and Saturn, nearly follow the SHA lines throughout the whole year. In other words, they have very little east-west motion among the stars. But the inner planets, Venus and Mercury, always remain close to the shaded 1200-hour band, that is close to the sun. Looking at Figure 6.10, we can understand why this is by visualizing the view of Venus from earth as they both travel in their orbits about the sun. Venus never can be seen far from the sun as Jupiter and Saturn can, which, clearly, can be 180° from the sun as viewed from earth.

Another feature of the four planets' orbits is they all lie within a couple of degrees of the earth's orbit, as implied by Figure 6.10. This means that they are always close to the ecliptic, the sun's path, which is indicated by the dotted sinusoidal curve shown on our back-cover star chart.

So just as we located stars by combining the planet diagram and the star chart, we can do the same with planets to conveniently place them

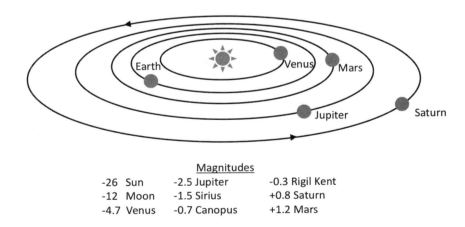

Magnitudes		
-26 Sun	-2.5 Jupiter	-0.3 Rigil Kent
-12 Moon	-1.5 Sirius	+0.8 Saturn
-4.7 Venus	-0.7 Canopus	+1.2 Mars

Figure 6.10 The four navigation planets in their orbits around the sun (not to scale). Mercury's orbit, now shown, lies inside Venus's and is not used in normal navigation.

among their backdrop of the stars: We transfer the planet's SHA from the planet diagram to the ecliptic on the star chart. For example, for all of 2005, Jupiter's SHA varies about 15° either side of 165°. Therefore for most of 2005, Jupiter is located near where the ecliptic intersects the 165° SHA near Spica, in the constellation of Virgo. Not much of a wandering body. In contrast, the two inner planets, Mercury and Venus, cross the SHA lines at sharp angles indicating much more rapid motion against the background of stars. If we want to know if Jupiter will be north or south of Spica, we can compare their declinations from the almanac's daily pages for the date of interest.

We can also get an idea of which planets might be viewable at our twilight from a quick look at the planet diagram alone. In our Rio de Janeiro example on 12 May 2005, looking at the diagram shows that Saturn will be 1:30 hours to the west of our meridian at the expected best viewing time of 1800 LMT. And at the same time Jupiter will be a little more than 2:00 hours east of our meridian. Under a clear sky both of these planets would be easily recognizable in early evening twilight when few, if any, stars are apparent to confuse the identification. This is particularly true of Jupiter which is almost half as bright as Sirius, the brightest star. As twilight settles in on a clear night, Jupiter should be the first "star" visible.

So we've now learned how to shoot the stars and planets, how to work up their sights, and how to predict where they'll be at their best observation times. Another great pay off is when you're on deck between evening and morning twilight, you can gather in the wonders of our universe. You can now recognize several of our solar system's planets, and many of its brightest stars that share our Milky Way galaxy. You can contemplate its vastness, Sirius, a meager 8.6 light years away (51 trillion miles), to the dying orange supergiant Enif at about 700 ly, one of our dimmest navigation stars. On a dark night at sea you can see up to 1,000 stars (looking on all sides of the rig). They may smite you with their charm and mystery, compelling you toward a little astronomy. You might learn about our 100,000 light-year-wide galaxy whose fuzzy disk, in the center of the Milky Way, hides a black hole controlling the galaxy's spiraling arms. Then there's the vast majority of the universe that lies beyond our galaxy, such as the galaxies Andromeda (3.5 million light-years) and Messier (3 million light years), both visible with the naked eye on a good night. The more we discover about our universe, large and small, the more we understand and appreciate our place in it. Sitting at the helm on a clear dark night with the caress of whispering waves and a force three gentle breeze, we steer her by a star while contemplating our existence in nature's majestic universe, musing on that age-old unanswered question—why?

7

SPECIAL SIGHTS

This chapter is a bag of tricks and a pile of fun, perhaps a relief from the standard St. Hilaire method discussed so far. We'll explain special sights that have their own particular advantages, such as simplified sight reductions, insensitivity to observation time, or the ability to determine UT. We'll see that some of these qualities make them invaluable in emergency situations, where we might be willing to relax our accuracy standards a bit, or where UT has been lost. Captain Joshua Slocum (1844–c1910) wrote in his account of sailing single-handed around the world in his sloop, *Spray*, that his time came from an old alarm clock that even lacked a minute hand. In addition to using lunar distance sights (see Chapter 8) for finding longitude, he probably employed good dead reckoning and some tricks of this chapter to safely navigate the globe.

Polaris

Polaris is special because it is always within 1° of the north celestial pole. If Polaris were exactly at the North Pole, its observed altitude would be equal to the observer's latitude, as shown in Figure 7.1. And since Polaris is very nearly at the North Pole, the ship's latitude is equal to the observed altitude of Polaris plus small corrections. This allows Polaris to be treated more simply than the other navigation bodies. Of course we can still reduce a Polaris sight by the standard St. Hilaire reduction using our universal sight reduction form as we did for the other stars. (However, note that the SHA and declination of Polaris is not included in the list of the 57 stars in the daily pages of the almanac. But they are listed separately near the back of the almanac.) We will discuss three simplified Polaris sight reductions, starting with the most accurate and proceeding to the least accurate. The least accurate, still useful at sea, requires only a sextant, and is therefore useful in emergency situations, or for showing off to your shipmates.

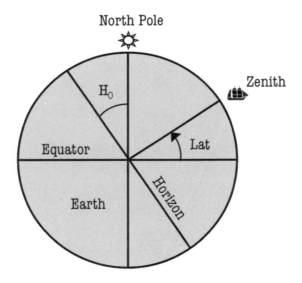

Figure 7.1 The observed altitude of a body exactly at the North Pole would be equal to the latitude of the observer.

Polaris by the Nautical Almanac

Near the back of the almanac, there is a table that lists three corrections to the observed altitude of Polaris to get the observer's latitude (see Appendix C). You enter the table with the LHA of Aries to get a_0, the largest correction, then you enter with your DR latitude and the month of the observation to get to get a_1 and a_2, two corrections that are usually less than a minute of arc.

For example, a sight reduction for an observation on 21 April 2005 at 23:18:56 and at a DR position N50° and W37° 14′ would look like this:

GHA of Aries at 23 hrs	195°	6.6′
Increment for 18:56	4°	44.8′
W lon	− 37°	14.0′
LHA Aries	162°	37.4′
H_O	49°	31.6′
a_0 for LHA 162° 37.4′	1°	22.3′
a_1 for Lat 50°		0.6′
a_2 for April		0.9°
Subtract 1°	− 1°	0.0°
Latitude	49°	55.4′

First the LHA of Aries is computed from the DR longitude and the observation time and date, just as in other star sights. Then the three corrections are found in the almanac's Polaris table. For convenience, the corrections are arranged so that they always add, resulting in a constant 1° always subtracted from the calculation. Note that the total correction is only 23.8′, and that the last two are each less than one minute of arc.

Polaris by H.O. 249, Vol. I

The next step in simplicity is to work only to one minute of accuracy by lumping the three above corrections into just one. This is done in

Table 6 at the back of the H.O. 249, Vol. I. where it lists a correction called Q, as shown in Figure 7.2. Entering the table with the same LHA of Aries of 162° 37.4´ as in the above example of the almanac sight reduction, gives a correction of +24´ for a final latitude of N49° 55.6´, within the expected agreement of one minute, compared to the above almanac Polaris reduction.

TABLE 6 — CORRECTION (Q) FOR POLARIS

LHA ϒ	Q	LHA ϒ	Q	LHA ϒ	Q	LHA ϒ	Q	LHA ϒ	Q	LHA ϒ	Q	LHA ϒ	Q	LHA ϒ	Q
359 20	-33	87 07	-28	124 18	-3	159 23	+22	241 30	+39	289 48	+14	324 00	-11	6 01	-36
1 27	-34	88 53	-27	125 39	-2	160 58	+23	244 52	+38	291 14	+13	325 23	-12	8 31	-37
3 40	-35	90 37	-26	127 00	-1	162 34	+24	247 52	+37	292 39	+12	326 47	-13	11 14	-38
6 01	-36	92 19	-25	128 20	0	164 12	+25	250 35	+36	294 03	+11	328 12	-14	14 11	-39
8 31	-37	93 58	-24	129 42	+1	165 52	+26	253 07	+35	295 27	+10	329 37	-15	17 31	-40
11 14	-38	95 36	-23	131 03	+2	167 34	+27	255 30	+34	296 50	+9	331 03	-16	21 26	-41
14 11	-39	97 11	-22	132 24	+3	169 19	+28	257 44	+33	298 12	+8	332 30	-17	26 25	-42
17 31	-40	98 45	-21	133 45	+4	171 07	+29	259 53	+32	299 35	+7	333 58	-18	35 29	-43
21 26	-41	100 18	-20	135 06	+5	172 57	+30	261 55	+31	300 56	+6	335 26	-19	43 16	-42
26 25	-42	101 49	-19	136 27	+6	174 51	+31	263 54	+30	302 18	+5	336 56	-20	52 20	-41
35 29	-43	103 19	-18	137 49	+7	176 50	+32	265 48	+29	303 39	+4	338 27	-21	57 19	-40
43 16	-42	104 47	-17	139 10	+8	178 52	+33	267 38	+28	305 00	+3	340 00	-22	61 14	-39
52 20	-41	106 15	-16	140 33	+9	181 01	+34	269 26	+27	306 21	+2	341 34	-23	64 34	-38
57 19	-40	107 42	-15	141 55	+10	183 15	+35	271 11	+26	307 42	+1	343 09	-24	67 31	-37
61 14	-39	109 08	-14	143 18	+11	185 38	+36	272 53	+25	309 03	0	344 47	-25	70 14	-36
64 34	-38	110 33	-13	144 42	+12	188 10	+37	274 33	+24	310 25	-1	346 26	-26	72 44	-35
67 31	-37	111 58	-12	146 06	+13	190 53	+38	276 11	+23	311 45	-2	348 08	-27	75 05	-34
70 14	-36	113 22	-11	147 31	+14	193 53	+39	277 47	+22	313 06	-3	349 52	-28	77 18	-33
72 44	-35	114 45	-10	148 57	+15	197 15	+40	279 22	+21	314 27	-4	351 38	-29	79 25	-32
75 05	-34	116 08	-9	150 23	+16	201 12	+41	280 55	+20	315 48	-5	353 28	-30	81 27	-31
77 18	-33	117 31	-8	151 55	+17	206 15	+42	282 27	+19	317 09	-6	355 21	-31	83 24	-30
79 25	-32	118 53	-7	153 19	+18	215 26	+43	283 57	+18	318 31	-7	357 18	-32	85 17	-29
81 27	-31	120 14	-6	154 48	+19	223 19	+42	285 26	+17	319 52	-8	359 20	-33	87 07	-28
83 24	-30	121 36	-5	156 18	+20	232 30	+41	286 54	+16	321 14	-9	1 27	-34	88 53	-27
85 17	-29	122 57	-4	157 50	+21	237 33	+40	288 22	+15	322 37	-10	3 40	-35	90 37	-26
87 07		124 18		159 23		241 30		289 48		324 00		6 01		92 19	

Figure 7.2 This table in H.O. 249, Vol. I, entered with the LHA of Aries, gives the correction (called Q) to be applied to the observed altitude to get latitude.

Polaris with only a Sextant

As seen in the above two reduction methods, if we're willing to sacrifice a little accuracy, there is really only one major altitude correction to get our latitude from Polaris. In fact, as we discuss in Exercise 2.16, it is easy to see that the great majority of the correction is given by

$$\text{Lat} = H_O - cd\,\cos(LHA_P) \tag{7.1a}$$

where LHA_P is Polaris's local hour angle and cd is its co-declination—

about 41 minutes. This provides a rare opportunity to use celestial navigation without tables (almanac or H.O. 249) and even without a knowledge of time, such as might occur under some emergency situations.

We can estimate the LHA of Polaris from our knowledge of the stars: As shown in Figure 7.3, we'll use two guide stars: Alkaid, the trailing star in the handle of the Big Dipper, and ε-Cassiopeia, the trailing star in the "W" of Cassiopeia. The line connecting ε-Cassiopeia and Alkaid will be our *guideline* for estimating the LHA of Polaris. Polaris is displaced from the true north pole by 41' toward ε-Cassiopeia, and trails this guideline by 13°. Therefore the LHA of Polaris is 13° less than the LHA of ε-Cassiopeia, or

$$\text{Lat} = H_O - 41' \cos(\text{LHA}\varepsilon - 13°) \tag{7.1b}$$

For example, when ε-Cassiopeia is exactly vertically above Alkaid, the LHA of ε-Cassiopeia is zero, giving Lat $= H_O - 41' \cos(-13') = H_O - 40'$.

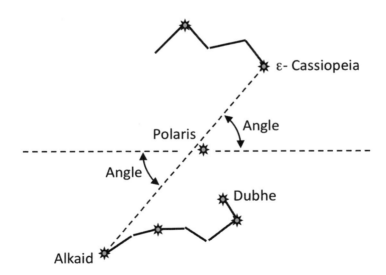

Figure 7.3 Polaris lies near the line connecting ε-Cassiopeia and Alkaid.

It's easy to express the correction given by Equation 7.1b pictorially, as shown in Figure 7.4. This diagram depicts positions of ε-Cassiopeia every 15° around the perimeter of a circle with Polaris at the center. We enter the diagram with our observed angle between the guideline and the horizontal. Then we read off the correction next to the corresponding location of ε-Cassiopeia: For example, when ε-Cassiopeia is 30° above the horizontal to the east of Polaris, the indicated correction is –12', negative because the observed altitude is too high. With ε-Cassiopeia to the west and 45° below the horizontal, the correction is +22', positive because Polaris's altitude is now too low. Note that when ε-Cassiopeia lies on the horizontal to the east, the correction is a plus 9' because now Polaris is below the horizontal, lagging by the 13°.

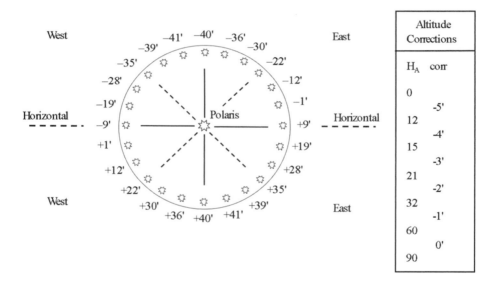

Figure 7.4 A diagram showing the correction to Polaris's altitude in terms of the locations of ε-Cassiopeia.

Sometimes ε-Cassiopeia is unobservable. It might be below the horizon, dimmed by haze, or obscured by clouds. We can always use the brighter Alkaid by just reading the opposite side of the circle: If we judged Alkaid to be 45° above the horizontal to the west of Polaris, the correction would not be –35', but the +35' read on the opposite side.

Polaris Altitude Corrections

in terms of the angle ε-Cassiopeia makes relative to Polaris and the horizontal.
For Alkaid, interchange east/west and above/below.

	ε-Cassiopeia West of Polaris			ε-Cassiopeia East of Polaris	
	Angle°	Corr´		Angle°	Corr´
ε Cassiopiea Above Horizontal	90	-40	ε Cassiopiea Above Horizontal	90	-40
	77	-41		85	-39
	59	-39		78	-37
	52	-37		72	-35
	46	-35		67	-33
	41	-33		62	-31
	36	-31		58	-29
	32	-29		54	-27
	28	-27		51	-25
	25	-25		47	-23
	21	-23		44	-21
	18	-21		41	-19
	15	-19		38	-17
	12	-17		35	-15
	9	-15		32	-13
	6	-13		29	-11
	3	-11		26	-9
	0	-9		23	-7
ε Cassiopiea Below Horizontal	-3	-7		20	-5
	-6	-5		17	-3
	-9	-3		15	-1
	-11	-1		12	1
	-14	1		9	3
	-17	3		6	5
	-20	5		3	7
	-23	7		0	9
	-26	9	ε Cassiopiea Below Horizontal	-2	11
	-28	11		-5	13
	-31	13		-8	15
	-34	15		-11	17
	-37	17		-14	19
	-40	19		-18	21
	-44	21		-21	23
	-47	23		-24	25
	-50	25		-28	27
	-54	27		-32	29
	-58	29		-36	31
	-62	31		-40	33
	-66	33		-45	35
	-71	35		-51	37
	-77	37		-58	39
	-84	39		-71	41
	-90	40		-90	40

Figure 7.5 A Polaris altitude correction table giving corrections to 2'.

We can see from Figure 7.4 that when ε-Cassiopeia is close to the horizontal, the angle measurement is most critical; a 15° error can produce a 10 mile error in our latitude. As ε-Cassiopeia moves away from the horizontal, accuracy is improved to the point where we can get our latitude to a couple of miles.

Those interested in increasing accuracy can try devising their own method to actually measure the angle of the guideline relative to the horizontal. Using a straight edge held against the protractor of a chart plotter is one possibility. A long-arm chart plotter works the same. Just hold it at a convenient distance from your eye with the protractor's center on Polaris, one side parallel to the horizon (the best you can), and the straight edge lined up with the two stars. Then read the angle from the horizontal. If you're able to significantly improve the measurement of the guideline angle, consult the more detailed table of Polaris altitude corrections shown in Figure 7.5. If you can squeeze out a 3° accuracy in your measurement, you are rewarded with a latitude within 2 minutes, even in the worst case. This is one example of the use of guide stars, which dates back many centuries. With its historical roots and simplicity, Polaris is hard to resist.

Meridian Sights

As we have just seen in our discussion of ε-Cassiopeia, a body crosses an observer's meridian in two ways; its upper transit occurs when its LHA = 0°, and its lower transit occurs when its LHA = 180°. (Note at lower transits, the body's altitude is a minimum, rather than maximum.) The best-known upper transit case is the noon sun shot, which made its debut when tables of its declination were published in the fifteenth century. The sun's altitude at local apparent noon (i.e., when the sun's altitude is a maximum), combined with the sun's declination gives latitude by simple addition and subtraction. In general there are two upper transit possibilities, depending on whether the body is north or south of you. As in any meridian transit, you can find the latitude by drawing a simple 2-D diagram in the meridian's plane.

By remembering that both latitude and declination carry negative signs in the southern hemisphere, you can easily verify that the following rule covers all upper transit cases (also see Exercise 1.21):

if the body is south of you, $L = dec + (90° - H_O)$ (7.2a)

if the body is north of you, $L = dec - (90° - H_O)$ (7.2b)

(Of course, we recognize that $90° - H_O$ is just the co-altitude, but we prefer this form because it relates directly to the measured altitude.) And for the less-common lower transit we get:

for northern latitudes, $L = \quad 90° - dec + H_O$ (7.2c)

for southern latitudes, $L = -90° - dec - H_O$ (7.2d)

So the meridian sights offer latitude with extreme simplicity, like Polaris, a feature so attractive that they are hard to pass up when they're available. (Note how all the equations give the expected result for the special cases of ± 90° declination.)

Furthermore, the result is insensitive to time because of the slow change in declination of most bodies. In the sun's worst case, at the equinox, its declination is changing about 1.0′ per hour. So a timing error of one hour would result in only a one-mile error in latitude. And at the solstices, you wouldn't even need to know what day it is; it would take a timing error of almost a week to produce a mile of error in latitude. This sight reduction is equally valid for any celestial body on your meridian. Timing is more critical for the moon because its declination changes more rapidly than the sun's. On the other hand, the stars change their declination only slightly over years. In fact, meridian sights of the stars, such as Polaris and others, have played an important role in the early history of sea voyages, as you can learn in the brief history of navigation in Appendix J, and from the titles in the bibliography in Appendix K.

This idea of using special stars (as we discussed above in connection with Alkaid and ε-Cassiopeia) as guide stars dates back to at least the fifteenth century when the Portuguese started exploring south of the equator, making Polaris unavailable. In the Southern Cross constellation, *Acrux* and *Gracrux* almost lie on the same meridian. So when the line connecting them is vertical, it's easy to judge when a meridian sight occurs. Furthermore at this time, the line connecting them gives the direction to true south (within 1°), another aid to the early explorers of the southern oceans.

Latitude without Meridian Shots or UT

It's also possible to obtain latitude from star shots, away from the meridian and without a knowledge of UT. The essentially simultaneous observation of two (or better, three or four) stars gives a fix, determining both latitude and longitude. And if the time used for reducing the sights were incorrect, the SHA of all the stars are incorrect, but all by the same amount, in the same direction. Hence their LHAs are also all incorrect by the same amount, in the same direction. This means that only the longitude is wrong, not the latitude. Thus we can find latitude from stars without meridian sights or UT. So without a knowledge of UT onboard, there are quite a few possibilities for obtaining latitude: daytime meridian shots of the sun, moon, and possibly Venus; nighttime meridian shots of the moon; and morning and evening twilight shots of the stars, whether they're on the meridian or not.

Latitude and Longitude from Meridian Sights

For centuries before John Harrison developed his sea-fairing chronometer, navigators relied on the noon sun shot for their latitude, accepting longitude as unknowable in the open ocean. Now, in the GPS age with our inexpensive quartz watches, we can easily determine longitude from our meridian sights. The latitude is relatively insensitive to the timing of a meridian sight, but the longitude is sensitive to time. This means we can use the time of meridian passing to determine longitude.

When a body is on the observer's meridian, the LHA is zero (for upper transit) and the observer's longitude is equal the GHA of the body at that time. Thus with the sun as an example, the local hour angle is zero at local apparent noon (LAN) and the longitude is equal to the GHA of the sun. So if you're going to take a noon sun shot, you could start recording altitudes a few minutes before LAN, and continue for a few minutes after. A plot of the altitudes versus time should show an increase in altitude toward the maximum at LAN, and a symmetrical decrease afterwards. A fair curve drawn though these points locates both the time of LAN and the noon altitude. The GHA of the sun at the time of your LAN is your longitude. (Of course, GHAs greater than 180° mean the longitude is east and it would be written as 360° − GHA.)

Figure 7.6 shows a plot of sun shots taken to the northwest after our departure from the Galapagos Islands, approaching the Juan Fernandez Island group off the coast of Chile, on 12 May 2005. We've drawn a smooth curve through the somewhat scattered data which serves to average the shots. (Looking through the paper folded about the vertical axis though LAN will average twice the data points over half the distance.) Note the scale's units. While the vertical scale is in

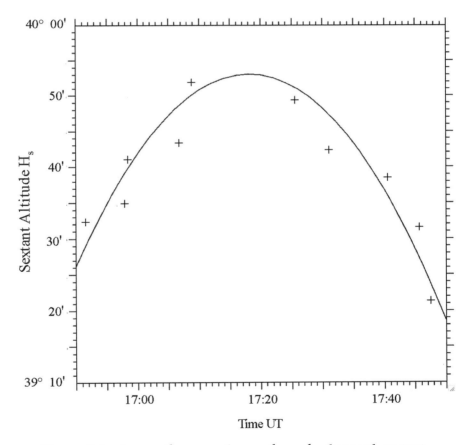

Figure 7.6 A smooth curve drawn through observed sextant altitudes, at times near local apparent noon, as we approached the Juan Fernandez Islands on 12 May 2005.

minutes of latitude, and the horizontal scale is minutes of time, their significance is quite different: a minute of time corresponds to 15′ of longitude. Plus inspecting the faired curve shows that the time of LAN can be determined to only within a few minutes of time, or tens of minutes of longitude. And this rather poor sensitivity to longitude gets worse at higher latitudes.

With careful inspection we can see from the plot that the meridian altitude is 39° 53.1′ at about 17:18:00 UT. Our height of eye is 9 feet and the sextant index correction is +2.3′. Using the simplified worksheet for this sight in Appendix E (for upper transits only) and the almanac data from Appendix C, we perform the sight reduction discussed above as follows:

Worksheet for Sun Meridian Lat & Lon	
Limb: *UL* **Date:** *12 May 05*	**Meridian time:** *17 :18 :00*
dec *N 18° 17.0'*	**H$_s$** *39° 53.1'*
d-corr *+0.2'* *d = +0.6*	*index* *+ 2.3'*
coH *−50° 24.4'* *(− body north)*	*dip* *− 2.9'*
Lat *S32° 7.2'*	**H$_A$** *39° 52.5'*
	Alt *− 16.9'*
GHA *75° 55.1'*	*Temp, P* _____
m s *4° 30.0'*	*− **H$_o$*** *−39° 35.6'*
GHA *80° 25.1'* *(− if >180°)*	*89° 60.0'*
(E lon) *359° 60'*	**coH** *50° 24.4'*
Lon *W80° 25.1'*	

On the right you see the normal altitude corrections, but now H$_o$ is subtracted from 90° to get the co-altitude, coH, which is then carried over to upper left side of the worksheet to compute the latitude. There's a reminder there to subtract the co-altitude from the declination if the body is observed to the north (otherwise it is added). Also remember we are observing our sign convention for declination and latitude, but we're not using our standard sign convention for longitude. Instead, the reminder in the bottom left-hand section tells us that if the GHA turns out to be greater than 180°, we subtract the GHA from 360°

because we have an east longitude.

This is a very simple sight reduction indeed. And it can be done without calculators, tables, or plotting. Besides, it even gives a fix. It also applies to any body on the meridian—using the appropriate corrections, of course. But its disadvantage is the narrow availability window of meridian shots and the extra work of determining the time of meridian passage. The sight can also have its accuracy limited by the determination of meridian passage time, which is particularly poor for low altitudes because of their slow rate of change in time, and for vessels having rapid northerly or southerly motion. These timing inaccuracies affect the longitude more than the latitude.

Some navigators call this a *time sight*. Historically, any sight that determines longitude was called a time sight because UT is always required to find longitude; the sight discussed in the next section is also called a time sight. At any rate, the latitude can be determined from the maximum altitude, as in the normal noon sun shot. So this combination provides a fix, instead of just an LOP—and by using simple arithmetic rather than solving the navigation triangle.

To help plan sights, the UTs of meridian passage *at Greenwich* for the sun, moon, planets, and Aries are shown on the bottom of the daily pages of the almanac. Although these times are for passage at the Greenwich meridian, they are approximately the local mean time on the local meridian.

Another complication of this sight is the distance covered by a moving vessel while we're taking successive sights. It turns out we need only consider the vessel's north-south velocity component because the east-west component has much less affect. So let's consider that the ship in our Juan Fernandez Island example were sailing north at 10 kn, then we would have recorded the solid-line plot as shown in Figure 7.7.

The dotted curve is the observation from the stationary ship (both curves are exact computer plots). As might be expected, since we'd be moving toward the sun during our observations, we see continuing increasing altitudes above the observations made when our vessel was stationary. These increasing altitudes also mean that the maximum altitude occurs a little later, as shown. If we were traveling south, these two effects would be reversed: we'd see a lower maximum altitude at an earlier time. Considering that 10 kn is a pretty good clip for many small vessels, the shift in LAN is not too extreme in latitude, the maximum has been shifted up about 3.5′. But the time of maximum altitude is later by about 3 min, or 45′ in longitude, a significant shift.

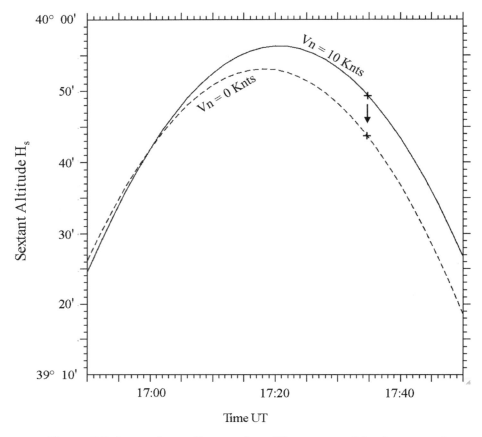

Figure 7.7 A vessel traveling north at 10kn sees an altitude versus time curve distorted by its change in latitude during the sextant observations. Correcting each observed H_s by the change in latitude of Vn x T brings the observations back to what a stationary vessel would obsrve at its latitude at 17:00.

This plot from the moving vessel can be easily corrected back to what would have been observed on a stationary vessel. By thinking that the increasing altitude is due to the ship's increasing latitude because of the northerly velocity, it makes sense that the correction ought to be Corr = Vn x T, where Vn is the northern velocity and T is the time referring back to an arbitrary reference position and time. As a point of mathematical interest, it's easy to show that our basic altitude equation (Equation A.1 of Appendix A) verifies our above intuition for reasonable altitudes and times. But this simple correction ignores the triangular geometry when the sun (or other body) is off the observer's meridian, producing an overcorrection for times either side of LAN. However, even though this correction is only an approximation, it's quite satisfactory for observations taken over less than an hour and at altitudes less than about 70°.

Now, to apply this simplified speed correction to our example, we'll write the velocity in minutes of latitude per minutes of time. With our Vn = 10 kn = 10′/60 min, the correction becomes Corr = (0.167′) T, where T is the time, in minutes, past our reference position. This correction has been used in Figure 7.7 to recover the altitude plot of a stationary reference vessel at 17:00 UT by subtracting (0.167′)T from the altitudes seen from the moving ship. For example, the downward black arrow represents the correction at 35 min past 17:00 UT, or (0.167′) times 35 min = 5.8′. In practice one would apply this correction to each sextant altitude before the smooth curve is drawn for measuring the altitude and time of local apparent noon. The position determined from the corrected Vn = 0 plot, was the vessel's position at 17:00 UT. This reference time at 17:00 is arbitrary: a different one produces different corrections with a corresponding different position at the selected reference time.

This may seem like a lot of fuss, or perhaps even antithetic for what is supposed to be a simple sight. But we have the option of handling this sight several ways, depending on our situation. After all, the desired accuracy in open ocean is quite different than making land fall on a small low island. The simplest and least accurate procedure is to just follow the body up to maximum altitude and mark the time when it just "hangs" there.

The next simplest, which still avoids data plotting, is to record an observation 20 to 30 minutes, depending on latitude, before LAN; catch the altitude at LAN as its maximum; reset the sextant to the first reading before LAN; and then record the time that the sun returns to this first altitude. The time of LAN is just the average of the time of the first observation and the time when the altitude returned to this same altitude.

Going a step further by plotting the data gives the additional advantage of averaging the sextant readings, producing a more accurate latitude and longitude. And even more fussy is correcting for the ship's north-south velocity component, as discussed above. Beyond that, you can carry it one more final step by including the declination change (for the sun, moon, and planets): just add (or subtract) d, the change in declination per hour listed in the almanac from the north-south component of velocity. So in our example the declination is increasing in time, so we'd use $(V_n + d)T$ for the correction (d in the same units as V_n). That's the ultimate treatment. The main advantage of this latitude and longitude meridian sight is it uses simple concepts and simple arithmetic without the need for sight reduction tables; and you can make it as simple as you want. The choice is yours.

Longitude from Altitude and Latitude

Longitude also can be calculated directly from a sight if the latitude is known. This is the Sumner case, discussed earlier, of computing longitude from altitude and latitude by

$$\cos LHA = (\sin H_o - \sin L \sin d) / (\cos L \cos d) \qquad (7.3)$$

which is nothing more than the altitude equation solved for cos LHA (we're using the same old altitude equation, as promised earlier). This time sight, as it was sometimes called, is mainly of historical interest. Latitude was found by any of the methods discussed above, and then the longitude was found from this time sight. Until Sumner's 1843 publication, a commitment to this traditional method prevented navigators, including the famous ones, from realizing that they were actually calculating one point on the equal-altitude LOP, as we discussed earlier in Chapters 1 and 2. Now it usually serves no useful purpose because the St. Hilaire method gives the best information possible from a single altitude observation and estimated position (as we also discuss in Chapter 10).

Time from a Lunar LOP and a Star Fix

Imagine you have an excellent star fix from, say, three or even more stars, whose LOPs cross almost at the same point, (meaning that the individual LOPs are in excellent agreement). Additionally, you have plotted a lunar LOP at essentially the same time as the star fix. But the lunar LOP doesn't run through the star fix. In fact, it's not even close enough to be explained by any of the usual suspects, such as sextant, abnormal refraction, or observation error. The situation is shown in Figure 7.8. What can be the problem?

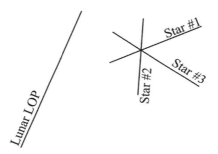

Figure 7.8 Three star LOPs agree to give a good fix. But the moon's LOP lies considerably to the west, indicating that the watch time is incorrect.

Without any other explanation, it no doubt means the time used to reduce the sight was incorrect. The quartz watch is wrong. This means that we can use the differential motion of the moon and stars to find the true UT of the sights. The stars move through the sky a bit faster than the sun's $15°$/hr. Their GHA increases at the Aries rate of $15.041667°$/hr (see exercise 2.2). The moon's motion is more complicated, with a GHA speed that varies somewhere between $13.6°$/hr and $14.6°$/hr. So as all navigators and students of the sky know, the stars come up a bit earlier each night, while the moon rises quite a bit later each night. These facts, combined with a good lunar LOP and a good star fix, allow us to determine UT independently of outside sources.

Figure 7.9 shows the two possible cases: the moon's LOP lies to the west of the star fix, or its LOP lies to the east of the fix. If we move the clock time forward from the one used to reduce the sights, both the LOP and the fix will advance westward. Then the stars, moving faster westward, will catch up to the moon's LOP case of LOP #1. On the other hand, if we retard the clock, the star fix will fall back eastward to the case of LOP #2. So if the lunar LOP is west of the star fix, the watch is slow; if it's east of the star fix, the watch is fast. Now that we know which way our watch is off, how do we determine how much?

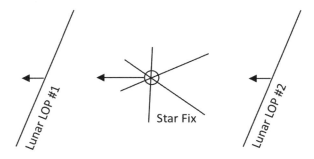

Figure 7.9 The horizontal arrows show that the star fix advances farther westward with an increased UT than does the lunar LOP. So advancing UT by the right amount will bring LOP#1 into agreement with the fix. Retarding UT will bring LOP#2 into agreement with the fix.

The key is to appreciate that both the lunar LOP and the star fix are correct except for the observation time, since all other sources of error have been eliminated. Therefore, if we correctly adjust the time of the two sights, the moon's LOP will pass through the star fix. In other words, the calculated moon's altitude, given by our usual relation,

$$\sin H_C = \sin L \sin d + \cos L \cos d \cos LHA \qquad (7.4)$$

will give the observed moon altitude H_O when computed using the *correct time and star fix location* to determine the moon's declination and LHA. Furthermore, the time-corrected star location has a new longitude, *but the same latitude*. (We saw this in our above discussion of obtaining latitude without UT.) However, there's a Catch 22 in trying to use this reasoning: We can't determine d or LHA for use in Equation

7.4 without knowing UT, which is what we're trying to find in the first place. Situations such as this, common enough in mathematics, call for a numerical solution rather than a simple closed-form equation. So we use interpolation.

We'll use our standard altitude equation above to calculate the moon's altitude from the position at the star fix at two times that are estimated to be somewhat before and somewhat after the true UT of the fix, and then interpolate between these times using the calculated altitudes compared to the actual measured altitude of the moon. When we select these two times we'll move the longitude of the star fix westward according to its LHA speed of 15.041667°/ hr (also 15.041667'/min) if we're advancing the clock, and eastward if we're retarding the clock. An example will show how easy it is to find UT from a moon LOP and a star fix.

Let's say on 10 May 2005, in the Pacific Ocean west of the Mexican coast, plotting a star fix puts us at W120° N20° (we're using some round numbers to simplify discussion), and a lunar observation gives a fully corrected altitude of 25° 40.7'. Although we know the clock is off of UT, we believe the observations were made between 0200 and 0300 UT. When the sights were worked up and plotted, the lunar LOP fell to the west of the star fix, indicating a clock slow on UT (the case of LOP #1 in Figure 7.9). First we calculate the moon's altitude that would be observed at 0200 at W120°, N20°. Then we calculate the altitude again from a location of the *same latitude* with the longitude advanced westward to the 0300 UT position of the star fix. Finally, we interpolate our actual observed lunar altitude between these two calculated altitudes and times. Using almanac data from Appendix C, our workup looks as follows:

At 0200 UT, 10 May 2005:		Latitude	20° 0.0'
Moon's GHA	190° 31.0'	dec	N25° 41.7'
Longitude	120° 0.0'		
LHA	70° 31.0'		

This gives $H_C = 25° 30.8'$ for the moon from direct calculation using the above latitude, declination, and LHA. Next we repeat the calculation at 0300 UT with our longitude increased by 15.041667°/hr x 1 hr = 15° 2.5´:

At 0300 UT, 10 May 2005:	Latitude 20° 0.0´
Moon's GHA 204° 59.5´	dec N25° 48.3´
advanced lon 135° 2.5´	
new LHA 69° 57.0´	

Now $H_C = 26° 2.1´$ at 0300 UT using the same latitude, but the time-advanced declination and LHA. So now we have an interpolation table of the moon's altitude versus time as follows:

H_C at 0200 UT: 25° 30.8´

H_O at time T: 25° 40.7´

H_C at 0300 UT: 26° 2.1´

The difference in the two altitudes one hour apart is 31.3´. And the altitude difference between the observed altitude and the 0200 UT altitude is 9.9´. So the interpolated unknown UT is found from the ratio T / 60 min = 9.9´ / 31.3´ or T = 60 x 9.9 / 31.3 = 18.9776 min = 18^m 59^s past the 0200 hour.   So our observations determined that the sights were observed at 02:18:59.

Note that the whole concept of finding UT from a moon's LOP and a star fix depends on the fact that stars don't change their declination in time and therefore the latitude determined by the fix is correct. Also we see that the sensitivity to the moon's altitude is only 31.3´ in an hour (about 0.5´ per minute). Furthermore, this sensitivity is near the maximum possible, so the sensitivity of UT to altitude is quite a bit less than we would like for setting our modern quartz watches. The exact sensitivity depends on the detailed geometry of a particular sight. If the moon were making a meridian passage, the sensitivity would be even worse, near zero. This low altitude sensitivity to UT means that in making these observations and sight reductions, we want to push for the ultimate accuracy. It also means that the one-hour interpolation interval used here is perfectly adequate, even when the moon's GHA and declination are changing rapidly. A more direct method of obtaining

UT is discussed in Chapter 8 on lunar distances, which is less sensitive to the vagaries of altitude observations, such as refraction corrections.

Position without St. Hilaire

The *Nautical Almanac* gives an iterative procedure for calculating a fix from several intercepts and azimuths determined from their St. Hilaire sight reductions. But it's possible to *directly calculate* your position from two simultaneous altitude sights, which can be implemented on a computer or hand calculator. Figure 7.10 shows the LOPs from observing two bodies. The observer, shown by a solid dot labeled Ship, is at one of the two intersections of these equal-altitude LOPs. The standard coordinates locate the observer and the GPs of the two bodies. The western most body is labeled number 1, and the eastern most body

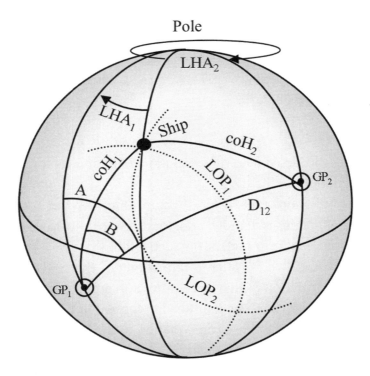

Figure 7.10 LOP_1 and LOP_2 from bodies 1 and 2 intersect at two points whose coordinates can be computed from the normal relationships of navigation triangles.

number 2. Also shown are the great-circle distance between the two bodies, D_{12}, and two bearing angles from the GP of body 1: Angle A is the angle between true north and D_{12}, and B is the angle between the co-altitude of body 1 and D_{12}.

By the generic application of our standard sight reduction equations (see the discussion in Appendix A), we can show that the latitude and longitude of the observer are given by sequentially solving the following equations:

$$\cos D_{12} = \sin d_1 \sin d_s + \cos d_1 \cos d_2 \cos (GHA_1 - GHA_2) \tag{7.5a}$$

$$\cos A = (\sin d_2 - \sin d_1 \cos D_{12}) \,/\, (\cos d_1 \sin D_{12}) \tag{7.5b}$$

$$\cos B = (\sin H_s - \cos D_{12} \sin H_1) \,/\, (\sin D_{12} \cos H_1) \tag{7.5c}$$

$$\sin Lat = \sin d_1 \sin H_1 + \cos d_1 \cos H_1 \cos (A - B) \tag{7.5d}$$

$$\cos LHA1 = (\sin H_1 - \sin d_1 \sin Lat) \,/\, (\cos d_1 \cos Lat) \tag{7.5e}$$

$$Lon = LHA_1 - GHA_1 \tag{7.5f}$$

The ship's latitude comes from Equation 7.5d, and its longitude from the last equation.

OK, so this looks like a lot of computing. And at first glance, it would seem that this is definitely not for those back-to-basics navigators who want to keep it simple. But in fact, it looks pretty favorable when compared to the two St. Hilaire reductions of the two observations. This direct calculation of this fix requires solving five trig equations of exactly the same form as the four needed for two St. Hilaire reductions. So by solving just one more trig equation of the same type, we get an exact computed fix, without plotting approximate straight lines or using APs. It's a sight reduction in its own right, completely avoiding the St. Hilaire intercept method.

Although the five equations may seem forbidding at first, they're really quite easy to understand. The first five are just repeated applications of our standard equations to three different spherical triangles in Figure 7.10 as follows: The first two are our great-circle equations applied to the triangle GP_1-GP_2-Pole. Equation 7.5c applies our standard azimuth equation to triangle GP_1-GP_2-ship. Equations 7.5d and 7.5e are the standard St. Hilaire equations applied to the triangle GP_1-ship-Pole. So we're standing behind our initial promise, that all our mathematical relationships are really just one equation, Equation A.0 of Appendix A.

From symmetry, you can see that the angle B has the same value for both fix possibilities. The argument $(A - B)$ for the cosine function in Equation 7.5d selects the fix shown in the figure. You can see from inspecting Figure 7.10 that the other fix uses $(A + B)$ for the cosine argument. Simply drawing a sketch for your particular sight, somewhat to scale, such as Figure 7.10, will immediately indicate which to use, $(A + B)$ or $(A - B)$, and how GHA_1 and LHA_1 are related to your ship's longitude.

Calculators and computers return only one of the two possible solutions for the inverse trig functions. The first three equations, requiring the inverse cosine, give angles from $0°$ to $180°$, which are valid solutions in all cases. The inverse sine in Equation 7.5d returns angles from $-90°$ to $+90°$, spanning the range of valid latitudes for the two fixes. In writing computer code, the easiest approach would be to simply calculate the latitudes and longitudes for both possible fixes and let the navigator select the correct fix. (After all, Equations 7.5 can't possibly know which fix is desired.)

For those readers who wish to write a general computer code, note that Equation 7.5f covers all possible relationships among LHA_1, GHA_1, and longitude. Our usual convention measures the LHA positive westward of the observer from $0°$ to $360°$. But the computer inverse cosine (Equation 7.5e) for LHA_1 returns positive angles from $0°$ to only $180°$. So if body 1 is east of the ship, the computer's returned LHA_1 must either be made negative or subtracted from $360°$ for use in Equation 7.5f. For example, if the body is east of the ship and $GHA_1 = 330°$ and LHA_1 returned by the inverse cosine is $170°$, then $Lon = -170° - 330° = -500°$. And adding one multiple of $360°$ gives longitude of $-140°$, or $140°W$, by our convention that west longitudes are negative. Of the two LHAs for body 1, the positive and the negative one, only one is valid. One way a computer code can decide between these two is to compare the computed altitudes from body 2 to the observed altitude H_2 for each of the two LHA possibilities. Alternatively, the navigator could just simply specify whether LHA_1 is positive (body 1 west) or negative (body 1 east).

Since Equations 7.5a through 7.5d depend only on the declinations and GHA differences of the two bodies, we can see that this direct calculation of latitude mathematically confirms our earlier discussion of finding latitude without a meridian sight or knowledge of UT. And since these don't change significantly with time for stars, any two-star observation gives latitude without knowing UT. Furthermore, we get latitude without selecting two APs and plotting two LOPs—and the equations are exactly the same form as a traditional two-star fix. More aspects of this sight reduction are discussed in Exercises 5.7 and 5.8.

St. Hilaire without a Sextant

Is it possible to work up a celestial LOP without a sextant? Sure, the one altitude that can be measured to useful accuracy without a sextant is zero altitude. Because of the normal haze on the horizon, plus their relatively low intensity, stars and planets are not candidates for a zero-altitude "shot". But under good viewing conditions the time the sun or moon crosses the horizon can be readily observed, giving us an LOP without a sextant. We certainly don't want to look directly at the sun's full disk as it approaches the horizon, and for that matter, the moon is sometimes too bright to view directly also. The simple and practical solution is to use the upper limb so that most of the body is well below the horizon when we finally take a direct look to mark the time. This means that sights of setting bodies are preferred because it can be tedious timing the upper limb's first appearance of a rising body.

Once the setting time is observed this zero observed-altitude is corrected as usual for dip (but of course, not for index error). The altitude correction for the sun's upper limb is − 49.6′ and the moon's is upper limb is + 4.5′ plus its parallax correction (see Appendix C). The sight reduction is a rather standard St. Hilaire, except for two things.

The altitude refraction correction is quite critical at this zero altitude. So be sure to use the Additional Correction Table from page

A4 of the Almanac (Appendix C). As you can see from the zero-altitude row, the additional temperature-pressure dependence can easily range over a few minutes of arc.

The sun's upper-limb negative altitude is not a problem when using H.O. 249 or when using a calculator. The H.O. 249 Aviation Navigation Tables were designed to handle the negative apparent altitudes possible from aircraft sights, and calculators automatically return negative altitudes from their inverse sign function. Even when using H.O. 229 you may only have to make a simple adjustment to your AP: When looking on the proper LHA page, following across the declination row and down the latitude column, you might find you're forced into the wrong "Contrary-Same" region of the table. Simply adjust your AP latitude one column over to stay in the proper region. This one-degree revision in AP latitude will not significantly affect the sight's accuracy. Finally, when plotting the intercept remember, for example, that an observed altitude of –53′ places the sun farther below the horizon than does the calculated altitude of – 27′. So in this case the intercept is plotted 26 nm away. Or if the calculated altitude were +3′, this intercept would be 56 nm away.

This ultimate low-altitude sight suffers from the vagaries of low-altitude refraction, not only for the body, but for the horizon which can sometimes be appreciable and is not accounted for in the dip correction. So be aware that this "sextantless" LOP might be off several miles in intercept, but the orientation of the LOP should be as reliable as a normal sight. Try this sight the next time you and your crew are watching for the green flash.

As an example, consider on 11 May 2005 we're now about 500 nm out of Las Palimas, in the Canary Islands, heading for our life-time dream of cruising the southern oceans. Our DR position is N24° 28′, W25° 17′, our height of eye is 9 ft, the temperature is a balmy 83°F, and the barometer is a nice steady 29.9″. While on a broad reach enjoying the north east trades, we time a lovely clear sunset at 20:19:18 UT.

Our workup using H.O. 249 follows: Even though we're using H.O. 249, which tabulates only to the nearest minute of arc, we do the rest of the calculation to 0.1′, just to avoid any unnecessary round off errors on our first non-sextant shot. Of course we could have easily used the calculator if we wanted to. The worksheet is the standard sun-worksheet in the Appendix, modified to accommodate the almanac's declination adjustment and to include the temperature and pressure corrections in the zero sextant altitude. Note that we have extrapolated the sun's upper limb altitude correction from the lowest tabulated apparent altitude of 0° 00' to our H_A of – 2.9' which is off the chart. We can easily see that the table's next lower H_A would be –0.3' with a correction of – 50.2'. (This extrapolation would be valid even on very large vessels where the dip correction could approach 6', giving a correction of –50.8'.) Because of the refraction uncertainties, it doesn't pay to get too fussy about these corrections.

Sun Worksheet for H.O. 249		
Limb *Upper Limb*	H_S	*0° 0'*
Date *11 May 2005*	index	
UT *20 : 19 : 18*	dip *– 2.9'*	*9 ft*
	H_A *– 2.9'*	
DR Lat *N24° 28'*	Alt *– 50.2'*	
DR Lon *N25° 17'*	Temp, P *+ 3.0'*	*83°F 29.9"*
AP Lat *N24°*		
AP Lon *W25° 44.4'*	H_O *– 47.2'*	
dec *N18° 3.9'*	GHA *120° 54.9'*	
+ 0.2' d=0.6	m s *4° 49.5'*	
N18° 4.1'	GHA *125° 44.4'*	
H_{TAB} *–1° 27'*	AP Lon *25° 44.4'* (E+, W–)	
Corr *+ 1.8' +4.1'x 27'/160'*	360°	
H_C *–1° 25.2'*	LHA *100°*	
H_O *– 47.2'*		
38 nm Z *70°*		
Toward Zn *290°*		

8

Lunar Distance Sights

In the previous chapter we obtained UT from a lunar LOP and a star fix, using the fact that the moon's GHA advances significantly slower than the star's. This is an indirect approach. Why not directly measure the great-circle distance between the moon and a star? For that matter, wouldn't the same idea apply to the distance between the moon and any other celestial body?

Well, this very idea was suggested, as early as 1472 by Johann Muller and by John Werner in 1514, to determine Greenwich time at sea and hence to find a ship's longitude. But the required mathematics was intractable for the average seaman until around the time Bowditch published his first edition of the *New American Practical Navigator* in 1802. Even though marine chronometers were perfected by John Harrison around 1760, they were impractical because they were expensive and impossible to check on long voyages. So lunar distances became the preferred method of determining longitude; their explanations and tables were included in Bowditch until 1914.

Today there's a renewed interest in lunar distances for the same reason that there's an interest in celestial navigation. Many people find celestial navigation interesting, challenging, of historical importance, satisfying to have mastered, and useful. All this can also be said of lunar distances, with an emphasis on satisfaction and a de-emphasis on useful. Nonetheless, there's always the possibility that accurate time at sea will be lost, along with radio and GPS, leaving us with no knowledge of UT. Lunars are just one more backup.

Because of its challenge, many see celestial navigation as the Holy Grail of navigation. If that's a fair evaluation, then it's fair to say that lunar distances are the Holy Grail of celestial navigation. Yet the explanation and use of lunars, as they are informally called, is straightforward. Their sight reductions use the same principles and equations that we've already discussed (as promised, no new equations). It is true that there are a couple more steps involved, but they are simple ones. Perhaps their largest drawback is their impracticality—and in a perverted way, perhaps that's their attraction. As in the previous chapter, we'll see that an observational precision of one minute of arc usually translates to about a two-minute time precision. With the one-second accuracy of reliable, cheap quartz watches, lunars fade in importance for the practical navigator. But the complete (elitist?) navigator couldn't ask for anything more than mastering the esoteric lunar.

Perhaps the value of lunars is best expressed by Captain Joshua Slocum in his account of his 1895-98 solo circumnavigation of the world in his sloop *Spray*: "The work of the lunarian, though seldom practiced in these days of chronometers, is beautifully edifying, and there is nothing in the realm of navigation that lifts one's heart up more in adoration."

The Concept

By measuring the great-circle distance between the moon and another celestial body (we'll use the sun in our discussion), we can determine UT. The moon's relative motion among the backdrop of other celestial bodies provides a clock because the *Nautical Almanac* tabulates the position of the moon versus UT. Better yet, UT could be tabulated versus the moon's position relative to other bodies. In fact, such tables, published in the *Nautical Almanac* until 1913, tabulated lunar distances at intervals of three hours for the sun and some stars near the ecliptic. The accurate measurement of these lunar distances was a major impetus for establishing the British Royal Observatory in Greenwich.

Today, anyone with a little computer savvy and the celestial navigation knowledge we've gained already could easily compute and tabulate the moon-sun arc distance versus UT. (Adapt Equation 5.1a by replacing the earth coordinates with appropriate celestial ones, and $\sin H_C$ with $\cos LD$, for lunar distance. Also see Appendix A and Equation 8.5 below.) Then a navigator could simply measure this lunar distance with a sextant, make some altitude corrections (naturally), page through this lunar table for the observed lunar distance, and read off the UT of the sight across from this lunar distance.

The UT thus obtained can be used to adjust clocks that keep time poorly, thus avoiding the need for expensive chronometers. Today, of course, an inexpensive quartz watch is all that's needed for celestial navigation, and it can be checked against outside time signals from radio or GPS. Historically, latitude was found by meridian sights that do not require accurate knowledge of UT (remember, time is only needed for the declination, which changes relatively slowly). Using the latitude previously obtained from a meridian sight, the LHA was calculated (Equation A.10, Appendix A). Then the longitude was extracted from this LHA and the GHA of the body, using the time found by lunars, or later by marine chronometers.

In keeping with our approach to celestial navigation, using modern developments, simple tools, and a full understanding of fundamental principles, we'll explain how lunars can be used to find UT without the use of specialized tables or mysterious rote procedures.

Taking the Lunar Sight

The principle observational difference between lunars and conventional sights is, of course, measuring the lunar distance itself. (The discussion on taking conventional sights is in Chapter 9.) The lunar measurement is made by bringing the near limbs of the sun and moon into coincidence with the sextant. Of course we always use the limb of the moon that is fully lit: the side toward the sun. Since we are measuring to these near limbs, we will need to add both semidiameters to the sextant reading. So the index-corrected reading LD is increased to the semidiameter-corrected distance, which we'll call LD_{SD}.

At first, taking a lunar distance sight may seem awkward, particularly at large sun-moon distances. I've found that the simplest idea for finding both bodies in the field of view works perfectly well: Set the index arm at an eyeball-estimate of the LD (point your arms and estimate the angle); set the sun shades; aim the telescope at the moon with the index mirror toward the sun; rotate the sextant about the telescope's axis so that the moon's terminator line (the light-dark boundary on the moon) is perpendicular to the sextant's frame. (This last step more accurately aims the index mirror at the sun.) Then while slightly rocking the sextant about the telescope's axis, swing the arm back and forth a bit. Soon the sun's image pops into view. From then on the sight is conventional: Rock the sextant while keeping the moon in the center of view, and adjust the near limbs so they just kiss. You'll soon notice how very slowly the LD changes compared to the more familiar altitude rate of change.

You might think that you can measure a lunar distance as large as the arc reads on your sextant (up to around 120° to 140°, depending on the sextant). But the limitation is on the foreshortening of the index mirror's projection onto the horizon mirror. At large angles this projection becomes smaller and smaller, making these wide-angle sights difficult. Also at wide angles the telescope's collimation error becomes more important, again see Chapter 9. (These considerations are equally important for any wide-angle shots, such as some terrestrial sights used in coastal navigation.)

Obviously, because lunar sights use two bodies, they have more availability limitations than other sights. Not only are two bodies required above the horizon, but both bodies also have to be clear of clouds; the new moon (its dark phase) puts it out of commission for three days a month; and in the crescent and gibbous phases, only one of its two limbs can be used for the required altitude shot.

Now we assume that we've overcome these lunar challenges, made the sights, and recorded the time of the observations with a watch set somewhere near UT, one that keeps time poorly and that we want to correct with lunars. Using the GHA and declination for the sun and the moon from the almanac, we calculate the lunar distance LD at two times, say the whole hour before our lunar sight and the whole hour after it. We also measure both the sun's and moon's altitudes at the time of the LD measurement. Using these two altitudes we somehow correct LD_{SD} for refraction and parallax. (As we've seen earlier, parallax is quite large for the moon, being as great as 61 minutes.)

Next we interpolate the UT of the lunar sight by using the two LDs that were calculated before and after the observed LD. Comparison of this interpolated time with the watch time of the sight tells how much the watch is fast or slow. For example, if the value of the observed LD is, say, 73 percent of the way between the LD calculated for the whole hour before the sight and the LD calculated for the whole hour after the sight, then the true UT of the sight was 73 percent of 60 minutes, or $0.73 \times 60m =$ 43.8m = 43m 48s past the hour. This determination of the time of the sight is, in fact, an interpolation between two LD values from a lunar table of our own making, one with just two entries, the only two that are needed. And that's all there is to lunars—well, except for that Holy Grail thing.

The Distance Clearing Concept

As for conventional sights, altitude corrections must be made to the sextant's measurement of the lunar distance. Since the measurement is between two celestial bodies, not referenced to the horizon, there is no dip correction. But corrections for refraction by the earth's atmosphere and parallax, particularly for the moon, must be applied to the semidiameter-corrected distance LD_{SD}. Historically, correcting the LD for altitude has been called *clearing the lunar distance*. Apparently the name comes from the idea of clearing the lunar distance of refraction and parallax effects. The situation is shown in Figure 8.1, where a navigator, located at Ob, observes the great-circle distance LD between the moon and the sun. The conventional altitude corrections for the sun and the moon adjust their individual altitudes, but how do they affect the LD observed at Ob?

To answer this question we redraw part of Figure 8.1 showing only the horizon system of coordinates as depicted in Figure 8.2a. The familiar co-altitudes extending from the body to the observer's zenith, and the altitudes extending from the body to the horizon, are along great circles, called *vertical circles*. They pass through the observer's zenith and the body, intersecting the horizon at right angles. We call

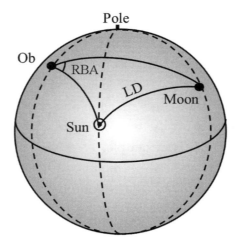

Figure 8.1 An observer at Ob sees the lunar distance LD. The relative bearing angle at Ob between the sun and the moon is RBA.

the angle between the two vertical circles the *relative bearing angle* (RBA), because it's the relative bearing between the sun and the moon observed at the observer's location Ob. As shown in the figure, the sun's altitude H_{SD} and the moon's altitude h_{SD} extend the apparent altitudes into the centers of the bodies to form a closed triangle having vertices sun-moon-Ob. Applying the refraction and parallax corrections gives us the conventional fully-corrected altitudes H_O and h_O. They alter the shape of the triangle by moving the sun and moon locations as shown in Figure 8.2b.

Exclusive of the semidiameter corrections, these altitude corrections always produce an increase in altitude for the moon and a decrease for the sun. Although the refraction correction is always negative while the parallax correction is always positive, the sun's parallax is always quite small, so its combined correction is always negative. On the other hand, the moon's parallax is so large that it always trumps refraction, producing a combined correction that is always positive. These corrections are shown in Figure 8.2b, where semidiameter-corrected LD_{SD} is cleared to produce LD_O. We can find the altitude corrections in the almanac. But we're left with a geometry question: How do we calculate the true lunar distance LD_O, given the lunar distance LD_{SD} and the altitude adjustments *along the vertical circles*?

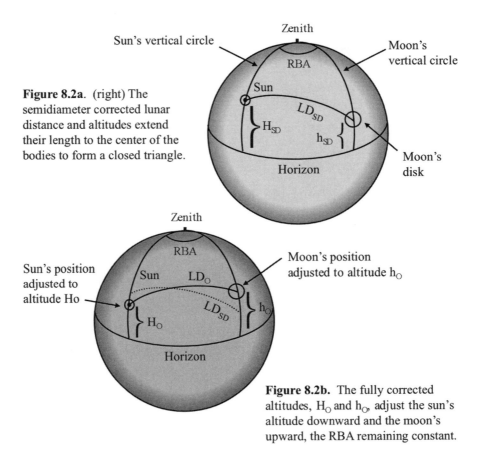

Figure 8.2a. (right) The semidiameter corrected lunar distance and altitudes extend their length to the center of the bodies to form a closed triangle.

Figure 8.2b. The fully corrected altitudes, H_O and h_O, adjust the sun's altitude downward and the moon's upward, the RBA remaining constant.

The answer to the above question lies in the observation that in altering LD_{SD} to LD_O, as shown in going from Figure 8.2a to 8.2b, the angle RBA remains constant. This fact is confirmed by thinking of how light from a celestial body is refracted in the plane of the vertical circle containing the body and the observer. This is emphasized in Figure 8.3, where the earth is shown very small compared to a greatly exaggerated atmosphere that bends the light rays. It's also easy to see that parallax operates in this same plane (see Figure 9.11 and its discussion). Thus if we adjust the altitudes of the sun and the moon along their vertical circles, the RBA must remain constant, as pictured in Figures 8.2 and 8.3. This constant RBA is the key to the geometry problem.

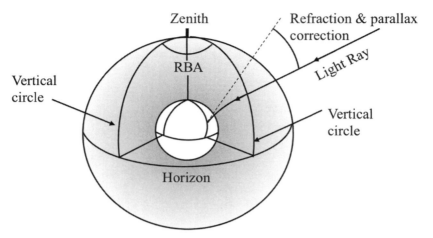

Figure 8.3 Because refraction in the earth's atmosphere (shaded) is confined to the plane of the vertical circle defined by the observer and the body, it does not alter the relative bearing angle RBA.

Clearing the Lunar Distance

All that remains is to transform our above verbal observation into a computational form useful for obtaining the LD altitude correction. As always, we need no new equations, only the ones already used in conventional sights (also see Appendix A). Our familiar altitude equation 5.1a gives exactly what we need; it gives the side of a spherical triangle in terms of the opposite angle and its adjacent sides. A minor detail is that Equation 5.1a solves for $\sin H_C$, which is the complement of the side. The side itself is given by the cosine. So with this modification, the generic application of Equation 5.1a to Figure 8.2a gives

$$\cos LD_{SD} = \sin H_{SD} \sin h_{SD} + \cos H_{SD} \cos h_{SD} \cos RBA \qquad (8.1)$$

where H_{SD} and h_{SD} are the sun's and moon's altitudes (respectively) corrected for index, dip, and semidiameter. These semidiameter corrections adjust the length of the LD and the altitude coordinates to close the triangle, making Equation 8.1 applicable. Now, if we further adjust H_{SD} and h_{SD} for refraction and parallax, we have the fully corrected altitudes H_O and h_O, which are obtained from the sextant altitudes in the conventional manner. And adapting our same great-circle distance Equation 8.1 to the fully-corrected triangle in Figure 8.2b gives the new lunar distance LD_O from

$$\cos LD_O = \sin H_O \sin h_O + \cos H_O \cos h_O \cos RBA \tag{8.2a}$$

where we have used the key fact that RBA has not changed. Furthermore, solving Equation 8.1 for cos RBA also gives

$$\cos RBA = (\cos LD_{SD} - \sin H_{SD} \sin h_{SD}) / \cos H_{SD} \cos h_{SD} \tag{8.2b}$$

So we substitute cos RBA from the above equation into 8.2a to get the final answer:

$$\cos LD_O = \sin H_O \sin h_O + \\ \cos H_O \cos h_O (\cos LD_{SD} - \sin H_{SD} \sin h_{SD}) / \\ \cos H_{SD} \cos h_{SD} \tag{8.3}$$

Thus we have the cleared lunar distance LD_O in terms of the lunar distance LD_{SD}, the semidiameter-corrected altitudes H_{SD} and h_{SD}, and the conventionally corrected altitudes H_O and h_O. This is a complete and exact result for clearing the lunar distance.

Equation 8.3 might appear complex, but in fact it consists of the same equations and thus requires the same work as a St. Hilaire sight reduction. First we solve Equation 8.2b, which is the azimuth equation in the St. Hilaire method. Then we substitute cos RBA into Equation 8.2a and solve for LD_O, which is the altitude equation in the St. Hilaire method—the same two equations, the same amount of work. In fact, historically these same solutions of the navigation triangle were first used to solve lunar distance problems, long before St. Hilaire thought of using them in his sight reductions.

To use a calculator, we store H_{SD} in [1] and h_{SD} in [2], then Equation 8.2b becomes in terms of keystroke instructions

$$[3] = (\cos LD_{SD} - \sin [1] \sin [2]) / \cos [1] \cos [2] \tag{8.4a}$$

where LD_{SD} is not stored because it's only entered once. The [3] means to store the result of the right-hand calculation in location [3] because cos RBA is used next in Equation 8.2a, which now reads

$$\cos LD_O = \sin [1] \sin [2] + \cos [1] \cos [2] \times [3] \qquad (8.4b)$$

after we've stored H_O in [1] and h_O in [2]. So the calculator operations are practically the same as in the St. Hilaire reduction.

There are other mathematical expressions for clearing the lunar distance. One method approximates Equation 8.3 by extracting the effects proportional to the relatively small differences in the sun and moon's altitude corrections $H_O - H_{SD}$ and $h_O - h_{SD}$ (and to their squares, when needed). But the two required proportionality constants are each calculated from equations just like Equation 8.2b. So that approach saves no effort and unnecessarily introduces approximations. With today's ten-digit accuracy of hand calculators, the above exact equations are easily evaluated accurately. (See Exercises 4.8 and 4.9.)

The Sight Reduction

As we've discussed earlier, high accuracy of sights might not be important in the open ocean where uncertainties of even 20 miles can be of no particular significance to navigation. But high accuracy in lunars is *always* useful for determining UT. This is because one minute of arc in the LD translates into about two minutes of UT, which is much poorer time resolution than our normally desired one second. Again, the sextant observation itself is clearly the limitation. But we don't want to compound this problem with inaccuracies in the sight reduction. So we'll aim for a sight reduction accuracy of 0.1´ of arc, which becomes a bit tricky when treating lunar altitude corrections because of the moon's relative closeness to the earth. Perhaps these subtleties add to the mystique of lunars.

The sight reduction procedure discussed above for reducing a lunar is summarized in the flow chart of Figure 8.4. We'll use this chart to keep the big picture in mind while we move through the individual steps.

The flow chart starts in the upper left-hand corner by demanding an impossibility: Measure the sun's altitude, moon's altitude, and sun-moon distance simultaneously. Well, who said lunars were easy? One way to approximate these simultaneous observations is to take several LD readings, say three. Then take the two altitudes, followed by three more LD readings. Average the six LD readings and their times to get an improved LD observation, which is really needed anyway. If the first group of LD observations took nearly the same time as the second group, their average time will satisfactorily approximate the time of the altitude readings. This is just one of many ways of approximating these simultaneous readings. Also, we could graph several observations of

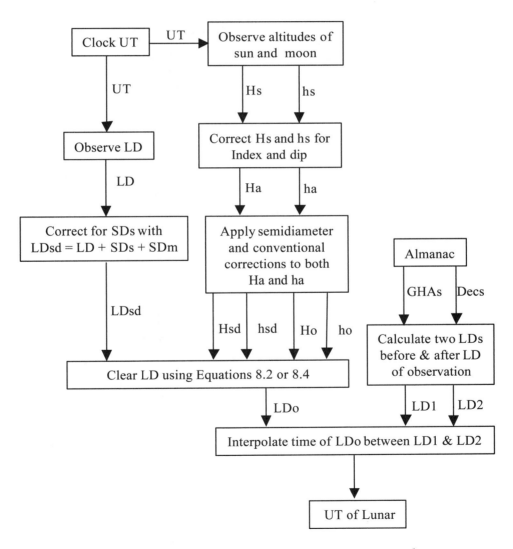

Figure 8.4 Flow chart for reducing a lunar-distance sight.

all three readings, draw the best curve through each of the three graphs, and read off the three measurements at one common time.

The three principle columns of the flowchart divide the sight reduction into its major tasks: The left column corrects the LD for semidiameters to get LD_{SD}. The middle column computes four altitude corrections to get H_{SD}, h_{SD}, H_O, and h_O. At the bottom of these two columns, these four altitudes are used to clear the lunar distance LD_{SD} to get LD_O.

Quite independently of these corrections for LD_O, the right column shows the calculation of the lunar distances that would be observed at times 1 and 2, before and after the expected time of the actual observation. And finally at the bottom, the cleared lunar distance is interpolated between the two calculated ones for times 1 and 2 to give us the actual UT of the observation.

Now, with the flowchart's big picture in mind, we can organize the details sequentially as shown in the worksheet of Figure 8.5. Before we give an example of an actual sight reduction, we'll describe the worksheet layout: The top block contains the observed data. It contains the date and time, the lunar distance, and the altitudes of the sun and moon. These blocks, or bins, containing the lunar calculations, we appropriately call loony bins.

The top loony bin calculates the semidiameters and the semidiameter-corrected lunar distance LD_{SD}. The second bin calculates the semidiameter corrected altitudes and uses them to calculate the cos(RBA) which it stores in calculator location [3]. The third loony bin calculates the conventional altitude corrections and uses them to clear the lunar distance, giving us LD_O.

Independently of these calculations, the fourth bin (second from the bottom) calculates the lunar distances that would be observed at times 1 and 2, the times before and after the expected time of observation. And finally, the bottom loony bin interpolates between these calculated lunar distances at times 1 and 2 to give the actual observation UT.

Date: *12 May 2005*		Estimated UT: *21:18:16*

$H_A = 38° 23.9' LL$ $h_A = 30° 21.3' LL$ $LD = 51° 52.3'$

$SD_{SUN} = 15.9'$ $SD_{MOON} = SD_{TAB} + 0.26' \sin(h_A)$

$SD_{MOON} = 14.9' + 0.26' \sin(30° 21.3) = 15.03'$

$LD_{SD} = 51° 52.3' + 15.9' + 15.0' = \boxed{52° 23.2'} = 52.38666667$ STO[3]

Sun SD alt correction: Moon SD alt correction:

H_A 38° 23.9' h_A 30° 21.3'

LL SD   <u>15.9'</u>   LL SD   <u>15.0'</u>

H_{SD} 38° 39.8'   STO[1] h_{SD} 30° 36.3'   STO[2]

STO[3] = $\cos RBA = ([3] - \sin[1] \sin[2]) / (\cos[1] \cos[2])$

Full sun alt correction: Full moon alt correction:

H_A 38° 23.9' h_A 30° 21.3'

alt   <u>+14.8'</u>   main   58.8'

H_O 38° 38.7'   STO[1]   LL   <u>1.3'</u>

                                    h_O 31° 21.4'   STO[2]

$\cos LD_O = \sin[1] \sin[2] + \cos[1] \cos[2] \times [3]$; $LD_O = 52° 2.9'$

Compute LD for *2100* UT:

Sun GHA   135° 55.2'   dec *N18° 19.5'*   STO[1]

Moon GHA <u>*79° 59.0'*</u>   dec *N27° 49.7'*   STO[2]

Diff GHA   55° 56.2'   STO[3]

$\cos LD_1 = \sin[1] \sin[2] + \cos[1] \cos[2] \cos[3]$; $LD1 = 51° 54.2'$

Compute LD for *2200* UT:

Sun GHA   150° 55.2'   dec *N18° 20.1'*   STO[1]

Moon GHA <u>*94° 27.8'*</u>   dec *N27° 46.7'*   STO[2]

Diff GHA   56° 27.4'   STO[3]

$\cos LD2 = \sin[1] \sin[2] + \cos[1] \cos[2] \cos[3]$; $LD2 = 52° 21.7'$

Interpolate for UT:

$\Delta T = 60 (LD_O - LD1) / (LD2 - LD1) = 60 (8.7'/27.5')$

$\Delta T = 18.982 min = 18:59$ $UT = 21:18:59$

Figure 8.5 Lunar distance worksheet.

A Lunar Example

Consider that on 12 May 2005 we've observed lunar distances in the moon's waxing phase using some averaging procedure to get the altitudes. This led to a LD of 51° 52.3′ at the averaged watch time of $21^h 18^m 16^s$ UT. Also we've found $H_A = 38° 23.9′$ for the sun's LL apparent altitude and $h_A = 30° 21.3′$ for the moon's LL apparent altitude. (Remember that apparent altitudes have been corrected for index error and dip.) We want to correct the watch's UT using lunar distances.

First we fill in the data at the top of the worksheet in the first loony bin. Because we've measured the LD from the nearest limbs of the sun and moon, we need to add their semidiameters to the LD to get the distance between the centers of the bodies. Looking at the bottom of the almanac's daily page, we find the sun's SD is 15.9′ on 12 May 2005 (Appendix C).

Finding the SD of the moon to within our accuracy requirement demands one more step because it appears larger at greater altitudes, since it's then closer to the observer. This tiny increase, called augmentation, can be approximated for our purposes by $0.26′ \sin(h_A)$. So we need to add this augmentation to the 14.9′ SD found in the daily page for 12 May 2005.

Next we enter bin 2, applying the semidiameters to the apparent altitudes, and storing H_{SD} and h_{SD} in calculator locations [1] and [2]. Then we use the keystroke reminder equation (which is Equation 8.4a) to calculate cos RBA and store that in location [3].

Loony bin 3 is next, where we calculate the observed altitudes H_O and h_O in the conventional manner from the almanac's sun and moon altitude-correction tables. These tables include corrections for parallax, augmentation, and refraction. So turning to the almanac's altitude correction tables (Appendix C), we enter with the sun's $H_A = 38° 23.9′$ and find a correction of 14.8′ and add it to H_A to get H_O. Looking in the moon's correction tables with $h_A = 30° 21.3′$, we find a main correction of 58.8′. Using the HP of 54.4′ from the daily pages, we interpolate the LL correction, getting 1.3′. Adding these to h_A gives h_O. Also remember that when we're being fussy about accuracy, we must include additional corrections when the temperature and pressure deviate from the standard atmosphere of 10° C and 1010 millibars

(Table A4 in the almanac).

Having found LD_{SD}, H_{SD}, h_{SD}, H_O, and h_O (the first five shaded items on the worksheet), we are ready to clear the lunar distance: Taking a calculator in hand, we execute the keystrokes as indicated by the reminder equation in bin 3 (which represents Equation 8.4b) to get the cleared distance $LD_O = 52°\ 2.9'$.

Now it's time to make our personal lunar distance table in bin 4. Looking in the almanac on the 12 May 2005 page, we extract the GHA and declination for the sun and moon for 2100 UT and 2200 UT, the hour before our sight and the hour after. Then using these declinations and the GHA differences, we execute the keystroke reminder equations to calculate LD1 and LD2. These equations represent the great-circle equation

$$\cos LD = \sin d_{sun} \sin d_{moon} + \\ \cos d_{sun} \cos d_{moon} \cos (GHA_{sun} - GHA_{moon}) \qquad (8.5)$$

Finally, we're at the bottom of the flow chart and worksheet. We are ready to find the sight time by interpolating the time of LD_O between the times of LD1 and LD2. (Notice how LD2 has increased from LD1 as expected with the moon east of the sun, trailing in its waxing phase.) The interpolation is done by equating the LD-difference ratios to their corresponding time-difference ratios: The difference $LD2 - LD1 = 27.5'$ corresponds to their 60-minute time difference. Similarly, the difference $LD_O - LD1 = 8.7'$ corresponds to the unknown time interval ΔT after 2100 UT. Therefore $\Delta T / 60 = 8.7' / 27.5'$. This gives $\Delta T = 60(8.7/27.5) = 18m\ 59s$ past 2100 UT. But the watch read $21^h\ 18^m\ 16^s$ UT at the sight time T. So the lunar indicates that the watch is 43 seconds slow on UT.

Accuracy

The interpretation of any observation requires thinking about the accuracy of the facts. Celestial navigation is no different. The above example shows the watch to be 43 seconds slow on UT. However, before we rush to advance the watch by this 43 seconds, we'd better think a bit.

Looking at the LD1-LD2 difference of 27.5' over 60 minutes means that about *one minute of LD corresponds to about two minutes of time*, an observation claimed at the beginning of our lunar discussion. So we see the hard, cruel fact that the lunar distance is not nearly as sensitive to time as we would like. And how accurate was the observation itself? At sea we expect sights to be within perhaps 1´ to 3´, depending on conditions and the observer's skill. Each of us must learn to evaluate our own accuracy capability; see the discussion at the end of Chapter 10. To conclude that the watch deserves resetting in this case, would mean that we can dependably measure to *much* better than one minute of arc. I would need proof of that assertion before tampering with the watch. Put another way, this lunar confirms that the watch is correct within the lunar's uncertainty.

Moreover, we need to take into account the possible accumulation of other errors. The almanac itself claims no more than 0.3´ accuracy for its tabulated coordinates of the moon. We've neglected the oblateness of the earth in the parallax correction, which can amount to a 0.2´ error. Even perfectly adjusted sextants have from 0.15´ to more than 0.33´ of arc error, depending on the quality of the instrument. So it's idealistic to think that any sight reduction, even with many averaged readings, is much better than one minute of arc.

Accepting this one-minute uncertainty in LD then gives us a two-minute uncertainty in UT. Remembering that the earth rotates 1.0´ in four seconds of time, this 120-second uncertainty in UT determines longitude to within only 30´. Maybe this explains how the British Parliament selected its accuracy requirement when it posted the £20,000 (millions in today's U.S. dollars) award for anyone who could determine longitude at sea to within 30´. It's practically impossible to do so by using lunars. Instead, John Harrison's marine chronometers came to the rescue.

So Why Lunars Today?

For appreciation and confidence. With cheap quartz watches (several, for reliability) we can do all the modern celestial navigation we could want. But learning and practicing lunars gives us deeper insight into celestial navigation; an appreciation for their historical importance and difficulty; and perhaps most significant of all, after conquering lunars we can appreciate the great convenience of St. Hilaire sights and modern quartz watches. Moreover, in the rare event of losing UT, with lunars and only a poor watch we can still be confident of finding our longitude at sea (well, OK, to within 30´).

Other Lunars

Lunar moon-star or moon-planet sights simply follow the above moon-sun example with, of course, no semidiameter corrections for stars or planets. So their apparent altitudes are used in place of the sun's semidiameter-corrected altitude. Select bodies near the ecliptic because they have the most lunar-distance sensitivity to time.

For practicing lunars, we can simplify a bit, thereby avoiding three simultaneous sights, altitude measurement errors, and interpolation for UT. And we don't require a horizon. From an accurately known location, make a LD observation (averaging for better accuracy, if you like). But then calculate the altitudes H_O and h_O for the time and location of the sight. Using the altitude correction tables, calculate the apparent altitudes corresponding to these corrected altitudes (i.e., we make the corrections in reverse). Then using these synthetic apparent altitudes find H_{SD} and h_{SD}, and clear the lunar distance. Next, calculate the lunar distance at the actual UT of the sight using the daily pages from the almanac. Comparison of the cleared lunar distance with the calculated one demonstrates the combined limitations of lunars and navigator skill.

Star-star sights offer an even better test of combined observational skill and sextant accuracy. The *Nautical Almanac* claims an accuracy better than 0.2´ for the coordinates of stars. And if two stars are selected with reasonably high altitudes, the refraction corrections will be very small and reliable. Therefore, comparing an observed star-star distance that is cleared of refraction with the calculated value is an excellent measure of combined navigator-sextant performance. For a simpler evaluation of navigator-sextant performance, Appendix G offers a direct approach. It tabulates the arc distance, already adjusted for refraction, between twelve star pairs. So your star-star distance reading corrected only for index error, should agree with those tabulated distances. You can also see from these tables how very insensitive is the refraction correction in the altitudes of the two stars.

9

THE ALTITUDE OBSERVATIONS

We've now covered sight reductions from keel to mast truck—sights by direct calculation and by tables; sights of all the navigational bodies;

and sights of all types, from St. Hilaire to lunar distance sights. That's the hard part of celestial navigation. As outlined much earlier, the other tasks of taking observations and plotting results pale in difficulty by comparison. But of course, they're of equal importance. Plotting and related issues come in the next chapter. Here we treat the important aspects of altitude observations: checking and adjusting the sextant, using it in observations, and correcting the altitude readings.

The Sextant

The marine sextant, shown in Figure 9.1, has three major optical parts: two mirrors, and an optional telescope. In addition there are separate shades for adjusting the brightness of the celestial body and the horizon. Beyond the obvious protection that shades provide for bright objects (the sun, moon, and sun-lit horizon), they can be very useful for getting optimum contrast under difficult conditions. The index mirror is located over the pivot point of the index arm. It reflects the image of the celestial body onto the horizon mirror. As shown in the figure, the horizon mirror is located in line with the observer's sight to the horizon; it not only reflects the body's image from the index mirror into the observer's eye, but also allows the observer to see the horizon directly. Thus, looking at the horizon mirror, you see both the horizon and the body in the same view. By looking at this composite view, the body and horizon are brought into coincidence by moving the index arm; then the altitude is read from the scale on the arc and the micrometer drum. Most sextants use a telescope, but sometimes a simple sight tube, or even just a peep sight, is used to view the horizon mirror (as in some antique octants). They all function perfectly well, but scopes have certain advantages discussed below.

The Horizon Mirror

There are two types of horizon mirrors that produce a composite view of the horizon and the celestial body. The older traditional mirror is silvered (or aluminized) on the right half (toward the frame), and clear on the left half. So you see a split image, the body on the right side of the horizon mirror, and the horizon on the left with a slight overlap of the two images in the middle. The newer type isn't divided into halves. Rather, its whole surface is uniformly treated with a thin film (dielectric or metal oxide) designed to give the mirror good reflectivity from the side facing the index-mirror, and good transmissivity from the side facing the horizon. Since both the horizon and the body are treated the same all the way across the mirror, there's no split image; the two are simply superimposed to make one combined image. Since there's no split in the image, these mirrors are called various names, such as *whole-horizon mirrors, allview mirrors,* or sometimes, *beamsplitters* (as Michelson and Morley called them in their famous 1887 experiment, showing the speed of light is a constant).

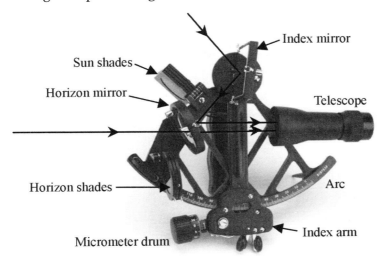

Figure 9.1 A marine sextant by Celestaire, showing the light rays from a celestial body and the horizon combining in the telescope to form a composite image. (Courtesy of Celestaire)

In bright-light conditions the whole-horizon mirror, with its two images completely superimposed across the field of view, is convenient for locating celestial bodies and is particularly nice for keeping them in view in rough weather on small boats. However, under certain conditions it produces a washed-out image. This occurs whenever the index-mirror image has little contrast between the body and its background, such as a dim star in a partially lit twilight sky. And it's further exacerbated when the direct image of the horizon has little contrast, such as in hazy conditions. Then superimposing this uniform wash from the index mirror with a low-contrast horizon-mirror image reduces the contrast in the combined images.

This loss of contrast is easily demonstrated with the whole-horizon sextant. Just look at a daytime horizon with the arc set just off of zero so that you see two horizons; then cover the index mirror with an opaque card, or the darkest sunshade. The increased contrast is dramatic. (Although the eye can just detect a 100 percent intensity change, it's sensitive to a mere 2 percent contrast change.)

Thus, the whole-horizon mirror makes high-contrast sights (such as the sun and stars against a dark sky) more convenient, but it makes low-contrast sights (such as dim stars against a twilight sky) more difficult—sometimes impossible. So with bright stars under reasonably good viewing conditions, the whole-horizon mirror's convenience outweighs the washout problem, but with poor viewing conditions, such as dim stars or haze, the traditional mirror can make the shot possible. Or to put it another way, the whole-horizon mirror makes easy sights easier, and hard sights harder.

The Telescope

Some common sextant telescopes are designated 3.5x40, 4x40, 6x30, 7x35, or 8x30, where the first number is the magnification and the second is the objective lens diameter in millimeters. Magnification is familiar to everyone. In sextant applications, as in all astronomical applications, the object is effectively at infinity, so all rays entering the objective lens from a given point on the object (*e.g.*, a point on the sun's disk) are parallel to each other, as diagramed in Figure 9.2. Those same rays exiting the eyepiece are also parallel to each other. These exiting rays leave the scope at a greater angle to the scope's axis than the entering rays. The ratio of the larger exiting angle to the smaller entering angle is called the angular magnification, or more simply, just magnification. A 4x scope will make the sun's 0.5-degree diameter appear to the observer as a 2-degree diameter. If, looking through a 4x scope, an observer looks at the sun's lower limb, and then shifts his eye to focus on the upper limb, he's rotated his eyeball 2 degrees.

Higher magnification helps to bring the celestial body more exactly into coincidence with the horizon. A person with 20/20 vision can resolve 1′ of arc. So with a 4x scope this person would theoretically be able to determine this coincidence to 0.25′, but other factors, such as instrument quality, atmospherics, and star patterns, can limit this resolution. (Parenthetically, quite a few people have 20/15, and very rarely, 20/10 vision.) Useful magnification is normally limited by ship motion with 3.5x or 4x useful on small boats, and 7x or 8x about the limit on large ships (or in many handheld applications, for that matter).

The diameter of the parallel rays exiting the eyepiece is called the *exit pupil*; see Figure 9.2. Simple geometric optics show that this exit pupil is equal to the objective lens diameter divided by the scope magnification. Hence a 4x40 scope has a 10mm exit pupil. The human eye pupil varies from 2-4mm (larger for older people) in bright light to 8mm in dim light, so even with the largest eye pupil of 8mm, this 4x40 scope wastes a little, although insignificant, light.

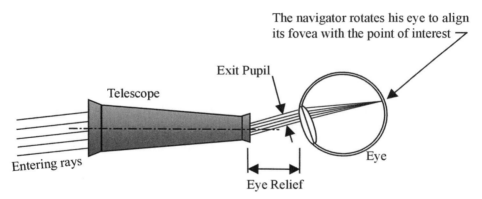

Figure 9.2 With the telescope focused at infinity, parallel rays from the distant object emerge from the eyepiece at a greater angle to the axis than they went in, producing an angular magnification. The exiting rays also have a smaller cross section than the entering rays, producing increased light intensity from a point source, such as a star.

Since the bundle of parallel light exiting a telescope's eyepiece is smaller than the corresponding parallel rays going in, the intensity (light per area) of the exiting rays has been increased. The eye focuses these parallel rays to a point on its retina. Thus the light-gathering power of a scope with a 40mm objective lens is much greater than the 8mm eye pupil: The ratio of this scope's aperture to the eye's is 40/8 = 5. The ratio of these areas is 5 squared, or 25. This is the ratio of brightness that the scope delivers compared to the unaided human eye when looking at a point source, such as a star. However, because of the logarithmic response of the human eye, this 25-fold increase in intensity doesn't seem that great. A single doubling of intensity is just detectable by the human eye. Thinking as the eye does, this 25-fold increase is only 4.64 doublings, which, although still appreciable, is not as great as you might have thought.

However, the above analysis of brightness versus aperture size is only for point sources, such as stars. Extended sources, such as the water and sky, also have their brightness altered by the telescope's magnification. For example, 3.5x40 scope and a 7x35 have an insignificant difference in aperture size. But the 3.5x has one-half the magnification of the 7x scope, producing an image of an extended source with one-half the linear dimensions of the 7x scope's image. Thus the light intensity (light per unit area again) of the 3.5x scope is four times the 7x scope's. In terms of the eye's log response, the 3.5x40 scope is two doublings brighter than the 7x35 (still neglecting aperture differences). Normally it's not the overall brightness that's important for detecting the horizon, but rather the sky-water contrast—and contrast is everything in taking difficult sights. But in dim light, the eye is more sensitive to slight contrast differentials when the brightness is increased. Therefore, the superior surface brightness of the lower magnification 3.5x scopes makes the horizon more visible for star sights with their dim light. However, I've found that this surface effect is somewhat subtle, verified only in the most difficult dim conditions. Nonetheless, some navigators call the 3.5x and 4x star scopes, and the higher magnification 6x, 7x, and 8x sun scopes. The star scopes work out well for both star and sun shots on small boats because the higher magnification of sun scopes isn't useful under small-boat conditions anyway. But having both is ideal for navigators of large ships.

We ignored pupil size in the above discussion because it's not critical: The nighttime eye pupil can effectively accommodate the 11 and 10mm exit pupils of the 3.5x40 and 4x40 scopes since the wasted light is negligible from the small aperture mismatch between the scope and eye pupil; and the wasted light is irrelevant for sun sights with the daytime's abundance of light. Also, the 5mm exit pupils of 6x30 and 7x35 scopes accommodate either night or day eye pupils. Thus all of these scopes accommodate all the eye pupil sizes (the same is true for the 8x30). But as we saw above, the low magnification scopes are better for seeing the horizon in dim light.

Eye Relief

The largest distance between the eyepiece's rear lens and the observer's eye for which the entire field of view can still be seen is called the *eye relief*. This is an important consideration for eye comfort, for rolling around in choppy seas, and for using eyeglasses. For a variety of reasons, some navigators will want to use their eyeglasses with their sextant. They may wear astigmatism-correcting eyeglasses (the scope's focus adjustment can't correct for this), or they may wish to avoid flipping their glasses on and off all the time. For them a minimum eye relief somewhere around 15mm is needed, which falls in the middle of the range of a few millimeters to 23mm found in sextant telescopes. Even without eyeglasses, too small an eye relief has the eyepiece bouncing off your eye in rough rides, and even in friendly seas it's uncomfortable having the eyepiece brushing your eyelashes. Normally, eye relief isn't specified for a sextant, but generally, telescopes having higher magnification tend to have the shorter eye relief. Just as with most binoculars, many sextants come with soft eyepieces, sometimes as an option, to help stabilize the sextant against your eyebrow.

Telescopes with Traditional Horizon Mirrors

So far we've discussed telescope properties common to all sextant scopes. But four quite different types of telescopes are found on sextants: two unusual ones, found on older sextants, are the terrestrial and the inverting telescopes. The terrestrial scope has an internal lens system to rotate the inverted image formed by the objective lens so that the viewer sees an upright image. This is the type of scope used on gun telescopic sights, for example. The second unusual type is called an inverting scope which lacks these internal lenses, making the image viewed by the observer upside down. These are frequently used in astronomical telescopes. At least one model of a Russian sextant uses this inverting scope. It apparently takes some practice to get accustomed to it.

By far the most common two scopes are the prism and the Galilean telescopes. The Galilean scope is the most common on modern sextants; the prism scope is sometimes an optional scope (usually the higher power 6x30 or 7x35). Each of these uses a different optical system to upright the inverted image that would be produced at the focal plane of the objective lens. As the name implies, the prism scope uses prisms, as commonly seen in binoculars. The Galilean scope uses a diverging lens for the eyepiece to make the final image upright. So it's the simplest, lightest, and least expensive design, having only two lenses. The significance of these different designs is that the prism and terrestrial scopes produce a very different view of a traditional half-silvered horizon mirror than does the Galilean scope.

The prism (and terrestrial) scopes have an internal focal plane where the separate views from each half of the traditional half-silvered mirror are superimposed to form one composite image: they produce a whole-horizon view, very similar to the thin-film whole-horizon mirrors. They can focus light anywhere across their entire field of view according to the entrance angle of the rays falling on only one-half of their objective lens. The ray tracing of Figure 9.3 shows how the entire horizon is imaged by using only half of the horizon mirror. The same is true for the silvered half of the horizon mirror; so the entire sun-sky image is produced all the way across the field of view. Therefore, a

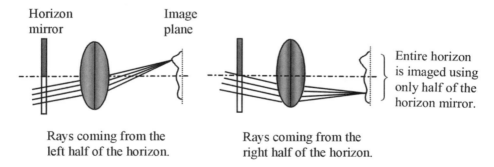

Rays coming from the left half of the horizon.

Rays coming from the right half of the horizon.

Entire horizon is imaged using only half of the horizon mirror.

Figure 9.3 Rays coming from both the left and right directions through just the left side of the horizon mirror form a complete image of the horizon. The same is true for rays coming from the silvered half of the horizon mirror, superimposing with the horizon's image. The eyepiece projects this composite image onto the eye's retina (not shown here). The ray's off-axis angles are exaggerated for clarity.

complete superposition of both sides of the horizon mirror is achieved, just as with the thin-film whole-horizon mirror. But the quality of the resulting superimposed image depends on the relative contrast between the images from each side of the horizon mirror. Since we're superimposing the light from the two images, a brighter image can wash out a dimmer one. But viewing two non-competing images will produce a complete overlap all across the field of view. For example, the bright sun viewed through the shades is perfectly dark except for the sun's disk. Thus we see a complete superposition of the sun and horizon all across the field of view, exactly as we do with the thin-film horizon mirror.

But many star sights have a relatively bright sky superimposed over dimly lit water. Light triumphs over darkness, so under these difficult contrast conditions the prism scope with the traditional mirror will produce a washed-out view, just as the thin-film whole-horizon mirror does. But rather than a uniform wash-out across the entire view, the horizon fades out toward the right edge of the view, and a body's image fades out toward the left edge of the view. Thus the whole-horizon effect grades gradually across the view. This effect is easily demonstrated by looking at a normal daytime horizon through one of these sextants using a prism scope: Split the horizon into two images, the directly viewed horizon and the one reflected from the index mirror. Then by blocking the light from the index mirror with an opaque card (or dark sunshade), the washed-out effect will be eliminated, leaving a complete horizon of the directly viewed image.

To help control this grading of the wash-out, some sextants have a lateral adjustment of the telescope that can be used to optimize the intensity contribution of the star-sky image relative to the directly viewed horizon. (Unfortunately, some scopes have a recessed seat for the scope's mounting screw that locks the scope in the center position. This can be modified with a little machining.) This slight change in relative intensities likewise produces only a slight change in contrasts. But as noted earlier, the eye is very sensitive to contrast differences in dim light, such as between similar sky and water illuminations. So this adjustment is effective in coaxing a difficult horizon into view, balancing a necessary horizon against an acceptable star brightness. In other words, it's possible to adjust the ratio of the effect of thin-film whole-horizon mirror to the effect of the traditional mirror. It's also somewhat possible to control the effect of the wash-out by simply sighting to the left or right of center. Frequently these controls over the composite image make possible an otherwise impossible star shot.

On the other hand, Galilean telescopes, with their simple optics having no internal focal plane, do not achieve this superposition. Hence they show a split view when used with the traditional half-silvered horizon mirror: The direct view from the horizon is seen on the left and the index mirror's image is seen on the right. Usually this combination of the traditional horizon-mirror viewed with a Galilean scope produces an overlap of the two images across about 1/2° in the middle of the field of view.

It's interesting, and perhaps somewhat surprising, to learn exactly how the Galilean scope works with the traditional horizon mirror. In high contrast sights, using horizon shades with a sun shot for example, you see the sun pretty much across the whole field of view, but only the horizon on the left. The sun's image on the left side is not from the silvered half of the horizon mirror. It's from the left side of the horizon mirror: it's the reflection from the horizon mirror's clear glass. You can easily verify this by covering the silvered half of the mirror with a piece of black paper. You'll see no difference in the image on the left where the sight is actually taken. Thus these high-contrast sun (and moon) sights don't actually use the silvered half of the horizon mirror. So with the sun seen across the whole field of view, but the horizon seen only on the left, the observer must bring the sun's disk tangent to the horizon slightly to the left of the center of the field of view.

But in star shots, where there's usually low contrast, no excess starlight, and no shades, the silvered half of the horizon mirror contributes all of the star's image. Again, you can verify this by blocking off the silvered half of the horizon mirror. In these shots there is only that small 1/2° overlap in the center, as shown in Figure 9.4, available for making the sight.

Incidentally, it follows that a perfectly acceptable whole-horizon mirror can be improvised from clear glass (optical quality, preferably). The normal reflection from the surface of the glass is more than adequate for sun (shades are still needed) and nighttime moon shots. But the reflected image is very dim for star shots and daytime moon shots. The challenge of improvising your own horizon mirror is not cutting the glass, but rather cutting it into a circle to fit the common mirror holder.

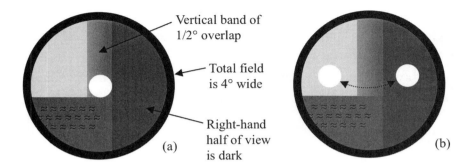

Figure 9.4 View of the traditional horizon mirror through a Galilean telescope. (a) In the center there is a small region of overlap between the left and right views. (b) Because of its brightness, the sun can be seen in the entire field of view.

Finally, we summarize this discussion of telescopes and horizon mirrors: The thin-film horizon mirror has the advantage of its full view of the horizon, making it easy to locate bodies and, as we discuss later in connection with Figure 9.7, making it easy to take the sight. Its disadvantage is taking sights in adverse contrast conditions, such as a relatively bright sky against a poorly defined horizon, which can occur frequently in star shots.

The behavior of the traditional half-silvered mirror depends on whether it's viewed with a Galilean scope or one with an internal focus, such as the prism scope. The Galilean scope has the advantage of low expense. But used with the traditional horizon mirror it has the disadvantage of the split view, which makes locating the body and taking the sight more difficult because the horizon is only seen in the left half of the view. However, this combination has the advantage of not exacerbating poor viewing conditions with the wash-out of the whole-horizon mirror. Finally, the traditional mirror viewed with the prism scope permits optimizing the advantage of both the whole-horizon view and the traditional mirror. Its disadvantage is more expense, and normal availability is limited to the higher 6x or 7x powers.

Field of View

The field of view (FOV) of a sextant is important for easily locating celestial bodies, particularly in star, wide-angle, and coastal navigation sights—concerns that are exacerbated in rough seas. Typically the FOV of Galilean scopes is around 4°. But since traditional horizon mirrors with these scopes show only the horizon on the left, these combinations have an effective working FOV of only about 2°, as shown in Figure 9.4. In some sextants, shade and mirror frames further obstruct the FOV. Since the shades aren't used on star shots, and frequently dim stars aren't sufficiently bright to show in the left half, then only about the middle 1/2° overlap remains to take the sight. On the other hand, prism scopes typically have a much wider FOV, around 7°, effectively, several times that of the lower power scopes.

Sextant Checks and Adjustments

A good celestial shot begins with a good sextant—and one properly adjusted. The three major optical parts discussed above—the telescope, the index mirror, and the horizon mirror—all require checking, and sometimes adjusting.

The Telescope

The telescope's axis should be parallel to the frame and centered on the middle of the horizon mirror. Some older sextants have one or two adjustments for this alignment, but improved manufacturing techniques have rendered this unnecessary, so that all modern sextants have only one or no adjustment for telescope alignment. However, for older sextants, ones that might have been damaged, or inexpensive ones, you might want to check the telescope alignment. Some sextants have an adjustment for centering of the telescope in the middle of the horizon glass. As mentioned earlier, this lateral adjustment can be used to vary the ratio between the intensity of images coming from the left and right sides of the traditional half-silvered horizon mirror when used with prism scopes. In any case, it's not critical and can be simply done visually.

Adjusting the telescope to be parallel to the frame, as mentioned above, is called *collimation*, and it requires a little more effort. This adjustment is particularly important for large angle measurements as sometimes encountered in terrestrial sights and lunar distance sights. One way to check this is to observe two stars at angles greater than 90°. If they move out of coincidence when moved from side to side in the field of view, the scope is not collimated correctly.

Another way is to find a flat surface, such as a dining room table, that is some distance from a wall. Sighting across the surface of the table at the wall, have an assistant place a mark (such as a piece of tape) on the wall at the elevation of the table's surface. Then place the sextant on the table and measure, as accurately as you can, the distance from the table to the center of the telescope. Place another mark on the wall this same distance above the first mark. This second mark will appear in the telescope's center of view if it's parallel to the frame. This, of course, assumes the surface defined by the end of the legs is parallel to the sextant's frame. Check this out when the sextant is on the table. Also, if a large adjustment was necessary, the distance from the table to the telescope's center might have changed significantly from the first adjustment, requiring repeating the procedure.

The Index Mirror

For proper optical alignment both mirrors must be perpendicular to the sextant's frame. The index mirror is checked for this by looking into the index mirror from the direction that a celestial body would "look" at it. By holding the sextant as shown in Figure 9.5, you should be able to see both the reflected image of the sextant's arc and the arc itself. You may have to place the index arm just right in order to expose the arc to your view. When you can see both the reflected image of the arc and the arc itself, they should appear as one continuous inline image. If they appear offset, the index mirror should be adjusted with the screws provided. Figure 9.5 shows what to look for: On the left, you see the direct view of the arc inline with its reflected image in the index mirror. But in the right-hand inset, the reflected arc image is offset (higher) from the direct image, indicating that adjustment of the index mirror is required.

This adjustment method assumes the reflecting surface of the index mirror is exactly over the center of the arc, i.e., over the pivot of the index arm. This is not true for all sextants, making this method an approximation for them. For those cases, this approximation is best when your line of sight is as parallel as possible to the sextant's frame. This is achieved when the arc appears as low as possible in the index mirror, unlike Figure 9.5, which shows the arc rather high in the mirror.

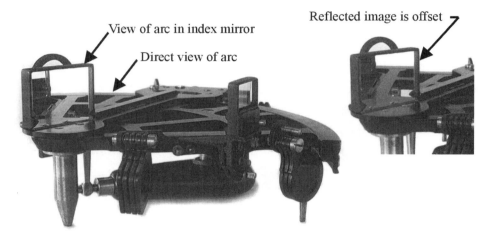

Figure 9.5 The index mirror is adjusted so that the reflected view of the arc in the index mirror is inline with its direct view. The telescope has been removed from the sextant for a better view of the arc. In the upper right inset, the reflected arc's image is misaligned with its direct image, indicating adjustment of the index mirror is required. (Photos by author.)

A more accurate approach is to place two objects of equal height (about half the height of the mirror) on the arc's perimeter so that they appear adjacent to each other in the mirror. Use identical objects, such as dice or machine nuts. You can also buy specially machined calibrating cylinders for this adjustment. Place one at point A, as shown in Figure 9.6, and the other somewhere near point B, so that its reflected image is adjacent to the direct image of the cylinder at A. When using these cylinders, sight level with their top surfaces, so that the top surfaces of the cylinders just disappear as you lower your line of sight from above (as shown in the figure). Adjust for no offset between the top of the directly viewed cylinder A and the top of the reflection of cylinder B, as shown in the figure.

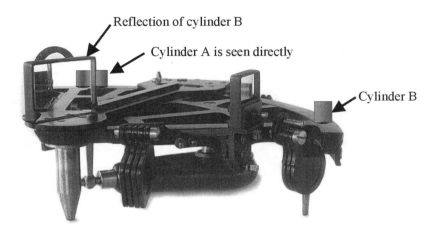

Reflection of cylinder B

Cylinder A is seen directly

Cylinder B

Figure 9.6   Correct alignment of the index mirror using calibrating cylinders. The top of the directly viewed cylinder and the top of the reflected cylinder are in line. (Photo by author.)

The Horizon Mirror

Two adjustments are required for the horizon mirror. One makes its plane perpendicular to the sextant's frame. The other adjusts its orientation so that the sextant reads zero when it's measuring a zero angle. A non-zero reading when the sextant is actually reading a zero angle is called the *index error*. The slickest way to make these two adjustments is to use a star. First, carefully set the arc to read exactly zero. Then (unless the sextant is extremely out of whack, or in exact adjustment), when observing a star (a fairly isolated one), you will see not one, but two images. One image is the direct view through the horizon mirror; the other is the reflected image from the index mirror. Usually, the reflected image will be separated a little from the direct image. Turning one of the two mirror-adjusting screws will move the reflected image left-right, the other will move it up-down. Tuning these screws until the two images coincide completes the horizon mirror adjustment.

There is another way of adjusting the horizon mirror that doesn't require a starry night. This approach divides the adjustment into two parts, one for the perpendicularity, and one for the index error. The perpendicularity adjustment is made by looking at the horizon and its reflected image. Bring these two horizon images into coincidence.

Then rotate the instrument about the telescope axis, observing whether or not the two horizons stay in alignment. If after rotating the sextant, the two images of the horizon go out of coincidence, the horizon mirror is not perpendicular to the frame. Adjust it with one of the two screws provided. Since these two screws provide movements that are orthogonal to one other, you should be able to distinguish between the two by inspecting your particular sextant.

Index Error

After adjusting the horizon mirror to be perpendicular to the frame, with the horizon and its reflected image in coincidence, we would like the sextant's arc to read exactly zero. This really never happens; instead, there's an index error. So carefully set the micrometer drum to zero. Then by adjusting the index correction screw on the horizon mirror, bring the two images into coincidence. This can affect the previous perpendicularity adjustment, so repeat that one. After readjusting these interacting adjustments a couple of times, quit when the index error is small—say, under a few minutes of arc. But the last adjustment you make should be the perpendicularity adjustment. Then just accept the remaining index error and apply it to your observation before any other corrections. This correction is listed on our sight reduction forms because we expect that it is always needed. A decent quality sextant will hold these adjustments for quite some time, but nonetheless, you should check the index error before each series of sights.

Another index correction method is to look at the sun and its reflected image. The best sensitivity is obtained not by aligning the sun's disk with itself, but by bringing one limb of the sun into coincidence with its other limb. Then do the reverse. A little thought, particularly with the aid of a sketch, shows that the sum of these two readings should be four times the sun's semidiameter, whereas the difference is twice the index error. I like this idea because of the sensitivity of aligning the edges of the sun's disk, the increased accuracy by dividing by two to get the index error, and the double check on the sextant by comparing the sun's semidiameter with the almanac's report for that date. (Some older sextants do not have a horizon shade sufficiently dark to look at the sun.)

Backlash

Many practical navigators satisfactorily ignore backlash. Backlash is lost motion, or play, among mechanical parts (such as a gear train) when reversing direction. In the marine sextant the micrometer-drum worm gear meshes with the arc's worm wheel, with the worm gear spring loaded against the arc to prevent backlash. Theoretically then, there would be no backlash; identical readings would occur when approaching the reading from either direction, i.e., from altitudes either higher or lower than the final reading. On the other hand (also theoretically), the slightest force on any material item, such as a gear or index arm, will deflect it, if only slightly.

Therefore, we can expect that, even though the worm gear is spring loaded, there might be a slight amount of backlash in a marine sextant. Depending on the direction of approach to the final reading, parts might deflect slightly; and the worm might ride slightly higher up one side of the arc's teeth than the other side. On a sextant with a 6.5" arc radius, an accumulation of these slight deflections to only one thousandth of an inch will produce a one-minute arc error (a good reason to keep the arc gear and worm very clean).

When you check for the index error, you can easily check for backlash by recording separate index errors, divided into two groups, one for approaching from each side of the reading. Take five to ten readings from each approach and average each group separately. If these two averages are identical, there is no backlash. Normally you don't get exactly zero, but you might find one or two minutes of backlash.

Some navigators believe that a directional bias, called personal error, can masquerade as backlash. The idea is that the observer might unconsciously achieve a slightly different visual coincidence when approaching the same reading from different directions. Also it could be different for different kinds of sights, such as using a star's point image compared to the sun's disc. Because this effect would appear the same as backlash, we needn't establish whether personal error is real. We just group the two effects together and call it all backlash. In any case, the navigator who is aiming for maximum accuracy can measure backlash and apply it with the index error according to the direction of approach taken to the reading. Others can happily ignore it, while those wishing to delve deeper into sextant mechanics can look at Morris's book cited in Appendix K.

Sextant Arc Error

No instrument is 100 percent accurate. Sextants have errors in the measured angle that varies along the arc, called arc error. With the exception of inexpensive plastic sextants, manufacturers of modern sextants usually certify a maximum arc error. Typically this maximum error ranges from 10 to 20 arc seconds, depending on the manufacturer. Many older sextants have a correction table of arc error versus angle, which may run from some small number to 35 seconds or more.

The arc error can be checked by measuring star-star distances as discussed at the end of Chapter 8, where we explain that to get the required accuracy, refraction corrections must be made by the same method used in clearing lunar distances. Using this method, Appendix G gives handy tables of precomputed star-star distances of twelve selected star pairs for checking sextant arc error. You only have to correct your sextant's reading for index error and then compare the result to the tabulated values of arc distances. These corrections are quite reliable, particularly when the star's altitudes are high, making the corrections small—say, under a few minutes of arc. This exercise will produce a useful and reliable indication of the combined observer-sextant accuracy capability—perhaps a humbling indication.

Sextant Observations

Observations at Home

Those not living on the ocean or a large body of water, yet wishing to practice sextant shots at home, have a couple of options for a substitute sea horizon. By far the nicest option, if convenient, is to use an inland lake. The distance to the natural sea horizon is given by

$$d = 1.169 \sqrt{h} \tag{9.1}$$

where h is the height of the observer's eye above the water in feet, and d is the distance to the natural horizon in nautical miles. If the distant shore is farther away than this, then that visible horizon can be used as is. But if the shore is closer, it's obstructing the true horizon, and a special dip correction must be substituted for the one in the almanac. This correction—dip short of the horizon, as it's called—is calculated from

$$Dip_s = 0.415767 \times d + 0.565786 \times h \, / \, d \qquad\qquad (9.2)$$

where the dip is in minutes of arc, d is the shore distance in nautical miles, and h is the observer's height in feet.

The table in Appendix H gives dip values calculated from this equation for a range of values. Notice that for shore distances less than about 0.5 nm, the correction is very sensitive to eye height, making it unreliable. Also note that, for a given eye height, as the distance increases, the correction becomes constant. At these distances, the lakeshore is over the natural horizon, and therefore the correction becomes equal to the normal correction in the almanac.

If a natural water horizon is unavailable, you can use several types of artificial horizons that fit onto the marine sextant. If all else fails, you can place a pan of water in an appropriate spot for viewing the body's reflection on the water's surface. Floating oil on the water's surface reduces the ripples, making better viewing. You aim the sextant at the reflected image from the water, then bring the image of the body from the index mirror into coincidence with the water image. Since you're bringing the two images into coincidence, their centers also coincide. So there's no semidiameter correction, which means use the star and planet altitude correction table in the almanac for the sun. And for the moon, follow the instructions for bubbles sextants given in the almanac's altitude correction table for the moon (Appendix C). Since this water surface is a true horizon, there is no dip correction. Observing the sun this way can be too bright for sextants that don't have very dark horizon shades, and stars can be difficult to see and identify. By drawing a simple sketch showing the body's rays reflected both from the water surface and the index mirror, you'll see that the sextant is measuring twice the true altitude. This is nice because when you divide the sextant altitude by two to get the true altitude, you also cut your observing error in half.

Taking a Sight

Conceptually, taking a sextant sight is as simple as pie. Looking through the telescope and adjusting the index arm, you bring two points into coincidence. Then, reading the angle from the arc and micrometer drum gives the angle subtended at your location by the two points.

But there's a catch. The horizon is not a distinct point—it's a line. The measurement we need in celestial navigation is the arc distance from the body to the horizon, measured perpendicular to the horizon. That's also the shortest distance between the two. So we use this fact to make sure the sextant is vertical, i.e., perpendicular to the horizon, when we make the measurement. This is done by rotating the sextant back and forth about an axis in the vertical plane, so that the observed body stays in the center of the field of view. When you keep the body stationary in the center of the field of view, you're rotating about the body's line of sight, making the body appear to describe an arc with the horizon zipping back and forth (and up and down) across the field of view. You'll find that to keep the body in the center of the view, you'll also have to turn slightly to the left and right (more so at high altitudes than low). You're looking for that one point on the horizon that is directly beneath the body. That lowest point on the arc occurs when the sextant is held vertically. That's the shortest distance, the measurement we want. So in taking the sight we continuously *swing the arc* or *rock the sextant*, as it's called, while simultaneously bringing the body down (or up) so that the lowest point of the arc just "kisses" the horizon. Figure 9.7 diagrams this view seen through the sextant's telescope when swinging the arc. For the sun or moon, we use the upper or lower limb of the body's disk, bringing it tangent to the horizon, as shown in the figure for the lower limb.

Swinging this arc is the most basic and important part of taking a sight. If it's not done carefully, taking a measurement with the sextant just slightly off of vertical can produce a considerable error: At a 45° altitude, a 5° error from vertical produces about a 13′ error in the observed altitude.

With experience come nuances. The arc's width may become smaller, approaching zero exactly at the time of the kiss. Sometimes, to avoid doing two things at once, I like to stop adjusting the sextant when the bottom of the arc and the horizon are not quite yet in coincidence and continuously swing the arc waiting for the exact second of coincide. This way, I make sure the sextant is vertical when I mark the time. With experience, both the width of the arc and the time interval are decreased.

Figure 9.7 Swinging the arc by keeping the body centered in the field of view of the sextant's telescope, viewed through a whole-horizon mirror. The index arm is properly set for reading when the body's disk just kisses the horizon at the lowest point of the arc. Then the sextant is vertical because it's reading the shortest distance from the body to the horizon.

Notice in comparing the whole-horizon view of Figure 9.7 with the traditional-mirror Galilean-scope sextant (see Figure 9.4), that the traditional-mirror sextant effectively has only half the field of view for swinging the arc—a four-degree field-of-view scope only gives you two degrees. This can be a serious disadvantage to any navigator aboard small boats in rough seas, a stumbling block for beginners on dry land, and an inconvenience for anyone at anytime.

Of course, the first job is to get both the body and the horizon in the same view. This is one place where a wide-view sextant really is nice. Several different methods are used by navigators. In the case of all celestial bodies, except for some minor stars and Venus, I have always found the common approach satisfactory: Set the sextant at zero; aim the telescope at the body, using appropriate shades; then in a coordinated fashion move the index arm outward as you move your aim downward toward the horizon, keeping the body centered in the view. As your aim approaches the horizontal, the horizon will come into view from below. Now both the horizon and the body are in view. A refinement of this idea that I use to avoid looking at the bright sun (or moon) with insufficiently dark horizon shades, is to set the index arm to just a little more than the field of view (about 6°). Then aiming just a little below the sun, I easily find the well-shaded index-mirror image of the sun in the center of view, rather than being blinded by the sun through the left side of the horizon mirror.

Beyond keeping the sextant vertical and locating the body in the field of view, the rest is common sense or personal preference. For example, some navigators believe that the sun's and moon's upper limbs provide a better sighting arrangement than the lower ones. One reason is that the gap between the disk and the horizon might be a confused cloud pattern when using the lower limb, but it's a nice clear view of the sea when using the upper limb.

There are other fairly obvious considerations: Pick a location on the vessel that is comfortable and has the least motion. Take that position and practice the body motion required to keep your upper body suspended in inertial space while holding the sextant steady in both hands. Time the sight to take the reading on the top of a wave crest so you're looking at the true horizon, rather than a nearby wave. (And don't add wave height to your eye height for the dip correction because when you're at the top of a wave, you're also looking at the tops of distant waves on the horizon.) Also, it might be interesting to note that inadvertent vertical motion of the sextant doesn't affect its reading, because the resulting dip correction would be negligible. Be alert to false horizons produced by various effects, such as fog, clouds, and wave patterns. Reflections from the water under the sun or moon can also produce a false horizon. Incorrect selection of both index and horizon shades can lead to problem sights. In fact, the proper selection of shades shouldn't be taken lightly. They can make all the difference in optimizing that all-important contrast in difficult sights.

High altitudes offer their own challenges. As altitudes approach 90°, the arc becomes very flat, which causes the body to run out of sight to left or right as you rock the sextant. Then you have to twist around in azimuth, searching for the low point of the arc while keeping the body in the center of the view. The reason for this is clear if you think about the azimuth behavior versus altitude. In fact, right at 90° altitude the azimuth becomes undefined, and the altitude is the same in all directions. Particularly in high seas, this simultaneous twisting around and rocking the sextant through large angles can result in quite a circus, to the amusement of your shipmates.

Furthermore, alignment of the sextant with the vertical becomes increasingly critical at high altitudes, as we see from the data below. Here we tabulate the altitude error (in minutes of arc) versus the altitude H, for three values of sextant misalignment. Note the rapid increase in altitude error, both with altitude (particularly above 45°), and with the sextant-off-vertical errors. Perhaps one saving grace is the split-view horizon mirror: I estimate that by carefully judging the vertical edge of the mirror to be perpendicular to the horizon, one can hold the sextant vertical to within 2°, considerably reducing the potential error at high altitudes. Even so, at altitudes above 75° you should probably forego those noon sun shots, substituting off-meridian sun lines. (The table's blank entry in the bottom right-hand corner is another example of our tricky spherical geometry: The more the body's altitude approaches 90°, the more every direction from it approaches right angles to the horizon. At an 85° altitude, it's impossible to have a great-circle arc from body-to-horizon deviate 6° from vertical at the horizon.)

Vertical Error 2°		Vertical Error 4°		Vertical Error 6°	
H°	H error	H°	H error	H°	H error
5	0	5	1	5	2
15	1	15	2	15	5
25	1	25	4	25	9
35	1	35	6	35	13
45	2	45	8	45	19
55	3	55	12	55	27
65	5	65	18	65	41
75	8	75	32	75	74
85	25	85	120	85	—

Averaging Sights

The first step in going all out for accuracy is, of course, to make sure the sextant is adjusted correctly, as discussed above. Then, under most conditions the altitude measurement itself limits the final accuracy. In addition to becoming ever more careful, experienced, and skillful, about the only way one can improve sextant observations is to average sights. The best method, although it's a bit of work, is to plot each individual altitude reading versus time. Simple quadrille graph paper will do. Be sure to use a scale that allows plotting to 0.1´ of arc and one second of time. Plot the data and draw through it a curve that you have eyeballed as a best fit. (With a computer, a best-fit curve can be exactly determined mathematically.) If the overall elapsed time of the observations is reasonably short, say ten minutes, and the sight is not near the meridian, the altitude-versus-time curve will be nearly a straight line. Figure 9.8 shows a plot of the five readings that produced the sextant altitude used in the Great Bahama Banks example of Chapter 5.

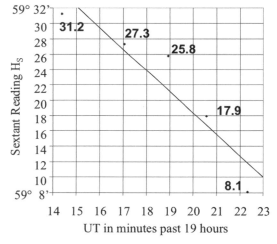

Figure 9.8 A plot of five sextant altitude readings versus observation time. Scatter from the best fit line varies from 0.2´ to 4.0´ of arc.

Such a plot has several advantages. First, we immediately see the scatter in readings from the best-fit line. This gives an indication of our accuracy limitation due to random errors in reading the sextant, and it also points out rogue readings that are suspect because of abnormal deviations from the best-fit line. In Figure 9.8 we see sextant readings that deviate from 0.1´ to 4.0´ from the line. Is the 59° 25.8´ reading, with its 4.0´ deviation from the line, an anomaly that should disqualify it? Judging by the other deviations, several of which are nearly as large, we conclude that it is a valid reading. On the other hand, if all the of the other four readings were, say, within only 1.0′ of the trend line, this deviation of four times that amount would indeed make it suspect. This brings us to two conclusions about the data shown: First, the fluctuations from the average seem to be normal random ones, and second, these fluctuations indicate about a 4.0′ random error.

Having come to this conclusion, we now can either read off the averaged reading from the best-fit line at anywhere near the middle of the plot, or we can average the five readings arithmetically. Figure 9.9 shows the arithmetic average. (Note how we average the minutes and seconds of UT separately for convenience, and how the 0.2 of the 18.2 minutes is carried over as 12 seconds. The same can be done with the degrees of altitude and hours when necessary.) For completely random fluctuations, by averaging N numbers we expect an improvement of a factor of one over the square root of N. So the average of five sights, each good to our maximum 4.0′ deviation, should provide an improvement of $1/\sqrt{5} = 0.45$, giving us now 0.45 times the 4.0′ random fluctuation, or about an accuracy of ±2.0′. Remember, of course, we are talking here about random observational error, not systematic errors.

Sextant	Universal Time		
59° 31.2′	19^H	14^M	23^S
27.3		17	03
25.8		18	56
17.9		20	34
8.1		22	20
59° 110.3′		91	136
		18.2	27
			12
H$_S$= 59° 22.1′	19	18	39

Figure 9.9 Averaging five sextant shots.

Plotting altitudes as in Figure 9.8 suggests comparing observed values with calculated ones at a known location. This exercise serves several purposes: Not only does it give practice calculating H$_C$, but it evaluates index, backlash, and arc errors. We might calculate sun altitudes, say every 20 to 30 minutes from noon to several hours afternoon for a fixed location. Then throughout that same time period, we take sun sights at about 20 minute intervals. At each time for evaluating backlash, we take readings by approaching the horizon-body coincidence from higher, and also from lower, altitudes, recording which is which. (Of course, it doesn't matter if we observe first, or calculate first.)

Next we plot the calculated values of altitude versus observation time, and carefully draw a fair curve though them producing a H_C *curve* similar to Figure 9.8; however, since this is H_C versus time, and is not a straight-line average, it will display some curvature, depending on latitude and azimuth of the body (according to Equation A.2b). Then after, reducing the sextant altitudes to H_O, we plot them on the same graph for evaluation. If the data extends over more than a few degrees of altitude, we'll have to break it up into several plots to resolve errors of the order of minutes of arc.

Comparing the H_C curved to the H_O observations will immediately show the amount of random and systematic errors. Random errors will show the observed altitudes scattered about the H_C curve, while systematic errors can show some type of correlation: For example, pure index error would show all the H_O data displaced vertically by a constant amount from the H_C curve. Pure backlash error would show the H_O data divided into two groups, one group consistently above and the other group consistently below the H_C curve. And pure arc error might show up as gradual divergence of the H_O data from the H_C curve. Of course, it's quite possible to have these systematic errors intertwined such that they can not be separated from one another. In that case, they combine to produce a random error which can't be corrected—but at least this exercise measures it.

A somewhat different approach to this same exercise is to measure star-star distances as mentioned early in Chapter 8 and in the previous section on Arc Errors in this chapter.

Altitude Corrections

All the required altitude corrections are provided in the *Nautical*

Almanac along with complete instructions for their use. They can be used quite blindly with no further knowledge than the directions for their use, as we did in our previous examples. But the curious celestial navigator wants to know more. A deeper knowledge of altitude effects will put these corrections into perspective, which is important for taking sights in various conditions and for judging accuracy. In other words, understanding them will make us better celestial navigators.

Dip

After the index correction, the first altitude correction applied to the sextant reading is for the height of the observer's eye above sea level. The higher the eye, the more the observer is looking over the true horizon, as shown in Figure 9.10. The *Nautical Almanac* includes the effect of refraction in its correction table using

Dip = 1.76 $\sqrt{h}$ when h is in meters,
or
Dip = 0.971$\sqrt{h}$, when h is in feet.

In these equations, the dip is in minutes of arc and h is the height of the observer's eye above sea level. Since this effect increases the observed altitude, the correction is always subtracted from the sextant reading.

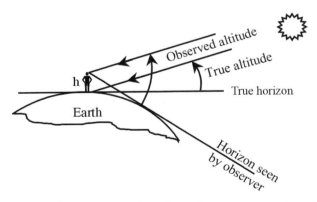

Figure 9.10 The observed altitude is always greater than the true altitude.

Refraction

Acute observers of the shoreline witness refraction. As waves approach the shore at an angle, the portion of the wave near the shore slows down in shallower water, while the portion farther out travels faster in the deeper water. This results in the portion farther out catching up with the portion nearer to shore, bending the wave toward the shore. This bending is particularly dramatic around a point where the wave can change direction more than 90°. This bending, called refraction, also occurs under normal conditions when light passing through the atmosphere encounters increasingly more dense air, which slows it down and bends the light downward toward the observer. This bending of the light rays makes the observed altitude appear higher than it really is. So this correction is subtracted from the observed altitude. The higher the altitude, the more the rays are making a 90° angle to the variations in density, so the correction is less with higher altitudes, becoming zero for 90° altitudes.

The almanac uses a formula for the refraction correction that is based on standard conditions of pressure and temperature, 1010 millibars, and 10° Celsius. When pressure and temperature deviate significantly from these conditions, additional corrections may have to be used. These additional altitude corrections are in a table on page A4 of the almanac, which shows deviations in altitude for non-standard conditions as great as 7.0′ for low altitudes and extreme conditions.

Atmospheric refraction becomes tricky to predict at low altitudes, where the effect is the greatest. So it's best to avoid observations below altitudes of about 10°. If you must use them, the almanac gives a table on page A3 for altitudes less than 10°, where you can see the correction getting as large as 33′. Remember that's 33 nautical miles, and it's at low altitudes where unpredictable abnormal refractive effects might occur.

Upper and Lower Limbs

All of the solutions to the navigation triangle assume that the location of the body is at the geometrical center of its optical disk. When we take a sight of either the sun or the moon, we measure the altitude either to the top or to the bottom of its disk, that is, either to its upper or lower limb, as they're called in astronomy. This is the simplest of corrections to understand. For example, if we shoot the lower limb, as is more frequently the case, we need to add the body's semidiameter to get from the horizon up to its center. This correction is included in the altitude correction table, so we don't need to account for it, except to make sure we're looking in the correct column in the table. Nonetheless, the semidiameter of the sun and the moon are also given at the bottom of the daily pages in the *Nautical Almanac*.

Parallax

Just as our computational geometry neglects the diameter of celestial bodies, assuming that we're measuring altitudes to their center, it likewise assumes that the observer is at the center of the earth. That is, the calculations have also neglected the diameter of the earth. In reality, because of the earth's diameter, the ray passing through the body's GP is not exactly parallel to the ray reaching the observer. This is shown in Figure 9.11, where we've drawn the case of maximum parallax, called the horizontal parallax (HP) when the body is on the horizon. When the body is overhead, the two rays coincide and the effect is zero. It's easy to calculate the HP with a little trig. Using the definition of the sine of an angle from Appendix F, we can write

$$\sin HP = R/d$$

where R is the radius of the earth and d is the distance to the body. Using an average earth-sun distance we get

$$\sin HP = 3440 \text{ nm} / 80{,}780{,}000 \text{ nm}$$

which gives us 0.146′ for the solar horizontal parallax. This small correction depends on the altitude and is therefore included in the solar altitude correction table. Jupiter, Saturn, and the stars are so far from the earth that their parallax is negligible, while Venus and Mars have a tiny additional correction listed in the altitude correction table on page A2. The correction depends on the time of year because their distance from the earth varies throughout the year.

The moon, being the closest to the earth, has the largest parallax, sufficiently large that its correction requires a special lunar table. Using our above equation for HP and using an average earth-moon distance gives

$$\sin HP = 3440 \text{ nm } / \text{ 207,559 nm}$$

which yields HP = 57.0′ for a typical lunar parallax, which is quite large for navigational purposes. Because the earth-moon distance varies throughout the month and year, the lunar HP is listed in the daily pages for each hour of UT. Inspection of these pages shows that the moon's HP varies somewhere between 53.9′ and 61.4′, our average calculated value being in the middle of this range. The parallax (PA) at altitudes above the horizon becomes less than HP, being zero at H = 90°, which is easily seen from Figure 9.11. In between it is given by PA = HP cos H. Since the parallax depends on the observed altitude, the lunar-altitude correction table in the back of the almanac tabulates both the upper and lower limb corrections versus altitude.

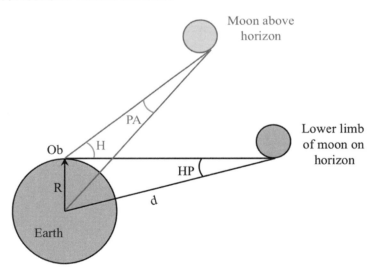

Figure 9.11 Parallax is due to the observer not being at the center of the earth. From the figure, an observer at Ob experiences horizontal parallax sin HP = R/d. When the body is above the horizon, the parallax PA = HP cos H.

10

Operations at Sea

In the late 1980s, navigation using range-range fixes from satellites came into widespread public use. Since this GPS can determine position anywhere on earth to an accuracy of tens of feet, the lore of the sextant no longer reigns supreme in guiding ships over the oceans. Nonetheless, celestial navigation remains unique. It is the only system completely independent of shipboard electronics and of signals originating from remote equipment. Thus modern navigation has shifted the importance and transformed the practice of celestial navigation.

Celestial before GPS

When celestial navigation is the primary mode of open ocean navigation, a rigorous daily routine should be followed, weather permitting. The day starts with a round of morning twilight star shots for a fix. These star sights are valuable because a round of stars can give good LOP crossings at nearly the same time, avoiding the uncertainty of dead reckoning required for running fixes. The same routine is followed in the evening twilight. Midmorning sun shots, a noon fix at LAN for latitude and longitude, and afternoon sun shots compose the standard observations. To these, when possible, are added day shots of the moon and Venus, and night shots of the moon and stars when the night horizon is useable. Bodies are always chosen with an awareness of the crossing angles of LOPs from other bodies and running fixes. In summary, all possible beneficial sights are taken.

These sights are augmented with running fixes as needed. For example, a noon sun latitude/longitude fix might be missed because of weather. Then the midmorning estimated position would be updated to an afternoon DR position, which would then be upgraded to a new EP from the next available LOP (as discussed later), using the sun, moon, or Venus.

Celestial with GPS

With today's normal GPS navigation, the above primary routine can be replaced with just a sufficient number, and type, of observations to keep the celestial navigator sufficiently skilled for backing up and checking the other navigational systems. This makes it less demanding—and more fun. Of course, a celestial navigator may choose to faithfully observe the primary routine, and even keep a separate chart for that purpose, complete with the whole suite of observations and running fixes.

But it's possible to simplify things, if desired. The first simplification is to skip averaging four or five sextant readings when the main goal is practice and proficiency. When really needed, or when evaluating the effect of averaging, it can easily be added to the routine, as discussed in Chapter 9.

Another simplification is to omit plotting every LOP, because that's rather perfunctory compared to honing and maintaining skills of sight observation and reduction. For that purpose the best approach is to use the GPS position for the DR position (which can't be done with the inspection tables). Then work up the sight and see how close H_O is to H_C. At sea we expect they should agree within one or two nautical miles, except under some poor conditions, such as rough seas or an indistinct horizon. Then, even a several-mile discrepancy might be expected. For sight quality checks, the observation and sight should be worked up within 0.1 nm so that we can be confident that altitude disparity is entirely due to other factors. The GPS also provides a method of discovering systematic errors. If the fluctuations between H_O and the H_C computed from the GPS position are truly due to random observer errors, then the algebraic differences between the two averaged over many observations should be zero. If they don't average to zero, there is a systematic error, such as an index error, which should be investigated. The azimuth cannot be checked accurately, but the calculated Zn should be compared to the ship's compass as a cross check on the compass and the navigator. Remember that the celestial Zn is a true bearing, not magnetic.

Usually three plotted LOPs wil not all intersect at the same point, but will enclose a triangle, sometimes called a *cocked hat*. Errors can cause the true position to fall outside of this triangle—a location that you might not intuitively expect. Even though the single most probable position is near the center of the cocked hat, with random altitude errors the probability can be quite high that the true position is somewhere outside. Moreover, many locations have equal, or nearly equal, probability of being the true position. All the practical navigator can do is to plot the position in the center of the cocked hat, realizing that the true position can be outside of the triangle as far as the possible random error extends beyond each LOP.

Perfect agreement among three LOPs, as shown in Figure 10.1a, tells us very little about the fix's accuracy. And just like random errors, systematic errors can easily cause the true position to lie outside of the cocked hat. Figure 10.1b shows how altitudes that are consistently too high can cause the true fix to lie outside of the resulting triangle. However, note that in the figure the azimuths of the bodies span less than 180° among themselves. Now if we switch the azimuth of body three by 180° in Figure 10.1b, the three azimuths will span more than 180°; and you can see that the true fix will would lie *inside* the cocked hat with the same altitude errors (all too high). Furthermore, the true fix lies at the center of the cocked hat (even if the constant altitude errors were all reversed). So a three-body fix with azimuths spread out more than 180° is preferable because the center position will cancel unknown constant altitude errors.

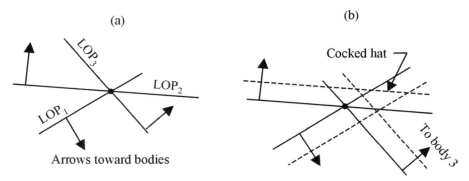

(a)

(b)

Figure 10.1 In **(a)**, a correct three-body fix with the arrows pointing toward the bodies. At **(b)**, the same altitude error for all three LOPs produces erroneous LOPs, the dotted lines, which leave the correct fix outside of the cocked hat.

In the old days, consistently tiny cocked hats were one of the celestial navigator's satisfying rewards. But this is deceiving because there are many kinds of errors. For example, the timing error (discussed in Chapter 7) in a multi-star fix alters the longitude but not the latitude, with the LOPs still intersecting at a point. In today's GPS age, there is no need to rely on cocked hats as a quality criterion. We modern navigators would do much better evaluating our skills by calculating, and recording, our intercept distances when using the GPS position as the AP. The distribution of many intercept distances about their average tells us the size of our random errors, and the deviation of this average from zero tells how well we agree with the GPS. Consistent agreement means the GPS is working right, and our celestial navigator is working well.

By acquiring this knowledge of expected errors, we become safer navigators. If we get a cocked hat unreasonably large compared to our known random-error potential, we suspect a mistake. If we get an usually tiny cocked hat, we know that we can't assume increased accuracy. But rather, its accuracy is still limited by the size of our known potential random errors. Cocked hats remind us that we can't be cock sure.

Those Special Sights

The use of the special sights discussed in Chapter 7 depends on the navigator's objective. Broader experience, understanding, flexibility, confidence, and satisfaction can be gained from learning and practicing special sights. But if the only interest is a reliable and simple backup system, it might be reasonable to forget about special sights. Particularly as a backup system for the part-time navigator, the advantage of having good proficiency in one method might trump the advantages of these additional sights. These special sights have lost their importance from the days when accurate sight timing was difficult and the calculations had to be worked out by hand, adding quite a few six-digit numbers (logarithms). But now they offer little advantage over using the St. Hilaire method with calculators or inspection tables. Moreover, meridian latitude shots require the extra job of finding the maximum altitude. Additionally, I think there has been an irrelevant historical carryover on the importance of determining latitude rather than a regular LOP. After all, a known latitude is just an east-west LOP. And if a sun shot is taken anywhere near local apparent noon, without regard to how near, and worked up as a regular St. Hilaire sight, the LOP will be nearly east-west anyhow. And that's the real consideration, the LOP crossing angle at noon relative to the morning and afternoon sun lines, used for running fixes.

Of course, some navigators are interested in delving deeper into the possibilities of celestial navigation for both pleasure and for novel emergency capabilities. For them, there are plenty of special sights to play with (as discussed in Chapter 7) such as the use of guide stars, and the meridian-latitude-longitude sight, which deserves special consideration because it requires neither a calculator nor sight reduction tables and it provides a fix instead of just an LOP.

The star sights retain their importance because of their ability to provide a fix from two or more nearly simultaneous observations. They should be practiced, plotted, and the resulting position reconciled with the GPS. Here again, the GPS simplifies the job of the backup celestial navigator. Since the GPS is the primary navigation, you can study the night sky at your leisure. One of the pleasures of celestial navigation is gaining familiarity with the stars. And of course, that can be done with any of the readily available star charts before you set out to sea. Once at sea, you can become familiar with the position of the navigation stars at your ship's location to discover which stars are appropriate for your sights. Except in poor weather conditions, there should be no need to precompute star positions and twilight times for star observations. But for those who want precomputed altitudes and azimuths, H.O. 249, Volume I, lists them according to the LHA of Aries and the observer's latitude. It even designates the stars with the preferred LOP crossing angles. See Chapter 6 for a discussion on indentifying and viewing stars and planets.

Plotting

The final step in most celestial navigation problems is plotting; using the St. Hilaire method, it's plotting the azimuth and intercept to arrive at the LOP. In order not to clutter up the primary navigation chart, particularly when just practicing sights, it's convenient to use plotting sheets. Universal plotting sheets (sometimes designated VP-OS), are available commercially in 13x14-inch sheets, 50 in a pad. Each sheet has a compass rose and unlabeled latitude lines, and a single meridian in the center. An example is shown in Figure 10.2. To customize this sheet for your use, first assign the meridian passing through the middle of the compass rose the desired longitude; then assign the parallels of latitude according to the scale you wish. Finally, scale the locations of the other meridians using the chart in the lower right-hand corner of the sheet.

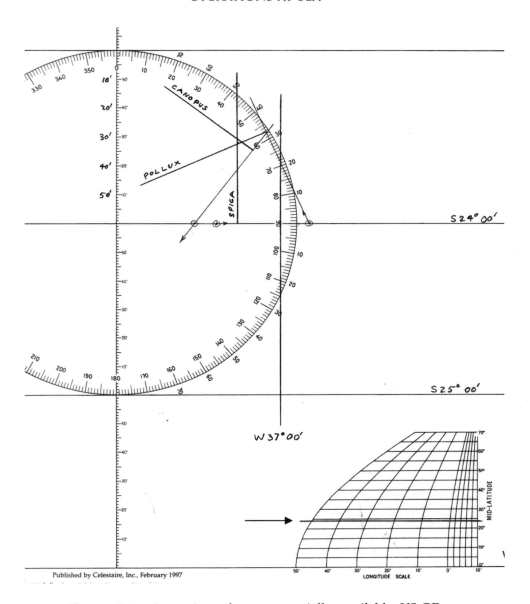

Figure 10.2 A portion of a commercially available VS-OP universal plotting sheet using S24° as the center latitude and W38° as center longitude. Three star lines are plotted from the H.O. 249, Vol. I, workup in Chapter 6.

In the figure's example the central latitude was chosen to be S24° for plotting three star lines from our example in Chapter 6. The parallel of latitude below the central S24° is thus labeled S25°. Next a horizontal line drawn at the 24° level through the small graph at the lower right-hand corner of the sheet provides the proper longitude scale according to a Mercator projection at the 24° mid latitude. Using a dividers to pick off a full 60′ along this 24° latitude line places the W37° meridian as shown, with the meridian passing through the rose's center at W38°. The layout of the universal plotting sheet is now complete, and the three LOPs are plotted using the latitude scale from the central meridian and the longitude scale from the lower right-hand graph (it's easy to forget this!). Remember all distances are plotted using the latitude scale—we all know that one minute of latitude equals one nautical mile.

Also we can use any physical distance scale we wish. For example, if we halved the scale from our above example (making distances appear larger), the lower parallel below the S24° central meridian would be at S24° 30′. And the latitude labeled W37° would become W37° 30′.

You can also make your own plotting sheets from scratch as shown in Figure 10.3. Plot three parallels of latitude using a scale of your choice. Then draw in the center meridian. Using a compass draw a circle with radius equal to the latitude spacing, centered on the middle latitude and meridian. Plot a line from the center of this circle at an angle to the horizontal equal to the chosen middle latitude, as shown. Then draw another meridian at the intersection of this line with the

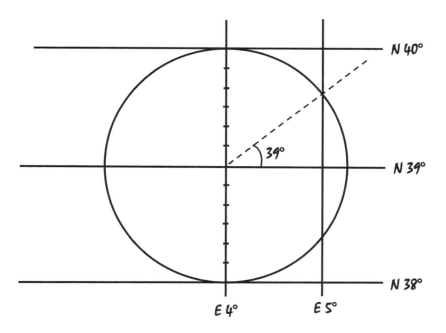

Figure 10.3 Construction of a plotting sheet centered at N39° E4°.

perimeter of the circle. Plot the remaining meridians with this spacing. The secondary minute longitude tics are placed by equally dividing the distance between 1° meridians.

This construction is a graphical method of arriving at the Mercator ratio of longitude to latitude according to

$$\text{Map Longitude Distance} = \text{Map Latitude Distance} \times \cos(\text{Lat}) \qquad (10.1)$$

So if in our construction, 3 inches were a degree of latitude, then a degree of longitude would be $3 \times \cos(24) = 2.74$ inches.

Whether you use the commercial plotting sheets or construct your own, for large-scale plotting, these sheets are a satisfactory approximation to a true Mercator projection, which requires the parallels of latitude to expand toward the poles, rather than being equally spaced.

Running Fixes

The position of a vessel determined by the intersection of two or more LOPs is called a fix. Because the vessel is usually moving, either all the LOPs would have to be acquired simultaneously, which rarely happens, the vessel is moving slowly enough that its motion can be ignored, or the fix is adjusted for the vessel's motion. The position determined by correcting for the ship's motion between LOPs acquired at different times, and hence different ship locations, is called a *running fix*.

Running fixes can mix very different kinds of navigation that have very different accuracies. In one case at sea, we might have taken a morning sun line which is followed by another sun line some hours later, perhaps in the afternoon when the sky cleared once again. In the *traditional running fix* the first LOP is advanced to the time of the second one by dead reckoning, DR, according to the speed and heading of the ship along the run between sights. In another case, the ship may have moved appreciably during a round of star shots, or shots among the sun, moon, or Venus.

These two cases, the long run between morning and afternoon shots, and the short run between a round of stars, are fundamentally the same running-fix problem. But they differ greatly in the relative accuracy of the DR and LOP positions. In the *long-run fix* the DR position may be off by many miles compared to the one or two mile accuracy of a celestial LOP. In the *short-run fix*, spanning perhaps under 20 minutes of time, the DR accuracy is usually considerably better than the LOP accuracy (at least in slow moving vessels). Because of the DR uncertainty and these accuracy limitations, we must treat running fixes as problems in estimation theory. And the rules for making the best estimation are simply common sense, that is the process of rational thinking: use all available information without invoking unnecessary assumptions or contradictions.

The Traditional Running Fix

An example of a long-run fix is the traditional running fix. It's used after a considerable run between LOPs where the assumption is the accuracies of the LOPs trump the accuracy of the estimated track. As shown in Figure 10.4, the fix is obtained by advancing the first LOP parallel to itself according to the DR estimated track made good between the two LOPs. The ship is placed where the advanced LOP intersects LOP2, shown by the point RFIX in the figure.

First note that this traditional running fix completely ignores any information about the location of the ship along LOP1. This means that any estimated track with the same component perpendicular to LOP1 yields the same RFIX, regardless of our knowledge of the ship's location along LOP1. And in actual reality, we always have *some* idea of where our ship is. Why not use this information?

Even more significant, as can be seen from the figure, this traditional running fix assumes that the component of estimated track perpendicular to LOP1 is exact; while on the other hand, it assumes that the component of the estimated track along LOP1 can have unlimited error. As can be visualized from the figure, this means that RFIX can even be forced in the opposite direction of the track component along LOP1. It's trapped into allowing arbitrary error along the advanced LOP1, otherwise LOP2 would necessarily pass through DR2. Thus it nonsensically allows the orientation of LOP1 to decree both the directions of exact information and of arbitrarily large error. Neither of which exist in dead reckoning. Furthermore, it's obvious that

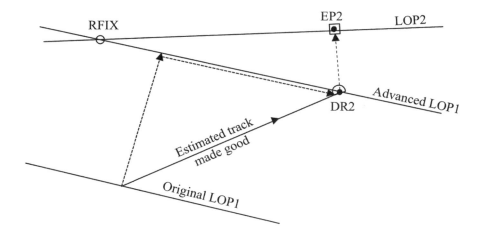

Figure 10.4 The traditional running fix at RFIX assumes that the component of the estimated track perpendicular to LOP1 is accurate, while the component of the estimated track parallel to LOP1 is completely ignored. But in reality, the reliability of the track estimate in different directions is entirely independent of the orientation of LOP1.

whatever the direction of dead-reckoning errors, they don't depend on LOP1's orientation. So that's a contradiction piled upon unjustified assumptions, all while disregarding available information. Is there a worse approach to rational reasoning—to estimation logic?

The Estimated Position Running Fix

We'll now take a quite different approach to the above problem by using estimation logic. We are still considering the situation where the LOP accuracy is substantially greater than the dead reckoning, as is usually the case after a run of some length. (Many kinds of LOPs will satisfy this, such as range, bearing, and celestial.) Let's first consider dead reckoning from a known departure point, followed by establishing an LOP. Figure 10.5 shows this situation with our position at DR1 when LOP1 was acquired. The information used to obtain DR1 can be speed, time, heading, current, and leeway. It's simply the best information we have, or that we believe is useable. We now wish to upgrade our DR position to an estimated position using the new and more accurate LOP1 information. We know that this new LOP1 only constrains our position perpendicular to itself, with no constraint whatsoever along it. So if we drop a line from DR1 to EP1 which is perpendicular to LOP1, we make full use of the LOP's perpendicular constraint, while retaining all of the DR information parallel to LOP1. So that is the best estimate, meeting all the logical criteria—it uses all available information without invoking unnecessary assumptions or contradictions.

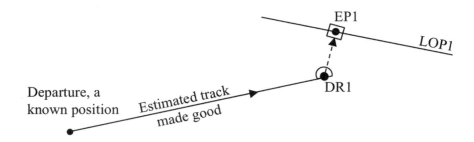

Figure 10.5 The newly acquired LOP improves the estimate of the ship's position by simultaneously constraining the ship's position to be as close as possible to DR1, while still fully honoring LOP1.

Next, let's say at some later time a second observation provides LOP2 when the ship's position is placed at DR2, as shown in Figure 10.6. Over time, the run from EP1 has degraded our position estimate into a DR position by using estimates of heading, distance, and perhaps other estimates. So we again have a DR position with a newly acquired LOP, just as in Figure 10.5. Therefore we again drop a perpendicular line to the new LOP to get our estimated position at EP2. This is an *EP running fix*. We use this method for each newly acquired LOP, continually improving our estimate with adding newly acquired LOPs, but always retaining DR information that has not been contradicted by the latest LOP.

So the EP running fix is the best estimate, meeting all our rational criteria—it uses all available information without invoking unnecessary assumptions or contradictions. Moreover, we see that for all crossing angles and dead reckoning uncertainty, the estimated position EP2 always lies closer (or equal) to our best previous estimate at DR2 than does RFIX. Indeed, you can see from Figure 10.4, that for sufficiently

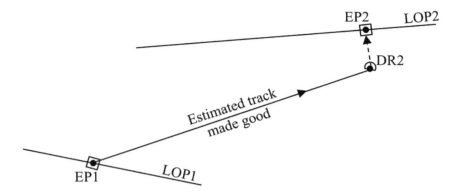

Figure 10.6 The same estimated position is used in a running fix by constraining the DR estimate perpendicular to LOP2, but retaining all the information in the DR estimate that is not constrained by LOP2.

small crossing angles, RFIX could be off by many miles, magnifying the DR error, rather than reducing it as the estimated position does. Thus the EP increases the value of LOPs having narrow crossing angles. After all, *any* new LOP must *improve* the dead-reckoned estimate by constraining it to a line. And this is exactly what the EP does—it always improves the DR estimate, while the traditional running fix can easily conflict with it.

On a leg of several running fixes, LOPs at different orientations will continually limit the DR error in the direction perpendicular to each new LOP. And successive LOPs as near as possible to right angles will continually limit the error the most. Note, as can be visualized from Figure 10.4, that as the angle between two successive LOPs approaches 90°, the results of the EP running fix and the traditional running fix approach one another.

The ultimate example of narrow LOP crossing angles is successive meridian shots in celestial navigation (such as the famous noon-sun shots). Since every sight gives a new latitude, these successive east-west LOPs never cross. Without even thinking about running fixes, navigators of old corrected their DR position by the newly observed latitude, but retained their dead reckoned longitude: in plotting terms, they're dropping a perpendicular from the DR position to the LOP – a perfect example of using the estimated position between successive LOPs.

The Short-Run Fix

On the opposite end of the accuracy spectrum we have the short-run fix, where the accuracy of the estimated track is greater than that of the LOPs. The most common example is a round of star shots. Other bodies, such as the sun, moon, and Venus, can also be shot within a very short time interval, providing another opportunity for a short-run fix. In many small vessels the speed is sufficiently slow, and the time between LOPs is short enough that the distance made good between observations can be ignored if the ultimate accuracy is not required, such as in the open ocean. But for large ships, making perhaps 10 kn or more, the short-run fix is the solution for the discriminating navigator.

When the time interval is short, the accuracy of the ship's travel between the first sight and the last can be as accurate, or more accurate, then the uncertainty in the LOP positions. For example, a one knot error in the ship's speed over a half-hour round of sights produces a 0.5 nm error, which is better than many celestial LOPs. So in this case the logic of the traditional running fix is valid. But instead of plotting each LOP and then advancing it to the latest one, it's easier to simply adjust the observed altitudes for the ship's position. We used the same treatment of the vessel's motion for meridian shots, where we adjusted the body's observed altitudes for the north-south motion of the observer along the meridian.

The only difference here is that the bearings to the bodies are in the direction of the calculated azimuths, Zn, rather than along the meridian. Figure 10.7a shows the direction to the body, Zn, and the ship track T. As diagrammed in Figure 10.7b, the component of velocity in the direction to the body is just Cos (T – Zn). (The cosine function is even, so it doesn't matter if we use T – Zn or Zn – T. See Appendix F for the concept of the cosine function.) Furthermore, when the angle T– Zn is greater than 90°, the cosine is negative, meaning that the velocity is away from the body. So as is easily visualized, when cos(T – Zn) is positive, the ship is moving toward the body, so that body's altitude is increasing. And conversely, when the cos(T – Zn) is negative, the ship is moving away from that body, so that body's altitude is decreasing.

So we'll adjust the sight's intercepts by the amount the ship has moved toward, or away from, that body during the time elapsed between when that body was shot and the time of the last sight (or any other reference sight). And we see that the ship has moved V cos(T – Zn) times the time difference between the sights, where V is the speed of the vessel.

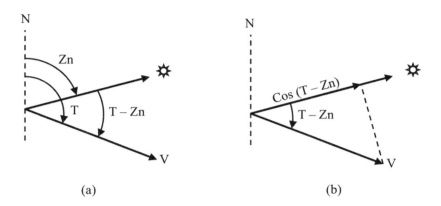

(a)   (b)

Figure 10.7 (a) The difference in the estimated track angle T from true north and the azimuth Zn determines the component of the ship's velocity V in the direction to the body. (b) This velocity component is Cos(T – Zn).

As an example, we'll use a round of four stars as shown in Figure 10.8, where the sight times, azimuths, and intercepts are shown that resulted from the standard work up. During the round of shots, the vessel had an estimated track of 270° true with a speed of 15 kn. Before plotting these azimuths and intercepts, we adjust the intercepts to be what would have resulted if all the stars were shot at the time of the last shot, that of Acrux.

The first four rows of the worksheet are the given results of the standard workup. The last six rows are the short-run fix calculations. The first entries in the second group are the tracks relative to the body's azimuths, T – Zn (its algebraic sign is irrelevant because the cosine is an even function). The third row contains the cos(T – Zn) factors, multiplied by the 15 kn ship's velocity. Note that for (T – Zn) angles greater than 90°, the velocity made good along the Zn direction is negative, that is, the ship is moving away from the body. The next row lists the our calculated time intervals of each of the first three sights relative to Acrux, the last sight. The times are in minutes and seconds. Multiplying each of these times by the entry just above it gives the adjustment to each intercept. This is easy using a calculator: First we convert the time interval to hours because V is in knots. For example, in the Sirius calculation take 37/60, add the 34 minutes, then divide this sum by 60 to get hours, and finally multiply by the 14.9 kn above, getting an intercept adjustment of + 8.6 nm. The plus sign means the distance is toward the body, as we can also see from the 5° relative bearing angle.

Finally, we apply these intercept adjustments to the original calculated intercepts, observing the *Toward/Away* directions. Of course when these directions are the same, they accumulate, as in the Betelgeuse case: the 12.1 *Toward* adjustment is added to the original 1.2 *Toward* intercept to give 13 *Toward* (rounding to the whole arc minute). But for Sirius the 8.6 *Toward* is subtracted from the 28.8 *Away* intercept since they're in opposite directions.

For those who don't want to think about cosines, or use a scientific calculator, Table 1 of H.O. 249 Sight Reduction Tables gives the product of the ship's speed with the cosine of the (T – Zn) angle. The table is constructed for aircraft speeds from 50 to 900 knots. But just mentally divide the speed by 10 or 100 and likewise the intercept adjustment to make it useful for marine use.

Short-Run Fix Worksheet				
Speed *15 kn*		Estimated Track *270° True*		
Body	*Regulus*	*Sirius*	*Betelgeuse*	*Acrux*
UT	*19:45:31*	*19:31:14*	*19:11:44*	*20:05:51*
Zn	*23°*	*275°*	*297°*	*154°*
Intercept	*27.2 Toward*	*26.8 Away*	*1.2 Toward*	*22 Away*
T – Zn	*–247°*	*+5°*	*+27°*	*–116°*
Cos(T – Zn)	*–0.391*	*+0.996*	*+0.891*	
V x Cos(T – Zn)	*–5.9*	*14.9*	*13.4*	
Time Difference	*20:20*	*34:37*	*54:07*	*– 0 –*
Correction	*–2.0 Away*	*+8.6 Toward*	*12.1 Toward*	
Final Intercept	*25 Toward*	*18 Away*	*13 Toward*	*22 Away*

Figure 10.8 The workup of a 4-star short-run fix.

Special LOP Orientations

The direction of LOPs is not only important for making accurate fixes (i.e., true fixes from simultaneous LOPs), but can also be useful in special situations. Suppose, for example, that you're on your final leg heading for your destination. Your arrival time is important. Then the best LOP orientation would be at, or nearly at, right angles to your course. On the other hand, suppose that the ETA isn't critical, but you want a landfall as accurate as possible, right on the button. Or, you may wish to clear an obstacle, such as a reef or a low island. Then an LOP that is parallel to your course would provide the best guidance. Of course, we're not at liberty to arbitrarily pick a given orientation of a celestial LOP. Generally, we could not pick an LOP to coincide with our course. However, in special situations, we may want to do the reverse—pick our course to coincide with an available LOP.

A primitive example of a course selected to match an LOP was the pre-nineteenth century practice of "chasing down the latitude" when no knowledge of the ship's longitude was available, but only the latitude was known from meridian or Polaris sights. So the navigator selected the port's latitude as the special LOP. Then, making sure the ship arrived at this latitude well ahead of time, the ship would sail along the parallel toward port, waiting for a landfall, not knowing when to expect it. Days or even weeks could be wasted at sea because of not knowing the longitude.

Francis Chichester carried this idea much further on his 1931 solo flight in his *Gypsy Moth* biplane across the Tasman Sea. Risking certain death in the open ocean, using only a marine sextant and dead reckoning, his challenge was finding a tiny speck in the Tasman Sea. His goal was Norfolk Island, 481 miles away from his departure at the northernmost tip of New Zealand. He laid out his course, not directly to the island, but to a point some 90 miles to the southwest of the island where he could intercept a precomputed sun line pointing right to the island. The 90-mile offset was selected to be sufficiently large that he could be assured, even with the uncertainties of dead reckoning, which way to head at the turning point. When Chichester reached the turning point, he made four extra sun shots to be sure he was on the precomputed sun line; then he changed course to match the sun line, heading straight for the island, where landfall dramatized the value of a little ingenuity applied to celestial navigation.

To see if Chichester's idea is adaptable to marine use, we'll explore an example from the mid-Pacific: The Midway Islands consist of two small, low islands (about 25 feet elevation) at the southern edge of a rounded atoll. We're approaching the atoll from northeast, on a southwesterly course, on the morning of 11 May 2005, expecting to be some 20 miles out around 2300 UT. Since we want to stay clear of the atoll's reefs, and the islands are to the south, we select a landfall target off the southeast corner of Eastern Island, located at N28° 13′, W177° 18′.

Following Chichester, we precompute several sun lines before and after 2300 UT, using our target location as the AP. (This exercise dramatizes our earlier claim that the AP is not an assumed position, as it's traditionally called. Rather, it is a *reference point* designating where we wish to draw the straight-line approximation to a given equal-altitude LOP.)

Plotting these precomputed sun lines, as sketched in Figure 10.9a, shows disappointing behavior. They are very fast moving targets, and as time goes on, they move faster and faster. The 9° orientation change between the 2200 and the 2230 UT line corresponds to a speed of 6 kn

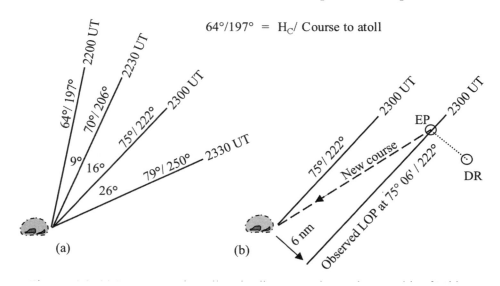

Figure 10.9 (a) Precomputed sun lines leading to a point on the east side of Midway Atoll. **(b)** An actual 2300 altitude of 75° 06′ places us on a LOP 6 nm southeast of the precomputer 2300 UT line.

at 20 nm from our landfall target. And at the same 20 nm out, the 26° orientation change from 2300 to 2330 UT corresponds to a speed of 18 kn. So timing arrival to intersect one of these sun lines, pointing right at the target, requires very sharp navigating indeed—or an airplane.

But all is not lost. As noted earlier, intentionally approaching the atoll so that our sun LOP is nearly parallel with our desired course vastly improves our estimated position, and subsequently improves our landfall.

Suppose now, while approaching the atoll our actual 2300 observation gives an 75° 06´ altitude LOP, instead of the desired 75°, as shown in Figure 10.9b. So using this, we find our estimated position, as discussed above under Running Fixes, by dropping a perpendicular to the LOP from our DR position. Then we plot our new course to the atoll, and use that to establish our new heading by converting to magnetic north and adjusting for estimated current and drift. Furthermore, we can continually monitor our progress toward the landfall. For example, we might repeat this procedure by taking another sight at 2315 UT, when the sun line pointing to the atoll has a 234° orientation (not shown in the figure, but you can compute any of these LOPs as exercises).

To demonstrate the superiority of this method, suppose that by not planning ahead, we approach the atoll in the afternoon with the sun's LOP running at nearly right angles to our course. Then the LOP would provide virtually no course guidance to the atoll. For example, in Figure 10.10 we show the same EP as Figure 10.9b, but with two different LOPs, having different orientations. On the left, LOP_1 is at right angles to our desired course, and on the right we have the same 222° LOP as in Figure 10.9b, which isn't quite aligned with the atoll, but falls six miles southeast. The figure shows the difference in course ambiguity generated by the two different LOP orientations. In both cases the EPs are in the same location, determined by dead reckoning updated with a sun line, and are 20 miles from the atoll. In both cases we have celestial accuracy perpendicular to the sun line, and an estimated 10-mile dead reckoning uncertainty (5 miles each side of the EP) along the sun line, as shown in the figures. We see that the celestial accuracy of LOP_1 is wasted in terms of improving the course estimate to the atoll; the course still has the DR uncertainty of 29°. On the other hand, the 222° LOP$_2$ has reduced the course uncertainty to just 9°, which is over three times better. So it pays to plan our landfall ahead of time.

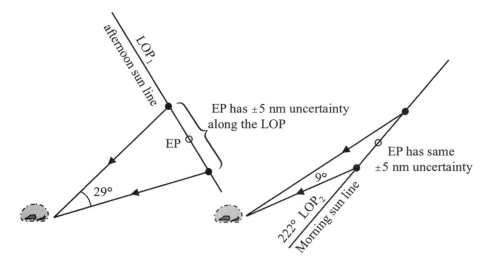

Figure 10.10 The effect of DR uncertainty and LOP orientation on the best estimated course to the atoll. In both cases the EP is 20 miles from the atoll. LOP$_2$, nearly directed at the atoll, has a 9° course uncertainty compared to the 29° course uncertainty of LOP$_1$.

Great-Circle Sailing

We've already seen many different applications of our basic altitude equation to great-circle problems, such as lunar distance clearing. One of the more obvious applications is computing the great-circle distance between two geographical locations.

The latitude and longitude of the AP is simply replaced with the coordinates of the first location. And the latitude and longitude of the GP is replaced with the coordinates of the second location. Then remember that the great-circle distance between the two is not H$_C$ given by the altitude equation, but corresponds to the co-altitude. So the angular distance between them is 90° minus H$_C$. Our rule for converting the angle A to Az gives the bearing from the first body to the second. This is not the reciprocal of the bearing from the second body to the first. Thus calling the great-circle distance D, replacing L with L$_1$, d with L$_2$, and identifying the LHA with the *longitude difference*, LonD, the great-circle-distance adaptation of the equations become

$$\cos D = \sin L_1 \sin L_2 + \cos L_1 \cos L_2 \cos (LonD) \qquad (10.2a)$$

and

$$\cos A = (\sin L_2 - \sin L_1 \cos D) / (\cos L_1 \sin D) \qquad (10.2b)$$

The first equation is symmetric in points one and two, but the second equation is not. The azimuth angle given by Equation 10.2b, combined with our rules for getting Zn from A, yields the azimuth at point one to point two. This bearing is not the reciprocal of the bearing at point two to point one. Again, a sketch (similar to Figure 3.1) will clarify relationships.

Calculating great circle courses is a case where the calculator trumps tabular methods. Instructions are included in H.O. 229, but they require plotting similar that of the intercept method, interpolation, and selecting among four different cases.

After the great-circle distance is calculated, multiply it by 60.04 nm per degree to get the great-circle distance in nautical miles. (For large distances we use the more accurate 60.04 rather than rounding off to 60 nm per degree.) The azimuth calculated by our rules is the initial course at the departure point, which, of course, changes along the great-circle track.

It's useful to know a few properties of great circles, both for visualizing great-circle tracks and for sketching other applications of the navigation triangle. A generic great circle can be envisioned as the equator rotated about a line connecting any two of its points 180° apart. On a Mercator chart great-circle tracks bow toward the nearest pole. At each meridian they have a greater latitude than the rhumb line connecting the same two points. If a great-circle track is sufficiently long, it reaches a maximum latitude where its direction is east-west, a point called its apex. The difference in distance between the great-circle track and the rhumb-line track is greatest at high latitudes; it's least for tracks near the equator where the meridians are nearly parallel. It's also greater for east-west courses than north-south courses. After all, a true north-south course lies on a meridian, which is a great circle. Great circles plot as straight lines on gnomonic charts (sometimes called great-circle charts). But distances are so distorted on these charts that they're limited primarily to planning routes. Once at sea, with our equations and a calculator it's easy to determine your great-circle course to your destination after each fix. You can't do better than heading directly toward your destination from wherever you are.

Time

The twentieth-century development of the digital quartz wristwatch has simplified celestial navigation. No longer are three expensive chronometers required to find longitude. These highly accurate and easy-to-read digital watches are so inexpensive and ubiquitous that just about every crewman has one. On a well-run ship, time-rating logs could be kept for at least three of these wristwatches. For each, regularly record its time relative to time from the GPS or other radio signals; establish a rate of gain, or loss, for each watch; and observe whether these rates remain constant. Any watch that doesn't keep a uniform rate should be replaced with another candidate. Then if the outside time signal fails, a comparison of at least three watches will reveal if one of them loses accurate time. Fortunately, these rates are usually very good, typically better than one second per several weeks. So for most voyages these rates can be ignored, rather being used to correct sight times. The digital watch is so easy to read that immediately after your sextant is aligned on the sight, you can quickly look at the seconds on the watch. This can be done in less than one second, requiring no help from another person.

Accurate time is available from the National Institute of Standards and Technology (NIST) via WWV (Boulder, CO) and WWVH (Hawaii) radio stations on 2.5, 5.0, 10.0, 15.0, and 20.0 MHz. Canada's station CHU broadcasts time signals similar to WWV's, on 3.33, 7.335, and 14.679 mHz. You can also set your quartz watch by using the NIST phone number. And at their website (see Appendix K) an animated clock displays the time, along with its current accuracy, which is typically 0.3 to 0.2 sec, determined by measuring the internet delay time to your particular computer.

Clocks that are synchronized to WWVB's low-frequency radio

signal on 60 kHz are convenient, small, portable, and inexpensive for use at home or at sea. Unfortunately, reception is only satisfactory in the vicinity of North America, having the largest coverage during nighttime hours. The delays along the 60 kHz propagation paths are less than 0.03 sec, but an actual clock's accuracy depends on its design. Although many manufactures don't give accuracy specs, most WWVB clocks should be plenty accurate for celestial navigation. The other obvious choice for checking your quartz watch is your GPS receiver.

As celestial navigators we've concentrated on using universal time, UT, in our sight workups. But aboard ship and on shore the commonly used time is zone time, ZT. Zone time is a crude attempt to make the sun reach its peak altitude at around 12:00 local time for every location on earth, which means we have to have different zone times at different longitudes. So for each hour difference in ZT, the longitudes would differ by 360°/ 24 hrs = 15°. These 15° wide time zones are reckoned from Greenwich with the zero-hour zone centered on Greenwich, extending 7.5° on each side of the *prime meridian*. The longitude in the middle of a time zone is exactly divisible by 15, called the *zone meridian*.

The twelve time zones west of Greenwich each have their ZT progressively an hour earlier than UT. And twelve zones east of Greenwich progressively each have their ZT an hour later than UT. For example, Papeete at 150° west longitude is right on the 10-hour zone meridian, so it has a ZT 10 hours behind UT, as do longitudes up to 7.5° on each side of the W150° meridian.

The time zone centered on 180° longitude has its western half 12 hours behind UT, and its eastern half 12 hours ahead of UT. So for example, as you sail west through 180° longitude your zone time goes from being 12 hours behind Greenwich to 12 hours ahead of Greenwich. Thus the zone time has increased by 24 hours, meaning the ZT clock hasn't changed, but the date has. It's increased by a day. As an example, Figure 10.11 shows the ZT in the 24 zones on a Sunday at 1500 UT. As the sun marches westward, the new day, Monday in this example, expands out of the international dateline, and the old day, Sunday, get absorbed at the dateline.

Instead of religiously following the time zone meridians spaced 15° apart, the boundaries of these 24 time zones frequently deviate around areas, such as island groups and political units, for the convenience of those region's inhabitants. And in some places they differ by half hour increments.

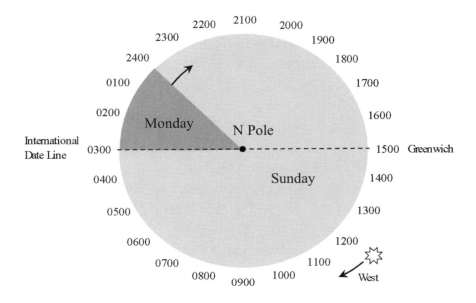

Figure 10.11 A diagram looking at the earth's Northern hemisphere, showing zone times on a Sunday when it's 1500 at Greenwich.

Accuracy

Three major factors limit the accuracy of celestial navigation: the sextant observation, the timing of the sight, and the sight reduction method. Under normal conditions the largest limitation, and hardest to control, is the altitude observation (which we've also discussed in Chapter 9). The human eye, limited by the performance of its optical nerve cells, provides navigators having 20/20 vision with 1.0′ resolution. A five-power scope increases this resolution to 0.2′. Quite a few people have 20/15 vision, giving them a resolution approaching 0.1′ with the same five-power scope. But these are theoretical values, achievable in the optometrist's office. Individual technique and conditions at sea can degrade these results immensely. Using star-star distance checks as discussed in Chapter 8 and altitude averaging as discussed in Chapter

9 will reveal your individual accuracy capability. You'll be doing great if you can consistently measure altitudes at sea to 1′ or 2′. Even averaging sights, as discussed in Chapter 9, will only improve this accuracy by a factor of two or so.

Usually the rest of the sight reduction procedure trumps the altitude measurements in accuracy, but these other errors certainly can accumulate: The three altitude corrections, index, dip, and refraction each should be within 0.1′, totaling 0.3′ if they all accumulated in the same direction (being somewhat generous on measuring index error, and neglecting extreme atmospheric conditions). Timing using today's quartz watches should be within one second, which translates into 0.25′ arc minutes (based on earth rate of 15°/hr). The almanac claims its GHA and declination data accurate to 0.25′ for the sun, 0.3′ for the moon, and better than 0.2′ for the stars and planets. Sight reduction tables H.O. 249 seem to have a maximum error of 0.5′ (that is, accurate to the nearest 1.0′), while H.O. 229, can perform their functions to within 0.2′ to 0.3′ of arc. Calculators and computers usually have a precision and accuracy greater than 0.01′ minutes of arc (with their 8 to 10 digit accuracy and precision), so they should not contribute to a loss of accuracy. The best combination of these errors comes from star and planet shots using a calculator for *all* of the calculations. With this combination, if all these possible errors accumulated in the same direction, the maximum possible error would be 0.95′. The worst combination would be moon shots using H.O. 249. The seven additions and subtractions of data, all accurate to only 0.5′, have a maximum possible error of 3.5′. Adding in the almanac's limitation of 0.3′ gives a 3.8′ maximum error.

To summarize, depending on the sight reduction used, the maximum possible error is between about 1′ and 4′ of arc. To these errors we must then add the observation error in the sextant altitude itself. Of course normally, many of these errors will cancel on the average, giving much better results. But in navigation it's essential to appreciate what the worst case can be.

So the next obvious question is, what is the best balance between these limitations and the need, or desire, for superior accuracy? For practicing observations and their sight reductions, we've maintained a precision of 0.1 minutes of arc throughout most of our discussion, believing it's easier to relax this requirement than to tighten it. Besides, this calculation precision allows you to evaluate your sights when practicing from a known location, knowing that any disagreement, beyond the reduction error discussed above, must be from observation error.

In actual practice at sea, under various situations and considering navigator preferences, we could reasonably relax this 1.0′ goal. Knowing position to within a mile is of little significance when 10 or even 20 miles would make little difference while far offshore. An old navigator's saw is, you don't need to know where you are; you just need to know where you are not. On the other hand, navigating ocean races, navigating near shallow reefs, or attempting a landfall to a small, low island are obviously different situations. Whatever the individual navigator's requirement, it is important to have a clear perception of the factors affecting accuracy.

Knowing the relationship between timing and accuracy will increase our overall understanding of celestial navigation—and increase its usefulness in unusual situations. Timing errors affect the values of declination and LHA that go into the calculation of H_C. Generally, the declination errors are negligible compared to the LHA errors, except for the moon when its declination is changing at the maximum rate. For example, at the equinox, where the sun's rate of change in declination is maximum, it would take a one-hour timing error to produce a one-mile latitude error due to a declination error in a noon sun shot. But a St. Hilaire sight of a body bearing east or west, feeling the full effect of the earth's rotation, would suffer the same one-mile error in only four seconds because of the resulting LHA error. Likewise, a whole minute timing error would produce a 15-mile error.

On the other hand, a St. Hilaire sight near the meridian is comparatively insensitive to errors in the LHA, and hence to timing. For example, at 40° latitude and an azimuth angle 8° off of the meridian, the same one-minute timing error would produce only a 1.6-mile error in the intercept distance. These errors can be seen from Equation A.2 of Appendix A, as explained in Exercises 2.17 and 2.18.

Relaxing accuracy requirements, to one or even several miles, permits simplified sight reduction procedures. Extracting data from the almanac can be simplified. Except for the moon, declination could be taken from the almanac with mental interpolation, or even no interpolation. You could forget the d and v corrections. Altitude corrections could likewise be simplified. For example, for the stars and planets a simple constant altitude correction of $-2.5'$ for altitudes greater than ten degrees would suffice if we were content with a 2.5-mile error. Taking this same approach, correct the sun's lower limb with $+13.5'$ and its upper limb with $-18.5'$. Tables, such as H.O. 249 or even custom-made ones, as suggested in Exercise 5.6, can also simplify the sight reduction.

These shortcuts offer advantages in special situations where a quick-and-dirty sight might be satisfactory: examples are beginning practice (as discussed in Chapter 13), experiencing lifeboat conditions, or just having fun at sea. This cavalier approach should still get you within several miles, depending on how you choose to carry it out. But under other conditions this computational advantage has to be weighed against the knowledge that the sight reduction is not as good as it could be.

Compass Deviation

In this GPS age, with its continuous readout of position, sailors can easily neglect the accuracy of the ship's compass. But the compass is the most fundamental navigation instrument on board; also the most reliable—when it's treated right. In addition to being ever mindful of magnetic *variation*, the difference between true north versus magnetic north, the navigator must measure and correct for the compass's *deviation* from magnetic north due to the magnetic disturbance of the vessel itself. Many modern fiberglass and aluminum boats have small to negligible deviation, but some have significant deviation errors that can seriously degrade your dead reckoning and your ability to travel the desired course.

Swinging the Ship

A compass deviation table is made by comparing the ship's compass to known magnetic headings. This means accurately observing the magnetic bearings of distant objects whose bearings are known independent of the ship's compass. This can be done with several different kinds of sighting vanes that mount over the ships compass to read the object's bearing relative to the ship's compass. But generally, such instruments are only available on large vessels, and would not be of much use on small boats where a view from the binnacle can be quite limited. Another option is the *Pelorus* (named after Hannibal's navigator on his trip to Italy, 203 BC). It's a portable compass card with no directional properties that can be set to various directions, such as the current ship's heading, with sighting vanes for taking bearings.

But perhaps the simplest method for small vessels is to use a handheld bearing compass aimed at a distant onshore object (greater than three miles away): The first step is to find an onboard location with no magnetic deviation. To do this, station a crew member at a prospective spot, such as on the forward deck away from magnetic objects. As the boat is slowly maneuvered in a tight circle, the handheld compass is kept steadied on the distance object. If there is no deviation at the location of the handheld compass, it will read a constant magnetic bearing as the boat is maneuvered around the circle.

Once a satisfactory location is found, the handheld is kept sighted straight forward as the boat is again maneuvered in a circle while the handheld reading and the ship's main compass are compared. The difference in the two readings is the ship's compass deviation. A tabulation of these differences, labeling them plus when the ship's compass reads more than the handheld and minus when it reads less, is the compass deviation table, giving the correct compass reading for a given desired magnetic heading. So in converting from magnetic heading to compass heading, follow the sign in the table. That is, if the sign is plus, add the correction to the magnetic heading to get the compass heading; if it's minus, subtract it to get the compass heading.

Note that when you tabulate the results, first apply the correction to the compass reading. That is, if the ship's compass were 10° too high when the compass was reading 120°, then you tabulate the compass correction +10° across from magnetic 110° (not across from 120°). Then when calculating the compass heading from a magnetic heading, apply the sign in your deviation correction table.

Sun Azimuths

As discussed above, in coastal waters, bearings to any distant object will do. In open waters one only has celestial bodies, and only bodies close to the horizon provide convenient sighting. And the rising and setting sun provide a convenient reference azimuth. Swinging the ship can be done with your sunrise coffee right after your morning Polaris shot. The other opportunity is at sunset with your evening grog, just before twilight sets in for updating your latitude from Polaris. This is a wonderful way to observe sunrises and sunsets, combining beauty with utility.

Of course, we now know how to calculate the azimuth of any of the navigation bodies from our known location. But for convenience, a table of Sunrise/Sunset Azimuths is provided in Appendix I. This table is constructed using our standard altitude equation with an altitude of −36.6′, which represents the zero altitude of the sun's center, corrected −33.8′ for refraction, plus a height-of-eye correction of − 2.8′ corresponding to 8.5 feet. (The effects of greater eye height would be negligible in practical cases.) The table can be used for both the sun's upper and lower limbs with negligible error, except at polar latitudes. For example, at latitude N65° on the summer solstice, the sun will change its azimuth by as much as 4° as its disk moves from its center (the tabulated value) to one of its limbs. Furthermore, we can easily visualize that for the right combination of polar latitudes and declinations, the sun can be very near the horizon while it sweeps out 360° of azimuth.

For lesser latitudes, the tables give the azimuth angle Z (used in sight reduction tables) from which the true-north azimuth Zn of the rising or setting sun is calculated. The table is entered with the sun's declination (from the almanac) and our current latitude. Note that neither must be precisely known. Then Z is extracted from the table (making sure you're in the correct table—same or contrary), and use the formulae at the top of the table to give the azimuth from *true north* at the instant the sun's center is on the horizon.

Say, for example, that we're at 18° north latitude and we want the sun's azimuth at sunset: At sunset on this date, suppose the almanac gives the sun's declination of S23° 15. 7'. Entering the contrary-name azimuth table with the 18° latitude and the declination rounded off to 23°, we find Z = 114°. Finally the relevant formula at the top of the table gives Zn = 360° − 114° = 246° at sunset. This true-north azimuth then is converted to magnetic by adding west magnetic variation, or subtracting east variation, as given by your chart.

Next the boat is held on a selected heading while the sun's azimuth is read from the compass sighting vanes (or from the handheld compass in a deviation-free location). The difference between the reading from the sighting vanes and the magnetic azimuth is the deviation error for the vessel's current heading. By recording these differences, for various ship's headings, you can construct a compass deviation table as discussed earlier. Label them plus when the compass reads more than the actual magnetic azimuth, otherwise, minus.

Ocean Pilot Charts

All of our studies of celestial navigation, including planning landfalls and great circle routes, might well be for naught if we don't select the proper route for a given passage. No sane mariner would set out on an offshore passage without considering the likely conditions to be found enroute. The likelihood of specific winds, currents, waves, fog, ice, temperatures, and storms all have to be considered in selecting the optimum route.

And fortunately, the U.S. National Geospatial-Intelligence Agency (NGA) publishes digital maps of the world's five ocean regions giving exactly this kind of vital information for planning ocean passages (See the Bibliography at the end of the book for their website). These maps, called *pilot charts*, are published for each month of the year, giving monthly average conditions of importance to mariners. The main body of the chart displays graphic information (in color) on winds, currents, wave heights, magnetic variation, and some great circle routes. Additional text includes further information on pressure, temperature, winds, cyclones, wave heights, and visibilities.

As an example, Figure 10.12 shows a small section (in gray scale here), south of the Cape of Good Hope, of the July pilot chart for the South Indian Ocean. The most prominent feature is the wind roses,

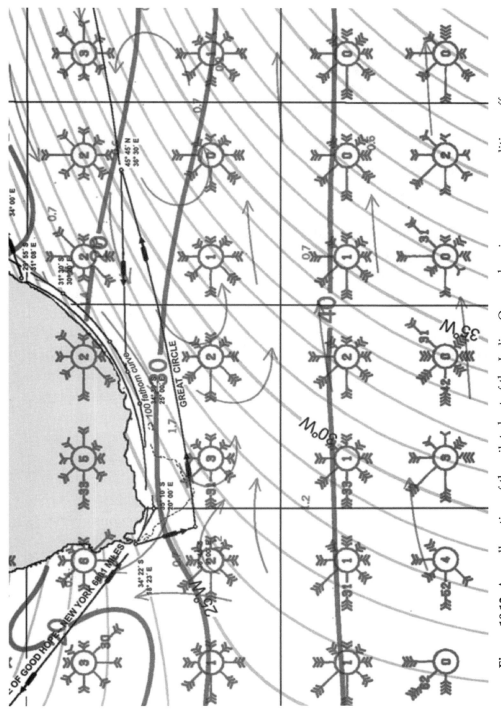

Figure 10.12 A small section of the pilot chart of the Indian Ocean, showing average conditions off the coast of the Cape of Good Hope in July.

with barbed arrows showing the average direction of winds for that month. The number of barbs on each arrow indicate the average wind force on the Beaufort scale. And the length of the arrow is proportional to the percent of time that wind blows this strength, with numbers given when the percentage is over 29% of the time. For example, just south of the Cape we expect a force six wind (22-27 kn) from the west 31% of the time. The number in the center of the rose indicates calm winds only 3% of the time. The thick semi-horizontal contour line (red when in color) indicates a wave height greater than 12 feet 30% of the time, and further south 40% of the time. The curvilinear arrows (green when in color) show current from the west at about 0.7 to 1.0 kn. The gray northeast-southwest trending contours indicate magnetic variation (one is marked 30°W here).

We see that the pilot chart offers readily digestible information that immediately tells us that an eastward trip around the Cape promises a fast lively winter passage in July, while a westward one would be a tough upwind slog. Of course pilot charts are just the "tip of the iceberg" in ocean passage planning. There are many cruising handbooks and passage-making guides available on the subject, beginning with Bowditch with its chapters on oceanography and marine meteorology, that the ocean passage maker should consult before weighing anchor.

11

TABLES, CALCULATORS, AND COMPUTERS: THE DEBATE

SIGHT REDUCTION TABLES
CALCULATORS AND COMPUTERS

Many experienced celestial navigators adopt one method of sight reduction, stick to it, and vigorously defend its use. But actually, all methods have their advantages and disadvantages. So why not become competent in a couple of them? As usual, in the interest of dependability and safety, the best answer is redundancy. Anyhow, here's more information on these methods—grist for debating comparisons among them.

Sight Reduction Tables

Using tables precludes even thinking about the navigation triangle equations and is therefore preferred for some purposes and by some navigators. An appreciation for the various types and uses of tables relates to their history, which is inextricably related to that of mathematics.

Our knowledge of trigonometry dates back to an Egyptian papyrus of Ahmes, c. 1550 B.C. Following centuries of mathematical advancement, an Arab astronomer, Al-Battani (c. 850-929), developed the essence of the equation for H_c that we use today. But this equation, with its three multiplications of numbers each having six or seven

187

digits, made maritime sight reductions impractical until Scottish mathematician John Napier published the first logarithm tables in 1614. Since multiplication of the required trig functions is equivalent to adding their logarithms, it then became practical to perform sight reductions at sea. By the late eighteenth century, several texts had been published on sight reduction methods. Then came the famous 1802 book *The New American Practical Navigator*, by Nathaniel Bowditch, a revision of a book first written and revised by two authors before him. The 2002 edition of Bowditch still carries the log-trig tables for those wishing to reenact this 200-year-old procedure.

This method of adding logarithms was the only method available until a large number of precomputed tabular solutions to the navigational triangle appeared near the end of the nineteenth century. Later the U.S. Hydrographic Office published H.O. 208 in 1928 and H.O. 211 in 1931. These short tables (as they are called now) break the navigation triangle into two right triangles. It's this division, not obvious to the normal user, that allows many fewer entries than otherwise. But this advantage is offset by tedium and obfuscation of concepts. For example, the *Nautical Almanac*'s short table, constructed by Admiral Thomas D. Davies, USN, requires extracting eight numbers from the tables, performing several additions, and applying about thirteen different rules. Bennett and Pepperday also offer similar versions of short tables in their books cited in Appendix K.

Much less tedious to use are the so-called inspection tables. The first was H.O. 214, published in 1936. Then came *Sight Reduction Tables for Air Navigation*, H.O. 249, (now called NIMA Pub. No. 249) with its Volume I published in 1947. The last was H.O. 229 (NIMA Pub. No. 229) called *Sight Reduction Tables for Marine Use*, which was computed on an IBM 1410 electronic computer. These tables give precomputed altitude and azimuth, limited to whole degrees of latitude, declination, and LHA. This whole-degree limitation is necessary to reduce the enormous number of entries that would otherwise be required. As a result (unless you are willing to consider three-dimensional interpolation), the whole-degree limitation prohibits some other uses, such as directly comparing the GPS with the celestial sights for accuracy and redundancy, and conveniently computing great-circle courses and distances. (Actually, these tables can be used to solve great-circle problems by using graphical methods at the end points to cover the non-whole degrees of latitude and longitude, though the whole process seems quite obtuse to the modern navigator. Details are given in H.O. 229.)

The H.O. 229 tables are published in six volumes, each covering 15° of latitude. These are the only inspection tables that cover all possible ranges of latitude, declination, and LHA. They tabulate H_C and Zn to 0.1 minutes, but their accuracy doesn't match their tabulated precision. At best they can only be relied upon to ±0.2′. And when using inconvenient second-order interpolation where required, their accuracy falls to ±0.31′.

Designed for air navigation, H.O. 249 is published in three volumes and gives results that are accurate to the nearest whole minute of arc (i.e., ±0.5′ accuracy), which is perfectly adequate for most marine applications. The real significance of H.O. 249 is the way it treats stars separately from the solar system bodies, which have limited ranges of declinations. Volume I, by internally accounting for each star's declination individually, directly gives H_C and Zn for each star according to the LHA of Aries and the latitude. Volumes 2 and 3 function just as does H.O. 229, giving the solutions to the navigation triangle. However, since Volume I covers the stars separately, Volumes 2 and 3 only cover the declinations of all the solar system bodies, so they only cover declinations up to 29°. That's a disadvantage to H.O. 249. And not only are Volumes 2 and 3 an incomplete set of tables, but Volume I inherently contains the declination of stars, making it somewhat ephemeral. Each edition covers an epoch of three years, and with certain corrections can be extended another three years. Epoch 2005.0 covers from 2004 though 2009, and can be used without corrections to 2007 with errors no greater than two minutes of arc.

One advantage of H.O. 249 is its organization, for it lists latitude by page openings, rather than listing one LHA for each page opening, as does H.O. 229, which has us flipping through about 180 pages for the particular LHA of each sight. With H.O. 249, the active pages change very slowly because a ship's latitude changes more slowly and uniformly than do the required LHAs. A handy bookmark will open H.O. 249 near the correct page every time.

Although tables have their disadvantages, they are relatively easy to use and have certain other advantages, such as being dependable and quite rugged (when not soaked in sea water). Also, they are particularly useful for quickly scanning values of H_c and Zn to learn about the behavior of the navigation triangle. The precomputed altitudes and azimuths for selected stars in Volume I of H.O. 249 is a real plus for star shots, providing easy sight planning, star identification, and a very simple sight reduction. Furthermore, unlike H.O. 229, with H.O. 249 we use the same AP for all stars in a fix, simplifying the plotting.

The availability of tables is shifting. With the role of celestial navigation diminishing in government and commercial service, continued Government Printing Office reproduction of these tables is uncertain. Some volumes of H.O. 229 are currently out of stock, and are not readily available on the used book market. Some used book sources are demanding prices three times the original price of H.O. 249. However, Celestaire publishes both H.O. 229 and H.O. 249, reprinted from government electronic files in soft cover at 90% of the original size. Furthermore, the U.S. National Geospatial-Intelligence Agency provides the complete H.O. 229 and H.O. 249 tables on their Web site. (See Appendix K.) They can be downloaded free of charge in Adobe PDF format, in whole or in selected sections.

For navigators who like to travel light, such as backpackers, boat delivery crews, or sailors jumping from leg to leg, labeling pages by latitude in H.O. 249 becomes an additional asset. There's no need to carry the weight and bulk of tables covering 40° or 50° of latitude, or of star tables that cover latitudes of the entire globe. Just remove the pages for the latitudes of your trip from both the star and the sight-reduction volumes, combine them into one binding, and you have one compact book, containing all that's needed and no more. Alternatively, with an Adobe Acrobat Reader, you can download H.O. 249 from the National Geospatial-Intelligence Agency's Web site and print out just the pages desired. (The government's printed version of H.O. 249, Volume I, also comes with a PDF CD of the complete star table.) I think that the ideal celestial navigator's go-kit should fit inside a sextant case.

Calculators and Computers

In today's world, when one thinks of solving the trig equations of the navigation triangle, computers naturally leap to mind. There's a range of possibilities, useable even at sea. The simplest is the inexpensive handheld scientific calculator. Then come programmable calculators, followed by handheld mini PCs, sometimes called Personal Digital Assistants, PDAs. The most powerful likely to be used is a laptop or full-size PC running on ship's power. Where Internet access is available, the National Geospatial-Intelligence Agency's Web site (see the bibliography, Appendix K) has a celestial navigation calculator, where you just type in L, d, and LHA, and it solves the equations for H_C and Zn.

Programs residing in PCs or programmable handheld calculators are very valuable for allowing the navigator to concentrate on other aspects, such as perfecting sextant observations, practicing different kinds of sights, and building confidence. However, those navigators who are attracted to the simplicity, independence, and redundancy of celestial navigation will want to try common handheld scientific calculators. They cost far less than tables, are available most anywhere, and are cheap enough to allow having several on board. Plus, such a calculator is no doubt already on board for a myriad of other uses, such as calculating speed and distance, making plotting sheets, computing ETAs, estimating the number of beer-days remaining, and so forth.

The scientific calculator has several other advantages over tables. With its ten-digit precision, interpolation is never needed for altitude or azimuth, for entering data to 0.1′ accuracy produces results to that accuracy. Mistakes, such as accidentally pressing the wrong key or entering the wrong number, are likely to result in large, and therefore detectable, errors. (An exception is a mistake in entering a low-significant digit.) In a table, being off just one column or row can produce undetectable, but significant errors. Once learned, a calculator's use is faster and less likely forgotten—especially when it's used for other applications. Sight reduction tables H.O. 249 don't cover all declinations, and H.O. 229 is a heavy, bulky set of six volumes. Only the calculator is inexpensive, complete, accurate, small, and light.

Furthermore, unlike all the precomputed tables, the calculator allows the selection of an arbitrary AP, as opposed to tables that are limited to whole-degree arguments. This means that inspection tables do not allow us to reduce many of the special sights discussed in Chapters 7 and 8, or to directly check our sight quality to within 0.1 nm when comparing H_O to H_C at a known position. Considering that our normal accuracy goal is 1 nm, we need a sight reduction with accuracy close to 0.1nm in order to evaluate degrading effects, such as sextant observation accuracy, ship motion, and false horizons. Cross-checking the celestial navigation with the GPS is an essential redundancy for affirming that both these independent systems are operating correctly. Also, the whole-degree requirement prohibits the convenient use of tables for the other applications, such as computing great-circle courses and distances. And as noted earlier, this same requirement of both H.O. 229 and H.O. 249 forces a different AP for each body, making calculating and plotting intercepts somewhat inconvenient, as in a fix from any of the solar system bodies. Only direct calculation (and some short tables) allows the same AP for all bodies in a fix.

Perhaps some people are frightened by the talk of sines and cosines, but using the calculator is really quite easy. It's said that Bowditch taught every crew member on the ships he commanded—even the cook—to use his log-haversine method. Surely our generation can use a calculator. With a little experience, its use will not only deepen our knowledge of navigational astronomy, but will also lead to other opportunities such as calculating great-circle distances, rhumb-line distances, star-star sextant accuracy checks, and lunar distance sights. These additional applications are prohibited by the whole-degree requirement of inspection tables. But with a calculator and an inquiring mind, a whole navigation world is open to us.

Quite a few manufacturers market appropriate scientific calculators. They use the term "scientific" to designate that their calculators have the necessary trig functions. Be sure to get one that has at least three memory locations. Most of the calculators in this category operate the same. The exception is HP calculators, which use the *Reverse Polish Notation*, RPN, some allowing selection of either RPN mode or the algebraic mode. The order of entries in the RPN mode is different than the algebraic mode, but it's easy and natural to use. Some people prefer it. In any case, become familiar with your calculator before attempting sight reductions.

Some people claim that the calculator doesn't have the reliability desired for a back-up system. In my more than three decades using calculators I have experienced one failure. I carry three at sea. And an inexpensive calculator is no more susceptible to damage than is an expensive sextant. The light-powered ones never have dead batteries, and they operate in light dimmer than is needed to read sight reduction tables. If you're concerned about moisture and salt water, keep your calculator inside a zip-lock sandwich bag. You can operate it perfectly well through the transparent bag.

The first step up in sophistication from the simple calculator is the more powerful, more expensive, programmable handheld scientific calculators, such as the HP-33s. After a short time with the instruction book, you can program the altitude and azimuth equations into memory. From then on, you only enter L, d, and the LHA, and out pops H_C and Zn. Also, other parts of the sight reduction can be programmed. This is by far the simplest and neatest method. It is inexpensive and easy to use compared to a set of tables. But on the other hand, it has the disadvantage of being more expensive, more specialized, more difficult to learn, and harder to replace than the common scientific calculator.

Climbing up the sophistication/expense ladder we next come to the PDAs and programmable graphic calculators such as the Texas Instruments TI-89 and TI-92 series. At this level, software is available that will do virtually everything, requiring only the entry of the DR position, observed altitude, and UT (some programs will even use this information to identify the observed body). Examples are the CelestNav software for the Palm OS series, and StarPilot for the TI series, which is the most comprehensive celestial navigation software available. You'll find it at many marine suppliers. The pre-programmed calculator has the advantage of convenience to the extreme—perhaps even to a fault. You don't have to know much about the fundamentals of celestial navigation, since everything is done for you. On the other hand, this convenience does allow concentration on other aspects, such as improving observation skills and using different types of sights. This convenience also allows the navigator to use celestial navigation when the details of sight reductions have been forgotten, or have been mentally blocked in a stressful situation at sea. Perhaps this is their greatest advantage.

Moving on to PCs, the vista opens even wider. But here, of course, we sacrifice handheld convenience and independence from ship power (even for laptops over the long term). There's a Starpilot version for the PC, called StarPilot-PC, which is operationally identical to the TI calculator version. Another PC software package is called simply Navigator. Her Majesty's *Nautical Almanac* Office also publishes a software package containing a book of algorithms and tables plus PC-compatible celestial navigation software called AstroNav PC. Even the U.S. Navy uses a PC-based program called STELLA (a somewhat strained acronym for "system to estimate latitude and longitude astronomically"). It's apparently very comprehensive, but not available to the general public.

And for computer-savvy do-it-yourselfers, there's almost no limit to what can be programmed into calculators such as the TI series, which can even run Basic. And on PC compatibles we can run high-level languages, such as Excel, Basic, Fortran, or C. The *Nautical Almanac* gives equations for complete sight reductions, including equations for altitude corrections and interpolation of GHA and declination. Direct plotting of LOPs can be done with Equations 13.1 of Exercise 1.22, as we did in Figure 2.7. You can compute fix coordinates directly from two or more simultaneous sights, without plotting or dead reckoning, as discussed at the end of Chapter 7. Carrying it even further, you can get the almanac data on a CD, or compute almanac data directly using the techniques in Jean Meeus's book, *Astronomical Algorithms* (see Appendix K). So you can create your own STELLA-like program, making it as sophisticated as you are able, or want to.

12

INSIGHTS FROM THE NAVIGATION TRIANGLE

EQUIVALENT TRIANGLES
THE AZIMUTH RULES
UNDERSTANDING INSPECTION TABLES
SPECIAL CASES OF THE AZIMUTH EQUATION

Before, sights; now, insights. This chapter isn't for everyone. Consider it optional. But for those who are interested, a closer look at the navigation triangle will provide a deeper understanding into navigational astronomy; an awareness of how sight reduction tables are designed; the reason for different azimuth rules for direct calculation and tabular methods; and simple ways to check the compass with celestial azimuths.

Equivalent Triangles

To reduce their size, sight reduction tables exploit the symmetry of the navigation triangle. These symmetries are all intuitively clear from looking at Figure 12.1: Beginning with figure 12.1a, we can see that the same triangle is produced by switching the GP and the AP meridians, as shown in Figure 12.1b. The two triangles are just flipped, but their co-altitudes and azimuth angles are identical. Also we see that exchanging the GP and AP is equivalent to changing the original LHA to 360° − LHA. So the LHAs are not the same in the two figures.

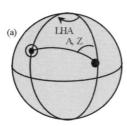

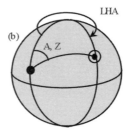

GP west of AP, LHA less than 180
Zn = 360 - A = 360 - Z

GP east of AP, LHA greater than 180
Zn = A = Z

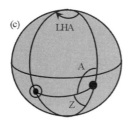

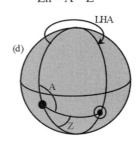

GP west of AP, LHA less than 180
Zn = 360 - A = 180 + Z

GP east of AP, LHA greater than 180
Zn = A = 180 - Z

Figure 12.1 Symmetry of the triangle equations produces four different triangles with the same co-altitudes and azimuth angles Z, but different angles A. The azimuth angle used in tables is Z, which equals A in the northern hemisphere, but differs in the southern hemisphere. Inspection of the figures provides a rule for obtaining Zn from both A and from Z.

We can also prove this intuitive observation by looking at the altitude equation

$$\sin H_C = \sin L \sin d + \cos L \cos d \cos LHA$$

where this exchange of GP and AP is only represented in the cos LHA term. We saw earlier that the cosine term is invariant under changing LHA to 360°– LHA. (You can also verify this by looking at the cosine curve in Appendix F.) So this exchange doesn't alter the above equation, which shows that the altitude H_C is the same in the two figures.

Furthermore, by remembering the azimuth equation for A

$$\cos A = (\sin d - \sin L \sin H_C) / (\cos L \cos H_C)$$

and observing that all the variables (L, d, and H_C) in this equation remain the same after switching the GP and AP, we see that A is also unchanged under this switch. So the equivalence of the top two triangles in Figure 12.1 is verified by the triangle equations.

The second symmetry property comes from reflecting the triangles in the top two figures (Figures 12.1 a and 12.1b) about their equators, which produces the bottom two figures (this is the same as negating both L and d). From the spherical symmetry of the figures, it should be clear that if we reckon the co-latitude and co-declination of these southern-hemisphere triangles from the South Pole, they are the identical triangles to the ones in the northern hemisphere that have their co-latitudes and co-declinations reckoned from the North Pole. Thus, all four triangles have identical altitudes.

However, the azimuths are a different story. The angle A used in our azimuth equation above is always defined relative to the North Pole, as shown in all four figures. But now we introduce an azimuth angle Z relative to the nearest pole (sometimes called the elevated pole). This definition makes Z equal to A in the northern hemisphere, but different than A in the southern hemisphere, as shown in the figure. Our above discussion, observing that A does not change when we interchange the GP and AP, is also valid in the southern hemisphere. Likewise, Z in the southern hemisphere doesn't change under the exchange of GP and AP, as shown in the lower figures.

In summary, then, the four cases in Figure 12.1 all have the same H_C, but the top two figures have different azimuth angles A than the bottom two. However, by introducing the azimuth angle Z, all four triangles are made identical, having the same altitude and angle Z. This allows a fourfold reduction in the size of precomputed sight-reduction tables, with one table entry for all four cases.

The Azimuth Rules

Because A and Z are not the same angle, different azimuth rules are needed for direct computation methods that use A, than for tabular methods which use Z. Inspection of Figure 12.1 shows that the rules for obtaining Zn from A are

if the LHA is greater than 180°, Zn = A,
if the LHA is less than 180°, Zn = 360° – A,

which are the rules used in our discussion of Figure 2.4 and the ones printed on the bottom of our calculator sight-reduction forms.

Also, we can now easily see the reason for the azimuth rules that are printed on each page of the tables, and why they're quite different from the rules used in direct calculation. Because Z is referenced to the nearest pole, four rules are needed, two for each hemisphere. Inspection of the figure shows that the rules for obtaining Zn from Z are as follows:

For northern latitudes, if LHA is greater than 180°..... Zn = Z,
                        if LHA is less than 180°…..........Zn = 360° – Z.

For southern latitudes, if LHA is greater than 180° ......Zn = 180° – Z,
                        if LHA is less than 180°…….......Zn = 180° + Z.

Understanding Inspection Tables

We've seen that because all four cases in Figure 12.1 have the same H_C and Z, they can be represented by just one table entry. Each entry of the tables represents two LHAs (the two that add to 360°) and two values of the declination and latitudes (the two that are both positive or negative). In H.O. 229 the pair of LHAs label the page openings. In H.O. 249 they label the rows, the smaller LHA on the left-hand side of the row, and 360° minus that LHA on the right-hand side of the row. The azimuth rules above are printed on each page opening for convenience. In both H.O. 229 and H.O. 249 no sign is given to the latitude and declination; rather, all four cases in Figure 12.1 are grouped under the section heading *Latitude Same Name as Declination* (meaning they are either both positive or both negative).

By drawing a sketch, you'll see that the above observations are also valid when the latitude and declination are in different hemispheres, but they require their own entries because their altitudes and azimuths are different from the Latitude-Same-as-Declination section. Therefore this section requires a separate listing labeled *Latitude Contrary Name to Declination*. In H.O. 229 these two sections occur on one page opening, divided on the right-hand page by a *Contrary-Same Line*, the C-S line, that separates them. In H.O. 249 they are either separated by a blank white space, or are on different pages.

By inspecting the H_C column (see H.O. 229 in Appendix D), you'll find that this C-S line occurs where the altitude falls to zero, i.e., the body is on the horizon. This also occurs for a body located at the antipode of the GP (i.e., exactly on the other side of the earth), where the declination has the same value but opposite name. Starting in the "Same-Name" section at the bottom of the page that contains both the "same" and "contrary" sections, and following a column upward in decreasing declination, we see that H_C decreases to zero where the body sets on the horizon. At that point a body located at the GP's antipode rises above the horizon as we cross the C-S Line, and its altitude increases as the declination of the GP continues to decrease. Because this antipode is on the same meridian as the original GP, but 180° in longitude from it, the LHAs for this Contrary-Name section are 180° different from the Same-Name section, as you see by comparing LHA headings at the top and bottom of the page.

By arranging the table in this fashion, all the solutions with altitudes above the horizon and with the same LHA are located on the same page opening. The Contrary-Name section is always smaller than the Same-Name section because the co-altitude (GP-RP distance) is necessarily larger (the altitude smaller) in opposite hemispheres than the Same-Name section, yielding fewer solutions above the horizon. Also as an appreciation of the navigation triangle, observe at the bottom of each page in H.O. 229 how the altitude becomes equal to the latitude when the declination reaches 90°. Exercises 2.9 to 2.11 of Chapter 13 will guide you in verifying these statements.

The third symmetry of the altitude equation is the obvious

invariance under exchanging the *values* of the latitude and declination while keeping the GP and AP on the same meridians. Interchanging L and d in the equation doesn't change the altitude equation. However, the azimuth equation is not invariant under this exchange, so A, and hence Z, are different. In Appendix D, you can verify this by comparing, for example, the two cases $L = 30°$, $d = 23°$, and $L = 23°$, $d = 30°$. You'll find they have the same H_c, but different Z.

We now see how the precalculated sight reductions tables are constructed and why their azimuth rules differ from the direct calculation method. The tables trade off a slightly more complicated treatment of LHA's and azimuth rules for a more compact compilation. These considerations are irrelevant for using a calculator to find H_C and A, where you just enter the latitude and declination according to the sign appropriate for the hemisphere and use the simpler azimuth rules for getting Zn from the azimuth angle A.

Special Cases of the Azimuth Equation

Further discussion of the azimuth equation

$$\cos A = (\sin d - \sin L \sin H) / (\cos L \cos H)$$

will give us insight into the workings of navigational astronomy. We consider what happens to the azimuth of the sun as the earth executes its daily rotation, keeping L and d constant. Figure 12.2 shows the navigation triangle for various times before noon. The particular case drawn here has the ship at a north latitude greater than the sun's declination, and the ship's longitude greater than the morning sun's GHA. So the first azimuth rule above applies, giving Zn = A and cos A = cos Zn. It will be convenient to start at noon and look at the sun's morning history, starting at noon and working backward to sunrise, and even earlier.

Figure 12.3 shows the corresponding behavior of the azimuth equation. Plotting cos Zn, Figure 12.3 also starts at noon with the Zn = 180° and works backward in time through sunrise and beyond. From the 3-D picture it's obvious that at local noon, the sun's LHA = 0°, and Zn = 180°. This is confirmed at the left side of the cosine curve in Figure

12.3, where we see that cos Zn = –1 corresponds to Zn = 180°. (See Appendix F for a short discussion of the cosine curve.)

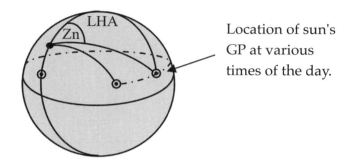

Location of sun's GP at various times of the day.

Figure 12.2 The relationship of the sun's azimuth to the sun's position.

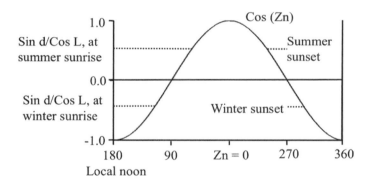

Figure 12.3 Cos (Zn) versus Zn for the case shown in Figure 12.2.

We see, both from the navigation triangle and from the cosine curve, that as the sun is moved eastward (backward toward sunrise) the azimuth decreases, going from 180° to 90° when the cosine is zero. At this point, since the cos 90° = 0, the equation must read

0 = (sin d – sin L sin H) / (cos L cos H)

which means that the numerator (sin d – sin L sin H) = 0, or that the altitude of the sun when its azimuth is due east is given by

sin H = sin d / sin L.   (12.1)

Also, we can look at the sun's azimuth at sunrise, i.e., when H = 0°. And we see from the azimuth equation that if we set H = 0°, then sin H = 0 and cos H = 1. So the sun's azimuth at sunrise must be given by

cos A = (sin d – 0) / cos L

or

cos A = sin d / cos L.   (12.2)

Both Equations 12.1 and 12.2 provide a simplified means of checking the ship's compass without recourse to computing H_C and Zn from the sight reduction equations. Assuming the ship's location is known, there are four possible checks, two at true east and west from Equation 12.1 (if the altitude isn't inconveniently high), and two at sunrise or sunset from Equation 12.2. The same is true for all other celestial bodies. Remember this Zn is relative to true north, not magnetic north, and the equations don't include the effects of dip or refraction.

We've just discussed two different events: the first was when Zn = 90°, which depends on the ratio sin d / sin L, and the second was when sunrise occurs, which depends on the ratio sin d / cos L. Which of these occurs earlier in the day depends on the relative value of these ratios. In the northern latitude's summer, the condition H = 0° occurs earlier than Zn = 90°. That is to say, the sun rises north of east. In the northern latitude's winter, the opposite is true and the sun rises south of east, as seen in Figure 12.3.

An interesting observation at this point is that at sunset or sunrise, at the time of the autumnal or vernal equinoxes, when the sun's declination is zero, sin d = 0, (since sin 0° = 0). Then Equation 12.2 gives cos A = 0, or Zn = 90° or 270° (remembering our rules for getting Zn from the azimuth angle A). That is to say, this gives us the somewhat curious result that at the time of the equinox, sunrise and sunset are due east and due west, respectively, for all people on earth, no matter what their location. See Exercise 2.3. Visualizing the relationship between these equations and the world we live in deepens our understanding and appreciation of navigational astronomy.

13

EXERCISES FOR UNDERSTANDING AND CONFIDENCE

SIGHT REDUCTION AND THE NAVIGATION TRIANGLE

NAVIGATIONAL ASTRONOMY

COURSES, DISTANCES, AND CHARTS

LUNAR DISTANCES

COMPUTER PROGRAMMING

The most obvious practice, the most appropriate for achieving proficiency, and perhaps the most fun, is to take many sextant shots and practice their sight reductions from a known location so the results can be evaluated. For this, of course, one needs all the celestial navigation tools: a sextant, a quartz digital watch with a means of setting it to accurate time, a *Nautical Almanac*, a method of solving the navigation triangle (calculator or tables), and a horizon. In some cases the horizon is the biggest problem. The first choice is a natural water horizon. Water horizons that are obstructed by a distant shore can be used if the short-horizon dip correction is not too severe, making it unreliable (see Chapter 9 and Appendix H). If a natural water horizon is unavailable, several types of artificial horizons can be used as discussed in Chapter 9.

If you use the calculator, at least a partial set of H.O. 229 or 249 is very valuable for checking your solutions to the navigation triangle. You can download these tables from the Internet, or you can buy them from the Government Printing Office, marine suppliers, or the used book market. Between hand calculators, excerpts in our Appendix D, printed tables, Internet tables, and the online navigation calculators at the National Geospatial-Intelligence Agency's and at the U.S. Naval Observatory's Web sites (see Appendix K), you have ample opportunity for practicing solving the navigation triangle by whichever method you prefer.

I recommend starting celestial navigation in a simple way that enhances understanding and confidence: First, if you want to use a calculator but are unfamiliar with or intimidated by them, practice solving the altitude and azimuth equations using only whole degrees, and compare your results with tabulated values (just use Appendix D). Then when you first move to real sights, stick to just whole degrees and whole minutes of time. Mentally interpolate GHA, its increment, and declination from the almanac to the nearest degree; forget about v and d corrections; and skip index and dip sextant corrections. From a known location, take a sight, recording the time to the nearest minute. For the sun, just center its disk on the horizon. Work up the sight; compare the result with your observed altitude and estimated azimuth. With consistent agreement to within one degree, practicing these quick-and-dirty sight reductions—say, a dozen times or so, particularly under different conditions—will give you familiarity and confidence with the whole procedure. After that accomplishment, it's time to move on to the full procedure, making all the corrections and working to a minute of arc and a second of time. For armchair practice there are the eight sights in the text in Chapters 5 and 6.

By making repeated and varied real-life sight reductions, you will achieve proficiency, though you will not necessarily deepen your understanding of celestial navigation. For that purpose, we present specially designed sight reductions and related exercises. Many are followed by comments that explain how to do the exercise, explain its significance, and frequently give the answer. The exercises are presented in five topical categories. Many provide sight reduction practice with results that make a particular point. Several exercises use the excerpts from H.O. 229 and 249 (Appendix D) to provide an insight to celestial navigation's spherical geometry.

The exercises vary in difficulty. Not every exercise is for everyone, but all are meant to be useful—even if you don't attempt an exercise, reading it along with its comment will enhance your understanding, confidence, and enjoyment of celestial navigation. Within each category the exercises vary in difficulty according to a star rating. Exercises with no star require only the standard understanding of nautical astronomy with no special math. One-star exercises are more challenging and may require thinking beyond standard sight reductions. Some require very simple algebra and plane trigonometry at the level discussed in Appendix F. Two-star exercises are more advanced; some require advanced high school trig, including common trig identities, and algebra. A few require elementary calculus. Some exercises require a chart, a *Nautical Almanac*, and a calculator or sight reduction tables. Have fun.

Sight Reduction and the Navigation Triangle

1.1.   Place Figure 2.7 under the upper right-hand corner of a sheet of paper and trace the figure onto the paper. Then extend the longitude axis westward past 82° and the latitude axis southward to 17°. Using dividers, copy the 0.1° tick marks from the figure. Then using the GP's location of GHA 82°, declination N17.8°, and the observed altitude of 83°, strike an arc of the LOP and compare it with the figure's arc. What is the maximum discrepancy between your mechanically drafted LOP and the computer-drawn one in the figure?

       Comment. This equal-altitude curve is the basic ingredient of celestial navigation. Remember to use the latitude scale to measure the co-altitude of 90° − 83° = 7°. For high altitudes such as this one, we expect a small error in substituting plane geometry for spherical geometry. So, not surprisingly, I get an error of several miles on the east end of the LOP.

1.2.   On 11 May 2005 1800 UT you observe a fully corrected sun altitude of 28°. Using the almanac's daily pages of Appendix C, a globe, and dividers or compass, find at least three places in the world where you might be.

       Comment. Of the infinity of places on this circular LOP, you could be at (or near) the island of Oahu, Hawaii; Montevideo,

Uruguay; St. Vicente Island in the Cape Verde Islands; Reykjavik, Iceland; or Barrow, Alaska.

1.3. While not moving (moored, becalmed, or grounded) eight hours after your sight in the above exercise, you next observe the sun at the same 28° altitude. At which of the above five locations are you?

Comment. Now you can only be two places in the world—the two intersections of these LOPs. One is somewhere roughly on the equator at 150° west longitude. The other is somewhere around Barrow, Alaska. A temperature reading should enable you to distinguish between these two.

1.4. Using either direct computation or tables, investigate the effect of the selected AP on the LOP. Choose three different positions that you can plot on your chart: (1) an actual position of your ship, (2) a first AP position, and (3) a second AP position. Select a reasonable local time, convert to UT, and look up the sun's GP in the almanac. Or more simply, just assume a reasonable LHA and sun's declination.

A. First, compute the altitude that would be observed at the ship's position.

B. Next, select the first AP position some 10 or 20 miles from the ship's position. Using this AP and the same GP data, work up the sight and plot the LOP. Compare this LOP to the actual ship's position.

C. Now select the second AP position, perhaps one degree north and one degree east of the first AP position. Plot the LOP corresponding to it. How does the LOP change and how does Zn change?

1.5. Take your AP at the body's GP and calculate H_c and the azimuth related angle A. Are your results reasonable?

Comment. The altitude should be 90°. The azimuth is undetermined. When you attempt division by cos H = cos 90° = 0 in the azimuth equation, you are dividing by zero, which the calculator can't do. So it gives an error. (Tables artificially list the azimuth angle as 90° to avoid writing "error" or "undefined.")

1.6.   * Venus was about at its maximum apparent distance from the sun on November 20, 2005 when the sun's GHA was 183° 36.8′ and declination was S19° 39.7′. At this same time Venus's GHA was 133° 53.0′ and its declination was S26° 15.9′. What was the angular separation between Venus and the sun at this time? You can find Venus in the daytime by setting your sextant's arc on this pre-computed angle and (using the darkest sunshade) swinging the sextant's frame toward Venus's expected position. For this time of year, should you look to the east or to the west of the sun?

Comment. This is one of several applications of our navigation-triangle solution beyond sight reductions. The altitude equation for calculating H_C can be used to calculate the angular distance between any two objects. Remember, the angular distance is represented by the co-altitude. Using the altitude equation you should find that the distance between the sun's *center* and Venus is 45° 59.5′. It may seem that a better method of finding Venus is to compute its altitude and azimuth from your DR position and sweep the sky around that altitude and azimuth with the sextant. Then you're ready to take the sight when you find Venus. But the altitude of Venus changes by the second, whereas its arc distance from the sun changes less than a degree/day. So your arc-distance calculation remains good for finding Venus, morning and night, over several days, while the altitude calculation doesn't.

1.7.   Determine the rate of change per minute of the sun's altitude on the summer equinox at the equator. Using a calculator or tables, find the sun's altitude at two different times, say five minutes apart. Repeat for a point at N45°. Repeat again for an extreme northern latitude, say N70°. Now repeat all three exercises for the sun at the summer solstice. Compare your results to sight reductions tables or to Equations A.2. You should see that the rate of change of altitude varies from zero to a maximum of one minute of arc per four seconds of time.

1.8. Using the St. Hilaire method, your calculated altitude at your DR position turns out to be exactly your observed altitude. Does this mean your ship is at the DR position?

Comment. This is a classic. The answer is a qualified no. Referring back to Figure 3.4, you can see that the ship could be *anywhere* on the LOP, according to the information gained from the sight. The single altitude measurement only determines a line of position, nothing more. However, the DR position does contain previously obtained information, and the LOP now constrains the DR information to a single line. Since the two pieces of information coincide, the DR position remains the best estimated position, having the old dead-reckoning uncertainty along the line, but new celestial accuracy perpendicular to the line.

1.9. Our example in Chapter 5 of reducing a sun sight by both direct computation and by H.O. 249 gives two different intercept distances (7 nm and 1 nm, respectively). Plot both of these showing that they produce the same LOP.

1.10. Why are the reduction tables H.O. 229 and H.O. 249 organized differently with H.O. 229 having LHA page headings, declination in rows, and latitude in columns, while H.O. 249 has latitude page headings, LHA in rows, and declination in columns?

1.11. Draw figures of the navigation triangle similar to Figure 2.3b for different combinations of the following: (a) Latitudes 0°, N45°, S45°, N85°, S85°, (b) Declinations 0°, N45°, S45°, N85°, S85°, and (c) LHAs 10°, 45°, 90°.

1.12.   The LHA convention used in tabular methods reckons the LHA westward toward the body from 0° to 360°. Draw a sketch of the type of Figure 2.3b with a LHA of 300°. If this LHA is thought of as the direction westward along a great-circle path to the body, what great-circle arc makes sense for the co-altitude? What is the meaning of the arc?

Comment. Looking westward along the great-circle path to the body would be looking 180° *away* from the body. Looking in this direction, the altitude of the body would be 360° minus the altitude from looking toward the body. The body would be below the horizon. Thus the concept of LHAs greater than 180° doesn't make much sense in terms of thinking about the navigation triangle. The convention is used to accommodate the tabular azimuth rules, which could equally well be done by distinguishing whether the GP is east or west of the AP. Then all LHAs could be less than 180°. You can verify this by looking at Figure 12.1.

1.13.   In our introductory chapters, we made a big fuss about a single altitude measurement's only constraining the observer's position to a line instead of a single point; furthermore, we pointed out that this LOP is a small circle, centered on the body's GP. However, the traditional noon sun sight also is a single altitude measurement, but it gives the observer's latitude, not an LOP centered on the sun's GP. Is this a contradiction, and if so, what is its resolution?

Comment. In our discussion of the equal-altitude LOP, it was assumed that we knew the GP of the sun. But in the noon sun sight we don't know the sun's GHA, only its declination. However, unlike the normal off-meridian sight, we do know the sun's azimuth at LAN: it's due north or south (and we know which, unless the sun is nearly overhead). Therefore, we still have knowledge of the same number of sight parameters as in the normal sight; we've lost the GHA information, but gained the azimuth. Thus, the sight still confines our location to a line—in this case, a parallel of latitude. This parallel of latitude is also a small circle, but it's not centered on the sun's GP like the normal equal-altitude LOP. Rather, it's an LOP where observers everywhere on it see identical sun's altitudes and azimuths, although at different times. That is, rather than being an equal-altitude LOP in the sense of a normal sight, it's an equal-altitude, equal-azimuth LOP.

1.14. The above discussion brings to mind the timed noon-sun shot (Chapter 7) where we measure the time of maximum altitude, thus getting both the latitude and longitude, a fix. Since we measure exactly the same information as in a St. Hilaire sight (time and altitude), how is it we get a fix instead of just an LOP?

Comment. The resolution of this paradox is that we measure not just any time, but the time when the body is on the meridian. In other words, we've been able to measure the body's azimuth, even if indirectly. This is the only case I know of at sea where it's practical to measure a body's azimuth sufficiently accurately to get a useful fix.

1.15. * In their direct calculation of sight reductions, the *Nautical Almanac* uses

$$\cos A = (\cos L \sin d - \sin L \cos d \cos LHA) / \cos H_c,$$

to calculate the azimuth angle A. Why do we use

$$\cos A = (\sin d - \sin L \sin H_c) / (\cos L \cos H_c)?$$

Comment. For simple non-programmable calculators, our equation is better because it requires only five trig function entries and three different variables (18 total keystrokes), while the almanac's version contains six trig functions and four different variables (22 total keystrokes). Plus, most inexpensive calculators only store three variables, not four.

1.16.   * Demonstrate that it's possible to exactly compute any number of points on a celestial LOP by computing just one point as an example: First, fabricate realistic data for a specific situation. For example, you could take a ship's position at N30.5° W150.5°, with the sun's declination of N21.75° and its GHA 90.25°. The observed altitude would then be 35° 49′ and its azimuth would be 84°. Now assume you don't know the ship's position, so you want to find a point on the LOP at a latitude of N30.5°. By using the observed altitude, calculate the longitude of a point on the LOP that has this latitude. Use Equation A.10 of Appendix A. Finally, check your answer with the known longitude.

Comment. This exercise and Exercise 1.17 are both good exercises in sight reduction plus solving trig equations with your calculator. Furthermore, they demonstrate that three different methods exactly compute the same point on the LOP.

1.17.   * Work the above exercise the other way around. Using Equation A.9 of Appendix A, assume the W150.5° longitude, and calculate the latitude on the LOP using the observed altitude.

1.18.   * The plot of the sine function in Appendix F shows that angles A and $(180° - A)$ have the same sine. In other words, the inverse sine function has two solutions (as does inverse cosine). The calculator only returns the angle whose sine is less than 90°. What is the meaning of the second solution in Equation 5.1a for the altitude H_c?

Comment. By drawing a diagram similar to Figure 1.2, you can see that this second solution is the altitude of the body measured by looking 180° away from it instead of toward it. Called a *back sight*, this solution is rarely used in practice, only being useful when the horizon is obscured in the direction of the body. But as we mentioned in discussing lunar distance sights, taking such sights with angles greater than 90° has its difficulties. How is Zn related to A for back sights?

1.19. * In our direct computation of the azimuth angle A, why don't we use the simpler Equation A.7 (Appendix A) rather than the more complicated Equation A.4 ?

Comment. Solving Equation A.7 for the inverse sine to get the azimuth angle A gives two different solutions for A either side of 90° (see Appendix F). Then we would need complicated azimuth rules for obtaining Zn from A. It's much easier just to use Equation A.4., which requires just knowing if the GP is east or west of the AP in order to find Zn. In fact, Equation A.7 was used in the old haversine method of Bowditch's time because it requires only multiplication and division, which converts to addition and subtraction of log trig functions. And it is still used in today's short tables along with its necessarily complicated azimuth rules.

1.20. ** In Equation 7.1 for reducing Polaris sights, the cos LHA term can be considered a correction due to Polaris not being exactly on the North Pole (if it were, cd would be zero and the correction would vanish). Instead of the simple formula above, the *Nautical Almanac* uses a table of observed altitude versus the LHA of Aries to give this correction. Pick a couple of dates and compare the results of Equation 7.1 with the almanac. (You need your own almanac for this one.)

Comment. The difference between these two sight reduction methods for Polaris seldom exceeds a mile or two, showing that Equation 7.1 is perfectly adequate for practical navigation at sea. And since it's so simple, it provides an emergency procedure, as discussed in Chapter 7.

1.21. By drawing simple sketches in the plane of the observer's meridian show that the rules,

if the body is south of you, $L = dec + (90° - H_O)$,
if the body is north of you, $L = dec - (90° - H_O)$.

correctly give the observer's latitude for upper-transit meridian sights. Mathematically inclined readers might want to confirm that our equation for altitude

$$\sin H_O = \sin L \sin d + \cos L \cos d \cos LHA$$

also reduces to these same two solutions when the LHA is zero.

Comment. Since LHA = 0°, cos LHA = 1. Then $\sin H_O = \cos (90° - H_C) = \sin L \sin d + \cos L \cos d$, and a trig identity reduces the right-hand side of this equation to cos (L – d). So then cos (90° – H_O) = cos (L – d). The arc cosine then gives two solutions, L = d + (90° – H_O) and L = d – (90° – H_O). The equations don't tell us how to apply these solutions. We get that by drawing a simple diagram showing that the first solution applies when the body is south of the observer, and that the second applies when the body is north. Similarly, for lower meridian transits (that's where LHA = 180°) drawing simple sketches or solving the altitude equation as above gives the two solutions:

$$L = \ \ 90° - dec + H_O \ \text{for northern latitudes}$$
$$L = - 90° - dec - H_O \ \text{for southern latitudes}$$

1.22.   ** The equations for tracing out an LOP by the method discussed in connection with Figure 2.6 can be obtained by applying the same generic relationship among the sides and angles of the navigation triangle that are shown by the equations in Appendix A. Equation A.1 of Appendix A solves for a side of the navigation triangle in terms of its opposite angle and its two adjacent sides. Show that applying this same relationship to Figure 2.6 gives

$$\sin L_X = \sin d \sin H_O + \cos d \cos H_O \cos B_X \tag{13.1a}$$

for finding the latitude L_X of a point on the LOP. And likewise from adapting Equation A.7, it follows that

$$\sin LHA_X = \cos H_O \sin B_X / \cos L_X \tag{13.1b}$$

for getting the longitude of this same point from its local hour angle.

1.23. ** Why is the above B_x method of computer plotting an LOP better than the St. Hilaire sight reduction, which also accurately locates a point on the LOP?

Comment. The St. Hilaire method doesn't yield latitude and longitude coordinates for direct plotting. Furthermore, it requires specifying a reference point for each calculation, which is an unnecessary complexity.

1.24. ** The St. Hilaire method requires solving two equations, the altitude and azimuth equations. We could also find a straight-line approximation by the Sumner method of specifying a latitude of a point on the LOP, then calculating its longitude. Repeating this for a second point and connecting the two points with a straight line gives an approximate LOP. Given that these two methods both require the same amount of calculation, why is the St. Hilaire method better?

Comment. This suggested Sumner procedure could be a little quirky, particularly for LOPs having an east-west orientation. You can see this by sketching LOP with a nearly east-west orientation and assuming a ship's DR position somewhat off the LOP. Then the specified latitudes can result in points on the LOP that are far from the region of interest (such as far from the DR position). Worse yet, the selected parallel of latitude might not even intersect the LOP, resulting in no solution. If the longitude were picked as the plotting variable, then the north-south LOPs have the same problem. This makes these methods too cumbersome to use as standard practice. In contrast, because the St. Hilaire method automatically results in an LOP segment that is nearest to the assumed position, it works under all situations.

Navigational Astronomy

2.1. Show that the table of Increments and Corrections in the *Nautical Almanac* gets its time increments for the sun and planets by simply using the fact that the sun goes around the earth once in 24 hours.

Comment. The earth's rotation is $360°/\text{day} = 360°/24$ hrs $= 15°/\text{hr} = 1°/4$ min $= 1'/4$ sec. Looking at the tables of *Increments and Correction* in the almanac, you see exactly these same increments.

2.2. Using the fact that the earth goes around the sun once a year while the stars don't, show that the stars should rise 3 min. 56.4 sec. earlier each night. Compare this result to the GHA of Aries listed in the *Nautical Almanac* on successive days.

Comment. Draw a diagram showing the earth in its orbit around the sun. Then imagine the earth doesn't rotate about its axis as it revolves around the sun. Notice that observers on this earth would then witness one solar day in one year, but no movement of the stars, which can be considered infinitely far away. Therefore, with the earth rotating on its axis, earthlings see one more solar day per year than they see sidereal days. This extra solar day means that the solar days are shorter than the sidereal day. The extra day is $24\text{hr}/\text{yr} = 1440\ \text{min}/365$ days $= 3.9452\ \text{min}/\text{day}$. This is 3 min. 56.7 sec. shorter than the sidereal day. So the stars rise that much earlier each night. By looking at the GHA of Aries on successive days, and converting the arc difference found there of 59.21′ to minutes and seconds of time, you'll verify this result.

2.3. Begin by sketching a 3-D representation of the navigation triangle, similar to Figure 2.3. Add a great circle that separates day from night, and show that on the vernal and autumnal equinoxes, the sun rises and sets east and west for everyone on earth.

Comment. This is an exercise in 3-D visualization. Draw a sketch of the earth with the sun's GP on the equator. Then draw the day-night boundary along a meridian 90° from the sun. Draw many 90° great-circle arcs extending from the sun to the day-night boundary. (These arcs should be analogous to the meridians that extend from the pole to the equator and that meet the equator everywhere at 90°.) Everyone located on the day-night boundary sees the sun at right angles to their local meridian, making the bearing to the sun east at sunrise and west at sunset. This exercise dramatizes how counterintuitive spherical geometry is to most of us.

2.4. By inspecting the daily pages of the almanac, determine the date and the amount of the minimum rate of change of the sun's declination. Do likewise for the maximum rate of change. Do these dates make sense? Note that the values for d are just the hourly change in declinations for that particular daily page. Also note that d never exceeds one minute of arc, so in many practical situations the d-correction can be ignored completely for the sun and planets. Address this same point for the moon.

2.5. Show that the values given in the *Nautical Almanac*'s Increments and Correction table for the v or d corrections are simply proportioned to the entry value of v or d throughout the hour according to the table's mid value of the minute entry (i.e., the minute plus 30 seconds).

Comment. The correction just multiplies the value of v or d by the ratio of the number of minutes to the 60 minutes of a whole hour. That is, the correction = (v or d) × (minutes + 0.5) / 60. For example, in the 19-minute table, the correction = (19.5/60) (v or d) = 0.325(v or d), which you can verify by comparing this result to the table.

2.6. Draw four figures similar to Figure 12.1 with the AP and the GP in opposite hemispheres and show that the same azimuth rules apply for computing Zn from the angle A.

2.7.   Notice from the *Nautical Almanac* that the SHA of Polaris varies much more than for other stars. Can you explain this?

Comment. It's a geometrical effect due to the convergence of the meridians. Since Polaris is very close to the Pole, a slight variation in its position can make large variations in its SHA, but not in its declination.

2.8.   In tables H.O. 229 and H.O. 249 the H_C remains the same while Z changes upon an interchange of the latitude and declination entries.   Why does the interpolation increment also change under this interchange?

Comment.   The rate of change of H_C depends on both the latitude and the declination, which become different under this exchange. You can see this from Equation A.1 because the rate of change of both sines and cosines is different for the same argument, as shown in the sine and cosine curves in Appendix F. These curves show that, in general, at any point the slope of the sine curve is different than the slope of the cosine curve. So when L and d are changed, the rate of change of H also changes.

2.9.   In Chapter 12 we saw how the tables in H.O. 229 have been efficiently arranged to include results of same-and-contrary latitudes and declinations in the same page opening. Make a careful 3-D sketch of the navigation triangle showing the complete 360° horizon (which, of course, is located 90° from the observer). Show the antipode of the GP. Then observe that as a body sets on the horizon, a body located at the GP's antipode would be rising. Therefore, all the above-the-horizon solutions for a given LHA and its supplement (i.e., 180° − LHA) efficiently occur on one page opening.

Comment. This sketch, also used in the next three exercises, can be challenging. It requires drawing four great circles, the equator, observer's meridian, body's meridian, and horizon. It's best to draw each one with a different colored pencil, making the lines dotted on the far side of the earth. Remember the observer's horizon is a great circle 90° from the observer's position. (Think of that geometry as analogous to the pole and the equator.) It's useful to realize that every two great circles intersect each other at two points, 180° apart, each in opposite hemispheres. Make sure this geometry is accurately reflected in your sketch for the equator, the body's meridian, and the horizon.

2.10.   Use the 3-D sketch from the above exercise to show that as the declination of a body approaches 90°, the observed altitude approaches the observer's latitude. Then verify this by looking at the bottom of the pages in H.O. 229, Appendix D. When the declination is exactly 90°, the altitude is exactly equal the observer's latitude (which would be the case for Polaris if it were exactly at the North Pole).

2.11.   Expand on the above two exercises by using the same sketch to continuously trace a body's path as its declination changes 360°, starting at 0° and moving initially northward, around 360° back to its starting point. Select the LHA = 32° and a mid latitude, such as N40°, so that your sketch corresponds to the H.O. 229 data in Appendix D. Mark the following locations on your sketch: the equator, the North Pole, where the body sets on the horizon, the South Pole, where the body rises above the horizon, and where the LHA suddenly changes 180°. Then starting in the Same-Name-Section of H.O. 229 (Appendix D) with dec = 0, follow this same 360° declination circuit. Verify that the body's altitude versus declination agrees with your sketch according to H.O. 229.

2.12.   Using the sketch from the above exercise, verify that the body's azimuth agrees with the result of H.O. 229. Where and why does the azimuth suddenly jump 180 degrees?

2.13.   * By inspecting the daily pages in the almanac, notice that the sun is hardly ever on the Greenwich meridian at 1200 UT. That is, local apparent noon does not occur at 12:00 noon, but a few minutes before or after 1200 UT. This difference is called the equation of time. Convert the sun's GHA at 1200 UT to time, getting the equation of time listed in the bottom right-hand page for that date. A plot of your result of this time difference from 1200 UT versus the sun's declination is the figure-eight diagram sometimes seen on globes (normally in the Pacific Ocean). It's called an *analemma*. And it contains all the information that the almanac does on the sun's GP, although not to the same precision.

2.14. * Find the latitude of the Arctic Circle using Equation 12.2, $\cos Zn = \sin d / \cos L$, for the azimuth of a body rising or setting, and realizing that $\cos Zn$ can't be greater than one (i.e., the sun doesn't set at all if Zn decreases all the way to 0°).

Comment. Set $\cos Zn = 1$, and solve for the latitude when the sun is at the summer solstice, i.e., when its declination is 23° 26.4′. (You can check this figure by finding the sun's maximum declination in the almanac.) The Arctic Circle is at N66° 33.6′.

2.15. * Using Equation 12.2, find the azimuth of sunrise on the summer and winter solstice on the equator.

Comment. The sun rises at Zn = 66°, considerably north of east. How far north of east does it rise at a location of N45° latitude?

2.16. ** Because Polaris is always less than 1° from the true North Pole, the navigation triangle for observations in the common latitudes, of, say, less than N60°, has a very long and narrow shape. Draw a picture like Figure 2.3 or 2.4, showing this property. Then, instead of using the normal spherical geometry, use simple plane geometry to show that an observer's latitude is given approximately by

$$L = H_o - cd \cos LHA, \qquad (13.2)$$

where LHA is Polaris's local hour angle and cd is its co-declination.

Comment. Draw the navigation triangle in plane geometry showing that the LHA is extremely small. Then approximate the co-latitude as the sum of two parts. One is the projection of Polaris's co-declination onto the co-latitude meridian, which is cos LHA times the co-declination. The other is Polaris's co-altitude. Approximate this projection with the co-altitude itself, because the bearing angle to Polaris is so tiny.

2.17. ** By differentiating Equation A.1 of Appendix A with respect to the LHA, and using Equation A.7, show that the rate of change of calculated altitude is

$$dH/d(LHA) = -\cos L \sin A \qquad (13.3)$$

2.18. ** Carrying the above exercise further, show that the total time rate of change of altitude with respect to time is

$$dH/dt = \pm(15'/\text{min}) \cos L \sin Zn \qquad (13.4)$$

when the contributions due to time-changing latitude of the observer, and the time change of declination, can be neglected. Show, however, that the moon is an exception when it's near its maximum rate of change of declination. Equation 13.4 gives the data on a pull-out card that comes with H.O. 249 called "Alternative Table 2—Altitude Correction for Change in Position of Body."

2.19. * By thinking of the navigation triangle and the altitude equation (Equation A.1), show that if you know the altitude of one star from a known location, you can calculate the altitudes of all other stars that would be observed from that same location.

Comment. This is really just calculating a star fix in reverse, i.e., you're finding star altitudes from a known position, instead of finding a position from known altitudes. Write down two altitude equations, one for each star. The two equations contain the one common latitude of the observer, but LHA_1 and LHA_2 for each star. The star #1 equation can be solved for LHA_1. And you should be able to show that $LHA_2 = SHA_2 - SHA_1 + LHA_1$. Therefore, you can calculate the altitude of star #2 because you know everything in its altitude equation: its declination, observer latitude, and LHA_2. Similarly, the altitude of any other star can be calculated.

Courses, Distances, and Charts

3.1.   * We like to believe that our celestial navigation is sometimes accurate to within one nautical mile. If we make landfall four nm out, what is the maximum course change we should have to make to lay the harbor, taking into consideration our celestial navigation error?

Comment. Using the definition of the sine of an angle, $\sin A = a/b$, take a to be one mile and b to be four miles. Draw a picture. So the maximum course change would be equal to arcsin $(1/4)$ = $14°$.

3.2.   * On your way from Auckland to Hobart, you've just plotted your position as S37° 24′, E179° 46′ from a running fix of the morning and noon sun shots. From your current position, what is the initial great-circle course and distance to the Hobart Tasman Island Light at S43° 14′, E148° 02′?

Comment. Applying our navigation triangle solutions to great-circle courses is another advantage of the calculator method. After each fix, why not calculate the new great-circle course and distance to your destination? Using the Tasman Island Light as our destination and our current plotted fix as our departure, Equations 10.2 give the initial great-circle course to the Light as 246° and the distance as 1483 nm.

3.3.   * We are on our way to Hobart from a point south of the Cape of Good Hope at S42° E18°, to a point that clears the southern tip of Tasmania at S42° E148°. Since this leg starts and ends on the same parallel of latitude, the rhumb-line course is 90°. Calculate the rhumb-line distance using Equation 10.1.

Comment. Since the rhumb-line course is due west along a parallel of latitude, we can use Equation 10.1 to get the rhumb-line distance = (60.04 nm/degree) × 130° × cos 42° = 5800 nm. (We use 60 nm per degree for short distances, such as the intercept distance.)

3.4. * Compute the great-circle distance between the two points of the leg described in the above exercise, and compare it to the rhumb-line distance. What are the initial and final courses of the great-circle route? What is the great-circle course at the midpoint of the leg?

Comment. Using Equation 10.2 to calculate the angular distance between the departure and arrival points gives 84.678° for this arc distance. Multiplying by 60.04 nm per degree gives 5084 nm for the great circle distance, which is 716 miles shorter than the rhumb line. The initial course is 145° true. The final course is 35° true. The midpoint course is 90°. Carefully make a sketch to show this.

3.5. * By using the same idea in the above two exercises, we can evaluate the St. Hilaire error in approximating the intercept's great-circle arc by a rhumb line. An extreme case would be a huge DR error with an intercept that is at high latitudes, running east or west. Take as an extreme case an intercept that runs all the way across a small-scale chart, which generally means something like ten degrees of arc. So use an intercept that runs from N60° W40° to N60° W30°. Compute and compare the rhumb-line and great-circle distances and azimuths to see how good this St. Hilaire approximation really is.

Comment. The rhumb-line track is 300.2 nm at 90.0° while the great-circle track is 299.9 nm at 85.7°. So even in this extreme case, approximating the intercept distance by a rhumb line contributes negligible error to the distance. However, the azimuth difference of 4.3° can contribute more error, depending on the distance along the straight-line LOP from the point of tangency with the true LOP. For example, at 15 nm from the tangent point, the error is 15 sin (4.3°) = 1.1 nm, not including the error due to curvature of the true LOP.

3.6.   ** Neglect the earth's eccentricity, thereby considering it a perfect sphere. Sketch a picture of the earth and show that the distance of a degree of longitude is related to the distance of a degree of latitude by Equation 10.1:

dist of degree of longitude = dist of degree of latitude × cos L

Comment. Draw a 2-D sketch of the earth in the plane of a meridian, and draw the radius of a parallel of latitude. See that this radius is $r = R_E \cos L$., where R_E is radius of the earth, 3440 nm. Then by multiplying both sides by $2\pi/360°$, the left side becomes the distance per degree of longitude. And the right side becomes the distance per degree of latitude times cos L.

3.7.   ** The Mercator projection artificially expands the converging meridians to make them parallel to one another while retaining the parallelism among the latitude lines. A straight line on such a rectangular grid thus crosses all parallels and meridians at the same angle. To compensate for this east-west expansion, a north-south expansion of latitude is necessary to keep the distances in each direction the same. Thus the parallels of latitude must be expanded according to 1/cos L. Show that starting at the equator, this incremental expansion in latitude results in the total distance from the equator to a latitude L being

$$\text{Dist} = R_{earth} \ln \tan(L/2 + 45°) \qquad (13.5)$$

where ln is the natural logarithm. These distances from the equator are called *meridional parts.*

Comment. This is a calculus exercise. To get the total expansion of latitude from the equator to any point of latitude L, integrate R_E / cos L along a meridian from the equator to latitude L. So we see that the parallels should continuously expand as latitude increases rather than having a constant spacing as in the construction of Mercator plotting sheets in Chapter 10. This expansion is readily apparent on small-scale charts covering tens of degrees, but is negligible on plotting charts covering only a few degrees.

3.8. The logic in drawing Figure 10.6 was that, in the absence of other knowledge, the DR position had equal uncertainty in all directions. That is, we could imagine the DR position in the middle of a circle of uncertainty. This is not always the case. Consider two extreme cases. First, we may have reason to believe that our distance made good from EP1 to DR2 is quite accurate, while the course made good is uncertain. In some cases the opposite might be true: the course made good is considered accurate, but distance is unreliable. Draw a figure similar to Figure 10.6 for each of these special cases.

Comment. In the first case, an arc of radius equal to the EP1-DR2 distance, centered on EP1, represents our knowledge of the DR2 location. Its intersection with LOP2 is the best estimated position. In the second case, the DR2 position is somewhere on the course line, or its extension. The intersection of this line with LOP2 is the best estimated position in this case.

3.9. Draw a figure similar to Figure 10.6 for the case where LOP2 is parallel to LOP1, showing that indeed the dead reckoning is corrected by the additional information provided by LOP2.

3.10. In advancing the previous LOP for a running fix as shown in Figure 10.3, what underlying assumption is being made about the uncertainty in the DR2 position?

Comment. The assumption must be that the dead reckoned

position DR2 is completely uncertain along the advanced LOP1, and completely certain perpendicular to it. It's difficult to imagine a dead reckoning technique that would lead to this result.

Lunar Distances

4.1. Show that the almanac's maximum error in the moon's coordinates of 0.3′ translates to an error of 36 seconds in time determined from lunar distance sights.

Comment. We saw in our LD discussion that generally one minute of error in LD translates into about a 2-minute time error. So an error of 0.3′ in the moon's position could produce a 120 sec × 0.3 = 36-second error in time.

4.2. Expand on Figure 8.1 to show how everyone on earth observes the same LD at the same time, and thus calculates the same UT from lunar-distance sights.

4.3. Draw figures similar to Figure 8.2b showing that clearing the lunar distance can produce a cleared LD that is greater than, less than, or equal to the original uncleared distance, depending on the specific geometry.

4.4. Lunars can also be taken with planets and stars. Using Appendix C, calculate the lunar distance to Capella on 10 May 2005 at 0200 UT. Then calculate the same LD at 0300 UT. By comparing these two LDs, find the sight's time sensitivity, in minutes of arc per minutes of UT. Compare this result with the 27.5′ per 60 minutes of time of the moon-sun example in Chapter 8. What do you conclude?

Comment. At 0200 UT, LD1 = 22° 23.7′. And at 0300 UT, LD2 = 22° 6.3′. So the time sensitivity is 17.4′ per hour, or 0.29′ per one minute of UT. The moon-sun shot, with its 0.46′ per minute of time, is about 50 percent more sensitive than the Capella shot.

This is a geometrical consequence of the Cappella being almost due north of the moon at this time, making the LD vary slowly in time, and thus making Capella a poor choice for the lunar. Lunars are best made with a body located near the ecliptic, which puts them nearly in the direct path of the moon's relative motion.

4.5.   * It's always good practice to check a newly found result, such as Equation 8.3, for special cases where we know what the answer must be. Show that when $H_O = H_{SD}$ and $h_o = h_{SD}$, (i.e., when there is no refraction or parallax correction), Equation 8.3 gives the expected result that $LD_O = LD_{SD}$.

4.6.   ** For the same reason given in the above problem, show that if the sun and moon have the same GHA (i.e., they're on the same meridian), Equation 8.3 gives the expected result $LD_O = \pm(H_O - h_o)$, the $\pm$ selected to make LD_O positive.

    The next three exercises are for mathematicians (these exercises really deserve a three-star rating), but the results and discussion should be of interest to all lunar fans.

4.7.   ** Draw a plane-geometry oblique triangle in the plane of the vertical circle containing the radius of the earth, the observer, and the moon. Calculate the moon's semidiameter in terms of its horizontal parallax, its altitude, the earth's radius, and the moon's radius. Show that using small angle approximations and a power-series expansion gives

$$SD = 0.2724 \, HP \, (1 + HP \sin h \, / 3438) \tag{13.6}$$

where 0.2724 = the ratio of the moon's radius to the earth's radius, HP is the horizontal parallax in minutes of arc, and h is the apparent altitude of the moon.

Comment. The first term, $0.2724 \, HP$, is the SD tabulated for the HP at 1200 UT of each of the three days in the almanac's daily pages. This tabulated value can be 0.1´ in error at the beginning or end of the day. The second term is the augmentation factor discussed in Chapter 8. Since it depends on the moon's altitude, it's included in the almanac's moon altitude correction tables, but not in the daily pages. In the text example, we used (0.26´) sin h by averaging $(0.2724/3438)HP^2$ between its maximum and minimum values of HP = 61.4´ and 53.9´. This approximation is good to 0.1´.

4.8. ** This exercise should be of interest to those who are familiar with approximate methods of clearing the lunar distance. Consider only the altitude correction $\Delta h = h_O - h_{SD}$ for the moon, which has the largest correction because of its parallax. Using power-series for trig functions correct to second order in Δh, show that, considering just the moon's correction alone, our Equation 8.3 can be approximated by

$$\cos LD_O = \cos LD + \cos A \sin LD \, \Delta h - \cos LD \, \Delta h^2 / 2 \qquad (13.7)$$

where

$$\cos A = (\sin H - \sin h \cos LD) / (\cos h \sin LD) \qquad (13.8)$$

and A is the angle between the moon's co-altitude and LD, and LD_O is the cleared lunar distance.

4.9. ** Another, perhaps simpler, approximate lunar-clearing formula is

$$LD_O = LD - \cos A \, \Delta h + 1/2 \cot LD \, (1 - \cos^2 A) \, \Delta h^2 / 3438 \qquad (13.9)$$

where the two correction terms and Δh are in minutes of arc. By taking the cosine of each side of this equation and expanding to second order in Δh, show that you get Equation 13.7, and hence that the two equations are equivalent approximations to our exact result, Equation 8.3.

Comment. Equation 13.9 might appear simpler than our Equation 8.3, but we need to add another term, – cos B ΔH, for the sun's altitude correction ΔH, with another calculation for B (which just has h and H interchanged from Equation 13.8). The second-order term in Equation 13.9 isn't necessary for the sun because its correction is so small. Likewise, the cross terms in Δh ΔH are negligibly small. So part of the calculation effort in using Equation 13.9 is calculating Equation 13.8 twice, once for cos A, and once for cos B. And that's exactly the same effort in calculating Equation 8.3. So the overall calculation effort is the same (or more) than required by Equation 8.3. Additionally, one must worry about the approximations when Equation 13.9 is used.

However, Equation 13.9 does furnish nice insight to the clearing process. The term cos A Δh is just the plane-geometry projection of Δh onto LD. This means that in the plane-geometry approximation, the clearing process does just what's expected—it uses the component of the altitude correction in the direction of LD. Also note how the negative sign of the cos A Δh term makes sense: There are four cases of the sign of the term, because geometrically, both cos A and Δh can be positive or negative, independently. One example is when the angle A is less than 90°, then cos A is positive. Then if Δh is positive, the correction is negative by Equation 13.9. But if Δh is negative, the correction is positive. A drawing like Figure 8.2b for these cases (and for the other two) will show that these results are, indeed, correct. When equations don't agree with simple observations that we know independently, it's disconcerting. When they agree, it's satisfying.

4.10. In our lunar-distance discussion of semidiameters we neglected the contraction of the moon's disk due to the difference in refraction from its center to one of its limbs. At what altitude could this change exceed 0.1′ of arc? What effect would a 0.1′ flattening have on the semidiameter correction to the lunar distance?

Comment. Looking in the almanac's altitude correction table for stars (because we just want refraction information), we see that in going from 12° 00′ to 12° 17′ of apparent altitude, the refraction changes 0.1′ for an increase of an altitude of 17′, an arc distance close to the semidiameter of the moon. Since this flattening is in the plane of the vertical circle, only a component of the 0.1′ would apply to the semidiameter in the direction of the lunar distance. In any case, we normally would avoid sights at the low altitude of 12°.

Computer Programming

For those navigators interested in an expanded use of calculators or computers, here are some ideas:

5.1.   The first step in sophistication is to implement the St. Hilaire altitude and azimuth equations on a programmable hand calculator, such as the HP-33s. This is quite easily done after a few minutes (or hours) with the instruction book. The next step might be to include the arc and index sextant corrections, followed by the dip and refraction corrections using the formulas in the *Nautical Almanac*. A programming decision must be made on how to handle the different altitude corrections for the sun, moon, stars, and planets. At this point, the inputs to the calculator would be the sextant altitude H_s, and the GHA and declination of the body. The outputs would be the intercept distance and the azimuth, Zn.

5.2.   The next level of sophistication might be to implement the whole sight reduction by computer, computing your own almanac data from methods given in the book by Jean Meeus, *Astronomical Algorithms* (see Appendix K). This ephemeral data can be made practically perpetual, valid for hundreds of years. With the power of PCs, or even the TI-89 series of programmable calculators, you can reproduce your own version of the Navy's STELLA computer program.

5.3.   Instead of using the St. Hilaire method, you could write a computer program using Equations 13.1 of Exercise 1.22 to compute latitude and longitude coordinates that trace out an LOP directly on a computer screen, just as in Figure 2.7. In using this technique, how would you decide which portion of the LOP to plot? How would you implement that plan?

Comment. The guts of the program is simply a loop over Equations 13.1 running the loop variable B_x, say 10′ or 15′ of arc, either side of the central bearing of interest. This central bearing has to be specified external to this plotting loop. So calculate the bearing from the GP to the DR position to find this central bearing to the ship. Remember this bearing angle is not the reciprocal of the DR-GP bearing, but is obtained from Equations 5.1a and 5.1b by interchanging the AP and GP latitude and declination. You can see this by drawing a diagram of the navigation triangle.

5.4.   * Automatic plotting of LOPs invites the idea of plotting running fixes by computer. This requires moving the previous position (from a fix or estimate) forward to a current estimated position, according to the estimated track made good. Show that the earlier position can be moved forward (or backward) to the current time by the equations

$$\text{Lon}_2 = \text{Lon}_1 + (V/60)t \sin T / \cos \text{Lat}_1 \qquad (13.10a)$$
$$\text{Lat}_2 = \text{Lat}_1 + (V/60)t \cos T \qquad (13.10b)$$

where Lat_1 and Lon_1 are the coordinates of the earlier position; Lat_2 and Lon_2 are the new coordinates of the point brought forward; V is the estimated speed over the ground in knots; t is the time of the run between the first and second positions; and T is the estimated true track angle made good.

Comment. These equations are based on distance = velocity × time, but they are modified to give degrees of latitude and longitude on a Mercator chart. By drawing a simple diagram showing the track angle (measured from true north), you'll verify Equation 13.10b. The convergence of the meridians is accounted for by using Equation 10.1, requiring the second term in Equation 13.10a to be divided by cos Lat_1. Of course, this assumes plane geometry, which is valid over the short distances used in running fixes.

5.5.   Computer plotting of LOPs and fixes brings up the question of map projections. What map projection would you use, and how would you implement it? Does it matter what map projection is used in the above suggested projects?

   Comment. If you're going to just plot LOPs and positions by their latitude and longitude coordinates, locations can be read off of the plot in terms of their coordinates without concern about map projections. A simple rectangular grid can be used. However, such a grid distorts rhumb lines into curves, so they cannot be plotted with a ruler.

5.6.   With the power of today's PCs, it's quite reasonable to consider computing and printing your own custom-made sight reduction tables. Consider making them cover just the latitudes of your next trip. Think about how to organize them, what print size to use, and what accuracy you would want.

5.7.   * Equations 7.5 tell us how to determine the latitude and longitude directly from the observed altitudes of two bodies without using the intercept concept. Using a programmable calculator or a high-level language, such as Basic, Excel, or C, write a computer program to solve these equations. Next, to test your work, using the almanac and your knowledge of celestial navigation, calculate the altitudes of two bodies that are simultaneously above the horizon at some hypothetical location, and that have a reasonable LOP crossing angle for a fix. Then use these two altitudes in your programmed equations to see if you recover the latitude and longitude of the hypothetical location.

5.8.   ** Expand the above program to compute a fix from altitude observations of three or more bodies, such as occurs in a round of star shots. How would you determine a single fix position from the different results of each pair of LOPs? How would you use the redundancy of the multiple altitude observations to the best advantage?

Comment. The answer to how to calculate the "best" fix location from the redundant information depends on the mathematical definition of "best." If there are N bodies involved, there are N (N − 1) / 2 two-body fixes. Four stars would produce six two-body fixes, and five stars would produce 10 fixes. One approach is to plot all of these two-body fixes on a chart. Then by eyeballing them you can make a subjective value judgment for the best location. It might seem that while making this judgment, you could exclude outlying rogue fixes. However, they might not be obvious because just one wacky altitude throws off N–1 fixes. In a four-body round of stars, three of the six fixes, 50 percent, would be rogue, making their identification difficult. However, if you thought all of the two-body fixes were valid, a simple average of the latitudes and longitudes is mathematically the best estimate if the errors are truly random. And this can be done without computer plotting facilities.

5.9   *If you prefer, you can program a computer to plot fixes by using the intercepts and azimuths from St. Hilaire sight reductions. The two equations

$$\tan A_1 = (I_2 - I_1 \cos A) / (I_1 \sin A)$$

$$R = I_1 / \cos A_1$$

locate the fix at the relative azimuth angle A_1 and radius R from an AP that is common to both LOPs, as shown in Figure 13.1. The angle A is known from the azimuth difference of the two azimuths of intercepts, I_1 and I_2.

Comment. The solution given by the above equations can also be written in terms of I_2 and A_2. That is, it's also true that $R = I_2$ / $\cos A_2$, and similarly for $\tan A_2$. If the fix is going to be plotted on a Mercator projection, remember that the radius R will have to be decomposed into latitude and longitude coordinates using Equation 10.1. At first, the above solution might seem simpler than using the five trig equations required in Exercise 5.7 above. But the above solution requires six trig equations, the two above, plus two each for each of the two St. Hilaire solutions. However, for computer use the number of equations is not particularly important. The more significant question is which method is less sensitive to special cases involving signs of angles and their inverse trig functions.

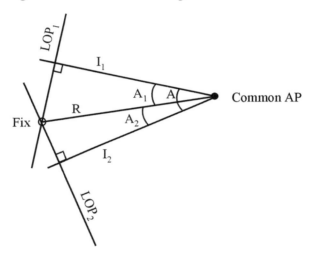

Figure 13.1 The relative azimuth angle A_1 (or A_2) and the radius R from the AP can be computed from the two LOP intercepts and their azimuth difference $A =$ $Zn_1 - Zn_2$ of the two LOP intercepts.

Because intercepts can be satisfactorily approximated by rhumb lines, plane geometry was assumed in deriving the above solutions. If you want to verify these solutions, I recommend drawing an auxiliary line from the intersection of LOP_1 and I_1 to the I_2 line, making it perpendicular to I_2. Then find the triangle that is similar to Fix-AP-(LOP$_1$-I$_1$-intersection). The rest is high school trig.

5.10.   ** The star pairs of Appendix G were selected to favor a wide range of arc distances; stars mostly observable worldwide; and stars with small proper motion. You might wish to write your own computer program that's not limited by these considerations. For example, you can select brighter stars that are more appropriate to your specific location; and you can automatically include stellar aberration by using the nautical almanac's coordinates for the observation date.

   The inputs to your program would be the SHAs and declinations of the star pairs observed at your observation time, along with the altitudes of each star. Then calculate their arc distance from Equation 10.2a (Equation 8.1 is this same equation). Next, using the refraction correction from the almanac

$$\text{Ref (refraction)} = 0.0167 \, / \, \tan(H + 7.32/(H + 4.32)),$$

where altitude H is in degrees, compute the observed altitudes H$_O$ from your measured apparent altitudes (the normal dip correction is so small that it can be neglected in these calculations). Then in applying the clearing equations 8.3, switch the altitudes H$_O$ and H$_A$ to get the star-star distance that includes refraction. This then gives the "uncleared" star-star distance that the sextant should read, after it's corrected for only index error.

Comment. Compare several of your results to entries in the Appendix G tables. For small star-star distances they should agree perhaps to 0.1´. But because the Appendix G data are not corrected for stellar aberration, and yours will be, the results may differ by as much as 1.0´ for some cases at large star-star distances.

APPENDICES

Appendix A. Navigation Triangle Formulae

Listed below are formulae that crop up in celestial navigation. But all of our *modern sight reductions* are based on just *one formula*, called the law of cosines. It gives the one side of a generic spherical triangle in terms of its two adjacent sides and its opposite angle—that is, the generic form of the equation is

$$\cos C = \cos A \cos B + \sin A \sin B \cos c \qquad\qquad A.0$$

where the sides and angles are shown in Figure A.1.

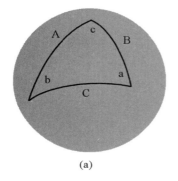 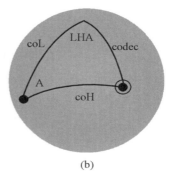

(a)   (b)

Figure A.1 **(a)** The sides of a spherical triangle, A, B, and C, are great circles. The angles opposite those sides are a, b, and c. Only one formula is used in all of our sight reductions: $\cos C = \cos A \cos B + \sin A \sin B \cos c$. **(b)** The same triangle labeled in terms of the familiar navigational triangle.

Clearly the same relation can be written with either the sides A or B in the cosine term on the left-hand side, giving three possible applications to a given triangle. Our familiar altitude and azimuth equations are both examples of this: Applying the above generic form to the navigation triangle in Figure A.1b gives

$$\cos(coH) = \cos(coL) \cos(codec) + \sin(coL) \sin(codec) \cos(LHA)$$

To make this equation more user-friendly to the navigator, we rewrite it in terms of the altitude, latitude, declination, remembering that $\cos(\text{coH}) = \sin(H)$, $\sin(\text{coL}) = \cos(L)$, etc. So it becomes

$$\sin H = \sin L \sin d + \cos L \cos d \cos LHA$$

our familiar altitude equation. The azimuth equation also comes from Equation A.0, but now we write $\cos(\text{codec})$ on the left-hand side in terms of its adjacent sides and opposite angle:

$$\cos(\text{codec}) = \cos(\text{coL}) \cos(\text{coH}) + \sin(\text{coL}) \sin(\text{coH}) \cos(A)$$

First converting to d and L in place of codec and coL, and then solving for $\cos A$ gives our azimuth equation:

$$\sin d = \sin L \sin H + \cos L \cos H \cos A$$

$$\cos A = (\sin d - \sin L \sin H) / (\cos L \cos H)$$

All of our navigation triangle equations, including the ones used in the direct calculation of fixes (end of Chapter 7), in clearing the lunar distance, and in great-circle sailing, are just the same old Equation A.0. There are many other spherical triangle relationships that can be expressed with many different equations. Many of them were important when logarithms had to be used for calculation, but we don't need them for our approach. A few of these alternative equations are listed below; these are useful for applications other than our standard sight reductions.

Altitude
$$\text{Sin } H = \sin L \sin d + \cos L \cos d \cos LHA \qquad \text{A.1}$$

Rate of change of altitude
$$dH/d(LHA) = -\cos L \sin A, \text{ per degree of LHA} \qquad \text{A.2a}$$
$$dH/dt = \pm 15' \cos L \sin A, \text{ per minute of time} \qquad \text{A.2b}$$

Altitude of a body bearing due east or west

$\text{Sin } H = \sin d \ / \sin L$ A.3

Azimuth

$\text{Cos } A = (\sin d - \sin L \sin H) \ / \ (\cos L \cos H)$ A.4

$\text{Cos } A = (\cos L \sin d - \sin L \cos d \cos LHA) \ / \ \cos H$ A.5

$\text{Tan } A = \sin LHA \ / \ (\cos L \tan d - \sin L \cos LHA)$ A.6

$\text{Sin } A = \cos d \sin LHA \ / \ \cos H$ A.7

Azimuth of a body at zero altitude, not including dip or refraction

$\text{Cos } Zn = \sin d \ / \cos L$ A.8

Latitude

$\text{Sin}(coL + G) = \sin H \sin G \ / \ \sin d$ A.9

where

$\tan G = \tan d \ / \ \cos LHA$, and coL is the co-latitude.

Longitude

$\text{Cos } LHA = (\sin H - \sin L \sin d) \ / \ (\cos L \cos d)$ A.10

and

Longitude is obtained from the LHA and GHA.

Meridian Sights

For upper transits

If the body is south of you, $L = dec + (90° - H_O)$ A.11a

If the body is north of you, $L = dec - (90° - H_O)$ A.11b

For lower transits

for northern latitudes, $L = \quad 90° - dec + H_O$ A.11c

for southern latitudes, $L = -90° - dec - H_O$ A.11d

Lunar Distance Sights

$\cos LD_O = \sin H_O \sin h_O + \cos H_O \cos h_O \cos RBA$ A.12a

where

$\cos RBA = (\cos LD_{SD} - \sin H_{SD} \sin h_{SD}) \ / \ (\cos H_{SD} \cos h_{SD})$ A.12b

Great-Circle Courses

$\cos D = \sin L_1 \sin L_2 + \cos L_1 \cos L_2 \cos (LonD)$ A.13a

$\cos A = (\sin L_2 - \sin L_1 \cos D) / (\cos L_1 \sin D)$ A.13b

Distance = 60.04 nm × D

if point 2 is east of point 1, Zn = A,

if point 2 is west of point 1, Zn = 306° – A

and

Zn is azimuth from point 1 to point 2

Hull Speed (in knots)

$Hs = 1.34\sqrt{WL}$ (in feet) $= 2.43 \sqrt{WL}$ (in meters) A.14

where

WL is the waterline length.

Distance to Visible Horizon (in nautical miles)

$D = 1.17 \sqrt{h}$ (in feet) $= 2.07 \sqrt{h}$ (in meters) A.15

where

h is height of eye.

Appendix B. Calculator Keystrokes

Calculators offer a modern alternative for finding H_C and Zn from the latitude, declination, and the LHA. The solutions are given by relatively simple equations. Writing L for latitude and d for declination, the two equations giving H_C and the azimuth angle A are:

$$\sin H_C = \sin L \sin d + \cos L \cos d \cos LHA \qquad \text{(B.1a)}$$

$$\cos A = (\sin d - \sin L \sin H_C) / (\cos L \cos H_C) \qquad \text{(B.1b)}$$

where the azimuth Zn is obtained from A by the rule:

if the LHA is greater than 180°, Zn = A,

if the LHA is less than 180°, Zn = 360° − A.

These equations might look forbidding. But by using the scientific calculator at a purely mechanical level, Equations B.1 can be thought of as a series of instructions, simply telling us which buttons to press on a calculator. In this view, the words "sin" (for sine) and "cos" (for cosine) are simply labels on calculator buttons. From this viewpoint, it's no different than a series of instructions telling us which column and row to search in a table for numbers, and how to combine those numbers to get an answer. While some calculators use reverse Polish notion, we'll assume the algebraic mode used by most calculators.

First of all, because the values of L, d, and LHA can be many digits long and they're used multiple times, it's efficient to store them in the calculator's three memory locations, designated one, two, and three, respectively. With any number in the display, pressing the STO (store) key followed by entering the number 1, will store that number in memory location 1. Pressing STO followed by entering 2, will store it in memory location No. 2, and likewise for location number three. So the first step is to store L, d, and the LHA in locations one through three respectively.

But as we store each of the values in memory, we need to convert them from degrees and decimal fractions of minutes to the decimal degrees required by calculators. Here's the best way: Say we want to enter a latitude of 21° 43.7′ into memory [1]. Just enter the 21°, and then add 43.7 divided by 60. The keystrokes are: Enter 21°, press +, enter 43.7, press ÷, enter 60, press =. The display should now read 21.72833333. Then immediately press STO, followed by entering 1, to store the latitude into location [1].

With the understanding that L, d, and LHA have been stored that way, and using [1] to mean memory location of the latitude, [2] the declination, and [3] the LHA, Equation B.1a can be expressed in the form

$$\sin H_C = \sin[1] \times \sin[2] + \cos[1] \times \cos[2] \times \cos[3] \qquad \text{(B.2a)}$$

This statement is simply a description of the actual keystrokes to use. We only need to know how to read this language. We start to the right of the equal sign with sin[1]. This means to take the sine of the value in location [1]. So we press RCL (recall), enter 1, and press the SIN key. Next, reading to the right, we press × for multiplication, then RCL, enter 2, press SIN, press +, and so on. The entire sequence is as follows:

Recall [1], press SIN, press ×, recall [2], press SIN, press +, recall [1], press COS, press ×, recall [2], press COS, press ×, recall [3], press COS, press =, press 2nd, press SIN.
Now H_C appears in the display in decimal degrees.

Sure, it looks complicated when written out like this. But when actually doing the calculation, we don't look at these words. Rather we look at Equation B.2a and view it as a code describing keystrokes. It's like playing a simple tune on a piano by knowing how to read notes. These 17 keystrokes use only six different keys. It is just as simple as learning to play about four bars of "Yankee Doodle" with one finger— and no timing! The repetition of keystrokes makes the whole thing incredibly simple after a little practice. You'll soon be a maestro.

To practice this language, turn to the excerpts from the H.O. 229 in Appendix D, where a multitude of solutions to Equation B.1a are tabulated. Select a set of whole degrees of latitude, declination, and LHA from the table. Enter these three variables into the calculator memories [1], [2], and [3], respectively. Then carefully execute the above keystrokes indicated by Equation B.2a to practice reproducing the H_C listed in these tables. (For now, ignore the interpolation factor, d, and the azimuth angle Z that are listed alongside H_C.) If you are unfamiliar with calculators, it may take a few attempts to get the H_C listed in the tables, but with a little practice it will soon seem simple. You might prefer following the keystroke table below, rather than the list of keystrokes above, but you should soon learn to read Equation B.2a directly.

For example, using L = 23°, d = – 35°, and LHA = 32°, you should get 24.54088395 in the calculator display for the altitude. Next we convert this decimal answer to degrees and minutes by subtracting the 24, then multiplying the decimal part by 60 to give 32.5'. So the result is 24° 32.5', which is what you find in H.O. 229, Appendix D. Note that this is a case of a latitude-contrary-name-as-declination, meaning they have opposite signs. (Use the + / – key on the calculator to negate the 35° after it's entered and before it's stored.) Practice various combinations using H.O. 229 until consistently correct answers are obtained. Then you're ready to go on to the azimuth equation.

The equation for A also has five trig functions, and contains L, d, and the just previously calculated H_C:

$$\cos A = (\sin d - \sin L \sin H_C) / (\cos L \cos H_C) \qquad \text{(B.1b)}$$

This expression for A requires the original latitude and declination values but not the LHA. So we can reuse memory location [3] to store H_C, which occurs twice in the azimuth calculation. Therefore right after H_C is calculated, hit the store [3] key *before* H_C is converted to degrees and minutes. Now in terms of the revised stored values, the azimuth equation reads

$$\cos A = (\sin[2] - \sin[1] \sin[3]) / (\cos[1] \cos[3]) \qquad \text{(B.2b)}$$

which tells us to perform the following keystrokes:

Recall [2] press SIN, press −, recall [1], press SIN, press ×, recall [3], press SIN, press =, press ÷, recall [1], press COS, press ÷, recall [3], press COS, press =, press INV, press COS. The calculator now displays A.

OK, so this amounts to another four bars on the one-finger piano, but again the routine has a simplifying pattern. To compare your calculator result with the table's, we need to make an adjustment because the calculated azimuth angle A is different than the tabulated angle Z. (See Figure 12.1 and its associated discussion.) In northern latitudes A = Z, but in southern latitudes A = 180° − Z. So in the above example you should get A = 151.5° = Z in the table. But if you now change L to − 23° for a southern latitude, you should get A = 120.6° and Z = 180°− 120° = 59.4°, which is the table Z for this L, d, and LHA. In practice, azimuths need not be carried out beyond whole degrees.

On the following page you will find the keystroke commands in tabular form. They assume that degrees and decimal minutes have been converted into decimal degrees, and that the latitude, declination, and LHA have been stored in memories [1], [2], and [3], respectively. The commands for A assume that right after H_C was calculated, it was stored in [3], while it's still in decimal form. At that point, I like to convert H_C to degrees and decimal minutes, write it down, then proceed to the azimuth calculation. See Keystroke Commands table, following page.

Keystroke Commands

H_C	A
recall [1]	recall [2]
press SIN	press SIN
press x	press −
recall [2]	recall [1]
press SIN	press SIN
press +	press x
recall [1]	recall [3]
press COS	press SIN
press x	press =
	press ÷
recall [2]	
press COS	recall [1]
press x	press COS
	press ÷
recall [3]	
press COS	recall [3]
press =	press COS
	press =
press 2nd	
press SIN	press 2nd
store [3]	press COS

The following eleven pages contain excerpts from the *Nautical Almanac*.

A2 Altitude Correction Tables 10°–90°—Sun, Stars, Planets

A3 Altitude Correction Tables 0°–10°—Sun, Stars, Planets

A4 Altitude Correction Tables—Additional Corrections

Planet Diagram, 2005

2005 May 10, 11, 12 (Tues. Wed. Thurs.)

2005 May 10, 11, 12 (Tues. Wed. Thurs.)

Conversion of Arc to Time

Increments and Corrections

Polaris (Pole Star) Table for LHA Aries 120°–239°

Altitude Correction Tables 0°–35°—Moon

Altitude Correction Tables 35°–90°—Moon

A2 ALTITUDE CORRECTION TABLES 10°-90°—SUN, STARS, PLANETS

OCT.—MAR. SUN APR.—SEPT.						STARS AND PLANETS				DIP					
App. Alt.	Lower Limb	Upper Limb	App. Alt.	Lower Limb	Upper Limb	App Alt.	Corrⁿ	App. Alt.	Additional Corrⁿ	Ht. of Eye	Corrⁿ	Ht. of Eye	Corrⁿ	Ht. of Eye	Corrⁿ
° ′	′	′	° ′	′	′	° ′	′		**2005**	m	′	ft.		m	′
9 33	+10·8	−21·5	9 39	+10·6	−21·2	9 55	−5·3		**VENUS**	2·4	−2·8	8·0		1·0	− 1·8
9 45	+10·9	−21·4	9 50	+10·7	−21·1	10 07	−5·2		Jan. 1–Sept. 23	2·6	−2·9	8·6		1·5	− 2·2
9 56	+11·0	−21·3	10 02	+10·8	−21·0	10 20	−5·1	°	′	2·8	−3·0	9·2		2·0	− 2·5
10 08	+11·1	−21·2	10 14	+10·9	−20·9	10 32	−5·0	60	+0·1	3·0	−3·1	9·8		2·5	− 2·8
10 20	+11·2	−21·1	10 27	+11·0	−20·8	10 46	−4·9			3·2	−3·2	10·5		3·0	− 3·0
10 33	+11·3	−21·0	10 40	+11·1	−20·7	10 59	−4·8	Sept. 24–Nov. 14		3·4	−3·3	11·2			
10 46	+11·4	−20·9	10 53	+11·2	−20·6	11 14	−4·7	°	′	3·6	−3·4	11·9		See table	
11 00	+11·5	−20·8	11 07	+11·3	−20·5	11 29	−4·6	41	+0·2	3·8	−3·5	12·6		←	
11 15	+11·6	−20·7	11 22	+11·4	−20·4	11 44	−4·5	76	+0·1	4·0	−3·6	13·3		m	′
11 30	+11·7	−20·6	11 37	+11·5	−20·3	12 00	−4·4			4·3	−3·7	14·1		20	− 7·9
11 45	+11·8	−20·5	11 53	+11·6	−20·2	12 17	−4·3	Nov. 15–Dec. 7		4·5	−3·8	14·9		22	− 8·3
12 01	+11·9	−20·4	12 10	+11·7	−20·1	12 35	−4·2	°	′	4·7	−3·9	15·7		24	− 8·6
12 18	+12·0	−20·3	12 27	+11·8	−20·0	12 53	−4·1	34	+0·3	5·0	−4·0	16·5		26	− 9·0
12 36	+12·1	−20·2	12 45	+11·9	−19·9	13 12	−4·0	60	+0·2	5·2	−4·1	17·4		28	− 9·3
12 54	+12·2	−20·1	13 04	+12·0	−19·8	13 32	−3·9	80	+0·1	5·5	−4·2	18·3			
13 14	+12·3	−20·0	13 24	+12·1	−19·7	13 53	−3·8			5·8	−4·3	19·1		30	− 9·6
13 34	+12·4	−19·9	13 44	+12·2	−19·6	14 16	−3·8	Dec. 8–Dec. 23		6·1	−4·4	20·1		32	−10·0
13 55	+12·5	−19·8	14 06	+12·3	−19·5	14 39	−3·7	°	′	6·3	−4·5	21·0		34	−10·3
14 17	+12·6	−19·7	14 29	+12·4	−19·4	15 03	−3·6	29	+0·4	6·6	−4·6	22·0		36	−10·6
14 41	+12·7	−19·6	14 53	+12·5	−19·3	15 29	−3·5	51	+0·3	6·9	−4·7	22·9		38	−10·8
15 05	+12·8	−19·5	15 18	+12·6	−19·2	15 56	−3·4	68	+0·2	7·2	−4·8	23·9			
15 31	+12·9	−19·4	15 45	+12·7	−19·1	16 25	−3·3	83	+0·1	7·5	−4·9	24·9		40	−11·1
15 59	+13·0	−19·3	16 13	+12·8	−19·0	16 55	−3·2			7·9	−5·0	26·0		42	−11·4
16 27	+13·1	−19·2	16 43	+12·9	−18·9	17 27	−3·1	Dec. 24–Dec. 31		8·2	−5·1	27·1		44	−11·7
16 58	+13·2	−19·1	17 14	+13·0	−18·8	18 01	−3·0	°	′	8·5	−5·2	28·1		46	−11·9
17 30	+13·3	−19·0	17 47	+13·1	−18·7	18 37	−2·9	26	+0·5	8·8	−5·3	29·2		48	−12·2
18 05	+13·4	−18·9	18 23	+13·2	−18·6	19 16	−2·8	46	+0·4	9·2	−5·4	30·4		ft.	
18 41	+13·5	−18·8	19 00	+13·3	−18·5	19 56	−2·7	60	+0·3	9·5	−5·5	31·5		2	− 1·4
19 20	+13·6	−18·7	19 41	+13·4	−18·4	20 40	−2·6	73	+0·2	9·9	−5·6	32·7		4	− 1·9
20 02	+13·7	−18·6	20 24	+13·5	−18·3	21 27	−2·5	84	+0·1	10·3	−5·7	33·9		6	− 2·4
20 46	+13·8	−18·5	21 10	+13·6	−18·2	22 17	−2·4	**MARS**		10·6	−5·8	35·1		8	− 2·7
21 34	+13·9	−18·4	21 59	+13·7	−18·1	23 11	−2·3	Jan. 1–July 5		11·0	−5·9	36·3		10	− 3·1
22 25	+14·0	−18·3	22 52	+13·8	−18·0	24 09	−2·1	°	′	11·4	−6·0	37·6		See table	
23 20	+14·1	−18·2	23 49	+13·9	−17·9	25 12	−2·0	60	+0·1	11·8	−6·1	38·9		←	
24 20	+14·2	−18·1	24 51	+14·0	−17·8	26 20	−1·9			12·2	−6·2	40·1		ft.	
25 24	+14·3	−18·0	25 58	+14·1	−17·7	27 34	−1·8	July 6–Sept. 16		12·6	−6·3	41·5		70	− 8·1
26 34	+14·4	−17·9	27 11	+14·2	−17·6	28 54	−1·7	Dec. 7–Dec. 31		13·0	−6·4	42·8		75	− 8·4
27 50	+14·5	−17·8	28 31	+14·3	−17·5	30 22	−1·6	°	′	13·4	−6·5	44·2		80	− 8·7
29 13	+14·6	−17·7	29 58	+14·4	−17·4	31 58	−1·6	41	+0·2	13·8	−6·6	45·5		85	− 8·9
30 44	+14·7	−17·6	31 33	+14·5	−17·3	33 43	−1·5	76	+0·1	14·2	−6·7	46·9		90	− 9·2
32 24	+14·8	−17·5	33 18	+14·6	−17·2	35 38	−1·4			14·7	−6·8	48·4		95	− 9·5
34 15	+14·9	−17·4	35 15	+14·7	−17·1	37 45	−1·3	Sept. 17–Dec. 6		15·1	−6·9	49·8			
36 17	+15·0	−17·3	37 24	+14·8	−17·0	40 06	−1·2	°	′	15·5	−7·0	51·3		100	− 9·7
38 34	+15·1	−17·2	39 48	+14·9	−16·9	42 42	−1·1	34	+0·3	16·0	−7·1	52·8		105	− 9·9
41 06	+15·2	−17·1	42 28	+15·0	−16·8	45 34	−1·0	60	+0·2	16·5	−7·2	54·3		110	−10·2
43 56	+15·3	−17·0	45 29	+15·1	−16·7	48 45	−0·9	80	+0·1	16·9	−7·3	55·8		115	−10·4
47 07	+15·4	−16·9	48 52	+15·2	−16·6	52 16	−0·8			17·4	−7·4	57·4		120	−10·6
50 43	+15·5	−16·8	52 41	+15·3	−16·5	56 09	−0·7			17·9	−7·5	58·9		125	−10·8
54 46	+15·6	−16·7	56 59	+15·4	−16·4	60 26	−0·6			18·4	−7·6	60·5			
59 21	+15·7	−16·6	61 50	+15·5	−16·3	65 06	−0·5			18·8	−7·7	62·1		130	−11·1
64 28	+15·8	−16·5	67 15	+15·6	−16·2	70 09	−0·4			19·3	−7·8	63·8		135	−11·3
70 10	+15·9	−16·4	73 14	+15·7	−16·1	75 32	−0·3			19·8	−7·9	65·4		140	−11·5
76 24	+16·0	−16·3	79 42	+15·8	−16·0	81 12	−0·2			20·4	−8·0	67·1		145	−11·7
83 05	+16·1	−16·2	86 31	+15·9	−15·9	87 03	−0·1			20·9	−8·1	68·8		150	−11·9
90 00			90 00			90 00	0·0			21·4		70·5		155	−12·1

ALTITUDE CORRECTION TABLES 0°-10°—SUN,STARS,PLANETS A3

App. Alt.	OCT.—MAR. SUN APR.—SEPT.				STARS PLANETS	App. Alt.	OCT.—MAR. SUN APR.—SEPT.				STARS PLANETS
	Lower Limb	Upper Limb	Lower Limb	Upper Limb			Lower Limb	Upper Limb	Lower Limb	Upper Limb	
° ′	′	′	′	′	′	° ′	′	′	′	′	′
0 00	− 17·5	− 49·8	− 17·8	− 49·6	− 33·8	3 30	+ 3·4	− 28·9	+ 3·1	− 28·7	− 12·9
0 03	16·9	49·2	17·2	49·0	33·2	3 35	3·6	28·7	3·3	28·5	12·7
0 06	16·3	48·6	16·6	48·4	32·6	3 40	3·8	28·5	3·6	28·2	12·5
0 09	15·7	48·0	16·0	47·8	32·0	3 45	4·0	28·3	3·8	28·0	12·3
0 12	15·2	47·5	15·4	47·2	31·5	3 50	4·2	28·1	4·0	27·8	12·1
0 15	14·6	46·9	14·8	46·6	30·9	3 55	4·4	27·9	4·1	27·7	11·9
0 18	− 14·1	− 46·4	− 14·3	− 46·1	− 30·4	4 00	+ 4·6	− 27·7	+ 4·3	− 27·5	− 11·7
0 21	13·5	45·8	13·8	45·6	29·8	4 05	4·8	27·5	4·5	27·3	11·5
0 24	13·0	45·3	13·3	45·1	29·3	4 10	4·9	27·4	4·7	27·1	11·4
0 27	12·5	44·8	12·8	44·6	28·8	4 15	5·1	27·2	4·9	26·9	11·2
0 30	12·0	44·3	12·3	44·1	28·3	4 20	5·3	27·0	5·0	26·8	11·0
0 33	11·6	43·9	11·8	43·6	27·9	4 25	5·4	26·9	5·2	26·6	10·9
0 36	− 11·1	− 43·4	− 11·3	− 43·1	− 27·4	4 30	+ 5·6	− 26·7	+ 5·3	− 26·5	− 10·7
0 39	10·6	42·9	10·9	42·7	26·9	4 35	5·7	26·6	5·5	26·3	10·6
0 42	10·2	42·5	10·5	42·3	26·5	4 40	5·9	26·4	5·6	26·2	10·4
0 45	9·8	42·1	10·0	41·8	26·1	4 45	6·0	26·3	5·8	26·0	10·3
0 48	9·4	41·7	9·6	41·4	25·7	4 50	6·2	26·1	5·9	25·9	10·1
0 51	9·0	41·3	9·2	41·0	25·3	4 55	6·3	26·0	6·1	25·7	10·0
0 54	− 8·6	− 40·9	− 8·8	− 40·6	− 24·9	5 00	+ 6·4	− 25·9	+ 6·2	− 25·6	− 9·8
0 57	8·2	40·5	8·4	40·2	24·5	5 05	6·6	25·7	6·3	25·5	9·7
1 00	7·8	40·1	8·0	39·8	24·1	5 10	6·7	25·6	6·5	25·3	9·6
1 03	7·4	39·7	7·7	39·5	23·7	5 15	6·8	25·5	6·6	25·2	9·5
1 06	7·1	39·4	7·3	39·1	23·4	5 20	7·0	25·3	6·7	25·1	9·3
1 09	6·7	39·0	7·0	38·8	23·0	5 25	7·1	25·2	6·8	25·0	9·2
1 12	− 6·4	− 38·7	− 6·6	− 38·4	− 22·7	5 30	+ 7·2	− 25·1	+ 6·9	− 24·9	− 9·1
1 15	6·0	38·3	6·3	38·1	22·3	5 35	7·3	25·0	7·1	24·7	9·0
1 18	5·7	38·0	6·0	37·8	22·0	5 40	7·4	24·9	7·2	24·6	8·9
1 21	5·4	37·7	5·7	37·5	21·7	5 45	7·5	24·8	7·3	24·5	8·8
1 24	5·1	37·4	5·3	37·1	21·4	5 50	7·6	24·7	7·4	24·4	8·7
1 27	4·8	37·1	5·0	36·8	21·1	5 55	7·7	24·6	7·5	24·3	8·6
1 30	− 4·5	− 36·8	− 4·7	− 36·5	− 20·8	6 00	+ 7·8	− 24·5	+ 7·6	− 24·2	− 8·5
1 35	4·0	36·3	4·3	36·1	20·3	6 10	8·0	24·3	7·8	24·0	8·3
1 40	3·6	35·9	3·8	35·6	19·9	6 20	8·2	24·1	8·0	23·8	8·1
1 45	3·1	35·4	3·4	35·2	19·4	6 30	8·4	23·9	8·2	23·6	7·9
1 50	2·7	35·0	2·9	34·7	19·0	6 40	8·6	23·7	8·3	23·5	7·7
1 55	2·3	34·6	2·5	34·3	18·6	6 50	8·7	23·6	8·5	23·3	7·6
2 00	− 1·9	− 34·2	− 2·1	− 33·9	− 18·2	7 00	+ 8·9	− 23·4	+ 8·7	− 23·1	− 7·4
2 05	1·5	33·8	1·7	33·5	17·8	7 10	9·1	23·2	8·8	23·0	7·2
2 10	1·1	33·4	1·4	33·2	17·4	7 20	9·2	23·1	9·0	22·8	7·1
2 15	0·8	33·1	1·0	32·8	17·1	7 30	9·3	23·0	9·1	22·7	6·9
2 20	0·4	32·7	0·7	32·5	16·7	7 40	9·5	22·8	9·2	22·6	6·8
2 25	− 0·1	32·4	− 0·3	32·1	16·4	7 50	9·6	22·7	9·4	22·4	6·7
2 30	+ 0·2	− 32·1	0·0	− 31·8	− 16·1	8 00	+ 9·7	− 22·6	+ 9·5	− 22·3	− 6·6
2 35	0·5	31·8	+ 0·3	31·5	15·8	8 10	9·9	22·4	9·6	22·2	6·4
2 40	0·8	31·5	0·6	31·2	15·4	8 20	10·0	22·3	9·7	22·1	6·3
2 45	1·1	31·2	0·9	30·9	15·2	8 30	10·1	22·2	9·9	21·9	6·2
2 50	1·4	30·9	1·2	30·6	14·9	8 40	10·2	22·1	10·0	21·8	6·1
2 55	1·7	30·6	1·4	30·4	14·6	8 50	10·3	22·0	10·1	21·7	6·0
3 00	+ 2·0	− 30·3	+ 1·7	− 30·1	− 14·3	9 00	+ 10·4	− 21·9	+ 10·2	− 21·6	− 5·9
3 05	2·2	30·1	2·0	29·8	14·1	9 10	10·5	21·8	10·3	21·5	5·8
3 10	2·5	29·8	2·2	29·6	13·8	9 20	10·6	21·7	10·4	21·4	5·7
3 15	2·7	29·6	2·5	29·3	13·6	9 30	10·7	21·6	10·5	21·3	5·6
3 20	2·9	29·4	2·7	29·1	13·4	9 40	10·8	21·5	10·6	21·2	5·5
3 25	3·2	29·1	2·9	28·9	13·1	9 50	10·9	21·4	10·6	21·2	5·4
3 30	+ 3·4	− 28·9	+ 3·1	− 28·7	− 12·9	10 00	+ 11·0	− 21·3	+ 10·7	− 21·1	− 5·3

A4 ALTITUDE CORRECTION TABLES—ADDITIONAL CORRECTIONS
ADDITIONAL REFRACTION CORRECTIONS FOR NON-STANDARD CONDITIONS

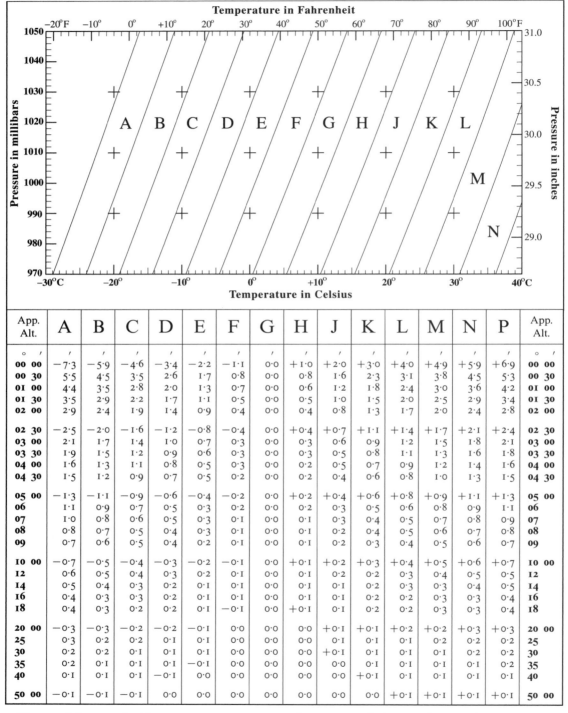

App. Alt.	A	B	C	D	E	F	G	H	J	K	L	M	N	P	App. Alt.
° ′	′	′	′	′	′	′	′	′	′	′	′	′	′	′	° ′
00 00	−7·3	−5·9	−4·6	−3·4	−2·2	−1·1	0·0	+1·0	+2·0	+3·0	+4·0	+4·9	+5·9	+6·9	00 00
00 30	5·5	4·5	3·5	2·6	1·7	0·8	0·0	0·8	1·6	2·3	3·1	3·8	4·5	5·3	00 30
01 00	4·4	3·5	2·8	2·0	1·3	0·7	0·0	0·6	1·2	1·8	2·4	3·0	3·6	4·2	01 00
01 30	3·5	2·9	2·2	1·7	1·1	0·5	0·0	0·5	1·0	1·5	2·0	2·5	2·9	3·4	01 30
02 00	2·9	2·4	1·9	1·4	0·9	0·4	0·0	0·4	0·8	1·3	1·7	2·0	2·4	2·8	02 00
02 30	−2·5	−2·0	−1·6	−1·2	−0·8	−0·4	0·0	+0·4	+0·7	+1·1	+1·4	+1·7	+2·1	+2·4	02 30
03 00	2·1	1·7	1·4	1·0	0·7	0·3	0·0	0·3	0·6	0·9	1·2	1·5	1·8	2·1	03 00
03 30	1·9	1·5	1·2	0·9	0·6	0·3	0·0	0·3	0·5	0·8	1·1	1·3	1·6	1·8	03 30
04 00	1·6	1·3	1·1	0·8	0·5	0·3	0·0	0·2	0·5	0·7	0·9	1·2	1·4	1·6	04 00
04 30	1·5	1·2	0·9	0·7	0·5	0·2	0·0	0·2	0·4	0·6	0·8	1·0	1·3	1·5	04 30
05 00	−1·3	−1·1	−0·9	−0·6	−0·4	−0·2	0·0	+0·2	+0·4	+0·6	+0·8	+0·9	+1·1	+1·3	05 00
06	1·1	0·9	0·7	0·5	0·3	0·2	0·0	0·2	0·3	0·5	0·6	0·8	0·9	1·1	06
07	1·0	0·8	0·6	0·5	0·3	0·1	0·0	0·1	0·3	0·4	0·5	0·7	0·8	0·9	07
08	0·8	0·7	0·5	0·4	0·3	0·1	0·0	0·1	0·2	0·4	0·5	0·6	0·7	0·8	08
09	0·7	0·6	0·5	0·4	0·2	0·1	0·0	0·1	0·2	0·3	0·4	0·5	0·6	0·7	09
10 00	−0·7	−0·5	−0·4	−0·3	−0·2	−0·1	0·0	+0·1	+0·2	+0·3	+0·4	+0·5	+0·6	+0·7	10 00
12	0·6	0·5	0·4	0·3	0·2	0·1	0·0	0·1	0·2	0·2	0·3	0·4	0·5	0·5	12
14	0·5	0·4	0·3	0·2	0·1	0·1	0·0	0·1	0·1	0·2	0·3	0·3	0·4	0·5	14
16	0·4	0·3	0·3	0·2	0·1	0·1	0·0	0·1	0·1	0·2	0·2	0·3	0·3	0·4	16
18	0·4	0·3	0·2	0·2	0·1	−0·1	0·0	+0·1	0·1	0·2	0·2	0·3	0·3	0·4	18
20 00	−0·3	−0·3	−0·2	−0·2	−0·1	0·0	0·0	0·0	+0·1	+0·1	+0·2	+0·2	+0·3	+0·3	20 00
25	0·3	0·2	0·2	0·1	0·1	0·0	0·0	0·0	0·1	0·1	0·1	0·2	0·2	0·2	25
30	0·2	0·2	0·1	0·1	0·1	0·0	0·0	0·0	+0·1	0·1	0·1	0·1	0·2	0·2	30
35	0·2	0·1	0·1	0·1	−0·1	0·0	0·0	0·0	0·0	0·1	0·1	0·1	0·1	0·2	35
40	0·1	0·1	0·1	−0·1	0·0	0·0	0·0	0·0	0·0	+0·1	0·1	0·1	0·1	0·1	40
50 00	−0·1	−0·1	−0·1	0·0	0·0	0·0	0·0	0·0	0·0	0·0	+0·1	+0·1	+0·1	+0·1	50 00

The graph is entered with arguments temperature and pressure to find a zone letter; using as arguments this zone letter and apparent altitude (sextant altitude corrected for index error and dip), a correction is taken from the table. This correction is to be applied to the sextant altitude in addition to the corrections for standard conditions (for the Sun, stars and planets from page A2–A3 and for the Moon from pages xxxiv and xxxv).

PLANETS, 2005

LOCAL MEAN TIME OF MERIDIAN PASSAGE

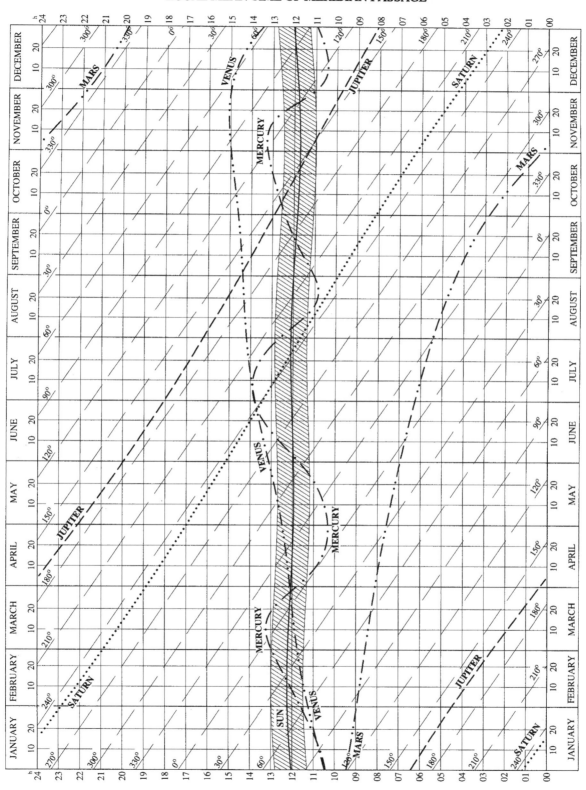

LOCAL MEAN TIME OF MERIDIAN PASSAGE

2005 MAY 10, 11, 12 (TUES., WED., THURS.)

UT	ARIES GHA	VENUS −3.8 GHA	Dec	MARS +0.5 GHA	Dec	JUPITER −2.3 GHA	Dec	SATURN +0.2 GHA	Dec	STARS Name	SHA	Dec
d h	° ′	° ′	° ′	° ′	° ′	° ′	° ′	° ′	° ′		° ′	° ′
10 00	227 53.5	170 17.2	N20 02.8	249 02.7	S10 47.7	38 08.7	S 2 32.5	113 35.1	N21 45.0	Acamar	315 23.5	S40 17.0
01	242 56.0	185 16.5	03.6	264 03.4	47.1	53 11.4	32.4	128 37.4	45.0	Achernar	335 31.7	S57 12.5
02	257 58.5	200 15.8	04.3	279 04.2	46.4	68 14.0	32.3	143 39.6	45.0	Acrux	173 16.3	S63 07.9
03	273 00.9	215 15.0 · ·	05.1	294 04.9 · ·	45.8	83 16.6 · ·	32.3	158 41.9 · ·	44.9	Adhara	255 17.8	S28 58.8
04	288 03.4	230 14.3	05.8	309 05.7	45.2	98 19.3	32.2	173 44.1	44.9	Aldebaran	290 57.0	N16 31.2
05	303 05.8	245 13.6	06.6	324 06.4	44.5	113 21.9	32.1	188 46.4	44.9			
06	318 08.3	260 12.9	N20 07.3	339 07.1	S10 43.9	128 24.6	S 2 32.1	203 48.6	N21 44.8	Alioth	166 25.5	N55 56.0
07	333 10.8	275 12.2	08.1	354 07.9	43.3	143 27.2	32.0	218 50.9	44.8	Alkaid	153 03.2	N49 17.2
T 08	348 13.2	290 11.5	08.8	9 08.6	42.6	158 29.9	31.9	233 53.1	44.8	Al Na'ir	27 51.6	S46 56.0
U 09	3 15.7	305 10.8 · ·	09.6	24 09.4 · ·	42.0	173 32.5 · ·	31.9	248 55.4 · ·	44.8	Alnilam	275 53.1	S 1 11.9
E 10	18 18.2	320 10.0	10.3	39 10.1	41.4	188 35.1	31.8	263 57.6	44.7	Alphard	218 02.4	S 8 40.9
S 11	33 20.6	335 09.3	11.1	54 10.9	40.8	203 37.8	31.7	278 59.9	44.7			
D 12	48 23.1	350 08.6	N20 11.8	69 11.6	S10 40.1	218 40.4	S 2 31.7	294 02.1	N21 44.7	Alphecca	126 16.0	N26 41.7
A 13	63 25.6	5 07.9	12.6	84 12.3	39.5	233 43.1	31.6	309 04.4	44.6	Alpheratz	357 50.4	N29 07.0
Y 14	78 28.0	20 07.2	13.3	99 13.1	38.9	248 45.7	31.5	324 06.6	44.6	Altair	62 14.3	N 8 52.7
15	93 30.5	35 06.4 · ·	14.0	114 13.8 · ·	38.2	263 48.3 · ·	31.5	339 08.9 · ·	44.6	Ankaa	353 22.1	S42 16.6
16	108 33.0	50 05.7	14.8	129 14.6	37.6	278 51.0	31.4	354 11.1	44.5	Antares	112 33.8	S26 26.8
17	123 35.4	65 05.0	15.5	144 15.3	37.0	293 53.6	31.3	9 13.4	44.5			
18	138 37.9	80 04.3	N20 16.3	159 16.1	S10 36.3	308 56.2	S 2 31.3	24 15.6	N21 44.5	Arcturus	146 01.1	N19 09.2
19	153 40.3	95 03.6	17.0	174 16.8	35.7	323 58.9	31.2	39 17.9	44.4	Atria	107 40.9	S69 02.3
20	168 42.8	110 02.8	17.7	189 17.6	35.1	339 01.5	31.2	54 20.1	44.4	Avior	234 21.0	S59 31.8
21	183 45.3	125 02.1 · ·	18.5	204 18.3 · ·	34.4	354 04.2 · ·	31.1	69 22.4 · ·	44.4	Bellatrix	278 39.1	N 6 21.3
22	198 47.7	140 01.4	19.2	219 19.0	33.8	9 06.8	31.0	84 24.6	44.4	Betelgeuse	271 08.5	N 7 24.5
23	213 50.2	155 00.7	19.9	234 19.8	33.2	24 09.4	31.0	99 26.8	44.3			
11 00	228 52.7	170 00.0	N20 20.7	249 20.5	S10 32.5	39 12.1	S 2 30.9	114 29.1	N21 44.3	Canopus	263 59.4	S52 42.0
01	243 55.1	184 59.2	21.4	264 21.3	31.9	54 14.7	30.8	129 31.3	44.3	Capella	280 44.3	N46 00.4
02	258 57.6	199 58.5	22.1	279 22.0	31.3	69 17.3	30.8	144 33.6	44.2	Deneb	49 35.8	N45 17.6
03	274 00.1	214 57.8 · ·	22.9	294 22.8 · ·	30.6	84 20.0 · ·	30.7	159 35.8 · ·	44.2	Denebola	182 39.9	N14 32.6
04	289 02.5	229 57.1	23.6	309 23.5	30.0	99 22.6	30.6	174 38.1	44.2	Diphda	349 02.4	S17 57.5
05	304 05.0	244 56.3	24.3	324 24.3	29.4	114 25.3	30.6	189 40.3	44.1			
06	319 07.5	259 55.6	N20 25.0	339 25.0	S10 28.7	129 27.9	S 2 30.5	204 42.6	N21 44.1	Dubhe	193 58.8	N61 43.6
W 07	334 09.9	274 54.9	25.8	354 25.8	28.1	144 30.5	30.4	219 44.8	44.1	Elnath	278 21.0	N28 36.8
E 08	349 12.4	289 54.2	26.5	9 26.5	27.5	159 33.2	30.4	234 47.1	44.0	Eltanin	90 48.7	N51 29.0
D 09	4 14.8	304 53.4 · ·	27.2	24 27.2 · ·	26.8	174 35.8 · ·	30.3	249 49.3 · ·	44.0	Enif	33 53.4	N 9 53.7
N 10	19 17.3	319 52.7	27.9	39 28.0	26.2	189 38.4	30.3	264 51.5	44.0	Fomalhaut	15 31.0	S29 35.6
E 11	34 19.8	334 52.0	28.7	54 28.7	25.6	204 41.1	30.2	279 53.8	44.0			
S 12	49 22.2	349 51.2	N20 29.4	69 29.5	S10 24.9	219 43.7	S 2 30.1	294 56.0	N21 43.9	Gacrux	172 07.9	S57 08.8
D 13	64 24.7	4 50.5	30.1	84 30.2	24.3	234 46.3	30.1	309 58.3	43.9	Gienah	175 58.7	S17 34.4
A 14	79 27.2	19 49.8	30.8	99 31.0	23.6	249 49.0	30.0	325 00.5	43.9	Hadar	148 56.7	S60 24.1
Y 15	94 29.6	34 49.1 · ·	31.5	114 31.7 · ·	23.0	264 51.6 · ·	29.9	340 02.8 · ·	43.8	Hamal	328 08.4	N23 29.2
16	109 32.1	49 48.3	32.3	129 32.5	22.4	279 54.2	29.9	355 05.0	43.8	Kaus Aust.	83 51.9	S34 23.0
17	124 34.6	64 47.6	33.0	144 33.2	21.7	294 56.9	29.8	10 07.3	43.8			
18	139 37.0	79 46.9	N20 33.7	159 34.0	S10 21.1	309 59.5	S 2 29.8	25 09.5	N21 43.7	Kochab	137 18.0	N74 08.0
19	154 39.5	94 46.1	34.4	174 34.7	20.5	325 02.1	29.7	40 11.7	43.7	Markab	13 44.9	N15 13.8
20	169 42.0	109 45.4	35.1	189 35.5	19.8	340 04.8	29.6	55 14.0	43.7	Menkar	314 22.0	N 4 06.6
21	184 44.4	124 44.7 · ·	35.8	204 36.2 · ·	19.2	355 07.4 · ·	29.6	70 16.2 · ·	43.6	Menkent	148 14.8	S36 23.9
22	199 46.9	139 43.9	36.5	219 37.0	18.6	10 10.0	29.5	85 18.5	43.6	Miaplacidus	221 41.5	S69 44.6
23	214 49.3	154 43.2	37.2	234 37.7	17.9	25 12.7	29.5	100 20.7	43.6			
12 00	229 51.8	169 42.5	N20 38.0	249 38.5	S10 17.3	40 15.3	S 2 29.4	115 23.0	N21 43.6	Mirfak	308 50.1	N49 52.8
01	244 54.3	184 41.7	38.7	264 39.2	16.7	55 17.9	29.3	130 25.2	43.5	Nunki	76 05.9	S26 17.5
02	259 56.7	199 41.0	39.4	279 40.0	16.0	70 20.5	29.3	145 27.4	43.5	Peacock	53 28.9	S56 43.0
03	274 59.2	214 40.3 · ·	40.1	294 40.7 · ·	15.4	85 23.2 · ·	29.2	160 29.7 · ·	43.5	Pollux	243 35.6	N28 01.0
04	290 01.7	229 39.5	40.8	309 41.5	14.7	100 25.8	29.1	175 31.9	43.4	Procyon	245 06.5	N 5 12.7
05	305 04.1	244 38.8	41.5	324 42.2	14.1	115 28.4	29.1	190 34.2	43.4			
06	320 06.6	259 38.1	N20 42.2	339 43.0	S10 13.5	130 31.1	S 2 29.0	205 36.4	N21 43.4	Rasalhague	96 12.1	N12 33.1
07	335 09.1	274 37.3	42.9	354 43.7	12.8	145 33.7	29.0	220 38.7	43.3	Regulus	207 50.2	N11 56.5
T 08	350 11.5	289 36.6	43.6	9 44.5	12.2	160 36.3	28.9	235 40.9	43.3	Rigel	281 18.5	S 8 11.7
H 09	5 14.0	304 35.8 · ·	44.3	24 45.2 · ·	11.6	175 38.9 · ·	28.8	250 43.1 · ·	43.3	Rigil Kent.	140 00.2	S60 51.6
U 10	20 16.5	319 35.1	45.0	39 46.0	10.9	190 41.6	28.8	265 45.4	43.2	Sabik	102 19.5	S15 44.0
R 11	35 18.9	334 34.4	45.7	54 46.7	10.3	205 44.2	28.7	280 47.6	43.2			
S 12	50 21.4	349 33.6	N20 46.4	69 47.5	S10 09.6	220 46.8	S 2 28.7	295 49.9	N21 43.2	Schedar	349 48.6	N56 33.7
D 13	65 23.8	4 32.9	47.1	84 48.2	09.0	235 49.5	28.6	310 52.1	43.1	Shaula	96 30.2	S37 06.5
A 14	80 26.3	19 32.1	47.8	99 49.0	08.4	250 52.1	28.5	325 54.3	43.1	Sirius	258 39.6	S16 43.4
Y 15	95 28.8	34 31.4 · ·	48.5	114 49.7 · ·	07.7	265 54.7 · ·	28.5	340 56.6 · ·	43.1	Spica	158 37.7	S11 11.5
16	110 31.2	49 30.7	49.2	129 50.5	07.1	280 57.3	28.4	355 58.8	43.0	Suhail	222 57.3	S43 27.4
17	125 33.7	64 29.9	49.9	144 51.2	06.5	296 00.0	28.4	11 01.1	43.0			
18	140 36.2	79 29.2	N20 50.6	159 52.0	S10 05.8	311 02.6	S 2 28.3	26 03.3	N21 43.0	Vega	80 43.0	N38 47.0
19	155 38.6	94 28.4	51.2	174 52.7	05.2	326 05.2	28.2	41 05.5	43.0	Zuben'ubi	137 12.2	S16 04.0
20	170 41.1	109 27.7	51.9	189 53.5	04.5	341 07.8	28.2	56 07.8	42.9		SHA	Mer. Pass.
21	185 43.6	124 26.9 · ·	52.6	204 54.2 · ·	03.9	356 10.5 · ·	28.1	71 10.0 · ·	42.9		° ′	h m
22	200 46.0	139 26.2	53.3	219 55.0	03.3	11 13.1	28.1	86 12.3	42.9	Venus	301 07.3	12 41
23	215 48.5	154 25.5	54.0	234 55.7	02.6	26 15.7	28.0	101 14.5	42.8	Mars	20 27.9	7 22
	h m									Jupiter	170 19.4	21 19
Mer. Pass. 8 43.1		v −0.7 d 0.7		v 0.7 d 0.6		v 2.6 d 0.1		v 2.2 d 0.0		Saturn	245 36.4	16 20

2005 MAY 10, 11, 12 (TUES., WED., THURS.)

UT	SUN GHA	SUN Dec	MOON GHA	MOON v	MOON Dec	MOON d	MOON HP
d h	° ′	° ′	° ′	′	° ′	′	′
10 00	180 54.1	N17 35.5	161 33.9	9.6	N25 28.0	6.9	55.6
01	195 54.2	36.1	176 02.5	9.5	25 34.9	6.8	55.6
02	210 54.2	36.8	190 31.0	9.5	25 41.7	6.6	55.6
03	225 54.2 ..	37.5	204 59.5	9.4	25 48.3	6.5	55.5
04	240 54.2	38.1	219 27.9	9.4	25 54.8	6.3	55.5
05	255 54.3	38.8	233 56.3	9.4	26 01.1	6.2	55.5
06	270 54.3	N17 39.4	248 24.7	9.4	N26 07.3	6.1	55.5
07	285 54.3	40.1	262 53.1	9.3	26 13.4	5.9	55.5
08	300 54.3	40.7	277 21.4	9.3	26 19.3	5.8	55.4
09	315 54.3 ..	41.4	291 49.7	9.3	26 25.1	5.7	55.4
10	330 54.4	42.0	306 17.9	9.3	26 30.8	5.5	55.4
11	345 54.4	42.7	320 46.2	9.2	26 36.3	5.3	55.4
12	0 54.4	N17 43.3	335 14.4	9.2	N26 41.6	5.3	55.3
13	15 54.4	44.0	349 42.6	9.1	26 46.9	5.1	55.3
14	30 54.4	44.6	4 10.7	9.2	26 52.0	4.9	55.3
15	45 54.5 ..	45.3	18 38.9	9.1	26 56.9	4.8	55.3
16	60 54.5	45.9	33 07.0	9.1	27 01.7	4.7	55.3
17	75 54.5	46.6	47 35.1	9.0	27 06.4	4.5	55.2
18	90 54.5	N17 47.2	62 03.1	9.1	N27 10.9	4.3	55.2
19	105 54.5	47.9	76 31.2	9.0	27 15.2	4.3	55.2
20	120 54.6	48.5	90 59.2	9.0	27 19.5	4.1	55.2
21	135 54.6 ..	49.2	105 27.2	9.0	27 23.6	3.9	55.2
22	150 54.6	49.8	119 55.2	9.0	27 27.5	3.8	55.1
23	165 54.6	50.4	134 23.2	9.0	27 31.3	3.6	55.1
11 00	180 54.6	N17 51.1	148 51.2	9.0	N27 34.9	3.5	55.1
01	195 54.6	51.7	163 19.2	8.9	27 38.4	3.4	55.1
02	210 54.7	52.4	177 47.1	9.0	27 41.8	3.2	55.1
03	225 54.7 ..	53.0	192 15.1	8.9	27 45.0	3.1	55.1
04	240 54.7	53.7	206 43.0	9.0	27 48.1	2.9	55.0
05	255 54.7	54.3	221 11.0	8.9	27 51.0	2.8	55.0
06	270 54.7	N17 54.9	235 38.9	8.9	N27 53.8	2.6	55.0
07	285 54.7	55.6	250 06.8	9.0	27 56.4	2.5	55.0
08	300 54.8	56.2	264 34.8	8.9	27 58.9	2.3	55.0
09	315 54.8 ..	56.9	279 02.7	8.9	28 01.2	2.2	54.9
10	330 54.8	57.5	293 30.6	9.0	28 03.4	2.1	54.9
11	345 54.8	58.1	307 58.6	8.9	28 05.5	1.9	54.9
12	0 54.8	N17 58.8	322 26.5	8.9	N28 07.4	1.7	54.9
13	15 54.8	17 59.4	336 54.4	9.0	28 09.1	1.7	54.9
14	30 54.9	18 00.0	351 22.4	8.9	28 10.8	1.4	54.9
15	45 54.9 ..	00.7	5 50.3	9.0	28 12.2	1.3	54.8
16	60 54.9	01.3	20 18.3	9.0	28 13.5	1.2	54.8
17	75 54.9	02.0	34 46.3	8.9	28 14.7	1.1	54.8
18	90 54.9	N18 02.6	49 14.2	9.0	N28 15.8	0.8	54.8
19	105 54.9	03.2	63 42.2	9.1	28 16.6	0.8	54.8
20	120 54.9	03.9	78 10.3	9.0	28 17.4	0.6	54.8
21	135 54.9 ..	04.5	92 38.3	9.0	28 18.0	0.4	54.7
22	150 55.0	05.1	107 06.3	9.1	28 18.4	0.3	54.7
23	165 55.0	05.8	121 34.4	9.1	28 18.7	0.2	54.7
12 00	180 55.0	N18 06.4	136 02.5	9.1	N28 18.9	0.0	54.7
01	195 55.0	07.0	150 30.6	9.1	28 18.9	0.1	54.7
02	210 55.0	07.6	164 58.7	9.1	28 18.8	0.3	54.7
03	225 55.0 ..	08.3	179 26.8	9.2	28 18.5	0.4	54.6
04	240 55.0	08.9	193 55.0	9.2	28 18.1	0.5	54.6
05	255 55.0	09.5	208 23.2	9.2	28 17.6	0.7	54.6
06	270 55.0	N18 10.2	222 51.4	9.3	N28 16.9	0.9	54.6
07	285 55.1	10.8	237 19.7	9.3	28 16.0	0.9	54.6
08	300 55.1	11.4	251 48.0	9.3	28 15.1	1.2	54.6
09	315 55.1 ..	12.0	266 16.3	9.4	28 13.9	1.2	54.6
10	330 55.1	12.7	280 44.7	9.3	28 12.7	1.4	54.6
11	345 55.1	13.3	295 13.0	9.5	28 11.3	1.6	54.5
12	0 55.1	N18 13.9	309 41.5	9.4	N28 09.7	1.6	54.5
13	15 55.1	14.5	324 09.9	9.5	28 08.1	1.9	54.5
14	30 55.1	15.2	338 38.4	9.5	28 06.2	1.9	54.5
15	45 55.1 ..	15.8	353 06.9	9.6	28 04.3	2.1	54.5
16	60 55.1	16.4	7 35.5	9.6	28 02.2	2.2	54.5
17	75 55.1	17.0	22 04.1	9.7	28 00.0	2.4	54.5
18	90 55.1	N18 17.7	36 32.8	9.6	N27 57.6	2.5	54.5
19	105 55.2	18.3	51 01.4	9.8	27 55.1	2.7	54.4
20	120 55.2	18.9	65 30.2	9.8	27 52.4	2.7	54.4
21	135 55.2 ..	19.5	79 59.0	9.8	27 49.7	3.0	54.4
22	150 55.2	20.1	94 27.8	9.9	27 46.7	3.0	54.4
23	165 55.2	20.8	108 56.7	9.9	N27 43.7	3.2	54.4
	SD 15.9	d 0.6	SD 15.1	15.0			14.9

Twilight / Sunrise / Moonrise

Lat.	Twilight Naut.	Twilight Civil	Sunrise	Moonrise 10	Moonrise 11	Moonrise 12	Moonrise 13
°	h m	h m	h m	h m	h m	h m	h m
N 72	▭	▭	▭	▭	▭	▭	▭
N 70	////	////	01 22	▭	▭	▭	▭
68	////	////	02 08	▭	▭	▭	▭
66	////	00 22	02 38	▭	▭	▭	▭
64	////	01 34	03 00	02 02	▭	▭	▭
62	////	02 08	03 17	03 01	02 51		04 52
60	00 20	02 32	03 32	03 34	03 51	04 33	05 46
N 58	01 24	02 51	03 44	03 59	04 25	05 11	06 18
56	01 55	03 07	03 55	04 19	04 50	05 37	06 42
54	02 18	03 20	04 04	04 36	05 10	05 59	07 01
52	02 36	03 31	04 12	04 50	05 27	06 16	07 17
50	02 51	03 41	04 20	05 03	05 41	06 31	07 31
45	03 20	04 02	04 36	05 29	06 11	07 01	08 00
N 40	03 41	04 18	04 49	05 50	06 34	07 25	08 22
35	03 58	04 32	05 00	06 07	06 53	07 44	08 41
30	04 12	04 43	05 09	06 22	07 09	08 01	08 56
20	04 34	05 02	05 26	06 47	07 37	08 29	09 23
N 10	04 52	05 18	05 40	07 09	08 01	08 53	09 46
0	05 06	05 31	05 53	07 30	08 23	09 16	10 07
S 10	05 18	05 44	06 06	07 51	08 45	09 38	10 29
20	05 30	05 57	06 20	08 13	09 09	10 03	10 52
30	05 41	06 10	06 35	08 39	09 37	10 31	11 18
35	05 47	06 18	06 44	08 55	09 54	10 47	11 34
40	05 53	06 26	06 55	09 12	10 13	11 07	11 52
45	06 00	06 35	07 07	09 34	10 37	11 30	12 14
S 50	06 07	06 46	07 21	10 02	11 07	12 01	12 41
52	06 10	06 51	07 28	10 15	11 22	12 16	12 55
54	06 13	06 56	07 36	10 31	11 40	12 33	13 10
56	06 17	07 02	07 44	10 49	12 01	12 54	13 28
58	06 20	07 09	07 53	11 12	12 28	13 21	13 51
S 60	06 25	07 16	08 04	11 42	13 07	13 58	14 19

Sunset / Twilight / Moonset

Lat.	Sunset	Twilight Civil	Twilight Naut.	Moonset 10	Moonset 11	Moonset 12	Moonset 13
°	h m	h m	h m	h m	h m	h m	h m
N 72	▭	▭	▭	▭	▭	▭	▭
N 70	22 38	////	////	▭	▭	▭	▭
68	21 49	////	////	▭	▭	▭	▭
66	21 18	////	////	▭	▭	▭	▭
64	20 55	22 24	////	00 22	▭	▭	▭
62	20 37	21 48	////	25 24	01 24	▭	03 01
60	20 23	21 23	////	24 23	00 23	01 32	02 07
N 58	20 10	21 04	22 34	23 49	24 54	00 54	01 35
56	19 59	20 48	22 01	23 25	24 28	00 28	01 11
54	19 50	20 34	21 37	23 05	24 06	00 06	00 51
52	19 41	20 23	21 19	22 48	23 49	24 35	00 35
50	19 34	20 13	21 04	22 34	23 34	24 21	00 21
45	19 18	19 52	20 34	22 05	23 03	23 52	24 30
N 40	19 05	19 35	20 12	21 42	22 40	23 29	24 10
35	18 54	19 21	19 55	21 24	22 20	23 10	23 53
30	18 44	19 10	19 41	21 08	22 04	22 54	23 39
20	18 27	18 51	19 19	20 40	21 35	22 27	23 14
N 10	18 13	18 35	19 01	20 17	21 11	22 03	22 52
0	18 00	18 22	18 47	19 55	20 49	21 41	22 32
S 10	17 47	18 09	18 34	19 34	20 26	21 19	22 11
20	17 33	17 56	18 23	19 11	20 02	20 55	21 49
30	17 17	17 42	18 11	18 44	19 33	20 27	21 24
35	17 08	17 35	18 05	18 28	19 17	20 11	21 09
40	16 58	17 27	17 59	18 09	18 57	19 52	20 51
45	16 46	17 17	17 53	17 47	18 33	19 28	20 30
S 50	16 31	17 06	17 45	17 19	18 03	18 58	20 03
52	16 24	17 01	17 42	17 05	17 48	18 43	19 50
54	16 17	16 56	17 39	16 49	17 30	18 26	19 35
56	16 08	16 50	17 36	16 30	17 09	18 05	19 17
58	15 59	16 43	17 31	16 07	16 42	17 39	18 55
S 60	15 48	16 36	17 27	15 37	16 03	17 01	18 27

SUN / MOON

Day	SUN Eqn. of Time 00ʰ	SUN Eqn. of Time 12ʰ	SUN Mer. Pass.	MOON Mer. Pass. Upper	MOON Mer. Pass. Lower	Age	Phase
d	m s	m s	h m	h m	h m	d	%
10	03 37	03 38	11 56	13 43	01 16	02	5
11	03 38	03 39	11 56	14 36	02 09	03	10
12	03 40	03 40	11 56	15 29	03 02	04	16

Appendix C, Excerpts from the Nautical Almanac
CONVERSION OF ARC TO TIME

0°–59°	h m	60°–119°	h m	120°–179°	h m	180°–239°	h m	240°–299°	h m	300°–359°	h m	0′00 ′	0′00 m s	0′25 m s	0′50 m s	0′75 m s
0	0 00	60	4 00	120	8 00	180	12 00	240	16 00	300	20 00	0	0 00	0 01	0 02	0 03
1	0 04	61	4 04	121	8 04	181	12 04	241	16 04	301	20 04	1	0 04	0 05	0 06	0 07
2	0 08	62	4 08	122	8 08	182	12 08	242	16 08	302	20 08	2	0 08	0 09	0 10	0 11
3	0 12	63	4 12	123	8 12	183	12 12	243	16 12	303	20 12	3	0 12	0 13	0 14	0 15
4	0 16	64	4 16	124	8 16	184	12 16	244	16 16	304	20 16	4	0 16	0 17	0 18	0 19
5	0 20	65	4 20	125	8 20	185	12 20	245	16 20	305	20 20	5	0 20	0 21	0 22	0 23
6	0 24	66	4 24	126	8 24	186	12 24	246	16 24	306	20 24	6	0 24	0 25	0 26	0 27
7	0 28	67	4 28	127	8 28	187	12 28	247	16 28	307	20 28	7	0 28	0 29	0 30	0 31
8	0 32	68	4 32	128	8 32	188	12 32	248	16 32	308	20 32	8	0 32	0 33	0 34	0 35
9	0 36	69	4 36	129	8 36	189	12 36	249	16 36	309	20 36	9	0 36	0 37	0 38	0 39
10	0 40	70	4 40	130	8 40	190	12 40	250	16 40	310	20 40	10	0 40	0 41	0 42	0 43
11	0 44	71	4 44	131	8 44	191	12 44	251	16 44	311	20 44	11	0 44	0 45	0 46	0 47
12	0 48	72	4 48	132	8 48	192	12 48	252	16 48	312	20 48	12	0 48	0 49	0 50	0 51
13	0 52	73	4 52	133	8 52	193	12 52	253	16 52	313	20 52	13	0 52	0 53	0 54	0 55
14	0 56	74	4 56	134	8 56	194	12 56	254	16 56	314	20 56	14	0 56	0 57	0 58	0 59
15	1 00	75	5 00	135	9 00	195	13 00	255	17 00	315	21 00	15	1 00	1 01	1 02	1 03
16	1 04	76	5 04	136	9 04	196	13 04	256	17 04	316	21 04	16	1 04	1 05	1 06	1 07
17	1 08	77	5 08	137	9 08	197	13 08	257	17 08	317	21 08	17	1 08	1 09	1 10	1 11
18	1 12	78	5 12	138	9 12	198	13 12	258	17 12	318	21 12	18	1 12	1 13	1 14	1 15
19	1 16	79	5 16	139	9 16	199	13 16	259	17 16	319	21 16	19	1 16	1 17	1 18	1 19
20	1 20	80	5 20	140	9 20	200	13 20	260	17 20	320	21 20	20	1 20	1 21	1 22	1 23
21	1 24	81	5 24	141	9 24	201	13 24	261	17 24	321	21 24	21	1 24	1 25	1 26	1 27
22	1 28	82	5 28	142	9 28	202	13 28	262	17 28	322	21 28	22	1 28	1 29	1 30	1 31
23	1 32	83	5 32	143	9 32	203	13 32	263	17 32	323	21 32	23	1 32	1 33	1 34	1 35
24	1 36	84	5 36	144	9 36	204	13 36	264	17 36	324	21 36	24	1 36	1 37	1 38	1 39
25	1 40	85	5 40	145	9 40	205	13 40	265	17 40	325	21 40	25	1 40	1 41	1 42	1 43
26	1 44	86	5 44	146	9 44	206	13 44	266	17 44	326	21 44	26	1 44	1 45	1 46	1 47
27	1 48	87	5 48	147	9 48	207	13 48	267	17 48	327	21 48	27	1 48	1 49	1 50	1 51
28	1 52	88	5 52	148	9 52	208	13 52	268	17 52	328	21 52	28	1 52	1 53	1 54	1 55
29	1 56	89	5 56	149	9 56	209	13 56	269	17 56	329	21 56	29	1 56	1 57	1 58	1 59
30	2 00	90	6 00	150	10 00	210	14 00	270	18 00	330	22 00	30	2 00	2 01	2 02	2 03
31	2 04	91	6 04	151	10 04	211	14 04	271	18 04	331	22 04	31	2 04	2 05	2 06	2 07
32	2 08	92	6 08	152	10 08	212	14 08	272	18 08	332	22 08	32	2 08	2 09	2 10	2 11
33	2 12	93	6 12	153	10 12	213	14 12	273	18 12	333	22 12	33	2 12	2 13	2 14	2 15
34	2 16	94	6 16	154	10 16	214	14 16	274	18 16	334	22 16	34	2 16	2 17	2 18	2 19
35	2 20	95	6 20	155	10 20	215	14 20	275	18 20	335	22 20	35	2 20	2 21	2 22	2 23
36	2 24	96	6 24	156	10 24	216	14 24	276	18 24	336	22 24	36	2 24	2 25	2 26	2 27
37	2 28	97	6 28	157	10 28	217	14 28	277	18 28	337	22 28	37	2 28	2 29	2 30	2 31
38	2 32	98	6 32	158	10 32	218	14 32	278	18 32	338	22 32	38	2 32	2 33	2 34	2 35
39	2 36	99	6 36	159	10 36	219	14 36	279	18 36	339	22 36	39	2 36	2 37	2 38	2 39
40	2 40	100	6 40	160	10 40	220	14 40	280	18 40	340	22 40	40	2 40	2 41	2 42	2 43
41	2 44	101	6 44	161	10 44	221	14 44	281	18 44	341	22 44	41	2 44	2 45	2 46	2 47
42	2 48	102	6 48	162	10 48	222	14 48	282	18 48	342	22 48	42	2 48	2 49	2 50	2 51
43	2 52	103	6 52	163	10 52	223	14 52	283	18 52	343	22 52	43	2 52	2 53	2 54	2 55
44	2 56	104	6 56	164	10 56	224	14 56	284	18 56	344	22 56	44	2 56	2 57	2 58	2 59
45	3 00	105	7 00	165	11 00	225	15 00	285	19 00	345	23 00	45	3 00	3 01	3 02	3 03
46	3 04	106	7 04	166	11 04	226	15 04	286	19 04	346	23 04	46	3 04	3 05	3 06	3 07
47	3 08	107	7 08	167	11 08	227	15 08	287	19 08	347	23 08	47	3 08	3 09	3 10	3 11
48	3 12	108	7 12	168	11 12	228	15 12	288	19 12	348	23 12	48	3 12	3 13	3 14	3 15
49	3 16	109	7 16	169	11 16	229	15 16	289	19 16	349	23 16	49	3 16	3 17	3 18	3 19
50	3 20	110	7 20	170	11 20	230	15 20	290	19 20	350	23 20	50	3 20	3 21	3 22	3 23
51	3 24	111	7 24	171	11 24	231	15 24	291	19 24	351	23 24	51	3 24	3 25	3 26	3 27
52	3 28	112	7 28	172	11 28	232	15 28	292	19 28	352	23 28	52	3 28	3 29	3 30	3 31
53	3 32	113	7 32	173	11 32	233	15 32	293	19 32	353	23 32	53	3 32	3 33	3 34	3 35
54	3 36	114	7 36	174	11 36	234	15 36	294	19 36	354	23 36	54	3 36	3 37	3 38	3 39
55	3 40	115	7 40	175	11 40	235	15 40	295	19 40	355	23 40	55	3 40	3 41	3 42	3 43
56	3 44	116	7 44	176	11 44	236	15 44	296	19 44	356	23 44	56	3 44	3 45	3 46	3 47
57	3 48	117	7 48	177	11 48	237	15 48	297	19 48	357	23 48	57	3 48	3 49	3 50	3 51
58	3 52	118	7 52	178	11 52	238	15 52	298	19 52	358	23 52	58	3 52	3 53	3 54	3 55
59	3 56	119	7 56	179	11 56	239	15 56	299	19 56	359	23 56	59	3 56	3 57	3 58	3 59

The above table is for converting expressions in arc to their equivalent in time; its main use in this Almanac is for the conversion of longitude for application to LMT (*added* if *west*, *subtracted* if *east*) to give UT or vice versa, particularly in the case of sunrise, sunset, etc.

18ᵐ INCREMENTS AND CORRECTIONS 19ᵐ

m 18	SUN PLANETS	ARIES	MOON	v or d Corrⁿ	v or d Corrⁿ	v or d Corrⁿ	m 19	SUN PLANETS	ARIES	MOON	v or d Corrⁿ	v or d Corrⁿ	v or d Corrⁿ
s	° ′	° ′	° ′	′ ′	′ ′	′ ′	s	° ′	° ′	° ′	′ ′	′ ′	′ ′
00	4 30·0	4 30·7	4 17·7	0·0 0·0	6·0 1·9	12·0 3·7	00	4 45·0	4 45·8	4 32·0	0·0 0·0	6·0 2·0	12·0 3·9
01	4 30·3	4 31·0	4 17·9	0·1 0·0	6·1 1·9	12·1 3·7	01	4 45·3	4 46·0	4 32·3	0·1 0·0	6·1 2·0	12·1 3·9
02	4 30·5	4 31·2	4 18·2	0·2 0·1	6·2 1·9	12·2 3·8	02	4 45·5	4 46·3	4 32·5	0·2 0·1	6·2 2·0	12·2 4·0
03	4 30·8	4 31·5	4 18·4	0·3 0·1	6·3 1·9	12·3 3·8	03	4 45·8	4 46·5	4 32·7	0·3 0·1	6·3 2·0	12·3 4·0
04	4 31·0	4 31·7	4 18·7	0·4 0·1	6·4 2·0	12·4 3·8	04	4 46·0	4 46·8	4 33·0	0·4 0·1	6·4 2·1	12·4 4·0
05	4 31·3	4 32·0	4 18·9	0·5 0·2	6·5 2·0	12·5 3·9	05	4 46·3	4 47·0	4 33·2	0·5 0·2	6·5 2·1	12·5 4·1
06	4 31·5	4 32·2	4 19·1	0·6 0·2	6·6 2·0	12·6 3·9	06	4 46·5	4 47·3	4 33·4	0·6 0·2	6·6 2·1	12·6 4·1
07	4 31·8	4 32·5	4 19·4	0·7 0·2	6·7 2·1	12·7 3·9	07	4 46·8	4 47·5	4 33·7	0·7 0·2	6·7 2·2	12·7 4·1
08	4 32·0	4 32·7	4 19·6	0·8 0·2	6·8 2·1	12·8 3·9	08	4 47·0	4 47·8	4 33·9	0·8 0·3	6·8 2·2	12·8 4·2
09	4 32·3	4 33·0	4 19·8	0·9 0·3	6·9 2·1	12·9 4·0	09	4 47·3	4 48·0	4 34·2	0·9 0·3	6·9 2·2	12·9 4·2
10	4 32·5	4 33·2	4 20·1	1·0 0·3	7·0 2·2	13·0 4·0	10	4 47·5	4 48·3	4 34·4	1·0 0·3	7·0 2·3	13·0 4·2
11	4 32·8	4 33·5	4 20·3	1·1 0·3	7·1 2·2	13·1 4·0	11	4 47·8	4 48·5	4 34·6	1·1 0·4	7·1 2·3	13·1 4·3
12	4 33·0	4 33·7	4 20·6	1·2 0·4	7·2 2·2	13·2 4·1	12	4 48·0	4 48·8	4 34·9	1·2 0·4	7·2 2·3	13·2 4·3
13	4 33·3	4 34·0	4 20·8	1·3 0·4	7·3 2·3	13·3 4·1	13	4 48·3	4 49·0	4 35·1	1·3 0·4	7·3 2·4	13·3 4·3
14	4 33·5	4 34·2	4 21·0	1·4 0·4	7·4 2·3	13·4 4·1	14	4 48·5	4 49·3	4 35·4	1·4 0·5	7·4 2·4	13·4 4·4
15	4 33·8	4 34·5	4 21·3	1·5 0·5	7·5 2·3	13·5 4·2	15	4 48·8	4 49·5	4 35·6	1·5 0·5	7·5 2·4	13·5 4·4
16	4 34·0	4 34·8	4 21·5	1·6 0·5	7·6 2·3	13·6 4·2	16	4 49·0	4 49·8	4 35·8	1·6 0·5	7·6 2·5	13·6 4·4
17	4 34·3	4 35·0	4 21·8	1·7 0·5	7·7 2·4	13·7 4·2	17	4 49·3	4 50·0	4 36·1	1·7 0·6	7·7 2·5	13·7 4·5
18	4 34·5	4 35·3	4 22·0	1·8 0·6	7·8 2·4	13·8 4·3	18	4 49·5	4 50·3	4 36·3	1·8 0·6	7·8 2·5	13·8 4·5
19	4 34·8	4 35·5	4 22·2	1·9 0·6	7·9 2·4	13·9 4·3	19	4 49·8	4 50·5	4 36·6	1·9 0·6	7·9 2·6	13·9 4·5
20	4 35·0	4 35·8	4 22·5	2·0 0·6	8·0 2·5	14·0 4·3	20	4 50·0	4 50·8	4 36·8	2·0 0·7	8·0 2·6	14·0 4·6
21	4 35·3	4 36·0	4 22·7	2·1 0·6	8·1 2·5	14·1 4·3	21	4 50·3	4 51·0	4 37·0	2·1 0·7	8·1 2·6	14·1 4·6
22	4 35·5	4 36·3	4 22·9	2·2 0·7	8·2 2·5	14·2 4·4	22	4 50·5	4 51·3	4 37·3	2·2 0·7	8·2 2·7	14·2 4·6
23	4 35·8	4 36·5	4 23·2	2·3 0·7	8·3 2·6	14·3 4·4	23	4 50·8	4 51·5	4 37·5	2·3 0·7	8·3 2·7	14·3 4·6
24	4 36·0	4 36·8	4 23·4	2·4 0·7	8·4 2·6	14·4 4·4	24	4 51·0	4 51·8	4 37·7	2·4 0·8	8·4 2·7	14·4 4·7
25	4 36·3	4 37·0	4 23·7	2·5 0·8	8·5 2·6	14·5 4·5	25	4 51·3	4 52·0	4 38·0	2·5 0·8	8·5 2·8	14·5 4·7
26	4 36·5	4 37·3	4 23·9	2·6 0·8	8·6 2·7	14·6 4·5	26	4 51·5	4 52·3	4 38·2	2·6 0·8	8·6 2·8	14·6 4·7
27	4 36·8	4 37·5	4 24·1	2·7 0·8	8·7 2·7	14·7 4·5	27	4 51·8	4 52·5	4 38·5	2·7 0·9	8·7 2·8	14·7 4·8
28	4 37·0	4 37·8	4 24·4	2·8 0·9	8·8 2·7	14·8 4·6	28	4 52·0	4 52·8	4 38·7	2·8 0·9	8·8 2·9	14·8 4·8
29	4 37·3	4 38·0	4 24·6	2·9 0·9	8·9 2·7	14·9 4·6	29	4 52·3	4 53·1	4 38·9	2·9 0·9	8·9 2·9	14·9 4·8
30	4 37·5	4 38·3	4 24·9	3·0 0·9	9·0 2·8	15·0 4·6	30	4 52·5	4 53·3	4 39·2	3·0 1·0	9·0 2·9	15·0 4·9
31	4 37·8	4 38·5	4 25·1	3·1 1·0	9·1 2·8	15·1 4·7	31	4 52·8	4 53·6	4 39·4	3·1 1·0	9·1 3·0	15·1 4·9
32	4 38·0	4 38·8	4 25·3	3·2 1·0	9·2 2·8	15·2 4·7	32	4 53·0	4 53·8	4 39·7	3·2 1·0	9·2 3·0	15·2 4·9
33	4 38·3	4 39·0	4 25·6	3·3 1·0	9·3 2·9	15·3 4·7	33	4 53·3	4 54·1	4 39·9	3·3 1·1	9·3 3·0	15·3 5·0
34	4 38·5	4 39·3	4 25·8	3·4 1·0	9·4 2·9	15·4 4·7	34	4 53·5	4 54·3	4 40·1	3·4 1·1	9·4 3·1	15·4 5·0
35	4 38·8	4 39·5	4 26·1	3·5 1·1	9·5 2·9	15·5 4·8	35	4 53·8	4 54·6	4 40·4	3·5 1·1	9·5 3·1	15·5 5·0
36	4 39·0	4 39·8	4 26·3	3·6 1·1	9·6 3·0	15·6 4·8	36	4 54·0	4 54·8	4 40·6	3·6 1·2	9·6 3·1	15·6 5·1
37	4 39·3	4 40·0	4 26·5	3·7 1·1	9·7 3·0	15·7 4·8	37	4 54·3	4 55·1	4 40·8	3·7 1·2	9·7 3·2	15·7 5·1
38	4 39·5	4 40·3	4 26·8	3·8 1·2	9·8 3·0	15·8 4·9	38	4 54·5	4 55·3	4 41·1	3·8 1·2	9·8 3·2	15·8 5·1
39	4 39·8	4 40·5	4 27·0	3·9 1·2	9·9 3·1	15·9 4·9	39	4 54·8	4 55·6	4 41·3	3·9 1·3	9·9 3·2	15·9 5·2
40	4 40·0	4 40·8	4 27·2	4·0 1·2	10·0 3·1	16·0 4·9	40	4 55·0	4 55·8	4 41·6	4·0 1·3	10·0 3·3	16·0 5·2
41	4 40·3	4 41·0	4 27·5	4·1 1·3	10·1 3·1	16·1 5·0	41	4 55·3	4 56·1	4 41·8	4·1 1·3	10·1 3·3	16·1 5·2
42	4 40·5	4 41·3	4 27·7	4·2 1·3	10·2 3·1	16·2 5·0	42	4 55·5	4 56·3	4 42·0	4·2 1·4	10·2 3·3	16·2 5·3
43	4 40·8	4 41·5	4 28·0	4·3 1·3	10·3 3·2	16·3 5·0	43	4 55·8	4 56·6	4 42·3	4·3 1·4	10·3 3·3	16·3 5·3
44	4 41·0	4 41·8	4 28·2	4·4 1·4	10·4 3·2	16·4 5·1	44	4 56·0	4 56·8	4 42·5	4·4 1·4	10·4 3·4	16·4 5·3
45	4 41·3	4 42·0	4 28·4	4·5 1·4	10·5 3·2	16·5 5·1	45	4 56·3	4 57·1	4 42·8	4·5 1·5	10·5 3·4	16·5 5·4
46	4 41·5	4 42·3	4 28·7	4·6 1·4	10·6 3·3	16·6 5·1	46	4 56·5	4 57·3	4 43·0	4·6 1·5	10·6 3·4	16·6 5·4
47	4 41·8	4 42·5	4 28·9	4·7 1·4	10·7 3·3	16·7 5·1	47	4 56·8	4 57·6	4 43·2	4·7 1·5	10·7 3·5	16·7 5·4
48	4 42·0	4 42·8	4 29·2	4·8 1·5	10·8 3·3	16·8 5·2	48	4 57·0	4 57·8	4 43·5	4·8 1·6	10·8 3·5	16·8 5·5
49	4 42·3	4 43·0	4 29·4	4·9 1·5	10·9 3·4	16·9 5·2	49	4 57·3	4 58·1	4 43·7	4·9 1·6	10·9 3·5	16·9 5·5
50	4 42·5	4 43·3	4 29·6	5·0 1·5	11·0 3·4	17·0 5·2	50	4 57·5	4 58·3	4 43·9	5·0 1·6	11·0 3·6	17·0 5·5
51	4 42·8	4 43·5	4 29·9	5·1 1·6	11·1 3·4	17·1 5·3	51	4 57·8	4 58·6	4 44·2	5·1 1·7	11·1 3·6	17·1 5·6
52	4 43·0	4 43·8	4 30·1	5·2 1·6	11·2 3·5	17·2 5·3	52	4 58·0	4 58·8	4 44·4	5·2 1·7	11·2 3·6	17·2 5·6
53	4 43·3	4 44·0	4 30·3	5·3 1·6	11·3 3·5	17·3 5·3	53	4 58·3	4 59·1	4 44·7	5·3 1·7	11·3 3·7	17·3 5·6
54	4 43·5	4 44·3	4 30·6	5·4 1·7	11·4 3·5	17·4 5·4	54	4 58·5	4 59·3	4 44·9	5·4 1·8	11·4 3·7	17·4 5·7
55	4 43·8	4 44·5	4 30·8	5·5 1·7	11·5 3·5	17·5 5·4	55	4 58·8	4 59·6	4 45·1	5·5 1·8	11·5 3·7	17·5 5·7
56	4 44·0	4 44·8	4 31·1	5·6 1·7	11·6 3·6	17·6 5·4	56	4 59·0	4 59·8	4 45·4	5·6 1·8	11·6 3·8	17·6 5·7
57	4 44·3	4 45·0	4 31·3	5·7 1·8	11·7 3·6	17·7 5·5	57	4 59·3	5 00·1	4 45·6	5·7 1·9	11·7 3·8	17·7 5·8
58	4 44·5	4 45·3	4 31·5	5·8 1·8	11·8 3·6	17·8 5·5	58	4 59·5	5 00·3	4 45·9	5·8 1·9	11·8 3·8	17·8 5·8
59	4 44·8	4 45·5	4 31·8	5·9 1·8	11·9 3·7	17·9 5·5	59	4 59·8	5 00·6	4 46·1	5·9 1·9	11·9 3·9	17·9 5·8
60	4 45·0	4 45·8	4 32·0	6·0 1·9	12·0 3·7	18·0 5·6	60	5 00·0	5 00·8	4 46·3	6·0 2·0	12·0 3·9	18·0 5·9

POLARIS (POLE STAR) TABLES, 2005

FOR DETERMINING LATITUDE FROM SEXTANT ALTITUDE AND FOR AZIMUTH

LHA ARIES	120° – 129°	130° – 139°	140° – 149°	150° – 159°	160° – 169°	170° – 179°	180° – 189°	190° – 199°	200° – 209°	210° – 219°	220° – 229°	230° – 239°
	a_0	a_0	a_0	a_0	a_0	a_0	a_0	a_0	a_0	a_0	a_0	a_0
°	° ′	° ′	° ′	° ′	° ′	° ′	° ′	° ′	° ′	° ′	° ′	° ′
0	0 52·2	0 59·6	1 07·0	1 14·1	1 20·7	1 26·7	1 31·9	1 36·0	1 39·0	1 40·8	1 41·4	1 40·7
1	52·9	1 00·3	07·7	14·8	21·4	27·3	32·3	36·4	39·3	41·0	41·4	40·5
2	53·6	01·1	08·4	15·5	22·0	27·8	32·8	36·7	39·5	41·1	41·4	40·4
3	54·4	01·8	09·1	16·1	22·6	28·4	33·2	37·0	39·7	41·1	41·3	40·2
4	55·1	02·5	09·8	16·8	23·2	28·9	33·6	37·3	39·9	41·2	41·3	40·0
5	0 55·9	1 03·3	1 10·6	1 17·5	1 23·8	1 29·4	1 34·1	1 37·7	1 40·1	1 41·3	1 41·2	1 39·9
6	56·6	04·0	11·3	18·1	24·4	29·9	34·5	38·0	40·3	41·3	41·1	39·6
7	57·3	04·8	12·0	18·8	25·0	30·4	34·9	38·2	40·4	41·4	41·0	39·4
8	58·1	05·5	12·7	19·4	25·6	30·9	35·3	38·5	40·6	41·4	40·9	39·2
9	58·8	06·2	13·4	20·1	26·2	31·4	35·6	38·8	40·7	41·4	40·8	39·0
10	0 59·6	1 07·0	1 14·1	1 20·7	1 26·7	1 31·9	1 36·0	1 39·0	1 40·8	1 41·4	1 40·7	1 38·7

Lat.	a_1	a_1	a_1	a_1	a_1	a_1	a_1	a_1	a_1	a_1	a_1	a_1
°	′	′	′	′	′	′	′	′	′	′	′	′
0	0·3	0·3	0·3	0·3	0·4	0·4	0·5	0·5	0·6	0·6	0·6	0·6
10	·3	·3	·4	·4	·4	·5	·5	·6	·6	·6	·6	·6
20	·4	·4	·4	·4	·5	·5	·5	·6	·6	·6	·6	·6
30	·4	·4	·4	·5	·5	·5	·5	·6	·6	·6	·6	·6
40	0·5	0·5	0·5	0·5	0·5	0·6	0·6	0·6	0·6	0·6	0·6	0·6
45	·5	·5	·6	·6	·6	·6	·6	·6	·6	·6	·6	·6
50	·6	·6	·6	·6	·6	·6	·6	·6	·6	·6	·6	·6
55	·7	·7	·7	·7	·6	·6	·6	·6	·6	·6	·6	·6
60	·7	·7	·7	·7	·7	·7	·6	·6	·6	·6	·6	·6
62	0·8	0·8	0·8	0·7	0·7	0·7	0·7	0·6	0·6	0·6	0·6	0·6
64	·8	·8	·8	·8	·7	·7	·7	·6	·6	·6	·6	·6
66	·9	·9	·9	·8	·8	·7	·7	·6	·6	·6	·6	·6
68	0·9	0·9	0·9	0·9	0·8	0·8	0·7	0·7	0·6	0·6	0·6	0·6

Month	a_2	a_2	a_2	a_2	a_2	a_2	a_2	a_2	a_2	a_2	a_2	a_2
	′	′	′	′	′	′	′	′	′	′	′	′
Jan.	0·6	0·6	0·6	0·6	0·6	0·5	0·5	0·5	0·5	0·5	0·5	0·5
Feb.	·8	·8	·7	·7	·7	·6	·6	·5	·5	·5	·4	·4
Mar.	0·9	0·9	0·9	0·8	·8	·8	·7	·7	·6	·6	·5	·5
Apr.	1·0	1·0	1·0	1·0	0·9	0·9	0·9	0·8	0·7	0·7	0·6	0·6
May	0·9	1·0	1·0	1·0	1·0	1·0	1·0	0·9	0·9	·8	·8	·7
June	·8	0·9	0·9	1·0	1·0	1·0	1·0	1·0	1·0	0·9	·9	·8
July	0·7	0·7	0·8	0·8	0·9	0·9	0·9	1·0	1·0	1·0	0·9	0·9
Aug.	·5	·5	·6	·7	·7	·8	·8	0·9	0·9	0·9	·9	·9
Sept.	·3	·4	·4	·5	·5	·6	·6	·7	·7	·8	·8	·9
Oct.	0·3	0·3	0·3	0·3	0·3	0·4	0·4	0·5	0·6	0·6	0·7	0·7
Nov.	·2	·2	·2	·2	·2	·2	·3	·3	·4	·4	·5	·6
Dec.	0·3	0·2	0·2	0·2	0·1	0·1	0·2	0·2	0·2	0·3	0·3	0·4

Lat.	AZIMUTH											
°	°	°	°	°	°	°	°	°	°	°	°	°
0	359·3	359·3	359·3	359·4	359·4	359·5	359·6	359·7	359·8	359·9	0·1	0·2
20	359·2	359·2	359·3	359·3	359·4	359·5	359·6	359·7	359·8	359·9	0·1	0·2
40	359·1	359·1	359·1	359·2	359·3	359·4	359·5	359·6	359·8	359·9	0·1	0·2
50	358·9	358·9	358·9	359·0	359·1	359·2	359·4	359·6	359·7	359·9	0·1	0·3
55	358·8	358·8	358·8	358·9	359·0	359·1	359·3	359·5	359·7	359·9	0·1	0·3
60	358·6	358·6	358·6	358·7	358·9	359·0	359·2	359·4	359·7	359·9	0·1	0·4
65	358·3	358·3	358·4	358·5	358·7	358·8	359·1	359·3	359·6	359·9	0·2	0·4

ILLUSTRATION

On 2005 April 21 at 23ʰ 18ᵐ 56ˢ UT in longitude W 37° 14′ the apparent altitude (corrected for refraction), H_O, of Polaris was 49° 31·6

From the daily pages:	°	′
GHA Aries (23ʰ)	195	06·6
Increment (18ᵐ 56ˢ)	4	44·8
Longitude (west)	−37	14
LHA Aries	162	37

	°	′
H_O	49	31·6
a_0 (argument 162° 37′)	1	22·4
a_1 (Lat 50° approx.)		0·6
a_2 (April)		0·9
Sum − 1° = Lat =	49	55·5

ALTITUDE CORRECTION TABLES 0°–35°— MOON

App. Alt.	0°–4° Corrⁿ	5°–9° Corrⁿ	10°–14° Corrⁿ	15°–19° Corrⁿ	20°–24° Corrⁿ	25°–29° Corrⁿ	30°–34° Corrⁿ	App. Alt.
00	0° 34.5	5° 58.2	10° 62.1	15° 62.8	20° 62.2	25° 60.8	30° 58.9	00
10	36.5	58.5	62.2	62.8	62.2	60.8	58.8	10
20	38.3	58.7	62.2	62.8	62.1	60.7	58.8	20
30	40.0	58.9	62.3	62.8	62.1	60.7	58.7	30
40	41.5	59.1	62.3	62.8	62.0	60.6	58.6	40
50	42.9	59.3	62.4	62.7	62.0	60.6	58.5	50
00	1° 44.2	6° 59.5	11° 62.4	16° 62.7	21° 62.0	26° 60.5	31° 58.5	00
10	45.4	59.7	62.4	62.7	61.9	60.4	58.4	10
20	46.5	59.9	62.5	62.7	61.9	60.4	58.3	20
30	47.5	60.0	62.5	62.7	61.9	60.3	58.2	30
40	48.4	60.2	62.5	62.7	61.8	60.3	58.2	40
50	49.3	60.3	62.6	62.7	61.8	60.2	58.1	50
00	2° 50.1	7° 60.5	12° 62.6	17° 62.7	22° 61.7	27° 60.1	32° 58.0	00
10	50.8	60.6	62.6	62.6	61.7	60.1	57.9	10
20	51.5	60.7	62.6	62.6	61.6	60.0	57.8	20
30	52.2	60.9	62.7	62.6	61.6	59.9	57.8	30
40	52.8	61.0	62.7	62.6	61.6	59.9	57.7	40
50	53.4	61.1	62.7	62.6	61.5	59.8	57.6	50
00	3° 53.9	8° 61.2	13° 62.7	18° 62.5	23° 61.5	28° 59.7	33° 57.5	00
10	54.4	61.3	62.7	62.5	61.4	59.7	57.4	10
20	54.9	61.4	62.7	62.5	61.4	59.6	57.4	20
30	55.3	61.5	62.8	62.5	61.3	59.5	57.3	30
40	55.7	61.6	62.8	62.4	61.3	59.5	57.2	40
50	56.1	61.6	62.8	62.4	61.2	59.4	57.1	50
00	4° 56.4	9° 61.7	14° 62.8	19° 62.4	24° 61.2	29° 59.3	34° 57.0	00
10	56.8	61.8	62.8	62.4	61.1	59.3	56.9	10
20	57.1	61.9	62.8	62.3	61.1	59.2	56.9	20
30	57.4	61.9	62.8	62.3	61.0	59.1	56.8	30
40	57.7	62.0	62.8	62.3	61.0	59.1	56.7	40
50	58.0	62.1	62.8	62.2	60.9	59.0	56.6	50

HP	L	U	L	U	L	U	L	U	L	U	L	U	L	U	HP
54.0	0.3	0.9	0.3	0.9	0.4	1.0	0.5	1.1	0.6	1.2	0.7	1.3	0.9	1.5	54.0
54.3	0.7	1.1	0.7	1.2	0.8	1.2	0.8	1.3	0.9	1.4	1.1	1.5	1.2	1.7	54.3
54.6	1.1	1.4	1.1	1.4	1.1	1.4	1.2	1.5	1.3	1.6	1.4	1.7	1.5	1.8	54.6
54.9	1.4	1.6	1.5	1.6	1.5	1.6	1.6	1.7	1.6	1.8	1.8	1.9	1.9	2.0	54.9
55.2	1.8	1.8	1.8	1.8	1.9	1.8	1.9	1.9	2.0	2.0	2.1	2.1	2.2	2.2	55.2
55.5	2.2	2.0	2.2	2.0	2.3	2.1	2.3	2.1	2.4	2.2	2.4	2.3	2.5	2.4	55.5
55.8	2.6	2.2	2.6	2.2	2.6	2.3	2.7	2.3	2.7	2.4	2.8	2.4	2.9	2.5	55.8
56.1	3.0	2.4	3.0	2.5	3.0	2.5	3.0	2.5	3.1	2.6	3.1	2.6	3.2	2.7	56.1
56.4	3.3	2.7	3.4	2.7	3.4	2.7	3.4	2.7	3.4	2.8	3.5	2.8	3.5	2.9	56.4
56.7	3.7	2.9	3.7	2.9	3.8	2.9	3.8	2.9	3.8	3.0	3.8	3.0	3.9	3.0	56.7
57.0	4.1	3.1	4.1	3.1	4.1	3.1	4.1	3.1	4.2	3.2	4.2	3.2	4.2	3.2	57.0
57.3	4.5	3.3	4.5	3.3	4.5	3.3	4.5	3.3	4.5	3.3	4.5	3.4	4.6	3.4	57.3
57.6	4.9	3.5	4.9	3.5	4.9	3.5	4.9	3.5	4.9	3.5	4.9	3.5	4.9	3.6	57.6
57.9	5.3	3.8	5.3	3.8	5.2	3.8	5.2	3.7	5.2	3.7	5.2	3.7	5.2	3.7	57.9
58.2	5.6	4.0	5.6	4.0	5.6	4.0	5.6	4.0	5.6	3.9	5.6	3.9	5.6	3.9	58.2
58.5	6.0	4.2	6.0	4.2	6.0	4.2	6.0	4.2	6.0	4.1	5.9	4.1	5.9	4.1	58.5
58.8	6.4	4.4	6.4	4.4	6.4	4.4	6.3	4.4	6.3	4.3	6.3	4.3	6.2	4.2	58.8
59.1	6.8	4.6	6.8	4.6	6.7	4.6	6.7	4.6	6.7	4.5	6.6	4.5	6.6	4.4	59.1
59.4	7.2	4.8	7.1	4.8	7.1	4.8	7.1	4.8	7.0	4.7	7.0	4.7	6.9	4.6	59.4
59.7	7.5	5.1	7.5	5.0	7.5	5.0	7.5	5.0	7.4	4.9	7.3	4.8	7.2	4.8	59.7
60.0	7.9	5.3	7.9	5.3	7.9	5.2	7.8	5.2	7.8	5.1	7.7	5.0	7.6	4.9	60.0
60.3	8.3	5.5	8.3	5.5	8.2	5.4	8.2	5.4	8.1	5.3	8.0	5.2	7.9	5.1	60.3
60.6	8.7	5.7	8.7	5.7	8.6	5.7	8.6	5.6	8.5	5.5	8.4	5.4	8.2	5.3	60.6
60.9	9.1	5.9	9.0	5.9	9.0	5.9	8.9	5.8	8.8	5.7	8.7	5.6	8.6	5.4	60.9
61.2	9.5	6.2	9.4	6.1	9.4	6.1	9.3	6.0	9.2	5.9	9.1	5.8	8.9	5.6	61.2
61.5	9.8	6.4	9.8	6.3	9.7	6.3	9.7	6.2	9.5	6.1	9.4	5.9	9.2	5.8	61.5

DIP

Ht. of Eye (m)	Corrⁿ	Ht. of Eye (ft)	Ht. of Eye (m)	Corrⁿ	Ht. of Eye (ft)
2.4	−2.8	8.0	9.5	−5.5	31.5
2.6	−2.9	8.6	9.9	−5.6	32.7
2.8	−3.0	9.2	10.3	−5.7	33.9
3.0	−3.1	9.8	10.6	−5.8	35.1
3.2	−3.2	10.5	11.0	−5.9	36.3
3.4	−3.3	11.2	11.4	−6.0	37.6
3.6	−3.4	11.9	11.8	−6.1	38.9
3.8	−3.5	12.6	12.2	−6.2	40.1
4.0	−3.6	13.3	12.6	−6.3	41.5
4.3	−3.7	14.1	13.0	−6.4	42.8
4.5	−3.8	14.9	13.4	−6.5	44.2
4.7	−3.9	15.7	13.8	−6.6	45.5
5.0	−4.0	16.5	14.2	−6.7	46.9
5.2	−4.1	17.4	14.7	−6.8	48.4
5.5	−4.2	18.3	15.1	−6.9	49.8
5.8	−4.3	19.1	15.5	−7.0	51.3
6.1	−4.4	20.1	16.0	−7.1	52.8
6.3	−4.5	21.0	16.5	−7.2	54.3
6.6	−4.6	22.0	16.9	−7.3	55.8
6.9	−4.7	22.9	17.4	−7.4	57.4
7.2	−4.8	23.9	17.9	−7.5	58.9
7.5	−4.9	24.9	18.4	−7.6	60.5
7.9	−5.0	26.0	18.8	−7.7	62.1
8.2	−5.1	27.1	19.3	−7.8	63.8
8.5	−5.2	28.1	19.8	−7.9	65.4
8.8	−5.3	29.2	20.4	−8.0	67.1
9.2	−5.4	30.4	20.9	−8.1	68.8
9.5		31.5	21.4		70.5

MOON CORRECTION TABLE

The correction is in two parts; the first correction is taken from the upper part of the table with argument apparent altitude, and the second from the lower part, with argument HP, in the same column as that from which the first correction was taken. Separate corrections are given in the lower part for lower (L) and upper(U) limbs. All corrections are to be **added** to apparent altitude, *but 30′ is to be subtracted from the altitude of the upper limb.*

For corrections for pressure and temperature see page A4.

For bubble sextant observations ignore dip, take the mean of upper and lower limb corrections and subtract 15′ from the altitude.

App. Alt. = Apparent altitude = Sextant altitude corrected for index error and dip.

ALTITUDE CORRECTION TABLES 35°–90°— MOON

App. Alt.	35°–39° Corrⁿ	40°–44° Corrⁿ	45°–49° Corrⁿ	50°–54° Corrⁿ	55°–59° Corrⁿ	60°–64° Corrⁿ	65°–69° Corrⁿ	70°–74° Corrⁿ	75°–79° Corrⁿ	80°–84° Corrⁿ	85°–89° Corrⁿ	App. Alt.
00	35 56.5	40 53.7	45 50.5	50 46.9	55 43.1	60 38.9	65 34.6	70 30.0	75 25.3	80 20.5	85 15.6	00
10	56.4	53.6	50.4	46.8	42.9	38.8	34.4	29.9	25.2	20.4	15.5	10
20	56.3	53.5	50.2	46.7	42.8	38.7	34.3	29.7	25.0	20.2	15.3	20
30	56.2	53.4	50.1	46.5	42.7	38.5	34.1	29.6	24.9	20.0	15.1	30
40	56.2	53.3	50.0	46.4	42.5	38.4	34.0	29.4	24.7	19.9	15.0	40
50	56.1	53.2	49.9	46.3	42.4	38.2	33.8	29.3	24.5	19.7	14.8	50
00	36 56.0	41 53.1	46 49.8	51 46.2	56 42.3	61 38.1	66 33.7	71 29.1	76 24.4	81 19.6	86 14.6	00
10	55.9	53.0	49.7	46.0	42.1	37.9	33.5	29.0	24.2	19.4	14.5	10
20	55.8	52.9	49.5	45.9	42.0	37.8	33.4	28.8	24.1	19.2	14.3	20
30	55.7	52.8	49.4	45.8	41.9	37.7	33.2	28.7	23.9	19.1	14.2	30
40	55.6	52.6	49.3	45.7	41.7	37.5	33.1	28.5	23.8	18.9	14.0	40
50	55.5	52.5	49.2	45.5	41.6	37.4	32.9	28.3	23.6	18.7	13.8	50
00	37 55.4	42 52.4	47 49.1	52 45.4	57 41.4	62 37.2	67 32.8	72 28.2	77 23.4	82 18.6	87 13.7	00
10	55.3	52.3	49.0	45.3	41.3	37.1	32.6	28.0	23.3	18.4	13.5	10
20	55.2	52.2	48.8	45.2	41.2	36.9	32.5	27.9	23.1	18.2	13.3	20
30	55.1	52.1	48.7	45.0	41.0	36.8	32.3	27.7	22.9	18.1	13.2	30
40	55.0	52.0	48.6	44.9	40.9	36.6	32.2	27.6	22.8	17.9	13.0	40
50	55.0	51.9	48.5	44.8	40.8	36.5	32.0	27.4	22.6	17.8	12.8	50
00	38 54.9	43 51.8	48 48.4	53 44.6	58 40.6	63 36.4	68 31.9	73 27.2	78 22.5	83 17.6	88 12.7	00
10	54.8	51.7	48.3	44.5	40.5	36.2	31.7	27.1	22.3	17.4	12.5	10
20	54.7	51.6	48.1	44.4	40.3	36.1	31.6	26.9	22.1	17.3	12.3	20
30	54.6	51.5	48.0	44.2	40.2	35.9	31.4	26.8	22.0	17.1	12.2	30
40	54.5	51.4	47.9	44.1	40.1	35.8	31.3	26.6	21.8	16.9	12.0	40
50	54.4	51.2	47.8	44.0	39.9	35.6	31.1	26.5	21.7	16.8	11.8	50
00	39 54.3	44 51.1	49 47.7	54 43.9	59 39.8	64 35.5	69 31.0	74 26.3	79 21.5	84 16.6	89 11.7	00
10	54.2	51.0	47.5	43.7	39.6	35.3	30.8	26.1	21.3	16.4	11.5	10
20	54.1	50.9	47.4	43.6	39.5	35.2	30.7	26.0	21.2	16.3	11.4	20
30	54.0	50.8	47.3	43.5	39.4	35.0	30.5	25.8	21.0	16.1	11.2	30
40	53.9	50.7	47.2	43.3	39.2	34.9	30.4	25.7	20.9	16.0	11.0	40
50	53.8	50.6	47.0	43.2	39.1	34.7	30.2	25.5	20.7	15.8	10.9	50

HP	L	U	L	U	L	U	L	U	L	U	L	U	L	U	L	U	L	U	L	U	L	U	HP
54.0	1.1	1.7	1.3	1.9	1.5	2.1	1.7	2.4	2.0	2.6	2.3	2.9	2.6	3.2	2.9	3.5	3.2	3.8	3.5	4.1	3.8	4.5	54.0
54.3	1.4	1.8	1.6	2.0	1.8	2.2	2.0	2.5	2.2	2.7	2.5	3.0	2.8	3.2	3.1	3.5	3.3	3.8	3.6	4.1	3.9	4.4	54.3
54.6	1.7	2.0	1.9	2.2	2.1	2.4	2.3	2.6	2.5	2.8	2.7	3.0	3.0	3.3	3.2	3.5	3.5	3.8	3.8	4.0	4.0	4.3	54.6
54.9	2.0	2.2	2.2	2.3	2.3	2.5	2.5	2.7	2.7	2.9	2.9	3.1	3.2	3.3	3.4	3.5	3.6	3.8	3.9	4.0	4.1	4.3	54.9
55.2	2.3	2.3	2.5	2.4	2.6	2.6	2.8	2.8	3.0	2.9	3.2	3.1	3.4	3.3	3.6	3.5	3.8	3.7	4.0	4.0	4.2	4.2	55.2
55.5	2.7	2.5	2.8	2.6	2.9	2.7	3.1	2.9	3.2	3.0	3.4	3.2	3.6	3.4	3.7	3.5	3.9	3.7	4.1	3.9	4.3	4.1	55.5
55.8	3.0	2.6	3.1	2.7	3.2	2.8	3.3	3.0	3.5	3.1	3.6	3.3	3.8	3.4	3.9	3.6	4.1	3.7	4.2	3.9	4.4	4.0	55.8
56.1	3.3	2.8	3.4	2.9	3.5	3.0	3.6	3.1	3.7	3.2	3.8	3.3	4.0	3.4	4.1	3.6	4.2	3.7	4.4	3.8	4.5	4.0	56.1
56.4	3.6	2.9	3.7	3.0	3.8	3.1	3.9	3.2	3.9	3.3	4.0	3.4	4.1	3.5	4.3	3.6	4.4	3.7	4.5	3.8	4.6	3.9	56.4
56.7	3.9	3.1	4.0	3.1	4.1	3.2	4.1	3.3	4.2	3.3	4.3	3.4	4.3	3.5	4.4	3.6	4.5	3.7	4.6	3.8	4.7	3.8	56.7
57.0	4.3	3.2	4.3	3.3	4.3	3.3	4.4	3.4	4.4	3.4	4.5	3.5	4.5	3.5	4.6	3.6	4.7	3.6	4.7	3.7	4.8	3.8	57.0
57.3	4.6	3.4	4.6	3.4	4.6	3.4	4.6	3.5	4.7	3.5	4.7	3.5	4.7	3.6	4.8	3.6	4.8	3.6	4.8	3.7	4.9	3.7	57.3
57.6	4.9	3.6	4.9	3.6	4.9	3.6	4.9	3.6	4.9	3.6	4.9	3.6	4.9	3.6	4.9	3.6	5.0	3.6	5.0	3.6	5.0	3.6	57.6
57.9	5.2	3.7	5.2	3.7	5.2	3.7	5.2	3.7	5.2	3.7	5.1	3.6	5.1	3.6	5.1	3.6	5.1	3.6	5.1	3.6	5.1	3.6	57.9
58.2	5.5	3.9	5.5	3.8	5.5	3.8	5.4	3.8	5.4	3.7	5.4	3.7	5.3	3.7	5.3	3.6	5.3	3.6	5.2	3.6	5.2	3.5	58.2
58.5	5.9	4.0	5.8	4.0	5.8	3.9	5.7	3.9	5.6	3.8	5.6	3.8	5.5	3.7	5.5	3.6	5.4	3.6	5.3	3.5	5.3	3.4	58.5
58.8	6.2	4.2	6.1	4.1	6.0	4.1	6.0	4.0	5.9	3.9	5.8	3.8	5.7	3.7	5.6	3.6	5.5	3.5	5.4	3.5	5.3	3.4	58.8
59.1	6.5	4.3	6.4	4.3	6.3	4.2	6.2	4.1	6.1	4.0	6.0	3.9	5.9	3.8	5.8	3.6	5.7	3.5	5.6	3.4	5.4	3.3	59.1
59.4	6.8	4.5	6.7	4.4	6.6	4.3	6.5	4.2	6.4	4.1	6.2	3.9	6.1	3.8	6.0	3.7	5.8	3.5	5.7	3.4	5.5	3.2	59.4
59.7	7.1	4.7	7.0	4.5	6.9	4.4	6.8	4.3	6.6	4.1	6.5	4.0	6.3	3.8	6.1	3.7	6.0	3.5	5.8	3.3	5.6	3.2	59.7
60.0	7.5	4.8	7.3	4.7	7.2	4.5	7.0	4.4	6.9	4.2	6.7	4.0	6.5	3.9	6.3	3.7	6.1	3.5	5.9	3.3	5.7	3.1	60.0
60.3	7.8	5.0	7.6	4.8	7.5	4.7	7.3	4.5	7.1	4.3	6.9	4.1	6.7	3.9	6.5	3.7	6.3	3.5	6.0	3.2	5.8	3.0	60.3
60.6	8.1	5.1	7.9	5.0	7.7	4.8	7.6	4.6	7.3	4.4	7.1	4.2	6.9	3.9	6.7	3.7	6.4	3.4	6.2	3.2	5.9	2.9	60.6
60.9	8.4	5.3	8.2	5.1	8.0	4.9	7.8	4.7	7.6	4.5	7.3	4.2	7.1	4.0	6.8	3.7	6.6	3.4	6.3	3.2	6.0	2.9	60.9
61.2	8.7	5.4	8.5	5.2	8.3	5.0	8.1	4.8	7.8	4.5	7.6	4.3	7.3	4.0	7.0	3.7	6.7	3.4	6.4	3.1	6.1	2.8	61.2
61.5	9.1	5.6	8.8	5.4	8.6	5.1	8.3	4.9	8.1	4.6	7.8	4.3	7.5	4.0	7.2	3.7	6.9	3.4	6.5	3.1	6.2	2.7	61.5

APPENDIX D. SIGHT REDUCTION TABLES

The following 18 pages contain excerpts from sight reduction tables for:

H.O. 229, Volume II, LHA 32°, 328°

H.O. 229, Volume II, LHA 37, 323°

H.O. 249, Volume I, Lat 24°S

H.O. 249, Volume II, Lat 24°

H.O. 249, Volume II, Table 5—Correction to Tabulated Altitudes for Minutes of Declination

32°, 328° L.H.A.   LATITUDE SAME NAME AS DECLINATION

N. Lat. { L.H.A. greater than 180° ..... Zn=Z ; L.H.A. less than 180° .... Zn=360°−Z }

Dec.	23° Hc	d	Z	24° Hc	d	Z	25° Hc	d	Z	26° Hc	d	Z	27° Hc	d	Z	28° Hc	d	Z	29° Hc	d	Z	30° Hc	d	Z	Dec.
0	51 19.1	+37.1	122.0	50 46.8	+38.3	123.1	50 13.7	+39.2	124.1	49 39.6	+40.3	125.1	49 04.8	+41.2	126.0	48 29.1	+42.2	126.9	47 52.7	+43.1	127.8	47 15.6	+43.9	128.7	0
1	51 56.2	+36.3	120.8	51 25.1	+37.4	121.8	50 52.9	+38.6	122.9	50 19.9	+39.6	123.9	49 46.0	+40.6	124.9	49 11.3	+41.6	125.8	48 35.8	+42.5	126.8	47 59.5	+43.4	127.7	1
2	52 32.5	+35.4	119.5	52 02.5	+36.6	120.6	51 31.5	+37.7	121.7	50 59.5	+38.9	122.7	50 26.6	+39.9	123.7	49 52.9	+40.9	124.7	49 18.3	+41.9	125.7	48 42.9	+42.8	126.6	2
3	53 07.9	+34.4	118.1	52 39.1	+35.7	119.3	52 09.2	+36.9	120.4	51 38.4	+38.0	121.5	51 06.5	+39.2	122.6	50 33.8	+40.2	123.6	50 00.2	+41.2	124.6	49 25.7	+42.2	125.5	3
4	53 42.3	+33.5	116.7	53 14.8	+34.8	118.1	52 46.1	+36.1	119.1	52 16.4	+37.3	120.2	51 45.7	+38.4	121.3	51 14.0	+39.5	122.4	50 41.4	+40.6	123.4	50 07.9	+41.6	124.4	4
5	54 15.8	+32.5	115.3	53 49.6	+33.8	116.6	53 22.2	+35.1	117.8	52 53.7	+36.4	118.9	52 24.1	+37.6	120.1	51 53.5	+38.8	121.2	51 22.0	+39.8	122.3	50 49.5	+40.9	123.3	5
6	54 48.3	+31.4	113.9	54 23.4	+32.8	115.2	53 57.3	+34.1	116.4	53 30.1	+35.6	117.6	53 01.7	+36.7	118.8	52 32.3	+37.9	120.0	52 01.8	+39.1	121.1	51 30.4	+40.1	122.1	6
7	55 19.7	+30.3	112.4	54 56.2	+31.8	113.7	54 31.5	+33.2	115.0	54 05.5	+34.6	116.3	53 38.4	+35.8	117.5	53 10.2	+37.1	118.8	52 40.9	+38.2	119.8	52 10.5	+39.4	120.9	7
8	55 50.0	+29.2	110.9	55 28.0	+30.7	112.2	55 04.5	+32.0	113.6	54 40.1	+33.5	114.9	54 14.2	+34.9	116.1	53 47.3	+36.1	117.5	53 19.1	+37.5	118.5	52 49.9	+38.7	119.7	8
9	56 19.2	+27.9	109.3	55 58.7	+29.5	110.7	55 36.8	+31.0	112.1	55 13.6	+32.5	113.4	54 49.1	+33.9	114.7	54 23.4	+35.3	116.1	53 56.6	+36.5	117.2	53 28.6	+37.7	118.4	9
10	56 47.1	+26.7	107.7	56 28.2	+28.2	109.1	56 07.8	+29.8	110.5	55 46.1	+31.3	111.9	55 23.0	+32.8	113.3	54 58.7	+34.2	114.6	54 33.1	+35.6	115.9	54 06.3	+36.9	117.1	10
11	57 13.8	+25.3	106.0	56 56.4	+27.0	107.5	56 37.6	+28.7	109.0	56 17.4	+30.2	110.4	55 55.8	+31.8	111.8	55 32.9	+33.2	113.1	55 08.7	+34.6	114.5	54 43.2	+36.0	115.8	11
12	57 39.1	+24.0	104.4	57 23.4	+25.7	105.9	57 06.3	+27.4	107.4	56 47.6	+28.9	108.8	56 27.6	+30.5	110.3	56 06.1	+32.1	111.7	55 43.3	+33.5	113.0	55 19.2	+34.9	114.4	12
13	58 03.1	+22.5	102.6	57 49.1	+24.4	104.2	57 33.7	+26.0	105.7	57 16.5	+27.8	107.2	56 58.1	+29.4	108.7	56 38.2	+30.9	110.1	56 16.8	+32.5	111.5	55 54.1	+34.0	112.9	13
14	58 25.6	+21.1	100.9	58 13.5	+22.8	102.5	57 59.7	+24.7	104.0	57 44.4	+26.4	105.6	57 27.5	+28.1	107.1	57 09.1	+29.8	108.6	56 49.3	+31.3	110.0	56 28.1	+32.8	111.4	14
15	58 46.7	+19.5	99.1	58 36.3	+21.5	100.7	58 24.4	+23.2	102.3	58 10.8	+25.0	103.9	57 55.6	+26.8	105.4	57 38.9	+28.5	107.0	57 20.6	+30.1	108.4	57 00.9	+31.7	109.9	15
16	59 06.2	+17.9	97.2	58 57.8	+19.8	98.9	58 47.6	+21.8	100.5	58 35.8	+23.6	102.1	58 22.4	+25.4	103.7	58 07.4	+27.1	105.3	57 50.7	+28.9	106.8	57 32.6	+30.5	108.3	16
17	59 24.1	+16.4	95.4	59 17.6	+18.3	97.1	59 09.4	+20.2	98.7	58 59.4	+22.1	100.4	58 47.8	+24.0	102.0	58 34.5	+25.8	103.6	58 19.6	+27.5	105.2	58 03.1	+29.2	106.7	17
18	59 40.5	+14.6	93.5	59 35.9	+16.7	95.2	59 29.6	+18.6	96.9	59 21.5	+20.6	98.6	59 11.8	+22.4	100.2	59 00.3	+24.3	101.9	58 47.1	+26.2	103.5	58 32.3	+27.9	105.1	18
19	59 55.1	+13.0	91.6	59 52.6	+14.9	93.3	59 48.2	+17.0	95.0	59 42.1	+19.0	96.7	59 34.2	+21.0	98.4	59 24.6	+22.8	100.1	59 13.3	+24.7	101.7	59 00.2	+26.6	103.4	19
20	60 08.0	+11.2	89.6	60 07.5	+13.3	91.3	60 05.2	+15.3	93.1	60 01.1	+17.3	94.8	59 55.2	+19.3	96.5	59 47.4	+21.3	98.2	59 38.0	+23.2	99.9	59 26.8	+25.0	101.6	20
21	60 19.2	+9.4	87.6	60 20.8	+11.5	89.4	60 20.5	+13.6	91.1	60 18.4	+15.7	92.9	60 14.5	+17.6	94.6	60 08.7	+19.7	96.4	60 01.2	+21.6	98.1	59 51.8	+23.6	99.8	21
22	60 28.6	+7.6	85.6	60 32.3	+9.7	87.4	60 34.1	+11.8	89.2	60 34.1	+13.8	90.9	60 32.1	+16.0	92.7	60 28.4	+18.0	94.5	60 22.8	+20.0	96.2	60 15.4	+22.0	98.0	22
23	60 36.2	+5.8	83.6	60 42.0	+7.9	85.4	60 45.9	+10.0	87.2	60 47.9	+12.1	88.9	60 48.1	+14.2	90.7	60 46.4	+16.3	92.5	60 42.8	+18.4	94.2	60 37.4	+20.4	96.1	23
24	60 42.0	+3.9	81.6	60 49.9	+6.0	83.3	60 55.9	+8.1	85.1	61 00.0	+10.3	86.9	61 02.3	+12.4	88.7	61 02.7	+14.5	90.5	61 01.2	+16.6	92.3	60 57.8	+18.7	94.1	24
25	60 45.9	+2.0	79.5	60 55.9	+4.1	81.3	61 04.0	+6.3	83.1	61 10.3	+8.4	84.9	61 14.7	+10.6	86.7	61 17.2	+12.7	88.5	61 17.8	+14.8	90.4	61 16.5	+16.9	92.2	25
26	60 47.9	+0.2*	77.5	61 00.0	+2.3	79.2	61 10.3	+4.4	81.0	61 18.7	+6.6	82.9	61 25.3	+8.7	84.9	61 29.9	+10.9	86.3	61 32.6	+13.0	88.3	61 33.4	+15.1	90.2	26
27	60 48.1	−1.7	75.4	61 02.3	+0.4	77.2	61 14.7	+2.5	79.0	61 25.3	+4.6	80.8	61 34.0	+6.8	82.6	61 40.8	+8.9	84.4	61 45.6	+11.2	86.3	61 48.5	+13.3	88.1	27
28	60 46.4	−3.6	73.4	61 02.7	−1.5	75.1	61 17.2	+0.6	76.9	61 29.9	+2.7	78.7	61 40.8	+4.8	80.5	61 49.7	+7.1	82.3	61 56.8	+9.2	84.2	62 01.8	+11.5	86.1	28
29	60 42.8	−5.4	71.3	61 01.2	−3.4	73.1	61 17.8	−1.3	74.8	61 32.6	+0.8	76.6	61 45.6	+2.9	78.4	61 56.8	+5.0	80.2	62 06.0	+7.3	82.1	62 13.3	+9.5*	84.0	29
30	60 37.4	−7.3	69.3	60 57.8	−5.3	71.0	61 16.5	−3.3	72.7	61 33.4	−1.2	74.5	61 48.5	+1.0	76.3	62 01.8	+3.2	78.1	62 13.3	+5.3*	80.0	62 22.8	+7.5*	81.8	30
31	60 30.1	−9.1	67.3	60 52.5	−7.1	68.9	61 13.2	−5.1	70.6	61 32.2	−3.1	72.4	61 49.5	−1.0	74.2	62 05.0	+1.1*	76.0	62 18.6	+3.3*	77.8	62 30.3	+5.5	79.7	31
32	60 21.0	−10.9	65.3	60 45.4	−9.0	66.9	61 08.1	−7.0	68.6	61 29.2	−5.0	70.3	61 48.5	−2.9	72.0	62 06.1	−0.8	73.8	62 21.9	+1.4*	75.7	62 35.8	+3.6*	77.5	32
33	60 10.2	−12.7	63.3	60 36.4	−10.8	64.9	61 01.1	−8.9	66.5	61 24.2	−6.9	68.2	61 45.6	−4.9	69.9	62 05.3	−2.8	71.7	62 23.3	−0.7*	73.5	62 39.4	+1.5*	75.4	33
34	59 57.5	−14.3	61.3	60 25.6	−12.6	62.9	60 52.2	−10.7	64.5	61 17.3	−8.8	66.1	61 40.7	−6.8	67.8	62 02.5	−4.7	69.6	62 22.6	−2.7	71.4	62 40.9	−0.5*	73.2	34
35	59 43.2	−16.0	59.4	60 13.0	−14.2	60.9	60 41.5	−12.6	62.5	61 08.5	−10.6	64.1	61 33.9	−8.7	65.7	61 57.8	−6.7*	67.4	62 19.9	−4.6	69.2	62 40.4	−2.6*	71.0	35
36	59 27.2	−17.5	57.5	59 58.8	−16.0	59.0	60 29.0	−14.2	60.5	60 57.9	−12.5	62.0	61 25.2	−10.5	63.7	61 51.1	−8.7	65.3	62 15.3	−6.6*	67.1	62 37.8	−4.5*	68.8	36
37	59 09.5	−19.2	55.6	59 42.8	−17.7	57.1	60 14.8	−16.0	58.5	60 45.4	−14.2	60.0	61 14.7	−12.4	61.6	61 42.4	−10.5	63.2	62 08.7	−8.6	64.9	62 33.3	−6.6*	66.7	37
38	58 50.3	−20.8	53.8	59 25.1	−19.2	55.2	59 58.8	−17.6	56.6	60 31.2	−16.0	58.1	61 02.3	−14.2	59.6	61 31.9	−12.4	61.2	62 00.1	−10.5	62.8	62 26.7	−8.5	64.5	38
39	58 29.5	−22.3	52.0	59 05.9	−20.8	53.3	59 41.2	−19.3	54.7	60 15.2	−17.6	56.1	60 48.1	−16.0	57.6	61 19.5	−14.2	59.1	61 49.6	−12.4	60.7	62 18.2	−10.5	62.4	39
40	58 07.2	−23.7	50.2	58 45.1	−22.3	51.5	59 21.9	−20.8	52.8	59 57.6	−19.3	54.2	60 32.1	−17.7	55.6	61 05.3	−15.9	57.1	61 37.2	−14.2	58.7	62 07.7	−12.3	60.3	40
41	57 43.5	−25.1	48.5	58 22.8	−23.8	49.7	59 01.1	−22.4	51.0	59 38.3	−20.9	52.3	60 14.4	−19.3	53.7	60 49.4	−17.8	55.1	61 23.0	−16.0	56.6	61 55.4	−14.3	58.2	41
42	57 18.4	−26.4	46.8	57 59.0	−25.1	48.0	58 38.7	−23.8	49.2	59 17.4	−22.4	50.5	59 55.1	−20.9	51.8	60 31.6	−19.3	53.1	61 07.0	−17.8	54.6	61 41.1	−16.1	56.1	42
43	56 52.0	−27.7	45.2	57 33.9	−26.5	46.3	58 14.9	−25.2	47.4	58 55.0	−23.9	48.6	59 34.2	−22.5	49.9	60 12.3	−21.0	51.3	60 49.2	−19.4	52.6	61 25.0	−17.8	54.1	43
44	56 24.3	−29.0	43.5	57 07.4	−27.8	44.6	57 49.7	−26.6	45.7	58 31.1	−25.3	46.9	59 11.7	−24.0	48.1	59 51.3	−22.6	49.4	60 29.8	−21.1	50.7	61 07.2	−19.5	52.1	44

23°   24°   25°   26°   27°   28°   29°   30°

32°, 328° L.H.A.

Dec	23° Hc	23° d	23° Z	24° Hc	24° d	24° Z	25° Hc	25° d	25° Z	26° Hc	26° d	26° Z	27° Hc	27° d	27° Z	28° Hc	28° d	28° Z	29° Hc	29° d	29° Z	30° Hc	30° d	30° Z
45	55 55.3	−30.1	42.0	56 39.6	−29.0	43.0	57 23.1	−27.9	44.0	58 05.8	−26.6	45.2	58 47.7	−25.4	46.3	59 28.7	−24.1	47.5	60 08.7	−22.7	48.8	60 47.7	−21.2	50.2
46	55 25.2	−31.2	40.4	56 10.6	−30.2	41.4	56 55.2	−29.1	42.4	57 39.2	−28.0	43.5	58 22.3	−26.8	44.6	59 04.6	−25.5	45.8	59 46.0	−24.2	47.0	60 26.5	−22.8	48.3
47	54 54.0	−32.3	38.9	55 40.4	−31.3	39.9	56 26.1	−30.3	40.8	57 11.2	−29.3	41.8	57 55.5	−28.1	42.9	58 39.1	−26.9	44.0	59 21.8	−25.6	45.2	60 03.7	−24.4	46.4
48	54 21.7	−33.3	37.5	55 09.1	−32.5	38.4	55 55.8	−31.4	39.3	56 41.9	−30.4	40.2	57 27.4	−29.4	41.2	58 12.2	−28.3	42.3	58 56.2	−27.1	43.4	59 39.3	−25.8	44.6
49	53 48.4	−34.3	36.1	54 36.6	−33.4	36.9	55 24.4	−32.6	37.8	56 11.5	−31.6	38.7	56 58.0	−30.5	39.6	57 43.9	−29.5	40.6	58 29.5	−28.4	41.7	59 13.6	−27.2	42.8
50	53 14.1	−35.2	34.7	54 03.2	−34.4	35.5	54 51.8	−33.5	36.3	55 39.9	−32.7	37.2	56 27.5	−31.8	38.1	57 14.4	−30.7	39.0	58 00.7	−29.7	40.0	58 46.3	−28.6	41.1
51	52 38.9	−36.1	33.3	53 28.8	−35.4	34.1	54 18.3	−34.6	34.9	55 07.2	−33.7	35.7	55 55.7	−32.8	36.5	56 43.7	−31.9	37.4	57 31.0	−30.9	38.4	58 17.7	−29.9	39.4
52	52 02.8	−37.0	32.0	52 53.4	−36.2	32.7	53 43.7	−35.5	33.5	54 33.5	−34.7	34.2	55 22.9	−33.9	35.0	56 11.8	−33.1	35.9	57 00.1	−32.1	36.8	57 47.8	−31.1	37.7
53	51 25.8	−37.8	30.8	52 17.2	−37.1	31.4	53 08.2	−36.4	32.1	53 58.8	−35.6	32.8	54 49.0	−34.9	33.6	55 38.7	−34.0	34.4	56 28.0	−33.2	35.3	57 16.7	−32.3	36.2
54	50 48.0	−38.5	29.5	51 40.1	−37.9	30.1	52 31.8	−37.2	30.8	53 23.2	−36.6	31.5	54 14.1	−35.8	32.2	55 04.7	−35.1	33.0	55 54.8	−34.3	33.8	56 44.4	−33.4	34.6
55	50 09.5	−39.2	28.3	51 02.2	−38.7	28.9	51 54.6	−38.1	29.5	52 46.6	−37.4	30.2	53 38.3	−36.7	30.8	54 29.6	−36.0	31.6	55 20.5	−35.2	32.3	56 11.0	−34.4	33.1
56	49 30.3	−40.0	27.1	50 23.5	−39.4	27.7	51 16.5	−38.8	28.3	52 09.2	−38.2	28.9	53 01.6	−37.6	29.5	53 53.6	−36.9	30.2	54 45.3	−36.2	30.9	55 36.6	−35.5	31.6
57	48 50.3	−40.6	26.0	49 44.1	−40.1	26.5	50 37.7	−39.6	27.1	51 31.0	−39.0	27.6	52 24.0	−38.4	28.2	53 16.7	−37.8	28.9	54 09.1	−37.2	29.5	55 01.1	−36.4	30.2
58	48 09.7	−41.2	24.9	49 04.0	−40.7	25.4	49 58.1	−40.2	25.9	50 52.0	−39.8	26.4	51 45.6	−39.2	27.0	52 38.9	−38.6	27.6	53 31.9	−37.9	28.2	54 24.7	−37.4	28.9
59	47 28.5	−41.9	23.8	48 23.3	−41.4	24.3	49 17.9	−40.9	24.7	50 12.2	−40.4	25.2	51 06.4	−39.9	25.8	52 00.3	−39.4	26.3	52 54.0	−38.8	26.9	53 47.3	−38.2	27.5
60	46 46.6	−42.3	22.8	47 41.9	−42.0	23.2	48 37.0	−41.6	23.6	49 31.8	−41.1	24.1	50 26.5	−40.6	24.6	51 20.9	−40.1	25.1	52 15.2	−39.6	25.6	53 09.1	−39.0	26.2
61	46 04.3	−43.0	21.7	46 59.9	−42.5	22.1	47 55.4	−42.1	22.5	48 50.7	−41.7	23.0	49 45.9	−41.3	23.4	50 40.8	−40.8	23.9	51 35.6	−40.3	24.4	52 30.1	−39.8	25.0
62	45 21.3	−43.6	20.7	46 17.4	−43.1	21.1	47 13.3	−42.7	21.4	48 09.0	−42.3	21.9	49 04.6	−41.9	22.3	50 00.0	−41.4	22.8	50 55.3	−41.1	23.2	51 50.3	−40.5	23.7
63	44 37.9	−43.9	19.8	45 34.3	−43.6	20.1	46 30.6	−43.3	20.5	47 26.7	−42.9	20.8	48 22.7	−42.5	21.2	49 18.6	−42.1	21.7	50 14.2	−41.6	22.1	51 09.8	−41.3	22.6
64	43 54.0	−44.4	18.8	44 50.7	−44.1	19.1	45 47.3	−43.7	19.5	46 43.8	−43.4	19.8	47 40.2	−43.0	20.2	48 36.5	−42.7	20.6	49 32.6	−42.3	21.0	50 28.5	−41.9	21.4
65	43 09.6	−44.9	17.9	44 06.6	−44.5	18.2	45 03.6	−44.3	18.5	46 00.4	−43.9	18.8	46 57.2	−43.6	19.2	47 53.8	−43.3	19.5	48 50.3	−42.9	19.9	49 46.6	−42.5	20.3
66	42 24.7	−45.2	17.0	43 22.1	−45.0	17.2	44 19.3	−44.6	17.5	45 16.5	−44.4	17.8	46 13.6	−44.1	18.2	47 10.5	−43.8	18.5	48 07.4	−43.5	18.8	49 04.1	−43.1	19.2
67	41 39.5	−45.6	16.1	42 37.1	−45.4	16.3	43 34.7	−45.2	16.6	44 32.1	−44.9	16.9	45 29.5	−44.6	17.2	46 26.7	−44.2	17.5	47 23.9	−44.0	17.8	48 21.0	−43.7	18.2
68	40 53.9	−46.1	15.2	41 51.7	−45.8	15.5	42 49.5	−45.5	15.7	43 47.2	−45.3	15.9	44 44.9	−45.1	16.2	45 42.5	−44.8	16.5	46 39.9	−44.5	16.8	47 37.3	−44.2	17.1
69	40 07.8	−46.1	14.4	41 05.9	−46.1	14.6	42 04.0	−46.0	14.8	43 01.9	−45.7	15.1	43 59.8	−45.4	15.3	44 57.7	−45.3	15.6	45 55.4	−45.0	15.8	46 53.1	−44.7	16.1
70	39 21.5	−46.8	13.6	40 19.8	−46.6	13.8	41 18.0	−46.3	14.0	42 16.2	−46.1	14.2	43 14.4	−45.9	14.4	44 12.4	−45.6	14.6	45 10.5	−45.5	14.9	46 08.4	−45.2	15.2
71	38 34.7	−47.0	12.7	39 33.2	−46.8	12.9	40 31.7	−46.7	13.1	41 30.1	−46.5	13.3	42 28.5	−46.3	13.5	43 26.8	−46.1	13.7	44 25.0	−45.8	14.0	45 23.2	−45.6	14.2
72	37 47.7	−47.4	12.0	38 46.4	−47.2	12.1	39 45.0	−47.0	12.3	40 43.6	−46.8	12.5	41 42.2	−46.7	12.7	42 40.7	−46.5	12.9	43 39.1	−46.3	13.1	44 37.6	−46.1	13.3
73	37 00.3	−47.6	11.2	37 59.2	−47.5	11.3	38 58.0	−47.4	11.5	39 56.8	−47.2	11.7	40 55.5	−47.0	11.8	41 54.2	−46.8	12.0	42 52.9	−46.7	12.2	43 51.5	−46.5	12.4
74	36 12.7	−47.9	10.4	37 11.7	−47.8	10.6	38 10.6	−47.6	10.7	39 09.6	−47.5	10.9	40 08.5	−47.4	11.0	41 07.4	−47.2	11.2	42 06.2	−47.0	11.4	43 05.0	−46.8	11.5
75	35 24.8	−48.2	9.7	36 23.9	−48.1	9.8	37 23.0	−47.9	9.9	38 22.1	−47.8	10.1	39 21.1	−47.6	10.2	40 20.2	−47.4	10.4	41 19.2	−47.4	10.5	42 18.2	−47.3	10.7
76	34 36.6	−48.5	9.0	35 35.8	−48.3	9.1	36 35.1	−48.3	9.2	37 34.3	−48.1	9.3	38 33.5	−48.0	9.4	39 32.7	−47.9	9.6	40 31.8	−47.7	9.7	41 30.9	−47.5	9.9
77	33 48.1	−48.7	8.2	34 47.5	−48.6	8.3	35 46.8	−48.5	8.4	36 46.2	−48.4	8.6	37 45.5	−48.3	8.7	38 44.8	−48.2	8.8	39 44.1	−48.0	8.9	40 43.4	−48.0	9.0
78	32 59.4	−48.9	7.5	33 58.9	−48.8	7.6	34 58.3	−48.7	7.7	35 57.8	−48.6	7.8	36 57.2	−48.5	7.9	37 56.1	−48.4	8.0	38 56.1	−48.4	8.1	39 55.4	−48.2	8.3
79	32 10.5	−49.2	6.9	33 10.1	−49.1	6.9	34 09.6	−49.0	7.0	35 09.2	−48.9	7.1	36 08.7	−48.8	7.2	37 08.2	−48.7	7.3	38 07.7	−48.6	7.4	39 07.2	−48.5	7.5
80	31 21.3	−49.3	6.2	32 21.0	−49.3	6.3	33 20.6	−49.2	6.3	34 20.3	−49.2	6.4	35 19.9	−49.1	6.5	36 19.5	−49.0	6.6	37 19.1	−48.9	6.6	38 18.7	−48.8	6.7
81	30 32.0	−49.6	5.5	31 31.7	−49.5	5.6	32 31.4	−49.4	5.6	33 31.1	−49.3	5.7	34 30.8	−49.3	5.8	35 30.5	−49.2	5.8	36 30.2	−49.1	5.9	37 29.9	−49.1	6.0
82	29 42.4	−49.7	4.9	30 42.2	−49.7	4.9	31 41.8	−49.6	5.0	32 41.8	−49.6	5.0	33 41.5	−49.5	5.1	34 41.5	−49.4	5.1	35 41.1	−49.3	5.2	36 40.8	−49.3	5.2
83	28 52.7	−49.9	4.2	29 52.5	−49.8	4.3	30 52.4	−49.8	4.3	31 52.2	−49.8	4.4	32 52.0	−49.7	4.4	33 51.8	−49.6	4.5	34 51.7	−49.7	4.5	35 51.5	−49.6	4.6
84	28 02.8	−50.1	3.6	29 02.7	−50.1	3.6	30 02.6	−50.1	3.7	31 02.4	−49.9	3.7	32 02.3	−49.9	3.7	33 02.2	−49.9	3.8	34 02.0	−49.8	3.8	35 01.9	−49.8	3.9
85	27 12.7	−50.2	3.0	28 12.6	−50.2	3.0	29 12.5	−50.2	3.0	30 12.5	−50.2	3.1	31 12.4	−50.2	3.1	32 12.5	−50.1	3.1	33 12.2	−50.1	3.2	34 12.1	−50.0	3.2
86	26 22.5	−50.4	2.4	27 22.4	−50.4	2.4	28 22.4	−50.4	2.4	29 22.3	−50.3	2.4	30 22.2	−50.3	2.5	31 22.2	−50.3	2.5	32 22.1	−50.2	2.5	33 22.1	−50.3	2.5
87	25 32.1	−50.6	1.8	26 32.0	−50.5	1.8	27 32.0	−50.5	1.8	28 32.0	−50.5	1.8	29 31.9	−50.4	1.8	30 31.9	−50.5	1.8	31 31.9	−50.5	1.9	32 31.8	−50.4	1.9
88	24 41.5	−50.7	1.2	25 41.5	−50.7	1.2	26 41.5	−50.7	1.2	27 41.5	−50.7	1.2	28 41.5	−50.7	1.2	29 41.5	−50.6	1.2	30 41.5	−50.6	1.2	31 41.4	−50.8	1.2
89	23 50.8	−50.8	0.6	24 50.8	−50.8	0.6	25 50.8	−50.8	0.6	26 50.8	−50.8	0.6	27 50.8	−50.8	0.6	28 50.8	−50.8	0.6	29 50.8	−50.8	0.6	30 50.8	−50.8	0.6
90	23 00.0	−50.9	0.0	24 00.0	−50.9	0.0	25 00.0	−50.9	0.0	26 00.0	−51.0	0.0	27 00.0	−51.0	0.0	28 00.0	−51.0	0.0	29 00.0	−51.0	0.0	30 00.0	−51.0	0.0

32°, 328° L.H.A.   LATITUDE SAME NAME AS DECLINATION

259

LATITUDE CONTRARY NAME TO DECLINATION **L.H.A. 32°, 328°**

Dec.	23° Hc	d	Z	24° Hc	d	Z	25° Hc	d	Z	26° Hc	d	Z	27° Hc	d	Z	28° Hc	d	Z	29° Hc	d	Z	30° Hc	d	Z	Dec.
0	51 19.1	-37.9	122.0	50 46.8	-38.9	123.1	50 13.7	-40.0	124.1	49 39.6	-40.9	125.1	49 04.8	-41.9	126.0	48 29.1	-42.8	126.9	47 52.7	-43.7	127.8	47 15.6	-44.5	128.7	0
1	50 41.2	-38.7	123.2	50 07.9	-39.7	124.3	49 33.7	-40.7	125.2	48 58.7	-41.6	126.2	48 22.9	-42.5	127.1	47 46.3	-43.3	128.0	47 09.0	-44.1	128.8	46 31.1	-45.0	129.6	1
2	50 02.5	-39.3	124.4	49 28.2	-40.4	125.4	48 53.0	-41.3	126.4	48 17.1	-42.2	127.3	47 40.4	-43.1	128.1	47 03.0	-43.9	129.0	46 24.9	-44.7	129.8	45 46.1	-45.4	130.6	2
3	49 23.2	-40.1	125.6	48 47.8	-41.0	126.5	48 11.7	-41.9	127.5	47 34.9	-42.8	128.3	46 57.3	-43.6	129.2	46 19.1	-44.4	130.0	45 40.2	-45.1	130.8	45 00.7	-45.8	131.5	3
4	48 43.1	-40.7	126.8	48 06.8	-41.6	127.6	47 29.8	-42.5	128.5	46 52.1	-43.3	129.4	46 13.7	-44.1	130.2	45 34.7	-44.9	131.0	44 55.1	-45.6	131.7	44 14.9	-46.3	132.4	4
5	48 02.4	-41.4	127.9	47 25.2	-42.2	128.7	46 47.3	-43.0	129.6	46 08.8	-43.8	130.4	45 29.6	-44.6	131.1	44 49.8	-45.3	131.9	44 09.5	-46.0	132.6	43 28.6	-46.7	133.3	5
6	47 21.0	-41.9	128.9	46 43.0	-42.8	129.8	46 04.3	-43.6	130.6	45 25.0	-44.4	131.3	44 45.0	-45.0	132.1	44 04.5	-45.7	132.8	43 23.5	-46.4	133.5	42 41.9	-47.0	134.2	6
7	46 39.1	-42.5	130.0	46 00.2	-43.3	130.8	45 20.7	-44.0	131.6	44 40.6	-44.7	132.3	44 00.0	-45.5	133.0	43 18.8	-46.2	133.7	42 37.1	-46.8	134.4	41 54.9	-47.4	135.0	7
8	45 56.6	-43.0	131.0	45 16.9	-43.7	131.8	44 36.7	-44.5	132.5	43 55.9	-45.3	133.2	43 14.5	-45.9	133.9	42 32.6	-46.5	134.6	41 50.3	-47.2	135.2	41 07.5	-47.8	135.8	8
9	45 13.6	-43.5	132.0	44 33.2	-44.3	132.7	43 52.2	-45.0	133.4	43 10.6	-45.6	134.1	42 28.6	-46.3	134.8	41 46.1	-46.9	135.4	41 03.1	-47.5	136.0	40 19.7	-48.0	136.6	9
10	44 30.1	-44.0	133.0	43 48.9	-44.7	133.7	43 07.2	-45.4	134.4	42 25.0	-46.0	135.0	41 42.3	-46.6	135.7	40 59.2	-47.3	136.3	40 15.6	-47.8	136.9	39 31.7	-48.4	137.4	10
11	43 46.1	-44.5	133.9	43 04.2	-45.2	134.6	42 21.8	-45.8	135.3	41 39.0	-46.5	135.9	40 55.7	-47.0	136.5	40 11.9	-47.5	137.1	39 27.8	-48.1	137.6	38 43.3	-48.7	138.2	11
12	43 01.6	-44.9	134.8	42 19.0	-45.5	135.5	41 36.0	-46.2	136.1	40 52.5	-46.7	136.7	40 08.7	-47.4	137.3	39 24.4	-47.9	137.9	38 39.7	-48.5	138.4	37 54.6	-48.9	138.9	12
13	42 16.7	-45.3	135.7	41 33.5	-46.0	136.4	40 49.8	-46.5	137.0	40 05.8	-47.1	137.5	39 21.3	-47.7	138.1	38 36.5	-48.2	138.6	37 51.2	-48.7	139.2	37 05.7	-49.2	139.7	13
14	41 31.4	-45.7	136.6	40 47.5	-46.3	137.2	40 03.3	-46.9	137.8	39 18.7	-47.5	138.4	38 33.6	-47.9	138.9	37 48.3	-48.5	139.4	37 02.5	-49.0	139.9	36 16.5	-49.5	140.4	14
15	40 45.7	-46.1	137.5	40 01.2	-46.6	138.1	39 16.4	-47.2	138.6	38 31.2	-47.7	139.1	37 45.7	-48.3	139.6	36 59.8	-48.8	140.1	36 13.5	-49.2	140.6	35 27.0	-49.7	141.1	15
16	39 59.6	-46.5	138.3	39 14.6	-47.0	138.9	38 29.2	-47.5	139.4	37 43.5	-48.1	139.9	36 57.4	-48.6	140.4	36 11.0	-49.0	140.9	35 24.3	-49.5	141.3	34 37.3	-49.9	141.8	16
17	39 13.1	-46.8	139.1	38 27.6	-47.4	139.7	37 41.7	-47.9	140.2	36 55.4	-48.3	140.7	36 08.8	-48.8	141.1	35 22.0	-49.3	141.6	34 34.8	-49.7	142.0	33 47.4	-50.1	142.5	17
18	38 26.3	-47.1	140.0	37 40.2	-47.6	140.5	36 53.8	-48.1	140.9	36 07.1	-48.6	141.4	35 20.0	-49.0	141.8	34 32.7	-49.5	142.3	33 45.1	-49.9	142.7	32 57.3	-50.3	143.1	18
19	37 39.2	-47.4	140.7	36 52.6	-47.9	141.2	36 05.7	-48.4	141.7	35 18.5	-48.9	142.1	34 31.0	-49.3	142.5	33 43.2	-49.7	143.0	32 55.2	-50.1	143.4	32 07.0	-50.6	143.7	19
20	36 51.8	-47.7	141.5	36 04.7	-48.2	142.0	35 17.3	-48.6	142.4	34 29.6	-49.0	142.8	33 41.7	-49.5	143.2	32 53.5	-49.9	143.6	32 05.1	-50.3	144.0	31 16.4	-50.7	144.4	20
21	36 04.1	-47.9	142.3	35 16.5	-48.4	142.7	34 28.7	-48.9	143.1	33 40.6	-49.4	143.5	32 52.2	-49.7	143.9	32 03.6	-50.1	144.3	31 14.8	-50.5	144.6	30 25.7	-50.9	145.0	21
22	35 16.2	-48.3	143.0	34 28.1	-48.7	143.4	33 39.8	-49.1	143.8	32 51.2	-49.5	144.2	32 02.5	-50.0	144.6	31 13.5	-50.4	144.9	30 24.3	-50.7	145.3	29 34.8	-51.0	145.6	22
23	34 27.9	-48.5	143.7	33 39.4	-48.9	144.1	32 50.7	-49.4	144.5	32 01.7	-49.7	144.9	31 12.5	-50.1	145.2	30 23.1	-50.4	145.6	29 33.6	-50.9	145.9	28 43.8	-51.2	146.2	23
24	33 39.4	-48.7	144.4	32 50.5	-49.2	144.8	32 01.3	-49.5	145.2	31 12.0	-50.0	145.5	30 22.4	-50.3	145.9	29 32.7	-50.7	146.2	28 42.7	-51.0	146.5	27 52.6	-51.4	146.8	24
25	32 50.7	-49.0	145.1	32 01.3	-49.3	145.5	31 11.8	-49.8	145.8	30 22.0	-50.1	146.2	29 32.1	-50.5	146.5	28 42.0	-50.8	146.8	27 51.7	-51.2	147.1	27 01.2	-51.5	147.4	25
26	32 01.7	-49.2	145.8	31 12.0	-49.6	146.2	30 22.0	-49.9	146.5	29 31.9	-50.3	146.8	28 41.6	-50.6	147.1	27 51.2	-51.0	147.4	27 00.5	-51.3	147.7	26 09.7	-51.6	148.0	26
27	31 12.5	-49.4	146.5	30 22.4	-49.7	146.8	29 32.1	-50.1	147.1	28 41.6	-50.4	147.4	27 51.0	-50.8	147.7	27 00.2	-51.2	148.0	26 09.2	-51.4	148.3	25 18.1	-51.7	148.5	27
28	30 23.1	-49.5	147.2	29 32.7	-50.0	147.5	28 41.6	-50.3	147.7	27 51.2	-50.7	148.0	27 00.2	-51.0	148.3	26 09.0	-51.2	148.6	25 17.8	-51.6	148.8	24 26.4	-51.9	149.1	28
29	29 33.6	-49.8	147.8	28 42.7	-50.1	148.1	27 51.7	-50.5	148.4	27 00.5	-50.8	148.7	26 09.2	-51.1	148.9	25 17.8	-51.4	149.2	24 26.2	-51.7	149.4	23 34.5	-52.0	149.6	29
30	28 43.8	-50.0	148.4	27 52.6	-50.3	148.7	27 01.2	-50.6	149.0	26 09.7	-50.9	149.2	25 18.1	-51.2	149.5	24 26.4	-51.6	149.7	23 34.5	-51.8	150.0	22 42.5	-52.1	150.1	30
31	27 53.8	-50.1	149.1	27 02.3	-50.4	149.3	26 10.6	-50.7	149.6	25 18.8	-51.0	149.8	24 26.9	-51.4	150.1	23 34.8	-51.6	150.3	22 42.7	-52.0	150.5	21 50.4	-52.2	150.7	31
32	27 03.7	-50.2	149.7	26 11.9	-50.6	149.9	25 19.9	-50.9	150.2	24 27.8	-51.2	150.4	23 35.5	-51.5	150.6	22 43.2	-51.8	150.8	21 50.7	-52.0	151.1	20 58.2	-52.3	151.2	32
33	26 13.5	-50.5	150.3	25 21.3	-50.6	150.5	24 29.0	-51.1	150.8	23 36.6	-51.4	151.0	22 44.0	-51.6	151.2	21 51.4	-51.9	151.4	20 58.7	-52.1	151.6	20 05.9	-52.4	151.7	33
34	25 23.0	-50.5	150.9	24 30.5	-50.8	151.1	23 37.9	-51.1	151.3	22 45.2	-51.4	151.5	21 52.4	-51.7	151.7	20 59.5	-51.9	151.9	20 06.6	-52.3	152.1	19 13.5	-52.5	152.3	34
35	24 32.5	-50.8	151.5	23 39.7	-51.0	151.7	22 46.8	-51.3	151.9	21 53.8	-51.5	152.1	21 00.7	-51.8	152.3	20 07.6	-52.1	152.5	19 14.3	-52.3	152.6	18 21.0	-52.6	152.8	35
36	23 41.7	-50.8	152.1	22 48.7	-51.1	152.3	21 55.5	-51.4	152.5	21 02.3	-51.7	152.7	20 08.9	-51.9	152.8	19 15.5	-52.2	153.0	18 22.0	-52.4	153.2	17 28.4	-52.6	153.3	36
37	22 50.9	-51.0	152.7	21 57.6	-51.3	152.9	21 04.1	-51.5	153.0	20 10.6	-51.7	153.2	19 17.0	-52.0	153.4	18 23.3	-52.2	153.5	17 29.6	-52.5	153.7	16 35.8	-52.7	153.8	37
38	21 59.9	-51.1	153.2	21 06.3	-51.3	153.4	20 12.6	-51.6	153.6	19 18.9	-51.9	153.7	18 25.0	-52.1	153.9	17 31.1	-52.3	154.0	16 37.1	-52.5	154.2	15 43.1	-52.8	154.3	38
39	21 08.9	-51.2	153.8	20 15.0	-51.5	154.0	19 21.0	-51.7	154.1	18 27.0	-51.9	154.3	17 32.9	-52.1	154.4	16 38.8	-52.4	154.5	15 44.6	-52.6	154.7	14 50.3	-52.8	154.8	39
40	20 17.7	-51.3	154.4	19 23.5	-51.5	154.6	18 29.3	-51.7	154.7	17 35.1	-52.0	154.8	16 40.8	-52.3	154.9	15 46.4	-52.5	155.1	14 52.0	-52.7	155.2	13 57.5	-52.9	155.3	40
41	19 26.4	-51.4	154.9	18 32.0	-51.6	155.1	17 37.6	-51.9	155.2	16 43.1	-52.1	155.3	15 48.5	-52.3	155.4	14 53.9	-52.5	155.6	13 59.3	-52.7	155.7	13 04.6	-53.0	155.8	41
42	18 35.0	-51.5	155.5	17 40.4	-51.8	155.6	16 45.7	-52.0	155.7	15 51.0	-52.2	155.8	14 56.2	-52.4	155.9	14 01.4	-52.6	156.1	13 06.5	-52.8	156.2	12 11.6	-53.0	156.2	42
43	17 43.5	-51.6	156.0	16 48.6	-51.8	156.1	15 53.7	-52.0	156.2	14 58.8	-52.3	156.3	14 03.8	-52.4	156.5	13 08.8	-52.6	156.5	12 13.7	-52.8	156.7	11 18.6	-53.0	156.7	43
44	16 51.9	-51.7	156.5	15 56.8	-51.9	156.6	15 01.7	-52.1	156.8	14 06.5	-52.3	156.9	13 11.4	-52.5	157.0	12 16.2	-52.7	157.0	11 20.9	-52.9	157.1	10 25.6	-53.1	157.2	44

| | **23°** | | | **24°** | | | **25°** | | | **26°** | | | **27°** | | | **28°** | | | **29°** | | | **30°** | | | |

L.H.A. 148°, 212° — LATITUDE SAME NAME AS DECLINATION

Dec. °	23° Hc	23° d	23° Z	24° Hc	24° d	24° Z	25° Hc	25° d	25° Z	26° Hc	26° d	26° Z	27° Hc	27° d	27° Z	28° Hc	28° d	28° Z	29° Hc	29° d	29° Z	30° Hc	30° d	30° Z	Dec. °
45	16 00.2	-51.7	157.1	15 05.0	-52.0	157.2	14 09.6	-52.1	157.3	13 14.3	-52.4	157.4	12 18.9	-52.6	157.4	11 23.5	-52.8	157.5	10 28.0	-52.9	157.6	9 32.5	-53.1	157.7	45
46	15 08.5	-51.8	157.6	14 13.0	-52.0	157.7	13 17.5	-52.2	157.8	12 21.9	-52.4	157.9	11 26.3	-52.6	157.9	10 30.7	-52.8	158.0	9 35.1	-53.0	158.1	8 39.4	-53.2	158.1	46
47	14 16.7	-51.9	158.1	13 21.0	-52.1	158.2	12 25.3	-52.3	158.3	11 29.5	-52.4	158.4	10 33.7	-52.6	158.4	9 37.9	-52.8	158.5	8 42.1	-53.0	158.6	7 46.2	-53.2	158.6	47
48	13 24.8	-51.9	158.6	12 28.9	-52.1	158.7	11 33.0	-52.3	158.8	10 37.1	-52.6	158.9	9 41.1	-52.7	158.9	8 45.1	-52.9	159.0	7 49.1	-53.1	159.0	6 53.0	-53.2	159.1	48
49	12 32.9	-52.0	159.1	11 36.8	-52.0	159.1	10 40.7	-52.3	159.3	9 44.5	-52.5	159.3	8 48.4	-52.7	159.4	7 52.2	-52.9	159.4	6 56.0	-53.0	159.5	5 59.8	-53.2	159.5	49
50	11 40.9	-52.1	159.6	10 44.6	-52.2	159.7	9 48.3	-52.4	159.8	8 52.0	-52.6	159.8	7 55.7	-52.8	159.9	6 59.3	-52.9	159.9	6 03.0	-53.1	160.0	5 06.6	-53.3	160.0	50
51	10 48.8	-52.1	160.2	9 52.4	-52.3	160.2	8 55.9	-52.5	160.3	7 59.4	-52.6	160.3	7 02.9	-52.8	160.4	6 06.4	-53.0	160.4	5 09.9	-53.2	160.4	4 13.3	-53.3	160.5	51
52	9 56.7	-52.1	160.7	9 00.1	-52.3	160.7	8 03.4	-52.5	160.7	7 06.8	-52.6	160.8	6 10.1	-52.8	160.9	5 13.4	-53.0	160.8	4 16.7	-53.1	160.9	3 20.0	-53.3	160.9	52
53	9 04.6	-52.2	161.2	8 07.8	-52.4	161.2	7 11.0	-52.6	161.3	6 14.1	-52.6	161.3	5 17.3	-52.8	161.3	4 20.5	-53.0	161.3	3 23.6	-53.1	161.4	2 26.7	-53.3	161.4	53
54	8 12.4	-52.3	161.7	7 15.4	-52.4	161.7	6 18.4	-52.5	161.7	5 21.5	-52.7	161.8	4 24.5	-52.8	161.8	3 27.5	-53.0	161.8	2 30.5	-53.2	161.8	1 33.4	-53.3	161.8	54
55	7 20.1	-52.2	162.2	6 23.0	-52.4	162.2	5 25.9	-52.6	162.2	4 28.8	-52.7	162.2	3 31.6	-52.8	162.3	2 34.5	-53.1	162.3	1 37.3	-53.2	162.3	0 40.1	-53.3	162.3	55
56	6 27.9	-52.3	162.7	5 30.6	-52.4	162.7	4 33.3	-52.6	162.7	3 36.0	-52.7	162.7	2 38.7	-52.8	162.7	1 41.4	-53.0	162.8	0 44.1	-53.1	162.8	0 13.2	+53.3	17.2	56
57	5 35.6	-52.3	163.1	4 38.2	-52.5	163.2	3 40.7	-52.6	163.2	2 43.3	-52.7	163.2	1 45.9	-52.9	163.2	0 48.4	-53.0	163.2	0 09.0	+53.2	16.8	1 06.5	+53.3	16.8	57
58	4 43.3	-52.3	163.6	3 45.7	-52.5	163.7	2 48.1	-52.6	163.7	1 50.6	-52.8	163.7	0 53.0	-52.9	163.7	0 04.6	+53.1	16.3	1 02.2	+53.2	16.3	1 59.8	+53.3	16.3	58
59	3 51.0	-52.4	164.1	2 53.2	-52.4	164.1	1 55.5	-52.6	164.2	0 57.8	-52.7	164.2	0 00.1	-52.9	164.2	0 57.6	+53.1	15.8	1 55.4	+53.1	15.9	2 53.1	+53.3	15.9	59
60	2 58.6	-52.3	164.6	2 00.8	-52.5	164.6	1 02.9	-52.6	164.6	0 05.1	-52.8	164.6	0 52.8	+52.9	15.4	1 50.7	+53.0	15.4	2 48.5	+53.1	15.4	3 46.4	+53.2	15.4	60
61	2 06.3	-52.4	165.1	1 08.3	-52.5	165.1	0 10.3	-52.6	165.1	0 47.7	+52.8	14.9	1 45.7	+52.8	14.9	2 43.7	+53.0	14.9	3 41.7	+53.1	14.9	4 39.6	+53.2	14.9	61
62	1 13.9	-52.4	165.6	0 15.8	-52.5	165.6	0 42.3	+52.7	14.4	1 40.5	+52.7	14.4	2 38.6	+52.8	14.4	3 36.7	+53.0	14.4	4 34.8	+53.1	14.5	5 32.9	+53.2	14.5	62
63	0 21.5	-52.4	166.1	0 36.7	+52.5	13.9	1 35.0	+52.6	13.9	2 33.2	+52.7	13.9	3 31.4	+52.8	13.9	4 29.7	+52.9	14.0	5 27.9	+53.0	14.0	6 26.1	+53.2	14.0	63
64	0 30.9	+52.3	13.4	1 29.2	+52.5	13.4	2 27.6	+52.6	13.4	3 25.9	+52.7	13.5	4 24.3	+52.8	13.5	5 22.6	+53.0	13.5	6 21.0	+53.0	13.5	7 19.3	+53.2	13.5	64
65	1 23.2	+52.4	12.9	2 21.7	+52.5	13.0	3 20.2	+52.6	13.0	4 18.7	+52.7	13.0	5 17.1	+52.8	13.0	6 15.6	+52.9	13.0	7 14.0	+53.1	13.1	8 12.5	+53.1	13.1	65
66	2 15.6	+52.4	12.5	3 14.2	+52.5	12.5	4 12.8	+52.6	12.5	5 11.4	+52.7	12.5	6 09.9	+52.7	12.6	7 08.5	+52.9	12.6	8 07.1	+53.0	12.6	9 05.6	+53.1	12.6	66
67	3 08.0	+52.3	12.0	4 06.7	+52.4	12.0	5 05.4	+52.6	12.0	6 04.0	+52.7	12.0	7 02.7	+52.8	12.0	8 01.4	+52.9	12.1	9 00.1	+52.9	12.1	9 58.7	+53.0	12.1	67
68	4 00.3	+52.3	11.5	4 59.1	+52.4	11.5	5 58.0	+52.5	11.5	6 56.7	+52.6	11.5	7 55.5	+52.7	11.6	8 54.3	+52.8	11.6	9 53.0	+53.0	11.6	10 51.8	+53.0	11.7	68
69	4 52.6	+52.4	11.0	5 51.5	+52.4	11.0	6 50.4	+52.5	11.0	7 49.3	+52.6	11.1	8 48.2	+52.7	11.1	9 47.1	+52.8	11.1	10 46.0	+52.8	11.1	11 44.8	+53.0	11.2	69
70	5 45.0	+52.2	10.5	6 43.9	+52.4	10.5	7 42.9	+52.5	10.5	8 41.9	+52.6	10.6	9 40.9	+52.7	10.6	10 39.9	+52.7	10.6	11 38.8	+52.9	10.7	12 37.8	+52.9	10.7	70
71	6 37.2	+52.3	10.0	7 36.3	+52.4	10.0	8 35.4	+52.4	10.0	9 34.5	+52.5	10.1	10 33.6	+52.6	10.1	11 32.6	+52.7	10.1	12 31.7	+52.8	10.2	13 30.7	+52.9	10.2	71
72	7 29.5	+52.2	9.5	8 28.7	+52.3	9.5	9 27.8	+52.4	9.6	10 27.0	+52.5	9.6	11 26.2	+52.5	9.6	12 25.3	+52.6	9.6	13 24.5	+52.7	9.7	14 23.6	+52.7	9.7	72
73	8 21.7	+52.2	9.0	9 21.0	+52.2	9.0	10 20.2	+52.4	9.1	11 19.5	+52.4	9.1	12 18.7	+52.5	9.1	13 17.9	+52.6	9.2	14 17.2	+52.6	9.2	15 16.4	+52.7	9.2	73
74	9 13.9	+52.1	8.5	10 13.2	+52.2	8.5	11 12.6	+52.3	8.6	12 11.9	+52.4	8.6	13 11.2	+52.4	8.6	14 10.5	+52.5	8.7	15 09.8	+52.6	8.7	16 09.1	+52.7	8.7	74
75	10 06.0	+52.1	8.0	11 05.4	+52.2	8.0	12 04.9	+52.2	8.1	13 04.3	+52.3	8.1	14 03.7	+52.3	8.1	15 03.0	+52.5	8.2	16 02.4	+52.6	8.2	17 01.8	+52.6	8.2	75
76	10 58.1	+52.1	7.5	11 57.6	+52.1	7.5	12 57.1	+52.2	7.6	13 56.6	+52.2	7.6	14 56.0	+52.3	7.6	15 55.5	+52.4	7.7	16 55.0	+52.4	7.7	17 54.4	+52.5	7.7	76
77	11 50.2	+52.0	7.0	12 49.7	+52.1	7.0	13 49.3	+52.1	7.1	14 48.8	+52.2	7.1	15 48.3	+52.3	7.1	16 47.9	+52.3	7.2	17 47.4	+52.4	7.2	18 46.9	+52.5	7.2	77
78	12 42.2	+52.0	6.5	13 41.8	+52.0	6.5	14 41.4	+52.0	6.5	15 41.0	+52.1	6.6	16 40.6	+52.2	6.6	17 40.2	+52.3	6.6	18 39.8	+52.3	6.7	19 39.4	+52.3	6.7	78
79	13 34.1	+51.9	6.0	14 33.8	+51.9	6.0	15 33.4	+52.0	6.0	16 33.1	+52.0	6.1	17 32.8	+52.0	6.1	18 32.4	+52.2	6.1	19 32.1	+52.2	6.2	20 31.7	+52.3	6.2	79
80	14 26.0	+51.7	5.5	15 25.7	+51.8	5.5	16 25.4	+51.9	5.5	17 25.1	+52.0	5.5	18 24.8	+52.0	5.6	19 24.6	+52.0	5.6	20 24.3	+52.1	5.6	21 24.0	+52.1	5.7	80
81	15 17.7	+51.8	4.9	16 17.5	+51.8	5.0	17 17.3	+51.8	5.0	18 17.1	+51.8	5.0	19 16.8	+51.9	5.0	20 16.6	+52.0	5.1	21 16.4	+52.0	5.1	22 16.1	+52.1	5.1	81
82	16 09.5	+51.6	4.4	17 09.3	+51.7	4.4	18 09.1	+51.7	4.5	19 08.9	+51.8	4.5	20 08.8	+51.8	4.5	21 08.6	+51.8	4.5	22 08.4	+51.9	4.6	23 08.2	+51.9	4.6	82
83	17 01.1	+51.6	3.9	18 01.0	+51.6	3.9	19 00.8	+51.7	3.9	20 00.7	+51.7	3.9	21 00.6	+51.8	4.0	22 00.4	+51.8	4.0	23 00.3	+51.8	4.0	24 00.1	+51.8	4.1	83
84	17 52.7	+51.5	3.3	18 52.6	+51.5	3.4	19 52.5	+51.5	3.4	20 52.4	+51.5	3.4	21 52.4	+51.6	3.4	22 52.1	+51.6	3.4	23 52.1	+51.6	3.5	24 51.9	+51.7	3.5	84
85	18 44.2	+51.3	2.8	19 44.1	+51.4	2.8	20 44.0	+51.4	2.8	21 43.9	+51.5	2.8	22 43.9	+51.4	2.9	23 43.8	+51.5	2.9	24 43.7	+51.5	2.9	25 43.6	+51.6	2.9	85
86	19 35.5	+51.3	2.2	20 35.5	+51.3	2.3	21 35.4	+51.3	2.3	22 35.4	+51.3	2.3	23 35.3	+51.4	2.3	24 35.3	+51.4	2.3	25 35.2	+51.4	2.4	26 35.2	+51.4	2.4	86
87	20 26.8	+51.2	1.7	21 26.8	+51.2	1.7	22 26.8	+51.2	1.7	23 26.7	+51.3	1.7	24 26.7	+51.2	1.7	25 26.7	+51.2	1.7	26 26.7	+51.1	1.8	27 26.6	+51.3	1.8	87
88	21 18.0	+51.1	1.1	22 18.0	+51.1	1.1	23 18.0	+51.0	1.2	24 18.0	+51.0	1.2	25 18.0	+51.1	1.2	26 18.0	+51.1	1.2	27 17.9	+51.1	1.2	28 17.9	+51.1	1.2	88
89	22 09.1	+50.9	0.6	23 09.1	+50.9	0.6	24 09.0	+51.0	0.6	25 09.0	+51.0	0.6	26 09.0	+51.0	0.6	27 09.0	+51.0	0.6	28 09.0	+51.0	0.6	29 09.0	+51.0	0.6	89
90	23 00.0	+50.8	0.0	24 00.0	+50.8	0.0	25 00.0	+50.8	0.0	26 00.0	+50.8	0.0	27 00.0	+50.8	0.0	28 00.0	+50.8	0.0	29 00.0	+50.8	0.0	30 00.0	+50.8	0.0	90

S. Lat. { L.H.A. greater than 180°.....Zn=180°-Z ; L.H.A. less than 180°.........Zn=180°+Z }

37°, 323° L.H.A. LATITUDE SAME NAME AS DECLINATION N. Lat.

{ L.H.A. greater than 180°......Zn=Z
{ L.H.A. less than 180°......Zn=360°−Z

Dec.	23° Hc	d	Z	24° Hc	d	Z	25° Hc	d	Z	26° Hc	d	Z	27° Hc	d	Z	28° Hc	d	Z	29° Hc	d	Z	30° Hc	d	Z	Dec.
0	47 19.2	+34.2	117.4	46 51.1	+35.3	118.4	46 22.2	+36.4	119.3	45 52.4	+37.5	120.2	45 21.9	+38.4	121.1	44 50.5	+39.4	121.9	44 18.4	+40.4	122.8	43 45.6	+41.3	123.6	0
1	47 53.4	+33.4	116.2	47 26.4	+34.6	117.2	46 58.6	+35.7	118.1	46 29.9	+36.7	119.1	46 00.3	+37.8	120.0	45 29.9	+38.9	120.9	44 58.8	+39.8	121.7	44 26.9	+40.7	122.6	1
2	48 26.8	+32.6	114.9	48 01.0	+33.8	116.0	47 34.3	+34.9	116.9	47 06.6	+36.1	117.9	46 38.1	+37.2	118.8	46 08.8	+38.1	119.8	45 38.6	+39.2	120.7	45 07.6	+40.1	121.5	2
3	48 59.4	+31.7	113.7	48 34.8	+32.9	114.7	48 09.2	+34.2	115.7	47 42.7	+35.3	116.7	47 15.3	+36.4	117.7	46 46.9	+37.5	118.6	46 17.8	+38.5	119.6	45 47.7	+39.6	120.5	3
4	49 31.1	+30.8	112.4	49 07.7	+32.1	113.4	48 43.4	+33.3	114.5	48 18.0	+34.5	115.5	47 51.7	+35.7	116.5	47 24.4	+36.8	117.5	46 56.3	+37.9	118.4	46 27.3	+38.9	119.4	4
5	50 01.9	+29.9	111.0	49 39.8	+31.3	112.1	49 16.7	+32.5	113.2	48 52.5	+33.8	114.3	48 27.4	+34.9	115.3	48 01.2	+36.1	116.3	47 34.2	+37.2	117.3	47 06.2	+38.3	118.3	5
6	50 31.8	+29.0	109.7	50 11.1	+30.2	110.8	49 49.2	+31.6	111.9	49 26.3	+32.8	113.0	49 02.3	+34.1	114.1	48 37.3	+35.3	115.1	48 11.4	+36.4	116.1	47 44.5	+37.5	117.1	6
7	51 00.8	+27.9	108.3	50 41.3	+29.4	109.5	50 20.8	+30.7	110.6	49 59.1	+32.0	111.7	49 36.4	+33.3	112.8	49 12.6	+34.5	113.9	48 47.8	+35.7	114.9	48 22.0	+36.9	116.0	7
8	51 28.7	+26.9	106.9	51 10.7	+28.3	108.1	50 51.5	+29.7	109.2	50 31.1	+31.1	110.4	50 09.7	+32.3	111.5	49 47.1	+33.7	112.6	49 23.5	+34.9	113.7	48 58.9	+36.1	114.8	8
9	51 55.6	+25.8	105.4	51 39.0	+27.3	106.6	51 21.2	+28.7	107.9	51 02.2	+30.1	109.0	50 42.0	+31.5	110.2	50 20.8	+32.7	111.4	49 58.4	+34.0	112.4	49 35.0	+35.2	113.5	9
10	52 21.4	+24.7	104.0	52 06.3	+26.2	105.2	51 49.9	+27.7	106.5	51 32.3	+29.1	107.7	51 13.5	+30.5	108.9	50 53.5	+31.9	110.0	50 32.4	+33.2	111.1	50 10.2	+34.5	112.3	10
11	52 46.1	+23.5	102.5	52 32.5	+25.1	103.7	52 17.6	+26.6	105.0	52 01.4	+28.1	106.2	51 44.0	+29.5	107.5	51 25.4	+30.9	108.7	51 05.6	+32.3	109.8	50 44.7	+33.6	111.0	11
12	53 09.6	+22.4	100.9	52 57.6	+23.9	102.1	52 44.2	+25.5	103.5	52 29.5	+27.0	104.8	52 13.5	+28.5	106.1	51 56.3	+29.9	107.3	51 37.9	+31.3	108.5	51 18.3	+32.7	109.7	12
13	53 32.0	+21.1	99.4	53 21.5	+22.8	100.7	53 09.7	+24.3	102.0	52 56.5	+25.9	103.3	52 42.0	+27.4	104.6	52 26.2	+28.9	105.9	52 09.2	+30.3	107.1	51 51.0	+31.7	108.3	13
14	53 53.1	+19.9	97.8	53 44.3	+21.5	99.2	53 34.0	+23.1	100.5	53 22.4	+24.7	101.8	53 09.4	+26.3	103.1	52 55.1	+27.8	104.4	52 39.5	+29.3	105.7	52 22.7	+30.7	106.9	14
15	54 13.0	+18.5	96.2	54 05.8	+20.2	97.6	53 57.1	+21.9	98.9	53 47.1	+23.5	100.3	53 35.7	+25.1	101.6	53 22.9	+26.7	102.9	53 08.8	+28.3	104.2	52 53.4	+29.7	105.5	15
16	54 31.5	+17.2	94.6	54 26.0	+19.0	96.0	54 19.0	+20.7	97.4	54 10.6	+22.3	98.7	54 00.8	+24.0	100.1	53 49.6	+25.6	101.4	53 37.1	+27.0	102.8	53 23.1	+28.6	104.1	16
17	54 48.7	+15.9	92.9	54 44.9	+17.6	94.3	54 39.7	+19.3	95.7	54 32.9	+21.0	97.1	54 24.8	+22.6	98.5	54 15.2	+24.3	99.8	54 04.1	+26.0	101.3	53 51.7	+27.6	102.6	17
18	55 04.5	+14.5	91.2	55 02.5	+16.2	92.7	54 59.0	+17.9	94.1	54 53.9	+19.7	95.5	54 47.4	+21.4	96.9	54 39.5	+23.1	98.3	54 30.1	+24.7	99.7	54 19.3	+26.3	101.1	18
19	55 19.0	+13.0	89.5	55 18.7	+14.8	91.0	55 16.9	+16.6	92.4	55 13.6	+18.4	93.9	55 08.8	+20.1	95.3	55 02.6	+21.8	96.7	54 54.8	+23.5	98.1	54 45.6	+25.1	99.5	19
20	55 32.0	+11.5	87.8	55 33.5	+13.3	89.3	55 33.5	+15.2	90.7	55 32.0	+16.9	92.2	55 28.9	+18.7	93.6	55 24.4	+20.4	95.1	55 18.3	+22.2	96.5	55 10.7	+23.9	98.0	20
21	55 43.5	+10.1	86.1	55 46.8	+11.9	87.5	55 48.7	+13.7	89.0	55 48.9	+15.5	90.5	55 47.6	+17.4	92.0	55 44.8	+19.1	93.4	55 40.5	+20.8	94.9	55 34.6	+22.6	96.3	21
22	55 53.6	+8.5	84.3	55 58.7	+10.4	85.8	56 02.4	+12.2	87.3	56 04.4	+14.1	88.8	56 05.0	+15.8	90.2	56 03.9	+17.7	91.7	56 01.3	+19.5	93.2	55 57.2	+21.2	94.7	22
23	56 02.1	+7.0	82.6	56 09.1	+8.9	83.9	56 14.6	+10.7	85.5	56 18.5	+12.5	87.0	56 20.8	+14.4	88.5	56 21.6	+16.2	90.0	56 20.8	+18.0	91.5	56 18.4	+19.9	93.0	23
24	56 09.1	+5.5	80.8	56 18.0	+7.3	82.3	56 25.3	+9.2	83.7	56 31.0	+11.1	85.3	56 35.2	+12.9	86.8	56 37.8	+14.8	88.3	56 38.8	+16.6	89.8	56 38.3	+18.4	91.3	24
25	56 14.6	+3.9	79.0	56 25.3	+5.7	80.5	56 34.5	+7.6	82.0	56 42.1	+9.5	83.5	56 48.1	+11.4	85.0	56 52.6	+13.2	86.5	56 55.4	+15.1	88.0	56 56.7	+16.9	89.6	25
26	56 18.5	+2.3	77.2	56 31.0	+4.2	78.7	56 42.1	+6.0	80.1	56 51.6	+7.9	81.7	56 59.5	+9.8	83.2	57 05.8	+11.7	84.7	57 10.5	+13.6	86.3	57 13.6	+15.5	87.8	26
27	56 20.8	+0.8	75.4	56 35.2	+2.6	76.8	56 48.1	+4.5	78.3	56 59.5	+6.3	79.8	57 09.3	+8.2	81.4	57 17.5	+10.1	82.9	57 24.1	+12.0	84.5	57 29.1	+13.9	86.0	27
28	56 21.6	−0.8	73.6	56 37.8	+1.0	75.0	56 52.6	+2.9	76.5	57 05.8	+4.7	78.0	57 17.5	+6.6	79.5	57 27.6	+8.5	81.1	57 36.1	+10.4	82.6	57 43.0	+12.3	84.2	28
29	56 20.8	−2.4	71.8	56 38.8	−0.5	73.2	56 55.4	+1.3	74.7	57 10.5	+3.1	76.2	57 24.1	+5.0	77.7	57 36.1	+6.9	79.2	57 46.5	+8.8	80.8	57 55.3	+10.7	82.4	29
30	56 18.4	−3.9	70.0	56 38.3	−2.2	71.4	56 56.7	−0.4	72.8	57 13.6	+1.5	74.3	57 29.1	+3.3	75.8	57 43.0	+5.2	77.4	57 55.3	+7.2	78.9	58 06.0	+9.1	80.5	30
31	56 14.5	−5.5	68.2	56 36.1	−3.7	69.6	56 56.3	−1.9	71.0	57 15.1	−0.1	72.5	57 32.4	+1.8	74.0	57 48.2	+3.6	75.5	58 02.5	+5.5	77.1	58 15.1	+7.4	78.6	31
32	56 09.0	−7.1	66.4	56 32.4	−5.4	67.8	56 54.4	−3.6	69.2	57 15.0	−1.8	70.6	57 34.2	0.0	72.1	57 51.8	+2.0	73.6	58 08.0	+3.8	75.2	58 22.5	+5.8	76.7	32
33	56 01.9	−8.5	64.6	56 27.0	−6.8	66.0	56 50.8	−5.1	67.4	57 13.2	−3.4	68.8	57 34.2	−1.6	70.3	57 53.8	+0.2	71.7	58 11.8	+2.1	73.3	58 28.3	+4.0	74.8	33
34	55 53.4	−10.1	62.8	56 20.2	−8.5	64.2	56 45.7	−6.8	65.5	57 09.8	−5.0	66.9	57 32.6	−3.2	68.4	57 54.0	−1.4	69.9	58 13.9	+0.5	71.4	58 32.3	+2.3	72.9	34
35	55 43.3	−11.6	61.1	56 11.7	−9.9	62.4	56 38.9	−8.3	63.7	57 04.8	−6.6	65.1	57 29.4	−4.8	66.5	57 52.6	−3.1	68.0	58 14.4	−1.3	69.5	58 34.6	+0.7	71.0	35
36	55 31.7	−13.0	59.3	56 01.8	−11.5	60.6	56 30.6	−9.8	61.9	56 58.2	−8.2	63.3	57 24.5	−6.4	64.7	57 49.5	−4.7	66.1	58 13.1	−2.9	67.6	58 35.3	−1.1	69.1	36
37	55 18.7	−14.4	57.6	55 50.3	−12.9	58.9	56 20.8	−11.4	60.1	56 50.0	−9.7	61.5	57 18.1	−8.1	62.8	57 44.8	−6.4	64.2	58 10.2	−4.6	65.7	58 34.2	−2.8	67.2	37
38	55 04.3	−15.9	55.9	55 37.4	−14.4	57.1	56 09.4	−12.9	58.4	56 40.3	−11.3	59.7	57 10.0	−9.7	61.0	57 38.4	−8.0	62.4	58 05.6	−6.3	63.8	58 31.4	−4.5	65.3	38
39	54 48.4	−17.2	54.2	55 23.0	−15.8	55.4	55 56.5	−14.3	56.6	56 29.0	−12.9	57.9	57 00.3	−11.3	59.2	57 30.4	−9.6	60.5	57 59.3	−7.9	61.9	58 26.9	−6.2	63.4	39
40	54 31.2	−18.6	52.6	55 07.2	−17.3	53.7	55 42.2	−15.8	54.9	56 16.1	−14.3	56.1	56 49.0	−12.7	57.4	57 20.8	−11.2	58.7	57 51.4	−9.6	60.1	58 20.7	−7.9	61.5	40
41	54 12.6	−19.9	51.0	54 49.9	−18.5	52.1	55 26.4	−17.2	53.2	56 01.8	−15.7	54.4	56 36.3	−14.3	55.6	57 09.6	−12.8	56.9	57 41.8	−11.2	58.2	58 12.8	−9.5	59.6	41
42	53 52.7	−21.1	49.3	54 31.4	−19.9	50.4	55 09.2	−18.6	51.5	55 46.1	−17.2	52.7	56 22.0	−15.8	53.8	56 56.8	−14.2	55.1	57 30.6	−12.7	56.4	58 03.3	−11.2	57.7	42
43	53 31.6	−22.0	47.8	54 11.5	−21.1	48.8	54 50.6	−19.9	49.9	55 28.9	−18.6	51.0	56 06.2	−17.2	52.1	56 42.6	−15.8	53.3	57 17.9	−14.3	54.6	57 52.1	−12.7	55.8	43
44	53 09.2	−23.5	46.2	53 50.4	−22.4	47.2	54 30.7	−21.1	48.2	55 10.3	−19.9	49.3	55 49.0	−18.6	50.4	56 26.8	−17.3	51.6	57 03.6	−15.8	52.8	57 39.4	−14.4	54.0	44

| | 23° | | | 24° | | | 25° | | | 26° | | | 27° | | | 28° | | | 29° | | | 30° | | | |

Dec	23° Hc	23° d	23° Z	24° Hc	24° d	24° Z	25° Hc	25° d	25° Z	26° Hc	26° d	26° Z	27° Hc	27° d	27° Z	28° Hc	28° d	28° Z	29° Hc	29° d	29° Z	30° Hc	30° d	30° Z	Dec
45	52 45.7	-24.8	44.7	53 28.0	-23.6	45.6	54 09.6	-22.5	46.6	54 50.4	-21.3	47.6	55 30.4	-20.0	48.7	56 09.5	-18.6	49.8	56 47.8	-17.3	51.0	57 25.0	-15.8	52.2	45
46	52 20.9	-25.8	43.2	53 04.4	-24.8	44.1	53 47.1	-23.7	45.0	54 29.1	-22.5	46.0	55 10.4	-21.3	47.1	55 50.9	-20.1	48.1	56 30.5	-18.7	49.3	57 09.2	-17.4	50.4	46
47	51 55.1	-26.9	41.7	52 39.6	-25.9	42.6	53 23.4	-24.8	43.5	54 06.6	-23.7	44.4	54 49.1	-22.6	45.4	55 30.8	-21.4	46.5	56 11.8	-20.2	47.5	56 51.8	-18.8	48.7	47
48	51 28.2	-28.0	40.3	52 13.7	-27.0	41.1	52 58.6	-26.0	42.0	53 42.9	-24.9	42.9	54 26.5	-23.8	43.8	55 09.4	-22.6	44.8	55 51.6	-21.5	45.9	56 33.0	-20.2	46.9	48
49	51 00.2	-28.9	38.9	51 46.7	-28.0	39.7	52 32.6	-27.1	40.5	53 18.0	-26.1	41.3	54 02.7	-25.1	42.3	54 46.8	-24.0	43.2	55 30.1	-22.8	44.2	56 12.8	-21.6	45.2	49
50	50 31.3	-29.9	37.5	51 18.7	-29.1	38.2	52 05.5	-28.1	39.0	52 51.9	-27.2	39.8	53 37.6	-26.2	40.7	54 22.8	-25.1	41.6	55 07.3	-24.0	42.6	55 51.2	-23.0	43.6	50
51	50 01.4	-30.9	36.1	50 49.6	-30.0	36.7	51 37.4	-29.1	37.6	52 24.7	-28.3	38.2	53 11.4	-27.3	39.2	53 57.7	-26.4	40.1	54 43.3	-25.3	41.0	55 28.2	-24.2	41.9	51
52	49 30.5	-31.7	34.8	50 19.6	-31.0	35.5	51 08.2	-30.1	36.2	51 56.4	-29.3	36.9	52 44.1	-28.4	37.7	53 31.3	-27.5	38.6	54 18.0	-26.5	39.4	55 04.0	-25.5	40.3	52
53	48 58.8	-32.6	33.5	49 48.6	-31.8	34.1	50 38.1	-31.1	34.8	51 27.1	-30.3	35.5	52 15.7	-29.4	36.3	53 03.8	-28.5	37.1	53 51.5	-27.7	37.9	54 38.5	-26.6	38.7	53
54	48 26.2	-33.5	32.2	49 16.8	-32.8	32.8	50 07.0	-32.0	33.5	50 56.8	-31.2	34.2	51 46.3	-30.5	34.9	52 35.3	-29.6	35.6	53 23.8	-28.7	36.4	54 11.9	-27.8	37.2	54
55	47 52.7	-34.2	31.0	48 44.0	-33.5	31.6	49 35.0	-32.9	32.2	50 25.6	-32.1	32.8	51 15.8	-31.4	33.5	52 05.7	-30.6	34.2	52 55.1	-29.8	34.9	53 44.1	-29.0	35.7	55
56	47 18.5	-34.9	29.8	48 10.5	-34.4	30.3	49 02.1	-33.7	30.9	49 53.5	-33.1	31.5	50 44.4	-32.3	32.1	51 35.1	-31.6	32.8	52 25.3	-30.8	33.5	53 15.1	-29.9	34.2	56
57	46 43.6	-35.7	28.6	47 36.1	-35.1	29.1	48 28.4	-34.5	29.6	49 20.4	-33.8	30.2	50 12.1	-33.2	30.8	51 03.5	-32.5	31.4	51 54.5	-31.8	32.1	52 45.2	-31.1	32.8	57
58	46 07.9	-36.4	27.4	47 01.0	-35.8	27.9	47 53.9	-35.2	28.4	48 46.6	-34.7	29.0	49 38.9	-34.0	29.5	50 31.0	-33.4	30.0	51 22.8	-32.7	30.7	52 14.1	-31.9	31.4	58
59	45 31.5	-37.1	26.3	46 25.2	-36.6	26.7	47 18.7	-36.0	27.2	48 11.9	-35.4	27.7	49 04.9	-34.9	28.2	49 57.6	-34.2	28.8	50 50.0	-33.6	29.4	51 42.2	-33.0	30.0	59
60	44 54.4	-37.7	25.1	45 48.6	-37.2	25.6	46 42.7	-36.8	26.0	47 36.5	-36.2	26.5	48 30.0	-35.6	27.0	49 23.4	-35.1	27.5	50 16.4	-34.4	28.1	51 09.2	-33.8	28.7	60
61	44 16.7	-38.3	24.0	45 11.4	-37.8	24.5	46 05.9	-37.3	24.9	47 00.3	-36.9	25.3	47 54.4	-36.4	25.8	48 48.3	-35.8	26.3	49 42.0	-35.3	26.8	50 35.4	-34.7	27.4	61
62	43 38.4	-38.9	23.0	44 33.6	-38.5	23.4	45 28.6	-38.0	23.8	46 23.4	-37.6	24.2	47 18.0	-37.0	24.6	48 12.5	-36.6	25.1	49 06.7	-36.0	25.6	50 00.7	-35.5	26.1	62
63	42 59.5	-39.4	21.9	43 55.1	-39.1	22.3	44 50.5	-38.6	22.7	45 45.8	-38.2	23.1	46 41.0	-37.8	23.5	47 35.9	-37.3	23.9	48 30.7	-36.8	24.4	49 25.2	-36.3	24.8	63
64	42 20.1	-40.0	20.9	43 16.0	-39.6	21.2	44 11.9	-39.2	21.6	45 07.6	-38.8	22.0	46 03.2	-38.4	22.3	46 58.6	-38.0	22.7	47 53.9	-37.6	23.2	48 48.9	-37.0	23.6	64
65	41 40.1	-40.5	19.9	42 36.4	-40.1	20.2	43 32.7	-39.8	20.5	44 28.8	-39.4	20.9	45 24.8	-39.0	21.2	46 20.6	-38.6	21.6	47 16.4	-38.2	22.0	48 11.9	-37.8	22.4	65
66	40 59.6	-41.0	18.9	41 56.3	-40.7	19.2	42 52.9	-40.3	19.5	43 49.4	-40.0	19.8	44 45.8	-39.7	20.2	45 42.0	-39.2	20.5	46 38.1	-38.8	20.9	47 34.1	-38.4	21.3	66
67	40 18.6	-41.5	18.0	41 15.6	-41.2	18.2	42 12.5	-40.8	18.5	43 09.4	-40.5	18.8	44 06.1	-40.2	19.1	45 02.8	-39.9	19.4	45 59.3	-39.5	19.8	46 55.7	-39.1	20.1	67
68	39 37.1	-41.9	17.0	40 34.4	-41.6	17.3	41 31.7	-41.3	17.5	42 28.9	-41.1	17.8	43 25.9	-40.7	18.1	44 22.9	-40.4	18.4	45 19.8	-40.0	18.7	46 16.6	-39.7	19.0	68
69	38 55.2	-42.4	16.1	39 52.8	-42.1	16.3	40 50.5	-41.8	16.6	41 47.8	-41.5	16.8	42 45.2	-41.2	17.1	43 42.5	-40.9	17.4	44 39.8	-40.7	17.7	45 36.9	-40.3	18.0	69
70	38 12.8	-42.7	15.2	39 10.7	-42.5	15.4	40 08.5	-42.2	15.6	41 06.3	-42.0	15.9	42 04.0	-41.8	16.1	43 01.6	-41.5	16.4	43 59.1	-41.2	16.6	44 56.6	-40.9	16.9	70
71	37 30.1	-43.1	14.3	38 28.2	-42.9	14.5	39 26.3	-42.7	14.7	40 24.3	-42.5	14.9	41 22.2	-42.2	15.1	42 20.1	-41.9	15.4	43 17.9	-41.6	15.6	44 15.7	-41.4	15.9	71
72	36 47.0	-43.6	13.4	37 45.3	-43.3	13.6	38 43.6	-43.1	13.8	39 41.8	-42.8	14.0	40 40.0	-42.6	14.2	41 38.2	-42.5	14.4	42 36.3	-42.2	14.6	43 34.3	-42.0	14.9	72
73	36 03.4	-43.8	12.6	37 02.0	-43.7	12.7	38 00.4	-43.5	12.9	38 59.0	-43.3	13.1	39 57.4	-43.1	13.3	40 55.7	-42.8	13.5	41 54.1	-42.7	13.7	42 52.3	-42.4	13.9	73
74	35 19.6	-44.3	11.7	36 18.3	-44.0	11.9	37 17.0	-43.9	12.0	38 15.7	-43.7	12.2	39 14.3	-43.5	12.4	40 12.9	-43.3	12.5	41 11.4	-43.1	12.7	42 09.9	-42.9	12.9	74
75	34 35.3	-44.5	10.9	35 34.3	-44.4	11.0	36 33.1	-44.2	11.2	37 32.0	-44.1	11.3	38 30.8	-43.9	11.5	39 29.6	-43.7	11.6	40 28.3	-43.5	11.8	41 27.0	-43.3	12.0	75
76	33 50.8	-44.9	10.1	34 49.9	-44.8	10.2	35 48.9	-44.6	10.3	36 47.9	-44.4	10.5	37 46.9	-44.3	10.6	38 45.9	-44.1	10.7	39 44.8	-43.9	10.9	40 43.7	-43.8	11.1	76
77	33 05.9	-45.1	9.3	34 05.1	-45.0	9.4	35 04.3	-45.0	9.5	36 03.5	-44.8	9.6	37 02.6	-44.6	9.8	38 01.8	-44.5	9.9	39 00.9	-44.4	10.0	39 59.9	-44.2	10.2	77
78	32 20.8	-45.4	8.5	33 20.1	-45.3	8.6	34 19.4	-45.2	8.7	35 18.7	-45.0	8.8	36 18.0	-44.9	8.9	37 17.3	-44.8	9.0	38 16.5	-44.7	9.2	39 15.7	-44.5	9.3	78
79	31 35.4	-45.8	7.7	32 34.8	-45.6	7.8	33 34.2	-45.5	7.9	34 33.7	-45.4	8.0	35 33.1	-45.3	8.1	36 32.5	-45.2	8.2	37 31.8	-45.0	8.3	38 31.2	-44.9	8.4	79
80	30 49.6	-45.9	7.0	31 49.2	-45.9	7.1	32 48.7	-45.8	7.2	33 48.3	-45.7	7.2	34 47.8	-45.6	7.3	35 47.3	-45.5	7.4	36 46.3	-45.4	7.5	37 46.3	-45.3	7.6	80
81	30 03.7	-46.3	6.2	31 03.3	-46.1	6.3	32 02.9	-46.0	6.4	33 02.6	-46.0	6.4	34 02.2	-45.9	6.5	35 01.8	-45.8	6.6	36 01.0	-45.7	6.7	37 01.0	-45.7	6.8	81
82	29 17.4	-46.4	5.5	30 17.2	-46.4	5.6	31 16.9	-46.3	5.6	32 16.6	-46.3	5.7	33 16.3	-46.2	5.7	34 16.0	-46.1	5.8	35 15.7	-46.1	5.9	36 15.3	-45.9	6.0	82
83	28 31.0	-46.7	4.8	29 31.0	-46.6	4.8	30 30.6	-46.6	4.9	31 30.3	-46.5	4.9	32 30.1	-46.4	5.0	33 29.9	-46.4	5.0	34 29.4	-46.3	5.1	35 29.4	-46.2	5.2	83
84	27 44.3	-46.8	4.1	28 44.1	-46.8	4.1	29 44.0	-46.8	4.2	30 43.8	-46.7	4.2	31 43.7	-46.7	4.2	32 43.5	-46.6	4.3	33 43.2	-46.6	4.3	34 43.2	-46.6	4.4	84
85	26 57.4	-47.1	3.4	27 57.3	-47.1	3.4	28 57.2	-47.0	3.4	29 57.1	-47.0	3.5	30 57.0	-47.0	3.5	31 56.9	-46.9	3.5	32 56.7	-46.8	3.6	33 56.6	-46.8	3.6	85
86	26 10.3	-47.3	2.7	27 10.2	-47.2	2.7	28 10.2	-47.3	2.7	29 10.1	-47.2	2.8	30 10.0	-47.2	2.8	31 10.0	-47.2	2.8	32 09.9	-47.1	2.8	33 09.8	-47.1	2.9	86
87	25 23.0	-47.5	2.0	26 23.0	-47.5	2.0	27 22.9	-47.4	2.0	28 22.9	-47.4	2.1	29 22.8	-47.4	2.1	30 22.8	-47.4	2.1	31 22.8	-47.4	2.1	32 22.7	-47.3	2.1	87
88	24 35.5	-47.7	1.3	25 35.5	-47.7	1.3	26 35.5	-47.6	1.3	27 35.5	-47.6	1.4	28 35.4	-47.6	1.4	29 35.4	-47.6	1.4	30 35.4	-47.6	1.4	31 35.4	-47.6	1.4	88
89	23 47.8	-47.8	0.7	24 47.8	-47.8	0.7	25 47.8	-47.8	0.7	26 47.8	-47.8	0.7	27 47.8	-47.8	0.7	28 47.8	-47.8	0.7	29 47.8	-47.8	0.7	30 47.8	-47.8	0.7	89
90	23 00.0	-48.0	0.0	24 00.0	-48.0	0.0	25 00.0	-48.0	0.0	26 00.0	-48.0	0.0	27 00.0	-48.0	0.0	28 00.0	-48.0	0.0	29 00.0	-48.0	0.0	30 00.0	-48.0	0.0	90
Dec	23°			24°			25°			26°			27°			28°			29°			30°			

37°, 323° L.H.A. LATITUDE SAME NAME AS DECLINATION

L.H.A. 37°, 323°

LATITUDE CONTRARY NAME TO DECLINATION

Dec.	23° Hc	d	Z	24° Hc	d	Z	25° Hc	d	Z	26° Hc	d	Z	27° Hc	d	Z	28° Hc	d	Z	29° Hc	d	Z	30° Hc	d	Z	Dec.
0	47 19.2	-35.0	117.4	46 51.1	-36.0	118.4	46 22.2	-37.1	119.3	45 52.4	-38.1	120.2	45 21.9	-39.1	121.1	44 50.5	-40.0	121.9	44 18.4	-40.9	122.8	43 45.6	-41.8	123.6	0
1	46 44.2	-35.7	118.6	46 15.1	-36.7	119.5	45 45.1	-37.7	120.4	45 14.3	-38.7	121.3	44 42.8	-39.7	122.1	44 10.5	-40.6	123.0	43 37.5	-41.5	123.8	43 03.8	-42.3	124.6	1
2	46 08.5	-36.3	119.8	45 38.3	-37.3	120.7	45 07.4	-38.4	121.5	44 35.6	-39.3	122.4	44 03.1	-40.2	123.2	43 29.9	-41.1	124.0	42 56.0	-41.9	124.8	42 21.5	-42.8	125.5	2
3	45 32.2	-37.1	120.9	45 01.0	-38.1	121.8	44 29.0	-39.0	122.6	43 56.3	-39.9	123.4	43 22.9	-40.8	124.2	42 48.8	-41.6	125.0	42 14.1	-42.4	125.7	41 38.7	-43.2	126.5	3
4	44 55.1	-37.7	122.0	44 22.9	-38.6	122.9	43 50.0	-39.5	123.7	43 16.4	-40.4	124.5	42 42.1	-41.3	125.2	42 07.2	-42.1	126.0	41 31.7	-42.9	126.7	40 55.5	-43.6	127.4	4
5	44 17.4	-38.3	123.1	43 44.3	-39.2	123.9	43 10.5	-40.1	124.7	42 36.0	-41.0	125.5	42 00.8	-41.7	126.2	41 25.1	-42.6	126.9	40 48.8	-43.4	127.6	40 11.9	-44.1	128.3	5
6	43 39.1	-38.9	124.2	43 05.1	-39.8	125.0	42 30.4	-40.7	125.7	41 55.0	-41.4	126.5	41 19.1	-42.3	127.2	40 42.5	-43.0	127.9	40 05.4	-43.7	128.5	39 27.8	-44.5	129.2	6
7	43 00.2	-39.4	125.2	42 25.3	-40.3	126.0	41 49.7	-41.1	126.7	41 13.6	-41.9	127.4	40 36.8	-42.7	128.1	39 59.5	-43.4	128.8	39 21.7	-44.1	129.4	38 43.3	-44.8	130.0	7
8	42 20.8	-40.0	126.3	41 45.0	-40.8	127.0	41 08.6	-41.6	127.7	40 31.7	-42.4	128.4	39 54.1	-43.1	129.1	39 16.1	-43.8	129.7	38 37.6	-44.6	130.3	37 58.5	-45.2	130.9	8
9	41 40.8	-40.5	127.3	41 04.2	-41.3	128.0	40 27.0	-42.1	128.6	39 49.3	-42.8	129.3	39 11.0	-43.5	129.9	38 32.3	-44.3	130.5	37 53.0	-44.9	131.1	37 13.3	-45.5	131.7	9
10	41 00.3	-41.0	128.2	40 22.9	-41.8	128.9	39 44.9	-42.5	129.6	39 06.5	-43.3	130.2	38 27.5	-43.9	130.8	37 48.0	-44.5	131.4	37 08.1	-45.2	132.0	36 27.8	-45.9	132.5	10
11	40 19.3	-41.4	129.2	39 41.1	-42.2	129.9	39 02.4	-42.9	130.5	38 23.2	-43.6	131.1	37 43.6	-44.3	131.7	37 03.5	-45.0	132.2	36 22.9	-45.6	132.8	35 41.9	-46.1	133.3	11
12	39 37.9	-41.9	130.2	38 58.9	-42.6	130.8	38 19.5	-43.3	131.4	37 39.6	-44.0	132.0	36 59.3	-44.7	132.5	36 18.5	-45.3	133.1	35 37.3	-45.8	133.6	34 55.8	-46.5	134.1	12
13	38 56.0	-42.4	131.1	38 16.3	-43.0	131.7	37 36.2	-43.7	132.3	36 55.6	-44.3	132.8	36 14.6	-44.9	133.4	35 33.2	-45.5	133.9	34 51.5	-46.2	134.4	34 09.3	-46.7	134.9	13
14	38 13.6	-42.7	132.0	37 33.3	-43.4	132.6	36 52.5	-44.1	133.1	36 11.3	-44.7	133.7	35 29.7	-45.4	134.2	34 47.7	-45.9	134.7	34 05.3	-46.5	135.2	33 22.6	-47.0	135.6	14
15	37 30.9	-43.1	132.9	36 49.9	-43.8	133.4	36 08.4	-44.4	134.0	35 26.6	-45.1	134.5	34 44.3	-45.6	135.0	34 01.8	-46.2	135.5	33 18.8	-46.7	135.9	32 35.6	-47.3	136.4	15
16	36 47.8	-43.5	133.8	36 06.1	-44.1	134.3	35 24.0	-44.8	134.8	34 41.5	-45.3	135.3	33 58.7	-45.9	135.8	33 15.6	-46.5	136.2	32 32.1	-47.0	136.7	31 48.3	-47.5	137.1	16
17	36 04.3	-43.9	134.6	35 21.9	-44.4	135.1	34 39.2	-45.0	135.6	33 56.2	-45.6	136.1	33 12.8	-46.2	136.5	32 29.1	-46.7	137.0	31 45.1	-47.3	137.4	31 00.8	-47.8	137.8	17
18	35 20.4	-44.2	135.4	34 37.5	-44.8	135.9	33 54.2	-45.4	136.4	33 10.6	-46.0	136.9	32 26.6	-46.4	137.3	31 42.4	-47.0	137.7	30 57.8	-47.4	138.1	30 13.0	-47.9	138.5	18
19	34 36.2	-44.6	136.3	33 52.7	-45.1	136.7	33 08.8	-45.7	137.2	32 24.6	-46.2	137.6	31 40.2	-46.8	138.1	30 55.4	-47.0	138.4	30 10.4	-47.7	138.8	29 25.1	-48.2	139.2	19
20	33 51.6	-44.8	137.1	33 07.5	-45.4	137.5	32 23.1	-45.9	138.0	31 38.4	-46.4	138.4	30 53.4	-46.9	138.8	30 08.2	-47.5	139.2	29 22.7	-48.0	139.5	28 36.9	-48.4	139.9	20
21	33 06.8	-45.2	137.9	32 22.1	-45.6	138.3	31 37.2	-46.2	138.7	30 52.0	-46.7	139.1	30 06.5	-47.2	139.5	29 20.7	-47.6	139.9	28 34.7	-48.1	140.2	27 48.5	-48.6	140.6	21
22	32 21.6	-45.4	138.7	31 36.5	-46.0	139.1	30 51.0	-46.5	139.5	30 05.3	-47.0	139.8	29 19.3	-47.4	140.2	28 33.1	-47.9	140.6	27 46.6	-48.3	140.9	26 59.9	-48.7	141.2	22
23	31 36.2	-45.7	139.4	30 50.5	-46.2	139.8	30 04.5	-46.7	140.2	29 18.3	-47.1	140.6	28 31.9	-47.7	140.9	27 45.2	-48.1	141.2	26 58.3	-48.5	141.6	26 11.2	-49.0	141.9	23
24	30 50.5	-46.0	140.2	30 04.3	-46.5	140.6	29 17.8	-46.9	140.9	28 31.1	-47.4	141.3	27 44.2	-47.8	141.6	26 57.1	-48.3	141.9	26 09.8	-48.7	142.2	25 22.2	-49.0	142.5	24
25	30 04.5	-46.2	140.9	29 17.8	-46.7	141.3	28 30.9	-47.2	141.6	27 43.7	-47.5	142.0	26 56.4	-48.0	142.3	26 08.8	-48.4	142.6	25 21.1	-48.9	142.9	24 33.2	-49.3	143.2	25
26	29 18.3	-46.4	141.7	28 31.1	-46.9	142.0	27 43.7	-47.3	142.3	26 56.2	-47.8	142.6	26 08.4	-48.2	142.9	25 20.4	-48.6	143.2	24 32.2	-49.0	143.5	23 43.9	-49.4	143.8	26
27	28 31.9	-46.7	142.5	27 44.2	-47.3	142.7	26 56.4	-47.6	143.0	26 08.4	-47.9	143.3	25 20.2	-48.4	143.6	24 31.8	-48.8	143.9	23 43.0	-49.2	144.1	22 54.5	-49.5	144.4	27
28	27 45.2	-46.9	143.1	26 57.1	-47.3	143.4	26 08.8	-47.7	143.7	25 20.4	-48.2	144.0	24 31.8	-48.6	144.3	23 43.0	-49.0	144.5	22 54.0	-49.3	144.8	22 05.0	-49.7	145.0	28
29	26 58.3	-47.1	143.8	26 09.8	-47.6	144.1	25 21.1	-47.9	144.4	24 32.2	-48.3	144.6	23 43.2	-48.7	144.9	22 54.0	-49.0	145.2	22 04.7	-49.4	145.4	21 15.3	-49.8	145.6	29
30	26 11.2	-47.3	144.5	25 22.2	-47.7	144.8	24 33.2	-48.1	145.0	23 43.9	-48.5	145.3	22 54.5	-48.9	145.5	22 05.0	-49.3	145.8	21 15.3	-49.6	146.0	20 25.5	-49.9	146.2	30
31	25 23.9	-47.5	145.2	24 34.5	-47.9	145.4	23 45.1	-48.3	145.7	22 55.4	-48.6	145.9	22 05.6	-49.0	146.2	21 15.7	-49.3	146.4	20 25.7	-49.7	146.6	19 35.6	-50.0	146.8	31
32	24 36.4	-47.7	145.9	23 46.7	-48.1	146.1	22 56.8	-48.4	146.3	22 06.8	-48.8	146.6	21 16.6	-49.1	146.8	20 26.4	-49.5	147.0	19 36.0	-49.8	147.2	18 45.5	-50.1	147.4	32
33	23 48.7	-47.8	146.5	22 58.6	-48.2	146.8	22 08.4	-48.6	147.0	21 18.0	-48.9	147.2	20 27.5	-49.3	147.4	19 36.9	-49.6	147.6	18 46.2	-49.9	147.8	17 55.4	-50.3	148.0	33
34	23 00.9	-48.0	147.2	22 10.4	-48.3	147.4	21 19.8	-48.7	147.6	20 29.1	-49.0	147.8	19 38.2	-49.3	148.0	18 47.3	-49.7	148.2	17 56.3	-50.1	148.4	17 05.1	-50.3	148.5	34
35	22 12.9	-48.1	147.8	21 22.1	-48.5	148.0	20 31.1	-48.8	148.2	19 40.0	-49.1	148.4	18 48.9	-49.5	148.6	17 57.6	-49.8	148.8	17 06.2	-50.1	149.0	16 14.8	-50.4	149.1	35
36	21 24.8	-48.3	148.5	20 33.6	-48.7	148.7	19 42.3	-49.0	148.9	18 50.9	-49.3	149.0	17 59.4	-49.6	149.2	17 07.8	-49.9	149.4	16 16.1	-50.2	149.5	15 24.4	-50.6	149.7	36
37	20 36.5	-48.5	149.1	19 44.9	-48.7	149.3	18 53.3	-49.1	149.5	18 01.6	-49.4	149.6	17 09.7	-49.7	149.8	16 17.9	-50.0	150.0	15 25.9	-50.3	150.1	14 33.8	-50.6	150.2	37
38	19 48.0	-48.5	149.7	18 56.2	-48.9	149.9	18 04.2	-49.2	150.1	17 12.2	-49.4	150.2	16 20.0	-49.8	150.4	15 27.8	-50.1	150.6	14 35.6	-50.4	150.7	13 43.2	-50.6	150.8	38
39	18 59.5	-48.7	150.4	18 07.3	-49.0	150.5	17 15.0	-49.3	150.7	16 22.7	-49.6	150.8	15 30.2	-49.9	151.0	14 37.7	-50.2	151.1	13 45.2	-50.5	151.2	12 52.6	-50.8	151.3	39
40	18 10.8	-48.8	151.0	17 18.3	-49.1	151.1	16 25.7	-49.4	151.3	15 33.1	-49.7	151.4	14 40.3	-49.9	151.5	13 47.6	-50.3	151.7	12 54.7	-50.5	151.8	12 01.8	-50.8	151.9	40
41	17 22.0	-48.9	151.6	16 29.2	-49.2	151.7	15 36.3	-49.5	151.9	14 43.4	-49.8	152.0	13 50.4	-50.1	152.1	12 57.3	-50.3	152.2	12 04.2	-50.6	152.3	11 11.0	-50.8	152.4	41
42	16 33.1	-49.0	152.2	15 40.0	-49.3	152.3	14 46.8	-49.6	152.4	13 53.6	-49.9	152.6	13 00.3	-50.1	152.7	12 07.0	-50.4	152.8	11 13.6	-50.7	152.9	10 20.2	-50.9	153.0	42
43	15 44.1	-49.2	152.8	14 50.7	-49.4	152.9	13 57.2	-49.7	153.0	13 03.7	-49.9	153.1	12 10.2	-50.2	153.2	11 16.6	-50.5	153.3	10 22.9	-50.7	153.4	9 29.3	-51.0	153.5	43
44	14 54.9	-49.2	153.4	14 01.3	-49.5	153.5	13 07.5	-49.7	153.6	12 13.8	-50.0	153.7	11 20.0	-50.3	153.7	10 26.1	-50.5	153.9	9 32.2	-50.7	154.0	8 38.3	-51.0	154.0	44

23°	24°	25°	26°	27°	28°	29°	30°

L.H.A. 143°, 217° — **LATITUDE SAME NAME AS DECLINATION**

Dec	23° Hc	d	Z	24° Hc	d	Z	25° Hc	d	Z	26° Hc	d	Z	27° Hc	d	Z	28° Hc	d	Z	29° Hc	d	Z	30° Hc	d	Z	Dec
45	14 05.7	-49.3	154.0	13 11.8	-49.6	154.1	12 17.8	-49.8	154.2	11 23.8	-50.1	154.3	10 29.7	-50.3	154.4	9 35.6	-50.6	154.4	8 41.5	-50.8	154.5	7 47.3	-51.1	154.6	45
46	13 16.4	-49.3	154.6	12 22.2	-49.6	154.7	11 28.0	-49.9	154.8	10 33.7	-50.1	154.8	9 39.4	-50.4	154.9	8 45.0	-50.6	155.0	7 50.8	-50.8	155.0	6 56.2	-51.0	155.1	46
47	12 27.1	-49.5	155.1	11 32.6	-49.7	155.2	10 38.1	-49.9	155.3	9 43.6	-50.2	155.4	8 49.0	-50.4	155.5	7 54.4	-50.6	155.5	6 59.8	-50.9	155.6	6 05.2	-51.2	155.6	47
48	11 37.6	-49.5	155.7	10 42.9	-49.7	155.8	9 48.2	-50.0	155.9	8 53.4	-50.2	155.9	7 58.6	-50.5	156.0	7 03.8	-50.7	156.1	6 08.9	-50.9	156.1	5 14.0	-51.1	156.1	48
49	10 48.1	-49.6	156.3	9 53.2	-49.9	156.4	8 58.2	-50.1	156.5	8 03.2	-50.1	156.5	7 08.1	-50.5	156.6	6 13.1	-50.7	156.6	5 18.0	-50.9	156.6	4 22.9	-51.2	156.7	49
50	9 58.5	-49.6	156.9	9 03.3	-49.8	157.0	8 08.1	-50.1	157.0	7 12.9	-50.3	157.1	6 17.6	-50.5	157.1	5 22.3	-50.7	157.2	4 27.0	-50.9	157.2	3 31.7	-51.1	157.2	50
51	9 08.9	-49.7	157.4	8 13.5	-49.9	157.5	7 18.0	-50.1	157.6	6 22.6	-50.4	157.6	5 27.1	-50.6	157.6	4 31.6	-50.8	157.7	3 36.1	-51.0	157.7	2 40.6	-51.2	157.7	51
52	8 19.2	-49.7	158.0	7 23.6	-50.0	158.1	6 27.9	-50.2	158.1	5 32.2	-50.4	158.1	4 36.5	-50.6	158.2	3 40.8	-50.8	158.2	2 45.1	-51.0	158.2	1 49.4	-51.2	158.2	52
53	7 29.5	-49.8	158.6	6 33.6	-50.0	158.6	5 37.7	-50.2	158.7	4 41.8	-50.4	158.7	3 45.9	-50.6	158.7	2 50.0	-50.8	158.7	1 54.1	-51.0	158.8	0 58.2	-51.2	158.8	53
54	6 39.7	-49.8	159.1	5 43.6	-50.0	159.2	4 47.5	-50.2	159.2	3 51.4	-50.4	159.2	2 55.3	-50.6	159.3	1 59.2	-50.8	159.3	1 03.1	-51.0	159.3	0 07.0	-51.2	159.3	54
55	5 49.9	-49.9	159.7	4 53.6	-49.9	159.7	3 57.3	-50.3	159.8	3 01.0	-50.4	159.8	2 04.7	-50.6	159.8	1 08.4	-50.8	159.8	0 12.1	-51.0	159.8	0 44.2	+51.2	20.2	55
56	5 00.0	-49.9	160.3	4 03.5	-50.0	160.3	3 07.0	-50.2	160.3	2 10.6	-50.5	160.3	1 14.1	-50.7	160.3	0 17.6	-50.9	160.3	0 38.9	+51.1	19.7	1 35.4	+51.2	19.7	56
57	4 10.1	-49.9	160.8	3 13.5	-50.0	160.8	2 16.8	-50.3	160.9	1 20.1	-50.5	160.9	0 23.4	-50.6	160.9	0 33.3	+50.9	19.1	1 30.0	+51.0	19.1	2 26.6	+51.2	19.2	57
58	3 20.2	-49.9	161.4	2 23.4	-50.1	161.4	1 26.5	-50.3	161.4	0 29.6	-50.4	161.4	0 27.2	+50.7	18.6	1 24.1	+50.8	18.6	2 21.0	+51.0	18.6	3 17.8	+51.2	18.6	58
59	2 30.3	-49.9	161.9	1 33.3	-50.2	161.9	0 36.2	-50.3	161.9	0 20.8	+50.5	18.1	1 17.9	+50.6	18.1	2 14.9	+50.8	18.1	3 12.0	+50.9	18.1	4 09.0	+51.1	18.1	59
60	1 40.4	-50.0	162.5	0 43.1	-50.1	162.5	0 14.1	+50.3	17.5	1 11.3	+50.4	17.5	2 08.5	+50.6	17.5	3 05.7	+50.8	17.5	4 02.9	+51.0	17.6	5 00.1	+51.2	17.6	60
61	0 50.4	-49.9	163.0	0 07.0	+50.1	17.0	1 04.4	+50.3	17.0	2 01.7	+50.5	17.0	2 59.1	+50.6	17.0	3 56.5	+50.7	17.0	4 53.9	+50.9	17.0	5 51.3	+51.1	17.1	61
62	0 00.5	-50.0	163.6	0 57.1	+50.0	16.4	1 54.6	+50.3	16.4	2 52.2	+50.4	16.4	3 49.7	+50.6	16.4	4 47.3	+50.7	16.5	5 44.8	+50.9	16.5	6 42.3	+51.1	16.5	62
63	0 49.5	+49.9	15.9	1 47.2	+50.1	15.9	2 44.9	+50.3	15.9	3 42.6	+50.4	15.9	4 40.3	+50.4	15.9	5 38.0	+50.7	15.9	6 35.7	+50.8	15.9	7 33.4	+51.0	16.0	63
64	1 39.4	+50.0	15.3	2 37.3	+50.1	15.3	3 35.2	+50.2	15.3	4 33.0	+50.4	15.3	5 30.9	+50.5	15.4	6 28.7	+50.6	15.4	7 26.6	+50.8	15.4	8 24.4	+51.0	15.5	64
65	2 29.4	+49.9	14.7	3 27.4	+50.1	14.8	4 25.4	+50.2	14.8	5 23.4	+50.4	14.8	6 21.4	+50.5	14.8	7 19.4	+50.7	14.9	8 17.4	+50.8	14.9	9 15.4	+50.9	14.9	65
66	3 19.3	+49.9	14.2	4 17.5	+50.0	14.2	5 15.6	+50.2	14.2	6 13.8	+50.3	14.3	7 11.9	+50.4	14.3	8 10.1	+50.6	14.3	9 08.2	+50.7	14.4	10 06.3	+50.9	14.4	66
67	4 09.2	+49.9	13.6	5 07.5	+50.0	13.7	6 05.8	+50.1	13.7	7 04.1	+50.3	13.7	8 02.4	+50.4	13.7	9 00.7	+50.5	13.8	9 58.9	+50.7	13.8	10 57.2	+50.8	13.9	67
68	4 59.1	+49.8	13.1	5 57.5	+49.9	13.1	6 56.0	+50.1	13.1	7 54.4	+50.2	13.2	8 52.8	+50.3	13.2	9 51.2	+50.5	13.2	10 49.6	+50.6	13.3	11 48.0	+50.8	13.3	68
69	5 48.9	+49.9	12.5	6 47.5	+49.9	12.5	7 46.1	+50.0	12.6	8 44.6	+50.2	12.6	9 43.2	+50.3	12.6	10 41.7	+50.5	12.7	11 40.2	+50.6	12.7	12 38.8	+50.7	12.8	69
70	6 38.8	+49.7	12.0	7 37.4	+49.9	12.0	8 36.1	+50.1	12.0	9 34.8	+50.2	12.0	10 33.5	+50.2	12.1	11 32.2	+50.3	12.1	12 30.8	+50.5	12.2	13 29.5	+50.6	12.2	70
71	7 28.5	+49.8	11.4	8 27.3	+49.9	11.4	9 26.2	+49.9	11.5	10 25.0	+50.1	11.5	11 23.7	+50.2	11.5	12 22.5	+50.3	11.6	13 21.3	+50.4	11.6	14 20.1	+50.5	11.7	71
72	8 18.3	+49.7	10.9	9 17.2	+49.8	10.9	10 16.1	+49.9	10.9	11 15.0	+50.0	11.0	12 13.8	+50.1	11.0	13 12.8	+50.3	11.0	14 11.7	+50.4	11.1	15 10.6	+50.5	11.1	72
73	9 08.0	+49.6	10.3	10 07.0	+49.7	10.3	11 06.0	+49.9	10.3	12 05.1	+49.9	10.4	13 04.1	+50.0	10.4	14 03.1	+50.1	10.5	15 02.1	+50.2	10.5	16 01.1	+50.3	10.5	73
74	9 57.6	+49.6	9.7	10 56.7	+49.7	9.7	11 55.9	+49.8	9.8	12 55.0	+49.8	9.8	13 54.1	+50.0	9.8	14 53.2	+50.1	9.9	15 52.3	+50.2	9.9	16 51.4	+50.3	10.0	74
75	10 47.2	+49.5	9.1	11 46.4	+49.6	9.2	12 45.7	+49.7	9.2	13 44.8	+49.9	9.2	14 44.1	+49.9	9.3	15 43.3	+50.0	9.3	16 42.5	+50.1	9.4	17 41.7	+50.2	9.4	75
76	11 36.7	+49.4	8.5	12 36.0	+49.6	8.6	13 35.4	+49.7	8.6	14 34.7	+49.7	8.7	15 34.0	+49.8	8.7	16 33.3	+49.9	8.7	17 32.6	+50.0	8.8	18 31.9	+50.1	8.8	76
77	12 26.1	+49.4	8.0	13 25.6	+49.4	8.0	14 25.0	+49.6	8.0	15 24.4	+49.6	8.1	16 23.8	+49.6	8.1	17 23.2	+49.8	8.2	18 22.6	+49.8	8.2	19 22.0	+49.9	8.3	77
78	13 15.5	+49.3	7.4	14 15.0	+49.4	7.4	15 14.5	+49.5	7.5	16 14.0	+49.5	7.5	17 13.5	+49.6	7.5	18 13.0	+49.6	7.6	19 12.4	+49.8	7.6	20 11.9	+49.8	7.7	78
79	14 04.8	+49.2	6.8	15 04.4	+49.3	6.8	16 04.0	+49.4	6.9	17 03.5	+49.4	6.9	18 03.1	+49.5	6.9	19 02.6	+49.6	7.0	20 02.2	+49.6	7.0	21 01.7	+49.8	7.1	79
80	14 54.0	+49.1	6.2	15 53.7	+49.1	6.2	16 53.3	+49.4	6.3	17 52.9	+49.4	6.3	18 52.6	+49.4	6.3	19 52.2	+49.5	6.4	20 51.8	+49.5	6.4	21 51.5	+49.5	6.5	80
81	15 43.1	+49.1	5.6	16 42.8	+49.1	5.6	17 42.6	+49.1	5.7	18 42.3	+49.2	5.7	19 42.0	+49.2	5.7	20 41.7	+49.3	5.8	21 41.3	+49.4	5.8	22 41.0	+49.5	5.9	81
82	16 32.2	+48.9	5.0	17 31.9	+49.0	5.0	18 31.7	+49.1	5.1	19 31.5	+49.0	5.1	20 31.2	+49.1	5.1	21 31.0	+49.2	5.2	22 30.7	+49.3	5.2	23 30.5	+49.3	5.2	82
83	17 21.1	+48.8	4.4	18 20.9	+48.8	4.4	19 20.7	+49.0	4.5	20 20.5	+49.0	4.5	21 20.3	+48.9	4.5	22 20.2	+49.0	4.5	23 20.0	+49.1	4.6	24 19.8	+49.1	4.6	83
84	18 09.9	+48.7	3.8	19 09.7	+48.8	3.8	20 09.6	+48.8	3.8	21 09.5	+48.8	3.9	22 09.2	+48.8	3.9	23 09.2	+48.9	3.9	24 09.1	+48.9	4.0	25 08.9	+49.0	4.0	84
85	18 58.6	+48.5	3.2	19 58.5	+48.6	3.2	20 58.4	+48.6	3.2	21 58.3	+48.6	3.2	22 58.0	+48.6	3.3	23 58.1	+48.7	3.3	24 58.0	+48.7	3.3	25 57.9	+48.8	3.3	85
86	19 47.1	+48.5	2.6	20 47.1	+48.4	2.6	21 47.0	+48.5	2.6	22 46.9	+48.6	2.6	23 46.6	+48.5	2.6	24 46.8	+48.6	2.7	25 46.7	+48.6	2.7	26 46.7	+48.6	2.7	86
87	20 35.6	+48.3	1.9	21 35.5	+48.3	1.9	22 35.5	+48.3	2.0	23 35.5	+48.3	2.0	24 35.1	+48.3	2.0	25 35.4	+48.4	2.0	26 35.3	+48.4	2.0	27 35.5	+48.4	2.0	87
88	21 23.9	+48.1	1.3	22 23.8	+48.2	1.3	23 23.8	+48.2	1.3	24 23.8	+48.2	1.3	25 23.4	+48.2	1.3	26 23.8	+48.2	1.3	27 23.8	+48.2	1.4	28 23.7	+48.3	1.4	88
89	22 12.0	+48.0	0.6	23 12.0	+48.0	0.7	24 12.0	+48.0	0.7	25 12.0	+48.0	0.7	26 12.0	+48.0	0.7	27 12.0	+48.0	0.7	28 12.0	+48.0	0.7	29 12.0	+48.0	0.7	89
90	23 00.0	+47.8	0.0	24 00.0	+47.8	0.0	25 00.0	+47.8	0.0	26 00.0	+47.8	0.0	27 00.0	+47.8	0.0	28 00.0	+47.8	0.0	29 00.0	+47.8	0.0	30 00.0	+47.8	0.0	90

S. Lat. { L.H.A. greater than 180°.....Zn=180°-Z
{ L.H.A. less than 180°..........Zn=180°+Z

LAT 24°S

LHA 90–134

LHA ϒ	CAPELLA Hc	Zn	◆ALDEBARAN Hc	Zn	◆ACHERNAR Hc	Zn	CANOPUS Hc	Zn	ACRUX Hc	Zn	◆REGULUS Hc	Zn	POLLUX Hc	Zn
90	19 19	352	44 37	331	33 09	216	60 56	172	18 20	152	19 28	067	32 06	028
91	19 11	351	44 10	330	32 37	216	61 03	174	18 46	152	20 18	066	32 31	027
92	19 03	351	43 42	329	32 05	216	61 08	175	19 12	152	21 08	065	32 55	026
93	18 53	350	43 13	328	31 32	216	61 13	176	19 38	151	21 58	065	33 18	025
94	18 44	349	42 43	327	31 00	216	61 16	177	20 04	151	22 47	064	33 41	024
95	18 33	349	42 13	326	30 27	216	61 17	179	20 31	151	23 37	064	34 03	023
96	18 21	348	41 41	324	29 55	216	61 17	180	20 57	151	24 26	063	34 24	022
97	18 10	347	41 09	323	29 22	216	61 18	181	21 24	151	25 15	063	34 44	021
98	17 58	346	40 36	322	28 50	216	61 16	183	21 50	151	26 03	062	35 03	020
99	17 44	346	40 02	321	28 17	216	61 13	184	22 17	151	26 51	061	35 21	019
100	17 31	345	39 27	320	27 45	216	61 09	185	22 44	151	27 39	061	35 38	018
101	17 16	344	38 52	319	27 12	216	61 03	186	23 11	151	28 27	060	35 55	017
102	17 01	344	38 16	318	26 40	216	60 57	187	23 38	151	29 14	059	36 10	016
103	16 45	343	37 37	317	26 07	216	60 45	189	24 05	151	30 01	059	36 24	015
104	16 29	342	37 02	317	25 35	216	60 40	190	24 32	150	30 48	058	36 38	014

LHA ϒ	BETELGEUSE Hc	Zn	◆RIGEL Hc	Zn	CANOPUS Hc	Zn	◆ACRUX Hc	Zn	Gienah Hc	Zn	◆REGULUS Hc	Zn	POLLUX Hc	Zn
105	54 52	331	60 18	298	60 30	191	24 59	150	16 47	102	31 34	057	36 50	013
106	54 25	330	59 29	297	60 19	192	25 26	150	17 41	102	32 20	057	37 02	012
107	53 57	328	58 40	296	60 07	193	25 53	150	18 34	101	33 06	056	37 12	010
108	53 27	327	57 50	295	59 54	195	26 20	150	19 28	101	33 51	055	37 22	009
109	52 57	325	57 00	294	59 39	196	26 47	150	20 22	100	34 36	054	37 30	008
110	52 25	324	56 09	293	59 24	197	27 14	150	21 16	100	35 20	054	37 37	007
111	51 53	323	55 19	291	59 08	198	27 41	150	22 10	100	36 04	053	37 44	006
112	51 19	321	54 27	290	58 51	199	28 08	150	23 04	099	36 47	052	37 49	005
113	50 44	320	53 36	290	58 32	200	28 36	150	23 58	099	37 30	051	37 53	004
114	50 09	319	52 44	289	58 13	201	29 03	150	24 52	099	38 13	050	37 56	003
115	49 32	318	51 53	288	57 54	202	29 30	150	25 46	099	38 55	049	37 58	002
116	48 55	317	51 01	288	57 33	203	29 57	151	26 40	098	39 36	049	37 59	001
117	48 17	315	50 08	287	57 11	204	30 24	151	27 34	098	40 17	048	37 59	359
118	47 38	314	49 15	286	56 49	204	30 51	151	28 29	098	40 57	047	37 58	358
119	46 58	313	48 23	285	56 26	205	31 17	151	29 23	097	41 37	046	37 56	357

LHA ϒ	POLLUX Hc	Zn	BETELGEUSE Hc	Zn	◆RIGEL Hc	Zn	CANOPUS Hc	Zn	◆ACRUX Hc	Zn	SPICA Hc	Zn	◆REGULUS Hc	Zn
120	37 52	356	46 18	312	47 30	285	56 02	206	31 44	151	12 14	097	42 15	045
121	37 48	355	45 37	311	46 37	284	55 37	207	32 11	151	13 14	097	42 54	044
122	37 42	354	44 57	310	45 43	283	55 12	208	32 38	151	14 10	096	43 31	043
123	37 36	353	44 13	309	44 50	283	54 46	208	33 04	151	15 03	096	44 08	042
124	37 28	352	43 30	308	43 57	282	54 20	209	33 31	151	15 58	095	44 44	041
125	37 20	350	42 47	307	43 03	282	53 53	210	33 57	151	16 52	095	45 19	039
126	37 10	349	42 03	306	42 09	281	53 25	211	34 23	152	17 47	095	45 54	038
127	37 00	348	41 18	305	41 15	281	52 57	211	34 49	152	18 41	094	46 27	037
128	36 48	347	40 33	305	40 21	280	52 29	212	35 15	152	19 36	094	47 00	036
129	36 35	346	39 48	304	39 27	280	52 00	212	35 41	152	20 31	093	47 32	035
130	36 22	345	39 02	303	38 33	279	51 30	213	36 07	152	21 26	093	48 02	033
131	36 07	344	38 16	302	37 38	278	51 00	214	36 32	152	22 20	092	48 32	032
132	35 51	343	37 30	301	36 44	278	50 29	214	36 58	153	23 15	092	49 01	031
133	35 35	342	36 42	301	35 49	277	49 59	215	37 23	153	24 10	092	49 28	030
134	35 18	341	35 55	300	34 56	277	49 27	215	37 48	153	25 05	091	49 55	028

LHA 0–44

LHA ϒ	◆Alpheratz Hc	Zn	Hamal Hc	Zn	◆RIGEL Hc	Zn	CANOPUS Hc	Zn	ACHERNAR Hc	Zn	◆Peacock Hc	Zn	Enif Hc	Zn
0	36 50	002	33 20	020	13 36	093	15 24	141	52 23	158	39 40	215	42 37	312
1	36 52	001	33 51	019	14 31	093	15 58	141	52 43	159	39 08	215	41 56	311
2	36 53	000	34 22	018	15 26	092	16 33	141	53 03	160	38 37	216	41 14	310
3	36 53	359	34 52	017	16 21	092	17 07	141	53 21	161	38 05	216	40 32	309
4	36 51	358	35 21	016	17 15	091	17 42	141	53 39	161	37 33	216	39 49	308
5	36 49	357	35 50	014	18 10	091	18 17	140	53 56	162	37 01	216	39 05	307
6	36 46	356	36 17	013	19 05	091	18 52	140	54 13	163	36 29	216	38 21	306
7	36 41	355	36 44	012	20 00	090	19 27	140	54 28	164	35 56	217	37 37	305
8	36 36	354	37 10	010	20 55	089	20 03	140	54 43	165	35 24	217	36 52	305
9	36 29	353	37 35	009	21 49	089	20 38	140	54 57	165	34 52	217	36 07	304
10	36 21	351	37 59	008	22 44	089	21 13	140	55 11	166	34 19	216	35 21	303
11	36 12	350	38 23	006	23 39	088	21 49	139	55 23	167	33 46	217	34 35	302
12	36 03	349	38 45	005	24 34	088	22 25	139	55 35	168	33 14	217	33 49	302
13	35 52	348	39 07	004	25 29	087	23 00	139	55 47	169	32 41	217	33 02	301
14	35 41	347	39 29	002	26 23	087	23 36	139	55 56	170	32 08	216	32 15	300

LHA ϒ	◆Hamal Hc	Zn	ALDEBARAN Hc	Zn	RIGEL Hc	Zn	CANOPUS Hc	Zn	ACHERNAR Hc	Zn	◆FOMALHAUT Hc	Zn	Alpheratz Hc	Zn
15	39 46	020	23 29	058	27 18	087	24 12	139	56 05	171	62 16	252	35 28	346
16	40 05	019	24 15	057	28 13	086	24 48	139	56 14	172	61 24	252	35 16	345
17	40 22	018	25 01	057	29 08	086	25 24	139	56 21	173	60 32	252	35 00	344
18	40 39	017	25 47	056	30 02	085	26 00	138	56 28	174	59 40	252	34 44	343
19	40 54	016	26 32	055	30 57	085	26 37	138	56 33	175	58 48	252	34 28	342
20	41 08	014	27 17	055	31 51	085	27 13	139	56 38	176	57 56	252	34 11	341
21	41 21	013	28 01	054	32 46	084	27 49	139	56 42	177	57 04	252	33 53	340
22	41 34	012	28 45	053	33 41	084	28 25	139	56 44	178	56 12	252	33 34	339
23	41 44	011	29 29	052	34 35	083	29 02	138	56 46	179	55 19	252	33 14	338
24	41 54	010	30 12	052	35 29	083	29 38	138	56 47	180	54 27	252	32 53	337
25	42 03	008	30 55	051	36 24	082	30 14	138	56 47	181	53 35	252	32 31	336
26	42 10	007	31 37	050	37 18	082	30 51	138	56 46	182	52 43	252	32 09	335
27	42 17	006	32 19	049	38 12	081	31 27	138	56 44	183	51 51	251	31 46	334
28	42 22	005	33 01	049	39 06	081	32 04	138	56 41	184	50 59	251	31 21	334
29	42 26	004	33 42	048	40 00	080	32 40	138	56 38	184	50 07	252	30 57	333

LHA ϒ	Hamal Hc	Zn	◆ALDEBARAN Hc	Zn	SIRIUS Hc	Zn	CANOPUS Hc	Zn	ACHERNAR Hc	Zn	◆FOMALHAUT Hc	Zn	Alpheratz Hc	Zn
30	42 29	002	34 22	047	23 23	099	33 16	139	56 33	185	49 14	252	30 31	332
31	42 30	001	35 01	046	24 17	098	33 52	139	56 27	186	48 22	252	30 05	331
32	42 31	000	35 41	045	25 11	098	34 29	139	56 21	187	47 30	252	29 38	330
33	42 30	359	36 20	044	26 06	098	35 05	139	56 13	188	46 38	252	29 10	329
34	42 28	357	36 58	044	27 00	097	35 41	139	56 05	189	45 46	252	28 41	328
35	42 25	356	37 35	043	27 55	097	36 17	139	55 56	191	44 54	251	28 12	327
36	42 21	355	38 12	042	28 49	097	36 53	139	55 47	191	44 02	251	27 43	327
37	42 15	354	38 48	041	29 44	096	37 29	139	55 35	192	43 11	251	27 12	326
38	42 09	353	39 24	040	30 38	096	38 05	139	55 25	193	42 19	251	26 41	325
39	42 01	351	39 58	039	31 33	095	38 41	139	55 10	194	41 27	251	26 09	324
40	41 52	350	40 32	038	32 27	095	39 16	140	54 57	195	40 35	251	25 37	324
41	41 42	349	41 06	037	33 22	095	39 52	140	54 42	195	39 43	250	25 04	323
42	41 30	348	41 38	036	34 16	094	40 27	140	54 24	196	38 52	250	24 31	322
43	41 18	346	42 10	035	35 11	094	41 02	140	54 12	197	38 00	250	23 57	321
44	41 05	345	42 40	034	36 06	094	41 38	140	53 55	198	37 09	250	23 22	321

LHA 135–149

LHA	◆POLLUX Hc Zn	BETELGEUSE Hc Zn	SIRIUS Hc Zn	◆CANOPUS Hc Zn	ACRUX Hc Zn	◆SPICA Hc Zn	REGULUS Hc Zn
135	34 59 340	35 07 299	57 42 277	48 56 215	38 13 153	25 59 091	50 20 027
136	34 40 339	34 19 298	56 48 276	48 44 216	38 38 153	26 54 091	50 46 025
137	34 20 338	33 31 298	55 53 275	47 51 216	39 02 154	27 49 090	51 07 024
138	33 59 337	32 42 297	54 58 275	47 19 217	39 26 154	28 44 090	51 29 023
139	33 37 336	31 53 296	54 04 274	46 46 217	39 50 154	29 39 089	51 50 021
140	33 14 335	31 04 296	53 09 274	46 13 217	40 14 154	30 33 089	52 09 020
141	32 50 334	30 14 295	52 15 273	45 39 218	40 38 155	31 28 089	52 26 018
142	32 26 333	29 24 294	51 20 273	45 05 218	41 01 155	32 23 088	52 43 017
143	32 01 332	28 34 294	50 25 273	44 31 218	41 24 155	33 18 088	52 58 015
144	31 35 331	27 44 293	49 30 272	43 57 219	41 46 156	34 13 087	53 11 013
145	31 08 330	26 54 293	48 35 272	43 23 219	42 09 156	35 07 087	53 23 012
146	30 41 330	26 03 292	47 41 271	42 48 219	42 31 156	36 02 086	53 33 010
147	30 13 329	25 12 291	46 46 271	42 14 219	42 54 157	36 57 086	53 42 008
148	29 44 328	24 21 291	45 51 270	41 39 220	43 14 157	37 51 086	53 50 007
149	29 14 327	23 29 290	44 56 270	41 04 220	43 35 158	38 46 085	53 56 005

LHA 150–164

LHA	◆PROCYON Hc Zn	SIRIUS Hc Zn	CANOPUS Hc Zn	◆ACRUX Hc Zn	SPICA Hc Zn	◆ARCTURUS Hc Zn	REGULUS Hc Zn
150	45 01 306	44 01 270	40 28 220	43 56 158	39 41 085	14 12 061	54 00 004
151	44 16 305	43 07 269	39 53 220	44 16 158	40 35 084	14 59 061	54 02 002
152	43 31 304	42 14 269	39 17 220	44 36 159	41 30 084	15 47 060	54 03 359
153	42 45 303	41 17 268	38 42 221	44 56 159	42 24 083	16 34 060	54 03 357
154	41 59 302	40 22 268	38 06 221	45 15 160	43 19 083	17 22 059	54 01 355
155	41 13 301	39 27 268	37 30 221	45 34 160	44 13 082	18 08 058	53 57 355
156	40 26 301	38 32 267	36 54 221	45 53 161	45 07 082	18 55 058	53 52 354
157	39 38 300	37 38 267	36 18 221	46 10 161	46 01 081	19 41 057	53 45 352
158	38 51 299	36 43 266	35 42 221	46 28 162	46 55 080	20 27 057	53 36 350
159	38 03 298	35 49 266	35 06 221	46 46 162	47 49 080	21 13 056	53 26 349
160	37 14 298	34 54 266	34 30 221	47 02 163	48 43 079	21 58 055	53 15 347
161	36 26 297	33 59 265	33 54 221	47 18 163	49 37 079	22 43 055	53 02 346
162	35 37 296	33 05 265	33 17 221	47 33 164	50 31 078	23 28 054	52 48 344
163	34 47 296	32 10 265	32 41 221	47 48 164	51 24 077	24 13 054	52 32 342
164	33 58 295	31 15 264	32 05 222	48 03 165	52 18 077	24 56 053	52 14 341

LHA 165–179

LHA	REGULUS Hc Zn	◆PROCYON Hc Zn	SIRIUS Hc Zn	CANOPUS Hc Zn	◆ACRUX Hc Zn	ANTARES Hc Zn	◆ARCTURUS Hc Zn
165	51 56 339	33 08 294	30 21 264	31 28 222	48 17 165	16 48 112	25 39 052
166	51 36 338	32 18 294	29 26 264	30 52 222	48 30 166	17 38 112	26 23 051
167	51 14 336	31 27 293	28 32 263	30 16 222	48 43 167	18 29 111	27 05 051
168	50 52 335	30 37 292	27 38 263	29 40 222	48 56 167	19 20 111	27 48 050
169	50 28 334	29 46 292	26 43 263	29 03 222	49 08 168	20 12 111	28 31 049
170	50 03 332	28 55 291	25 49 262	28 27 221	49 19 168	21 03 111	29 11 049
171	49 37 331	28 03 290	24 55 262	27 50 221	49 29 169	21 54 110	29 52 048
172	49 10 329	27 12 290	24 01 262	27 14 221	49 40 169	22 46 110	30 32 047
173	48 41 328	26 20 289	23 06 261	26 38 221	49 49 170	23 37 110	31 12 046
174	48 12 327	25 29 289	22 12 261	26 02 221	49 58 171	24 29 109	31 52 046
175	47 41 326	24 37 288	21 18 261	25 25 221	50 06 172	25 21 109	32 31 045
176	47 10 324	23 44 288	20 24 260	24 49 221	50 13 172	26 12 109	33 10 044
177	46 38 323	22 52 287	19 30 260	24 13 221	50 20 173	27 04 109	33 47 043
178	46 04 322	22 00 287	18 36 259	23 37 221	50 27 174	27 56 108	34 24 042
179	45 30 321	21 07 286	17 42 259	23 02 221	50 32 175	28 48 108	35 00 041

LHA 45–59

LHA	◆CAPELLA Hc Zn	BETELGEUSE Hc Zn	SIRIUS Hc Zn	CANOPUS Hc Zn	ACHERNAR Hc Zn	◆FOMALHAUT Hc Zn	Hamal Hc Zn
45	13 24 024	36 55 059	37 01 093	42 12 141	53 38 199	36 17 250	40 50 344
46	13 46 023	37 42 058	37 56 093	42 47 141	53 20 199	35 26 250	40 34 343
47	14 07 022	38 29 058	38 50 092	43 22 141	53 02 200	34 34 250	40 18 342
48	14 28 022	39 15 057	39 45 092	43 56 142	52 42 201	33 43 249	40 00 341
49	14 48 021	40 01 056	40 40 091	44 30 142	52 22 201	32 52 249	39 41 339
50	15 08 021	40 46 055	41 34 091	45 04 142	52 01 202	32 01 249	39 21 338
51	15 27 020	41 31 054	42 29 091	45 38 142	51 41 203	31 09 249	39 01 337
52	15 45 019	42 15 053	43 24 090	46 12 143	51 19 204	30 18 248	38 39 336
53	16 03 019	42 59 053	44 19 090	46 45 143	50 57 204	29 27 248	38 16 335
54	16 20 018	43 42 052	45 14 089	47 18 143	50 34 205	28 37 248	37 53 334
55	16 37 017	44 25 051	46 08 089	47 50 144	50 11 205	27 46 248	37 28 333
56	16 53 017	45 07 050	47 03 088	48 23 144	49 47 206	26 55 248	37 03 332
57	17 08 016	45 49 049	47 58 088	48 55 145	49 23 207	26 04 247	36 37 331
58	17 23 015	46 29 048	48 53 087	49 26 145	48 58 207	25 14 247	36 10 330
59	17 37 015	47 09 047	49 48 087	49 58 145	48 33 208	24 23 247	35 42 329

LHA 60–74

LHA	CAPELLA Hc Zn	BETELGEUSE Hc Zn	SIRIUS Hc Zn	CANOPUS Hc Zn	◆ACHERNAR Hc Zn	Diphda Hc Zn	Hamal Hc Zn
60	17 51 014	47 49 045	50 42 087	50 28 146	48 07 208	44 02 268	35 13 328
61	18 04 013	48 27 044	51 37 086	50 59 146	47 41 209	43 07 267	34 44 327
62	18 16 013	49 04 043	52 32 086	51 30 147	47 14 209	42 12 267	34 14 326
63	18 27 012	49 42 042	53 26 085	51 59 148	46 48 210	41 18 266	33 43 325
64	18 38 011	50 19 041	54 21 085	52 28 148	46 21 210	40 23 266	33 11 324
65	18 49 010	50 54 039	55 16 084	52 56 149	45 53 211	39 28 266	32 39 323
66	18 58 010	51 28 038	56 10 084	53 25 149	45 25 211	38 33 266	32 06 322
67	19 07 009	52 02 037	57 05 083	53 52 150	44 57 211	37 39 265	31 32 322
68	19 15 008	52 34 036	57 59 083	54 19 151	44 29 212	36 45 265	30 58 321
69	19 23 008	53 06 034	58 54 082	54 46 152	44 00 212	35 50 265	30 24 320
70	19 30 007	53 36 033	59 48 082	55 11 152	43 31 212	34 55 264	29 48 319
71	19 36 006	54 05 031	60 42 081	55 37 153	43 02 213	34 01 264	29 12 318
72	19 41 005	54 33 030	61 36 081	56 01 154	42 32 213	33 06 264	28 35 318
73	19 46 005	54 59 028	62 30 080	56 25 155	42 02 213	32 12 263	27 58 317
74	19 50 004	55 24 027	63 24 079	56 48 155	41 32 213	31 18 263	27 20 316

LHA 75–89

LHA	◆CAPELLA Hc Zn	POLLUX Hc Zn	◆PROCYON Hc Zn	◆Suhail Hc Zn	CANOPUS Hc Zn	◆ACHERNAR Hc Zn	Hamal Hc Zn
75	19 53 003	24 27 040	41 23 058	36 12 127	57 11 156	41 02 214	26 42 315
76	19 56 002	25 02 039	42 06 057	36 56 127	57 32 157	40 31 214	26 03 315
77	19 58 002	25 36 038	42 51 057	37 39 127	57 53 158	40 01 214	25 24 314
78	19 59 001	26 10 038	43 35 056	38 23 127	58 13 159	39 30 215	24 44 313
79	20 00 000	26 43 037	44 23 055	39 06 127	58 33 160	38 59 215	24 04 313
80	20 00 359	27 16 036	45 11 054	39 50 128	58 50 161	38 28 215	23 24 312
81	19 59 359	27 48 035	45 55 053	40 33 128	59 07 162	37 56 215	22 43 311
82	19 57 358	28 20 035	46 40 052	41 17 128	59 23 163	37 25 215	22 01 311
83	19 55 357	28 50 034	47 21 050	42 00 128	59 39 164	36 53 216	21 19 310
84	19 52 357	29 20 033	48 03 049	42 43 128	59 53 165	36 22 216	20 37 309
85	19 48 356	29 49 032	48 45 049	43 27 128	60 06 167	35 50 216	19 55 309
86	19 46 355	30 18 031	49 24 047	44 10 128	60 20 168	35 19 216	19 12 308
87	19 39 354	30 46 030	50 06 046	44 53 128	60 30 169	34 48 216	18 28 307
88	19 33 354	31 13 029	50 45 045	45 36 129	60 40 170	34 14 216	17 45 307
89	19 26 353	31 40 029	51 24 044	46 19 129	60 49 171	33 41 216	17 01 306

DECLINATION (15° – 29°)
SAME NAME AS LATITUDE

N. Lat. { L.H.A. greater than 180° .....Zn=Z
{ L.H.A. less than 180°.............Zn=360°−Z

LHA	15° Hc	d	Z	16° Hc	d	Z	17° Hc	d	Z	18° Hc	d	Z	19° Hc	d	Z	20° Hc	d	Z	21° Hc	d	Z	22° Hc	d	Z
0	81 00	60	180	82 00	60	180	83 00	60	180	84 00	60	180	85 00	60	180	86 00	60	180	87 00	60	180	88 00	60	180
1	80 57	60	174	81 57	59	173	82 56	60	172	83 56	59	171	84 55	59	169	85 54	58	167	86 52	56	163	87 48	51	155
2	80 48	59	168	81 47	58	166	82 45	58	165	83 43	57	162	84 40	55	159	85 35	54	155	86 29	48	148	87 17	38	137
3	80 34	57	162	81 31	56	160	82 27	56	158	83 23	53	154	84 16	52	150	85 08	47	145	85 55	40	137	86 35	29	125
4	80 15	55	157	81 10	54	154	82 04	52	151	82 56	50	147	83 46	47	143	84 33	41	136	85 14	35	128	85 49	23	118
5	79 51	53	151	80 44	51	149	81 35	49	145	82 24	46	141	83 10	43	136	83 53	37	130	84 30	29	122	84 59	19	112
6	79 22	51	147	80 13	49	144	81 02	46	140	81 48	42	136	82 30	39	131	83 09	33	125	83 42	26	117	84 08	16	109
7	78 51	48	143	79 39	46	139	80 25	43	136	81 08	40	131	81 48	35	126	82 23	29	120	82 52	23	114	83 15	15	106
8	78 16	46	139	79 02	43	135	79 45	40	132	80 25	37	127	81 02	33	122	81 35	27	117	82 02	20	111	82 22	14	104
9	77 38	44	135	78 22	41	132	79 03	38	128	79 41	34	124	80 15	30	119	80 45	25	114	81 10	19	108	81 29	12	102
10	76 59	41	132	77 40	39	129	78 19	36	125	78 55	32	121	79 27	27	116	79 54	23	111	80 17	18	106	80 35	12	100
11	76 17	39	129	76 56	37	126	77 33	34	122	78 07	30	118	78 37	26	114	79 03	21	109	79 24	17	104	79 41	11	99
12	75 34	37	126	76 11	35	123	76 46	32	120	77 18	28	116	77 46	25	112	78 11	20	107	78 31	16	103	78 47	10	98
13	74 49	36	124	75 25	33	121	75 58	30	117	76 28	27	114	76 55	23	110	77 16	18	106	77 38	14	101	77 52	10	97
14	74 03	34	122	74 37	32	119	75 09	29	115	75 38	25	112	76 03	21	108	76 26	18	104	76 44	14	100	76 58	09	96
15	73 16	33	120	73 49	30	117	74 19	28	114	74 47	24	110	75 11	21	107	75 32	18	103	75 50	13	99	76 03	10	95
16	72 28	31	118	72 59	30	115	73 29	26	112	73 55	24	109	74 19	20	105	74 39	17	102	74 56	13	98	75 09	09	95
17	71 39	30	116	72 09	28	113	72 38	25	111	73 03	23	107	73 26	19	104	73 45	16	101	74 01	13	97	74 14	09	94
18	70 49	30	115	71 19	27	112	71 46	25	109	72 11	21	106	72 32	19	103	72 51	16	100	73 07	12	97	73 19	09	93
19	69 59	29	113	70 28	26	111	70 54	24	108	71 18	21	105	71 39	18	102	71 57	15	99	72 12	13	96	72 25	09	93
20	69 09	27	112	69 36	26	109	70 02	23	107	70 25	20	104	70 45	18	101	71 03	15	98	71 18	12	95	71 30	09	92
21	68 17	27	111	68 44	25	108	69 09	22	106	69 31	20	103	69 51	18	100	70 09	14	98	70 23	12	95	70 35	09	92
22	67 26	26	109	67 52	24	107	68 16	22	105	68 38	19	102	68 57	17	99	69 14	15	97	69 29	11	94	69 40	09	91
23	66 34	26	108	67 00	23	106	67 23	21	104	67 44	19	101	68 03	17	99	68 20	14	96	68 34	11	93	68 45	09	91
24	65 42	25	107	66 07	23	105	66 30	20	103	66 50	19	100	67 09	16	98	67 25	14	95	67 39	12	93	67 51	09	90
25	64 49	25	106	65 14	22	104	65 36	20	102	65 56	19	100	66 15	16	97	66 31	13	95	66 44	12	92	66 56	09	90
26	63 57	24	105	64 21	21	103	64 42	20	101	65 02	18	99	65 20	16	97	65 36	14	94	65 50	11	92	66 01	09	90
27	63 04	23	105	63 27	22	102	63 49	19	100	64 08	18	99	64 26	15	96	64 41	14	94	64 55	11	91	65 06	09	89
28	62 11	22	104	62 33	22	102	62 55	19	100	63 14	17	98	63 31	16	95	63 47	13	93	64 00	11	91	64 11	10	89
29	61 17	23	103	61 40	20	101	62 00	19	99	62 19	18	97	62 37	15	95	62 52	13	93	63 05	11	91	63 17	09	88
30	60 24	22	102	60 46	20	100	61 06	19	98	61 25	17	96	61 42	15	94	61 57	13	92	62 10	12	90	62 22	09	88
31	59 30	22	101	59 52	20	100	60 12	18	98	60 30	17	96	60 47	15	94	61 02	14	92	61 16	11	90	61 27	10	88
32	58 36	22	101	58 58	20	99	59 18	18	97	59 35	17	95	59 53	15	93	60 08	13	91	60 21	11	89	60 32	10	87
33	57 42	22	100	58 04	19	98	58 23	18	96	58 41	17	95	58 58	15	93	59 13	13	91	59 26	12	89	59 38	09	87
34	56 48	21	99	57 09	20	98	57 29	18	96	57 47	16	94	58 03	15	92	58 18	13	90	58 31	12	89	58 43	10	87
35	55 54	21	99	56 15	19	97	56 34	18	95	56 52	16	94	57 08	15	92	57 23	13	90	57 36	12	88	57 48	10	86
36	55 00	20	98	55 20	20	97	55 40	17	95	55 57	17	93	56 14	14	91	56 28	14	90	56 42	11	88	56 53	11	86
37	54 06	20	98	54 26	19	96	54 45	18	94	55 03	16	93	55 19	14	91	55 33	14	89	55 47	12	88	55 59	10	86
38	53 11	20	97	53 31	19	95	53 50	18	94	54 08	16	92	54 24	15	91	54 39	13	89	54 52	12	87	55 04	11	85
39	52 17	20	96	52 37	19	95	52 56	17	93	53 13	16	92	53 29	15	90	53 44	13	89	53 57	12	87	54 09	11	85
40	51 22	20	96	51 42	19	94	52 01	17	93	52 18	16	91	52 34	15	90	52 49	14	88	53 03	12	87	53 15	11	85
41	50 28	20	95	50 48	18	94	51 06	17	92	51 23	16	91	51 39	15	89	51 54	14	88	52 08	12	86	52 20	11	85
42	49 33	20	95	49 53	18	93	50 11	18	92	50 29	16	90	50 45	15	89	51 00	13	87	51 13	13	86	51 26	11	84
43	48 39	19	94	48 58	18	93	49 16	16	92	49 32	16	90	49 50	15	88	50 05	14	87	50 19	12	86	50 31	12	84
44	47 44	19	94	48 03	19	93	48 22	17	91	48 39	16	90	48 55	15	88	49 10	14	87	49 24	13	85	49 37	11	84
45	46 49	20	93	47 09	18	92	47 27	17	91	47 44	16	89	48 00	15	88	48 15	14	86	48 29	13	85	48 42	12	83
46	45 55	19	93	46 14	18	92	46 32	17	90	46 49	17	89	47 06	15	87	47 21	14	86	47 35	13	85	47 48	12	83
47	45 00	19	93	45 19	18	91	45 37	18	90	45 55	16	88	46 11	15	87	46 26	14	86	46 40	13	84	46 53	12	83
48	44 05	19	92	44 24	18	91	44 42	18	89	45 00	16	88	45 16	15	87	45 31	15	85	45 46	13	84	45 59	12	83
49	43 10	19	92	43 29	18	90	43 48	17	89	44 05	16	88	44 21	16	86	44 37	14	85	44 51	14	84	45 05	12	82
50	42 16	19	91	42 35	18	90	42 53	17	89	43 10	17	87	43 27	15	86	43 42	15	85	43 57	13	83	44 10	13	82
51	41 21	19	91	41 40	18	90	41 58	17	88	42 15	17	87	42 32	16	86	42 48	14	84	43 02	14	83	43 16	13	82
52	40 26	19	90	40 45	18	89	41 03	18	88	41 21	16	87	41 37	16	85	41 53	15	84	42 08	14	83	42 22	13	81
53	39 31	19	90	39 50	19	88	40 09	17	88	40 26	17	86	40 43	16	85	40 59	15	84	41 14	14	82	41 28	13	81
54	38 36	19	90	38 55	19	88	39 14	17	87	39 31	17	86	39 48	16	85	40 04	15	83	40 19	15	82	40 34	13	81
55	37 41	20	89	38 01	18	88	38 19	18	87	38 37	17	86	38 54	16	84	39 10	15	83	39 25	14	82	39 39	14	81
56	36 47	19	89	37 06	18	88	37 24	18	86	37 42	17	85	37 59	16	84	38 15	16	83	38 31	14	82	38 45	14	80
57	35 52	19	88	36 11	19	87	36 30	17	86	36 47	18	85	37 05	16	84	37 21	16	82	37 37	14	81	37 51	15	80
58	34 57	19	88	35 16	19	87	35 35	18	85	35 53	17	85	36 10	17	83	36 27	15	82	36 42	15	81	36 57	15	80
59	34 02	20	88	34 22	18	86	34 40	18	85	34 58	18	84	35 16	16	83	35 32	16	82	35 48	16	81	36 04	14	79
60	33 08	19	87	33 27	19	86	33 46	18	85	34 04	17	84	34 21	17	82	34 38	16	82	34 54	16	80	35 10	14	79
61	32 13	19	87	32 32	19	86	32 51	18	85	33 09	18	84	33 27	17	82	33 44	16	81	34 00	16	80	34 16	15	79
62	31 18	20	87	31 38	19	85	31 57	18	84	32 15	18	83	32 33	17	82	32 50	16	81	33 06	16	80	33 22	16	78
63	30 23	20	86	30 43	19	85	31 02	18	84	31 20	18	83	31 38	18	82	31 56	16	81	32 12	16	79	32 28	16	78
64	29 29	19	86	29 48	20	85	30 08	18	84	30 26	18	82	30 44	18	81	31 02	16	80	31 18	17	79	31 35	15	78
65	28 34	20	85	28 54	19	84	29 13	19	83	29 32	18	82	29 50	18	81	30 08	17	80	30 25	16	79	30 41	16	78
66	27 39	20	85	27 59	20	84	28 19	18	83	28 37	19	82	28 56	18	81	29 14	17	80	29 31	17	79	29 48	16	77
67	26 45	20	85	27 05	19	84	27 24	19	83	27 43	19	81	28 02	18	80	28 20	17	79	28 37	17	78	28 54	17	77
68	25 50	20	84	26 10	20	83	26 30	19	82	26 49	19	82	27 08	18	80	27 26	18	79	27 44	17	78	28 01	17	77
69	24 56	20	84	25 16	20	83	25 36	19	82	25 55	19	81	26 14	18	80	26 32	18	79	26 50	17	78	27 07	17	77
	15°			16°			17°			18°			19°			20°			21°			22°		

S. Lat. { L.H.A. greater than 180° ....Zn=180°−Z
{ L.H.A. less than 180°...........Zn=180°+Z

DECLINATION (15° – 29°)
SAME NAME AS LATITUDE

LAT 24°

DECLINATION (15° – 29°)
SAME NAME AS LATITUDE

23° Hc	d	Z	24° Hc	d	Z	25° Hc	d	Z	26° Hc	d	Z	27° Hc	d	Z	28° Hc	d	Z	29° Hc	d	Z	LHA
89 00	60	180	90 00	−60	90	89 00	−60	0	88 00	−60	0	87 00	−60	0	86 00	−60	0	85 00	−60	0	360
88 39	26	137	89 05	−26	90	88 39	−51	42	87 48	−56	24	86 52	−58	17	85 54	−59	12	84 55	−59	10	359
87 55	15	118	88 10	−15	90	87 55	−37	61	87 18	−48	42	86 30	−53	31	85 37	−56	24	84 41	−57	19	358
87 04	12	109	87 16	−10	89	87 06	−29	69	86 37	−39	53	85 58	−47	41	85 11	−51	33	84 20	−54	28	357
86 12	09	104	86 21	−07	89	86 14	−22	74	85 52	−34	60	85 18	−41	49	84 37	−46	41	83 51	−50	35	356
85 18	08	101	85 26	−05	89	85 21	−18	77	85 03	−28	65	84 35	−36	55	83 59	−41	47	83 18	−46	41	355
84 24	07	99	84 31	−04	89	84 27	−15	78	84 12	−23	69	83 49	−32	60	83 17	−37	52	82 40	−42	46	354
83 30	06	97	83 36	−03	89	83 33	−12	80	83 21	−21	71	83 00	−27	63	82 33	−34	56	81 59	−38	50	353
82 36	06	96	82 42	−03	88	82 39	−10	81	82 29	−18	73	82 11	−24	66	81 47	−31	59	81 16	−35	53	352
81 41	06	95	81 47	−02	88	81 45	−09	81	81 36	−15	74	81 21	−22	68	80 59	−27	62	80 32	−33	56	351
80 47	05	94	80 52	−01	88	80 51	−08	82	80 43	−13	75	80 30	−20	70	80 10	−25	64	79 45	−29	59	350
79 52	05	93	79 57	00	88	79 57	−07	82	79 50	−12	77	79 38	−18	72	79 20	−22	66	78 58	−27	61	349
78 57	05	93	79 02	00	88	79 02	−05	82	78 57	−11	77	78 46	−16	72	78 30	−20	67	78 10	−25	62	348
78 02	05	92	78 08	00	87	78 03	−05	82	78 03	−09	78	77 54	−14	73	77 40	−19	68	77 21	−23	64	347
77 08	05	92	77 13	01	87	77 14	−04	83	77 10	−09	78	77 01	−13	74	76 48	−17	69	76 31	−21	65	346
76 13	05	91	76 18	01	87	76 19	−03	83	76 16	−07	78	76 09	−12	74	75 57	−16	70	75 41	−19	66	345
75 18	05	91	75 23	01	87	75 25	−03	83	75 22	−06	79	75 16	−11	75	75 05	−14	71	74 51	−18	67	344
74 23	06	90	74 29	02	87	74 31	−03	83	74 28	−05	79	74 23	−10	75	74 13	−13	72	74 00	−16	68	343
73 28	06	90	73 34	02	86	73 36	−01	83	73 35	−05	79	73 30	−09	76	73 21	−12	72	73 09	−15	69	342
72 34	05	89	72 39	03	86	72 42	−01	83	72 41	−05	79	72 36	−07	76	72 29	−11	73	72 18	−14	69	341
71 39	06	89	71 45	02	86	71 47	00	83	71 47	−04	80	71 43	−07	77	71 36	−09	73	71 27	−13	70	340
70 44	06	89	70 50	03	86	70 53	00	83	70 53	−03	80	70 50	−06	77	70 44	−09	74	70 35	−12	71	339
69 49	06	88	69 55	04	85	69 59	00	83	69 59	−02	80	69 57	−06	77	69 51	−08	74	69 43	−11	71	338
68 54	07	88	69 01	03	85	69 04	01	82	69 05	−02	80	69 03	−04	77	68 59	−08	74	68 51	−10	71	337
68 00	06	88	68 06	04	85	68 10	01	82	68 11	−01	80	68 10	−04	77	68 06	−07	74	67 59	−09	72	336
67 05	07	87	67 12	04	85	67 16	01	82	67 17	−01	80	67 16	−03	77	67 13	−06	75	67 07	−08	72	335
66 10	07	87	66 17	04	85	66 21	02	82	66 23	00	80	66 23	−03	77	66 20	−05	75	66 15	−07	72	334
65 15	07	87	65 22	05	84	65 27	02	82	65 29	01	80	65 30	−03	77	65 27	−04	75	65 23	−07	72	333
64 21	07	87	64 28	05	84	64 33	03	82	64 36	00	80	64 36	−01	77	64 35	−04	75	64 31	−06	73	332
63 26	07	86	63 33	06	84	63 39	03	82	63 42	01	80	63 43	−01	77	63 42	−04	75	63 38	−05	73	331
62 31	08	86	62 39	05	84	62 44	04	82	62 48	01	79	62 49	00	77	62 49	−03	75	62 46	−05	73	330
61 37	07	86	61 44	05	84	61 50	04	81	61 54	01	79	61 56	00	77	61 56	−02	75	61 54	−04	73	329
60 42	08	85	60 50	06	83	60 56	04	81	61 00	02	79	61 02	01	77	61 03	−02	75	61 01	−03	73	328
59 47	08	85	59 55	07	83	60 02	04	81	60 06	03	79	60 09	01	77	60 10	−01	75	60 09	−03	73	327
58 53	08	85	59 01	07	83	59 08	04	81	59 12	03	79	59 15	02	77	59 17	−01	75	59 16	−02	73	326
57 58	09	85	58 07	06	83	58 13	06	81	58 19	03	79	58 22	02	77	58 24	00	75	58 24	−02	73	325
57 04	08	84	57 12	07	82	57 19	06	81	57 25	04	79	57 29	02	77	57 31	00	75	57 31	−01	73	324
56 09	09	84	56 18	07	82	56 25	06	80	56 31	04	79	56 35	03	77	56 38	01	75	56 39	−01	73	323
55 15	09	84	55 24	07	82	55 31	06	80	55 37	05	79	55 42	03	77	55 45	01	75	55 46	00	73	322
54 20	09	84	54 29	08	82	54 37	07	80	54 44	05	78	54 49	03	77	54 52	02	75	54 54	00	73	321
53 26	09	83	53 35	08	82	53 43	07	80	53 50	05	78	53 55	04	77	53 59	02	75	54 01	01	73	320
52 31	10	83	52 41	08	81	52 49	07	80	52 57	06	78	53 02	05	77	53 06	03	75	53 09	01	73	319
51 37	10	83	51 47	08	81	51 55	08	80	52 03	06	78	52 09	04	76	52 13	04	75	52 17	01	73	318
50 43	10	82	50 53	09	81	51 02	07	79	51 09	06	78	51 15	05	76	51 20	04	75	51 24	03	73	317
49 48	11	82	49 59	09	81	50 08	08	79	50 16	06	78	50 22	06	76	50 28	04	74	50 32	03	73	316
48 54	10	82	49 04	10	80	49 14	08	79	49 22	07	77	49 29	06	76	49 35	04	74	49 39	04	73	315
48 00	10	82	48 10	10	80	48 20	09	79	48 29	07	77	48 36	06	76	48 42	05	74	48 47	04	73	314
47 05	11	81	47 16	10	80	47 26	09	79	47 35	08	77	47 43	06	75	47 49	06	74	47 55	04	73	313
46 11	11	81	46 22	11	80	46 33	09	78	46 42	08	77	46 50	07	75	46 57	05	74	47 02	05	72	312
45 17	12	81	45 29	11	79	45 39	09	78	45 48	09	77	45 57	07	75	46 04	06	74	46 10	05	72	311
44 23	12	81	44 35	10	79	44 45	10	78	44 55	09	77	45 04	07	75	45 11	07	74	45 18	05	72	310
43 29	12	80	43 41	11	79	43 52	10	78	44 02	09	76	44 11	08	75	44 19	07	73	44 26	06	72	309
42 35	12	80	42 47	11	79	42 58	11	77	43 09	09	76	43 18	08	75	43 26	08	73	43 34	06	72	308
41 41	12	80	41 53	12	79	42 05	10	77	42 15	10	76	42 25	09	74	42 34	07	73	42 41	07	72	307
40 47	13	80	41 00	11	78	41 11	11	77	41 22	10	76	41 32	09	74	41 41	08	73	41 49	08	72	306
39 53	13	79	40 06	12	78	40 18	11	77	40 29	10	75	40 39	10	74	40 49	08	73	40 57	08	72	305
38 59	13	79	39 12	13	78	39 25	11	77	39 36	11	75	39 47	09	74	39 56	09	73	40 05	08	71	304
38 06	13	79	38 19	12	78	38 31	12	76	38 43	11	75	38 54	10	74	39 04	09	73	39 13	09	71	303
37 12	13	79	37 25	13	77	37 38	12	76	37 50	11	75	38 01	11	74	38 12	10	72	38 22	08	71	302
36 18	14	79	36 32	13	77	36 45	12	76	36 57	12	75	37 08	11	73	37 20	10	72	37 30	09	71	301
35 24	15	78	35 39	13	77	35 52	13	76	36 05	11	74	36 16	12	73	36 28	10	72	36 38	10	71	300
34 31	14	78	34 45	14	77	34 59	13	75	35 12	12	74	35 24	12	73	35 36	10	72	35 46	10	71	299
33 37	15	77	33 52	14	76	34 06	13	75	34 19	13	74	34 32	11	73	34 43	12	71	34 55	10	70	298
32 44	15	77	32 59	14	76	33 13	13	75	33 26	13	73	33 39	13	73	33 52	11	71	34 03	11	70	297
31 50	16	77	32 06	14	76	32 20	14	75	32 34	13	73	32 47	13	72	33 00	12	71	33 12	11	70	296
30 57	15	77	31 12	15	75	31 27	14	74	31 41	14	73	31 55	13	72	32 08	12	71	32 20	12	70	295
30 04	15	76	30 19	15	75	30 34	15	74	30 49	14	73	31 03	13	72	31 16	13	71	31 29	12	70	294
29 11	15	76	29 26	16	75	29 42	15	74	29 57	14	73	30 11	13	72	30 24	13	70	30 37	13	69	293
28 17	17	76	28 34	15	75	28 49	15	74	29 04	15	72	29 19	14	72	29 33	13	70	29 46	13	69	292
27 24	17	75	27 41	16	74	27 57	15	73	28 12	15	72	28 27	14	71	28 41	14	70	28 55	13	69	291

| 23° | | | 24° | | | 25° | | | 26° | | | 27° | | | 28° | | | 29° | | | |

DECLINATION (15° – 29°)
SAME NAME AS LATITUDE

LAT 24°

N. Lat. { L.H.A. greater than 180° .....Zn=Z
{ L.H.A. less than 180°............Zn=360°–Z

DECLINATION (15° – 29°)
__SAME__ NAME AS LATITUDE

LAT 24°

LHA	15° Hc	d	Z	16° Hc	d	Z	17° Hc	d	Z	18° Hc	d	Z	19° Hc	d	Z	20° Hc	d	Z	21° Hc	d	Z	22° Hc	d	Z
70	24 01	21	84	24 22	19	83	24 41	20	82	25 01	19	80	25 20	18	79	25 38	19	78	25 57	17	77	26 14	17	76
71	23 07	20	83	23 27	20	82	23 47	20	81	24 07	19	80	24 26	19	79	24 45	18	78	25 03	18	77	25 21	17	76
72	22 12	21	83	22 33	20	82	22 53	20	81	23 13	19	80	23 32	19	79	23 51	19	78	24 10	18	77	24 28	17	76
73	21 18	21	83	21 39	20	81	21 59	20	80	22 19	19	79	22 38	20	78	22 58	18	77	23 16	19	76	23 35	18	75
74	20 24	21	82	20 45	20	81	21 05	20	80	21 25	19	79	21 45	19	78	22 04	19	77	22 23	19	76	22 42	18	75
75	19 29	21	82	19 50	21	81	20 11	20	80	20 31	20	79	20 51	19	78	21 11	19	77	21 30	19	76	21 49	18	75
76	18 35	21	81	18 56	21	80	19 17	21	79	19 38	20	78	19 58	19	77	20 17	20	76	20 37	19	75	20 56	19	74
77	17 41	21	81	18 02	21	80	18 23	21	79	18 44	20	78	19 04	20	77	19 24	20	76	19 44	19	75	20 03	19	74
78	16 47	21	81	17 08	21	80	17 29	21	79	17 50	21	78	18 11	20	77	18 31	20	76	18 51	20	75	19 11	19	74
79	15 53	21	80	16 14	22	79	16 36	21	78	16 57	21	77	17 18	20	76	17 38	20	75	17 58	20	74	18 18	20	73
80	14 59	22	80	15 21	21	79	15 42	21	78	16 03	21	77	16 24	21	76	16 45	20	75	17 05	20	74	17 25	20	73
81	14 05	22	80	14 27	21	79	14 48	22	78	15 10	21	77	15 31	21	76	15 52	21	75	16 13	20	74	16 33	20	73
82	13 11	22	79	13 33	22	78	13 55	22	77	14 17	21	76	14 38	21	75	14 59	21	74	15 20	21	73	15 41	20	72
83	12 17	22	79	12 39	23	78	13 02	22	77	13 23	22	76	13 45	21	75	14 06	22	74	14 28	21	73	14 49	21	72
84	11 23	23	79	11 46	22	78	12 08	22	77	12 30	22	76	12 52	22	75	13 14	21	74	13 35	22	73	13 56	21	72
85	10 30	22	78	10 52	23	77	11 15	22	76	11 37	22	75	11 59	22	75	12 21	22	73	12 43	21	72	13 04	22	71
86	09 36	23	78	09 59	22	77	10 22	22	76	10 44	23	75	11 07	22	74	11 29	22	73	11 51	22	72	12 12	22	71
87	08 43	23	77	09 06	23	76	09 29	22	76	09 51	23	75	10 14	22	74	10 36	23	73	10 59	22	72	11 21	22	71
88	07 49	23	77	08 12	24	76	08 36	23	76	08 59	22	74	09 21	23	73	09 44	23	72	10 07	22	71	10 29	22	70
89	06 56	23	77	07 19	24	76	07 43	23	75	08 06	23	74	08 29	23	73	08 52	23	72	09 15	22	71	09 37	23	70
90	06 03	23	76	06 26	24	75	06 50	23	74	07 13	24	73	07 37	23	73	08 00	23	72	08 23	23	71	08 46	23	70
91	05 09	24	76	05 33	24	75	05 57	24	74	06 21	23	73	06 44	24	72	07 08	23	71	07 31	23	70	07 54	24	69
92	04 16	24	75	04 40	24	75	05 04	24	74	05 28	24	73	05 52	24	72	06 16	24	71	06 40	23	70	07 03	24	69
93	03 23	25	75	03 48	24	74	04 12	24	73	04 36	24	72	05 00	24	71	05 24	24	70	05 48	24	70	06 12	24	69
94	02 30	25	75	02 55	24	74	03 19	25	73	03 44	24	72	04 08	25	71	04 33	24	70	04 57	24	69	05 21	24	68
95	01 38	24	74	02 02	25	73	02 27	25	72	02 52	24	72	03 17	24	71	03 41	25	70	04 06	24	69	04 30	25	68
96	00 45	25	74	01 10	25	73	01 35	25	72	02 00	25	71	02 25	25	70	02 50	25	69	03 15	25	68	03 40	24	68
97	−0 08	25	73	00 18	25	73	00 43	25	72	01 08	25	71	01 33	25	70	01 59	25	69	02 24	25	68	02 49	25	67
98	−1 00	25	73	−0 35	26	72	−0 09	25	71	00 16	26	70	00 42	26	69	01 08	25	69	01 33	26	68	01 59	26	67
99	−1 53	26	73	−1 27	26	72	−1 01	26	71	−0 35	26	70	−0 09	26	70	00 17	25	68	00 42	26	67	01 08	26	67
100	−2 45	26	72	−2 19	26	71	−1 53	26	71	−1 27	27	70	−1 00	26	70	−0 34	26	68	−0 08	26	67	00 18	26	66
101	−3 37	26	72	−3 11	27	71	−2 44	26	70	−2 18	27	69	−1 51	26	68	−1 25	26	67	−0 58	26	66	−0 32	27	66
102	−4 29	27	71	−4 02	26	70	−3 36	27	70	−3 09	27	69	−2 42	27	68	−2 15	26	67	−1 49	27	66	−1 22	27	65
103	−5 21	27	71	−4 54	27	70	−4 27	27	70	−4 00	27	68	−3 33	27	67	−3 06	27	66	−2 39	28	65	−2 11	27	65
104	−6 13	27	71	−5 46	28	70	−5 18	27	69	−4 51	28	68	−4 23	27	67	−3 56	28	66	−3 28	27	65	−3 01	28	64
105				−6 37	28	69	−6 09	27	68	−5 42	28	67	−5 14	28	67	−4 46	28	66	−4 18	28	65	−3 50	28	64
106										−6 32	28	67	−6 04	28	66	−5 36	29	65	−5 07	28	64	−4 39	28	63
107																−6 25	28	65	−5 57	29	64	−5 28	29	63
108																						−6 17	29	63
109																								

LHA	15° Hc	d	Z	16° Hc	d	Z	17° Hc	d	Z	18° Hc	d	Z	19° Hc	d	Z	20° Hc	d	Z	21° Hc	d	Z	22° Hc	d	Z
90	−6 03	−23	104	−6 26	−24	105	**270**																	
89	−5 09	−24	104	−5 33	−24	105	−5 57	−24	106	−6 21	−23	107	**271**											
88	−4 16	−24	105	−4 40	−24	105	−5 04	−24	106	−5 28	−24	107	−5 52	−24	108	−6 16	−24	109	−6 40	−23	110	**272**		
87	−3 23	−25	105	−3 48	−24	106	−4 12	−24	107	−4 36	−24	108	−5 00	−24	109	−5 24	−24	110	−5 48	−24	110	−6 12	−24	111
86	−2 30	−25	105	−2 55	−24	106	−3 19	−25	107	−3 44	−24	108	−4 08	−25	109	−4 33	−24	110	−4 57	−24	111	−5 21	−24	112
85	−1 38	−24	106	−2 02	−25	106	−2 27	−25	108	−2 52	−25	108	−3 17	−24	110	−3 41	−25	110	−4 06	−24	111	−4 30	−25	112
84	−0 45	−25	106	−1 10	−25	107	−1 35	−25	108	−2 00	−25	108	−2 25	−25	110	−2 50	−25	110	−3 15	−25	112	−3 40	−25	112
83	00 08	−25	107	−0 18	−25	107	−0 43	−25	108	−1 08	−25	109	−1 33	−26	110	−1 59	−25	111	−2 24	−25	112	−2 49	−25	113
82	01 00	−25	107	00 35	−26	107	00 09	−25	108	−0 16	−25	109	−0 42	−26	110	−1 08	−25	111	−1 33	−25	112	−1 59	−25	113
81	01 53	−26	107	01 27	−26	108	01 01	−26	109	00 35	−26	110	00 09	−26	111	−0 17	−26	112	−0 42	−25	113	−1 08	−26	114
80	02 45	−26	108	02 19	−26	109	01 53	−26	110	01 27	−26	110	01 00	−26	111	00 34	−26	112	00 08	−26	113	−0 18	−26	114
79	03 37	−26	108	03 11	−26	109	02 44	−26	110	02 18	−27	111	01 51	−26	111	01 25	−27	113	00 58	−27	113	00 32	−27	114
78	04 29	−27	109	04 02	−27	110	03 36	−27	110	03 09	−27	111	02 42	−27	112	02 15	−27	113	01 49	−27	114	01 22	−27	115
77	05 21	−27	109	04 54	−27	110	04 27	−27	111	04 00	−27	112	03 33	−27	113	03 06	−27	114	02 39	−28	114	02 11	−27	115
76	06 13	−27	109	05 46	−28	111	05 18	−27	111	04 51	−28	112	04 23	−28	113	03 56	−28	114	03 28	−28	115	03 01	−28	116
75	07 04	−27	110	06 37	−28	111	06 09	−27	112	05 42	−28	113	05 14	−28	113	04 46	−28	114	04 18	−28	115	03 50	−28	116
74	07 56	−28	110	07 28	−28	111	07 00	−28	112	06 32	−28	113	06 04	−28	114	05 36	−29	115	05 07	−28	116	04 39	−28	117
73	08 47	−28	111	08 19	−28	112	07 51	−29	113	07 22	−29	113	06 54	−29	114	06 25	−29	115	05 57	−29	116	05 28	−29	117
72	09 38	−28	111	09 10	−29	112	08 41	−29	113	08 13	−29	114	07 44	−29	115	07 15	−29	116	06 46	−29	117	06 17	−29	117
71	10 29	−29	112	10 00	−28	113	09 32	−29	114	09 03	−30	114	08 33	−29	115	08 04	−29	116	07 35	−30	117	07 05	−29	118
70	11 20	−29	112	10 51	−29	113	10 22	−30	114	09 52	−29	115	09 23	−30	116	08 53	−30	117	08 23	−29	118	07 54	−30	118
	15°			**16°**			**17°**			**18°**			**19°**			**20°**			**21°**			**22°**		

S. Lat. { L.H.A. greater than 180° ....Zn=180°–Z
{ L.H.A. less than 180°............Zn=180°+Z

DECLINATION (15° – 29°)
__CONTRARY__ NAME TO LATITUDE

DECLINATION (15° – 29°)
SAME NAME AS LATITUDE

LAT 24°

LAT 24°

23°			24°			25°			26°			27°			28°			29°			LHA
Hc	d	Z	Hc	d	Z	Hc	d	Z	Hc	d	Z	Hc	d	Z	Hc	d	Z	Hc	d	Z	
26 31	17	75	26 48	16	74	27 04	16	73	27 20	15	72	27 35	15	71	27 50	14	70	28 04	13	69	290
25 38	17	75	25 55	17	74	26 12	16	73	26 28	15	72	26 43	15	71	26 58	15	70	27 13	14	68	289
24 45	18	75	25 03	16	74	25 19	17	72	25 36	16	71	25 52	15	70	26 07	15	69	26 22	14	68	288
23 53	17	74	24 10	17	73	24 27	17	72	24 44	16	71	25 00	16	70	25 16	15	69	25 31	15	68	287
23 00	18	74	23 18	17	73	23 35	17	72	23 52	17	71	24 09	16	70	24 25	15	69	24 40	16	68	286
22 07	18	74	22 25	18	73	22 43	17	72	23 00	17	71	23 17	17	70	23 34	16	69	23 50	15	67	285
21 15	18	73	21 33	18	72	21 51	18	71	22 09	17	70	22 26	17	69	22 43	16	68	22 59	16	67	284
20 22	19	73	20 41	18	72	20 59	18	71	21 17	18	70	21 35	17	69	21 52	17	68	22 09	16	67	283
19 30	19	73	19 49	18	72	20 07	19	71	20 26	18	70	20 44	17	69	21 01	17	68	21 18	17	67	282
18 38	19	72	18 57	19	71	19 16	18	70	19 34	18	69	19 52	18	68	20 10	18	67	20 28	17	66	281
17 45	20	72	18 05	19	71	18 24	19	70	18 43	19	69	19 02	18	68	19 20	18	67	19 38	17	66	280
16 53	20	72	17 13	20	71	17 33	19	70	17 52	19	69	18 11	18	68	18 29	19	67	18 48	18	66	279
16 01	20	72	16 21	20	71	16 41	20	70	17 01	19	69	17 20	19	68	17 39	19	67	17 58	18	66	278
15 09	21	71	15 30	20	70	15 50	20	69	16 10	19	68	16 29	20	67	16 49	19	66	17 08	19	65	277
14 17	21	71	14 38	21	70	14 59	20	69	15 19	20	68	15 39	20	67	15 59	19	66	16 18	19	65	276
13 26	21	71	13 47	21	70	14 08	20	69	14 28	21	68	14 49	20	67	15 09	20	66	15 29	19	65	275
12 34	21	70	12 55	22	69	13 17	21	68	13 38	20	67	13 58	21	66	14 19	20	65	14 39	20	64	274
11 43	21	70	12 04	22	69	12 26	21	68	12 47	21	67	13 08	21	66	13 29	21	65	13 50	20	64	273
10 51	22	70	11 13	22	69	11 35	22	68	11 57	21	67	12 18	21	66	12 39	21	65	13 00	21	64	272
10 00	22	69	10 22	22	68	10 44	22	67	11 06	22	66	11 28	22	65	11 50	21	64	12 11	22	63	271
09 09	22	69	09 31	23	68	09 54	22	67	10 16	22	66	10 38	22	65	11 00	22	64	11 22	22	63	270
08 18	23	68	08 41	23	68	09 02	22	67	09 26	23	66	09 49	22	65	10 11	23	64	10 34	22	63	269
07 27	23	68	07 50	23	67	08 13	23	66	08 36	23	65	08 59	23	64	09 22	23	63	09 45	22	62	268
06 36	24	68	07 00	23	67	07 23	24	66	07 47	23	65	08 10	23	64	08 33	23	63	08 56	23	62	267
05 45	24	67	06 09	24	66	06 33	24	66	06 57	24	65	07 21	23	64	07 44	24	63	08 08	23	62	266
04 55	24	67	05 19	24	66	05 43	25	65	06 08	24	64	06 32	24	63	06 56	24	62	07 20	23	61	265
04 04	25	67	04 29	25	66	04 54	24	65	05 18	25	64	05 43	24	63	06 07	25	62	06 32	24	61	264
03 14	25	66	03 39	25	66	04 04	25	64	04 29	25	63	04 54	25	63	05 19	25	62	05 44	24	61	263
02 24	26	66	02 50	25	65	03 15	25	64	03 40	26	63	04 06	25	62	04 31	25	61	04 56	25	60	262
01 34	26	65	02 00	26	65	02 26	25	64	02 51	26	63	03 17	26	62	03 43	25	61	04 08	26	60	261
00 44	27	65	01 11	26	64	01 37	26	63	02 03	26	62	02 29	26	61	02 55	26	61	03 21	26	60	260
00 05	26	65	00 21	27	64	00 48	26	63	01 14	27	62	01 41	26	61	02 07	27	60	02 34	26	59	259
00 55	27	64	00 28	27	64	00 01	27	63	00 26	27	62	00 53	27	61	01 20	27	60	01 47	27	59	258
– 1 44	27	64	– 1 17	28	63	00 49	27	62	00 22	27	61	00 05	28	60	00 33	27	59	01 00	27	58	257
– 2 33	28	63	– 2 05	27	62	– 1 38	28	62	– 1 10	28	61	00 42	28	60	00 14	27	59	00 13	28	58	256
– 3 22	28	63	– 2 54	28	62	– 2 26	28	61	– 1 58	29	60	– 1 29	28	59	– 1 01	28	59	00 33	28	58	255
– 4 11	29	63	– 3 42	28	62	– 3 14	29	61	– 2 45	28	60	– 2 17	29	59	– 1 48	29	58	– 1 19	28	57	254
– 4 59	29	62	– 4 30	29	61	– 4 01	29	60	– 3 32	29	59	– 3 03	29	59	– 2 34	29	58	– 2 05	29	57	253
– 5 48	30	62	– 5 18	29	61	– 4 49	29	60	– 4 20	30	59	– 3 50	29	58	– 3 21	30	57	– 2 51	30	56	252
– 6 36	30	61	– 6 06	30	60	– 5 36	30	59	– 5 06	29	59	– 4 37	30	58	– 4 07	30	57	– 3 37	31	56	251
					110	– 6 23	30	59				– 5 23	31	57	– 4 52	30	56	– 4 22	31	56	250
											111	– 6 09	31	57	– 5 38	31	56	– 5 07	31	55	249
														112	– 6 23	31	55	– 5 52	32	55	248

23°			24°			25°			26°			27°			28°			29°			LHA
Hc	d	Z	Hc	d	Z	Hc	d	Z	Hc	d	Z	Hc	d	Z	Hc	d	Z	Hc	d	Z	
– 6 36	–24	112			273																
– 5 45	–24	113	– 6 09	–24	114	– 6 33	–24	114			274										
– 4 55	–24	113	– 5 19	–24	114	– 5 43	–25	115	– 6 08	–24	116	– 6 32	–24	117			275				
– 4 04	–25	113	– 4 29	–25	114	– 4 54	–24	115	– 5 18	–25	116	– 5 43	–24	117	– 6 07	–25	118	– 6 32	–24	119	276
– 3 14	–25	114	– 3 39	–25	115	– 4 04	–25	116	– 4 29	–25	117	– 4 54	–25	117	– 5 19	–25	118	– 5 44	–24	119	277
– 2 24	–26	114	– 2 50	–25	115	– 3 15	–25	116	– 3 40	–26	117	– 4 06	–25	118	– 4 31	–25	118	– 4 56	–25	120	278
– 1 34	–26	115	– 2 00	–26	115	– 2 26	–26	116	– 2 51	–26	117	– 3 17	–26	118	– 3 43	–25	119	– 4 08	–26	120	279
00 44	–27	115	– 1 11	–26	116	– 1 37	–26	117	– 2 03	–26	118	– 2 29	–26	119	– 2 55	–26	119	– 3 21	–26	120	280
00 05	–26	115	00 21	–27	116	00 48	–27	118	– 1 14	–27	118	– 1 41	–26	119	– 2 07	–27	120	– 2 34	–26	121	281
00 55	–27	116	00 28	–27	117	00 01	–27	118	00 26	–27	118	00 53	–27	119	– 1 20	–27	120	– 1 47	–27	121	282
01 44	–27	116	01 17	–28	117	00 49	–27	118	00 22	–27	119	00 05	–28	119	00 33	–27	120	– 1 00	–27	122	283
02 33	–28	117	02 05	–27	118	01 38	–28	118	01 10	–28	119	00 42	–28	120	00 13	–28	121	00 13	–28	122	284
03 22	–28	117	02 54	–28	118	02 26	–28	119	01 58	–29	120	01 29	–28	120	01 01	–28	121	00 33	–28	122	285
04 11	–29	117	03 42	–28	118	03 14	–29	119	02 45	–28	120	02 17	–29	121	01 48	–29	122	01 19	–28	123	286
04 59	–29	118	04 30	–29	118	04 01	–29	120	03 33	–29	120	03 03	–29	121	02 35	–29	122	02 05	–28	123	287
05 48	–30	118	05 18	–29	119	04 49	–30	120	04 20	–30	121	03 50	–30	122	03 21	–30	123	02 51	–30	124	288
06 36	–30	119	06 06	–30	120	05 36	–30	121	05 06	–29	121	04 37	–30	122	04 07	–30	123	03 37	–31	124	289
07 24	–30	119	06 54	–31	120	06 23	–30	121	05 53	–30	122	05 23	–31	123	04 52	–30	124	04 22	–31	124	290
23°			**24°**			**25°**			**26°**			**27°**			**28°**			**29°**			

DECLINATION (15° – 29°)
CONTRARY NAME TO LATITUDE

N. Lat. { L.H.A. greater than 180° .....Zn=Z
L.H.A. less than 180°............Zn=360°–Z

DECLINATION (15° – 29°) **CONTRARY** NAME TO LATITUDE

LHA	15° Hc	d	Z	16° Hc	d	Z	17° Hc	d	Z	18° Hc	d	Z	19° Hc	d	Z	20° Hc	d	Z	21° Hc	d	Z	22° Hc	d	Z
	° ′	′	°	° ′	′	°	° ′	′	°	° ′	′	°	° ′	′	°	° ′	′	°	° ′	′	°	° ′	′	°
69	12 11	-30	113	11 41	-29	114	11 12	-30	114	10 42	-30	115	10 12	-30	116	09 42	-30	117	09 12	-30	118	08 42	-31	119
68	13 01	-30	113	12 31	-29	114	12 02	-31	115	11 31	-30	116	11 01	-30	117	10 31	-31	118	10 00	-30	118	09 30	-31	119
67	13 51	-30	114	13 21	-30	115	12 51	-30	115	12 21	-31	116	11 50	-31	117	11 19	-31	118	10 48	-31	119	10 17	-31	120
66	14 42	-31	114	14 11	-30	115	13 41	-31	116	13 10	-31	117	12 39	-31	118	12 08	-32	119	11 36	-31	119	11 05	-32	120
65	15 31	-30	115	15 01	-31	116	14 30	-32	116	13 58	-31	117	13 27	-31	118	12 56	-32	119	12 24	-32	120	11 52	-32	121
64	16 21	-31	115	15 50	-31	116	15 19	-32	117	14 47	-32	118	14 15	-32	119	13 43	-32	120	13 11	-32	120	12 39	-33	121
63	17 11	-32	116	16 39	-32	117	16 07	-32	118	15 35	-32	118	15 03	-32	119	14 31	-33	120	13 58	-32	121	13 26	-33	122
62	18 00	-32	116	17 28	-32	117	16 56	-32	118	16 24	-33	119	15 51	-33	120	15 18	-33	121	14 45	-33	122	14 12	-33	122
61	18 49	-32	117	18 17	-33	118	17 44	-33	119	17 11	-33	119	16 38	-33	120	16 05	-33	121	15 32	-34	122	14 58	-34	123
60	19 38	-33	117	19 05	-33	118	18 32	-33	119	17 59	-33	120	17 26	-34	121	16 52	-34	122	16 18	-34	123	15 44	-34	123
59	20 26	-33	118	19 53	-33	119	19 20	-34	120	18 46	-34	121	18 12	-34	121	17 38	-34	122	17 04	-34	123	16 30	-35	124
58	21 15	-34	118	20 41	-34	119	20 07	-34	120	19 33	-34	121	18 59	-34	122	18 25	-35	123	17 50	-35	124	17 15	-35	125
57	22 03	-34	119	21 29	-34	120	20 55	-35	121	20 20	-35	122	19 45	-35	123	19 10	-35	123	18 35	-35	124	18 00	-36	125
56	22 50	-34	120	22 16	-35	121	21 41	-34	121	21 07	-36	122	20 31	-35	123	19 56	-36	124	19 20	-36	125	18 44	-36	126
55	23 38	-35	120	23 03	-35	121	22 28	-35	122	21 53	-36	123	21 17	-36	124	20 41	-36	125	20 05	-36	125	19 29	-37	126
54	24 25	-35	121	23 50	-36	122	23 14	-35	123	22 39	-36	124	22 03	-37	124	21 26	-36	125	20 50	-37	126	20 13	-37	127
53	25 12	-36	122	24 36	-36	122	24 00	-36	123	23 24	-36	124	22 48	-37	125	22 11	-37	126	21 34	-38	127	20 56	-37	128
52	25 59	-37	122	25 22	-36	123	24 46	-37	124	24 09	-37	125	23 32	-37	126	22 55	-38	126	22 17	-37	127	21 40	-38	128
51	26 45	-37	123	26 08	-37	124	25 31	-37	125	24 54	-37	125	24 17	-38	126	23 39	-38	127	23 01	-38	128	22 23	-39	129
50	27 31	-37	123	26 54	-38	124	26 16	-37	125	25 39	-38	126	25 01	-39	127	24 22	-38	128	23 44	-39	129	23 05	-39	129
49	28 16	-37	124	27 39	-38	125	27 01	-38	126	26 23	-39	127	25 44	-38	128	25 06	-39	128	24 27	-40	129	23 47	-39	130
48	29 01	-38	125	28 23	-38	126	27 45	-38	127	27 07	-39	127	26 28	-40	128	25 48	-39	129	25 09	-40	130	24 29	-40	131
47	29 46	-38	126	29 08	-39	126	28 29	-39	127	27 50	-40	128	27 10	-39	129	26 31	-40	130	25 51	-41	131	25 10	-40	131
46	30 31	-39	126	29 52	-40	127	29 12	-39	128	28 33	-40	129	27 53	-41	130	27 12	-40	131	26 32	-41	131	25 51	-41	132
45	31 15	-40	127	30 35	-40	128	29 55	-40	129	29 15	-40	130	28 35	-41	130	27 54	-41	131	27 13	-42	132	26 31	-41	133
44	31 58	-40	128	31 18	-40	129	30 38	-41	129	29 57	-41	130	29 16	-41	131	28 35	-42	132	27 53	-42	133	27 11	-42	134
43	32 41	-40	128	32 01	-41	129	31 20	-41	130	30 39	-42	131	29 57	-42	132	29 15	-42	133	28 33	-42	134	27 51	-43	134
42	33 24	-41	129	32 43	-41	130	32 02	-42	131	31 20	-42	132	30 38	-43	133	29 55	-42	133	29 13	-43	134	28 30	-43	135
41	34 06	-41	130	33 25	-42	131	32 43	-43	132	32 00	-42	133	31 18	-43	133	30 35	-43	134	29 52	-44	135	29 08	-44	136
40	34 48	-42	131	34 06	-43	132	33 23	-42	133	32 41	-44	133	31 57	-43	134	31 14	-44	135	30 30	-44	136	29 46	-44	137
39	35 29	-43	132	34 46	-43	133	34 03	-43	133	33 20	-44	134	32 36	-44	135	31 52	-44	136	31 08	-45	137	30 23	-44	137
38	36 10	-43	133	35 27	-44	133	34 43	-44	134	33 59	-44	135	33 15	-45	136	32 30	-45	137	31 45	-45	137	31 00	-45	138
37	36 50	-44	133	36 06	-44	134	35 22	-45	135	34 37	-44	136	33 53	-45	137	33 08	-46	138	32 22	-46	138	31 36	-46	139
36	37 29	-44	134	36 45	-45	135	36 00	-45	136	35 15	-45	137	34 30	-46	138	33 44	-46	138	32 58	-46	139	32 12	-46	140
35	38 08	-45	135	37 23	-45	136	36 38	-46	137	35 52	-45	138	35 07	-47	138	34 20	-46	139	33 34	-47	140	32 47	-47	141
34	38 47	-46	136	38 01	-46	137	37 15	-46	138	36 29	-46	139	35 43	-47	139	34 56	-47	140	34 09	-48	141	33 21	-47	142
33	39 24	-46	137	38 38	-46	138	37 52	-47	139	37 05	-47	140	36 18	-47	140	35 31	-48	141	34 43	-48	142	33 55	-48	143
32	40 01	-46	138	39 15	-47	139	38 28	-48	140	37 40	-47	140	36 53	-48	141	36 05	-48	142	35 17	-49	143	34 28	-49	143
31	40 38	-48	139	39 50	-47	140	39 03	-48	141	38 15	-48	141	37 27	-49	142	36 38	-49	143	35 49	-49	144	35 00	-49	144
30	41 13	-48	140	40 25	-48	141	39 37	-48	142	38 49	-49	142	38 00	-49	143	37 11	-49	144	36 22	-50	145	35 32	-50	145
29	41 48	-49	141	40 59	-48	142	40 11	-49	143	39 22	-50	143	38 32	-49	144	37 43	-50	145	36 53	-50	146	36 03	-50	146
28	42 22	-49	142	41 33	-49	143	40 44	-50	144	39 54	-50	144	39 04	-50	145	38 14	-50	146	37 24	-51	147	36 33	-51	147
27	42 55	-49	143	42 06	-50	144	41 16	-51	145	40 25	-50	145	39 35	-51	146	38 44	-51	147	37 53	-51	148	37 02	-51	148
26	43 28	-51	144	42 37	-50	145	41 47	-51	146	40 56	-51	147	40 05	-51	147	39 14	-52	148	38 22	-51	149	37 31	-52	149
25	43 59	-51	145	43 08	-51	146	42 17	-51	147	41 26	-52	148	40 34	-51	148	39 43	-52	149	38 51	-53	150	37 58	-52	150
24	44 30	-52	147	43 38	-51	147	42 47	-52	148	41 55	-52	149	41 03	-53	149	40 10	-52	150	39 18	-53	151	38 25	-53	151
23	44 59	-51	148	44 08	-53	148	43 15	-52	149	42 23	-53	150	41 30	-53	150	40 37	-53	151	39 44	-53	152	38 51	-53	152
22	45 28	-52	149	44 36	-53	150	43 43	-53	150	42 50	-53	151	41 57	-53	152	41 04	-54	152	40 10	-54	153	39 16	-54	153
21	45 56	-53	150	45 03	-53	151	44 10	-54	151	43 16	-53	152	42 23	-54	153	41 29	-54	153	40 35	-55	154	39 40	-54	154
20	46 23	-54	151	45 29	-54	152	44 35	-54	153	43 41	-54	153	42 47	-54	154	41 53	-55	154	40 58	-54	155	40 04	-55	156
19	46 49	-55	153	45 54	-54	153	45 00	-54	154	44 06	-55	154	43 11	-55	155	42 16	-55	156	41 21	-55	156	40 26	-56	157
18	47 13	-55	154	46 18	-54	155	45 24	-55	155	44 29	-56	156	43 33	-55	156	42 38	-55	157	41 43	-56	157	40 47	-56	158
17	47 37	-55	155	46 42	-56	156	45 46	-55	156	44 51	-56	157	43 55	-56	157	42 59	-56	158	42 03	-56	158	41 07	-56	159
16	47 59	-56	157	47 03	-55	157	46 08	-56	158	45 12	-57	158	44 15	-56	159	43 19	-56	159	42 23	-57	160	41 26	-56	160
15	48 20	-56	158	47 24	-56	158	46 28	-57	159	45 31	-56	159	44 35	-57	160	43 38	-57	160	42 41	-56	161	41 45	-57	161
14	48 40	-56	159	47 44	-57	160	46 47	-57	160	45 50	-57	161	44 53	-57	161	43 56	-57	162	42 59	-57	162	42 02	-58	162
13	48 59	-57	161	48 02	-57	161	47 05	-57	162	46 08	-58	162	45 10	-57	162	44 13	-58	163	43 15	-57	163	42 18	-58	164
12	49 17	-58	162	48 19	-57	163	47 22	-58	163	46 24	-58	163	45 26	-58	164	44 28	-57	164	43 31	-58	164	42 33	-58	165
11	49 33	-58	163	48 35	-58	164	47 37	-58	164	46 39	-58	165	45 41	-58	165	44 43	-58	165	43 45	-59	166	42 46	-58	166
10	49 48	-58	165	48 50	-59	165	47 51	-58	166	46 53	-58	166	45 55	-59	166	44 56	-58	167	43 58	-59	167	42 59	-59	167
9	50 01	-58	166	49 03	-59	167	48 04	-58	167	47 06	-59	167	46 07	-59	168	45 08	-59	168	44 09	-58	168	43 11	-59	169
8	50 13	-58	168	49 15	-59	168	48 16	-59	168	47 17	-59	169	46 18	-59	169	45 19	-59	169	44 20	-59	170	43 21	-59	170
7	50 24	-59	169	49 25	-59	170	48 26	-59	170	47 27	-59	170	46 28	-60	170	45 28	-59	171	44 29	-59	171	43 30	-59	171
6	50 34	-60	171	49 34	-59	171	48 35	-59	171	47 36	-60	172	46 36	-59	172	45 37	-60	172	44 37	-59	172	43 38	-60	172
5	50 42	-60	172	49 42	-59	173	48 43	-60	173	47 43	-60	173	46 43	-59	173	45 44	-60	173	44 44	-59	173	43 45	-60	174
4	50 48	-59	174	49 49	-60	174	48 49	-60	174	47 49	-60	174	46 49	-59	174	45 50	-60	175	44 50	-60	175	43 50	-60	175
3	50 53	-59	175	49 54	-60	176	48 54	-60	176	47 54	-60	176	46 54	-60	176	45 54	-60	176	44 54	-60	176	43 54	-59	176
2	50 57	-60	177	49 57	-60	177	48 57	-60	177	47 57	-60	177	46 57	-60	177	45 57	-60	177	44 57	-59	177	43 58	-60	177
1	50 59	-60	178	49 59	-60	179	48 59	-60	179	47 59	-60	179	46 59	-60	179	45 59	-60	179	44 59	-60	179	43 59	-60	179
0	51 00	-60	180	50 00	-60	180	49 00	-60	180	48 00	-60	180	47 00	-60	180	46 00	-60	180	45 00	-60	180	44 00	-60	180
	15°			16°			17°			18°			19°			20°			21°			22°		

LAT 24°

S. Lat. { L.H.A. greater than 180° ....Zn=180°–Z
L.H.A. less than 180°...........Zn=180°+Z

DECLINATION (15° – 29°) **CONTRARY** NAME TO LATITUDE

DECLINATION (15° – 29°)
CONTRARY NAME TO LATITUDE

23°			24°			25°			26°			27°			28°			29°			LHA
Hc	d	Z	Hc	d	Z	Hc	d	Z	Hc	d	Z	Hc	d	Z	Hc	d	Z	Hc	d	Z	
08 11	-30	120	07 41	-31	121	07 10	-30	121	06 40	-31	122	06 09	-31	123	05 38	-31	124	05 07	-31	125	291
08 59	-31	120	08 28	-31	121	07 57	-31	122	07 26	-32	123	06 54	-31	124	06 23	-31	125	05 52	-32	125	292
09 46	-31	121	09 15	-32	122	08 43	-31	122	08 12	-32	123	07 40	-32	124	07 08	-32	125	06 36	-32	126	293
10 33	-32	121	10 01	-32	122	09 29	-32	123	08 57	-32	124	08 25	-32	125	07 53	-32	125	07 21	-33	126	294
11 20	-32	122	10 48	-33	123	10 15	-32	123	09 43	-33	124	09 10	-33	125	08 37	-32	126	08 05	-33	127	295
12 06	-32	122	11 34	-33	123	11 01	-33	124	10 28	-33	125	09 55	-33	126	09 22	-34	126	08 48	-33	127	296
12 53	-34	123	12 19	-33	123	11 46	-33	124	11 13	-34	125	10 39	-33	126	10 06	-34	127	09 32	-34	128	297
13 39	-34	123	13 05	-34	124	12 31	-34	125	11 57	-34	126	11 23	-34	127	10 49	-34	127	10 15	-35	128	298
14 24	-34	124	13 50	-34	125	13 16	-34	125	12 42	-35	126	12 07	-34	127	11 33	-35	128	10 58	-35	129	299
15 10	-35	124	14 35	-34	125	14 01	-35	126	13 26	-35	127	12 51	-35	128	12 16	-36	129	11 40	-35	129	300
15 55	-35	125	15 20	-35	126	14 45	-35	127	14 09	-35	127	13 34	-36	128	12 58	-35	129	12 23	-36	130	301
16 40	-36	125	16 04	-35	126	15 29	-36	127	14 53	-36	128	14 17	-36	129	13 41	-37	130	13 04	-36	130	302
17 24	-36	126	16 48	-36	126	16 12	-36	128	15 36	-37	128	14 59	-36	129	14 23	-37	130	13 46	-37	131	303
18 08	-36	127	17 32	-37	127	16 55	-36	128	16 19	-37	129	15 42	-37	130	15 05	-38	131	14 27	-37	132	304
18 52	-37	127	18 15	-37	128	17 38	-37	129	17 01	-37	130	16 24	-38	130	15 46	-38	131	15 08	-38	132	305
19 36	-38	128	18 58	-37	129	18 21	-38	129	17 43	-38	130	17 05	-38	131	16 27	-38	132	15 49	-39	133	306
20 19	-38	128	19 41	-38	129	19 03	-38	130	18 25	-39	131	17 46	-38	132	17 08	-39	132	16 29	-39	133	307
21 02	-39	129	20 23	-38	130	19 45	-39	131	19 06	-39	131	18 27	-39	132	17 48	-40	133	17 08	-39	134	308
21 44	-39	130	21 05	-39	130	20 26	-39	131	19 47	-40	132	19 07	-39	133	18 28	-40	134	17 48	-40	134	309
22 26	-39	130	21 47	-40	131	21 07	-40	132	20 27	-40	133	19 47	-40	133	19 07	-40	134	18 27	-41	135	310
23 08	-40	131	22 28	-40	132	21 48	-41	133	21 07	-40	133	20 27	-41	134	19 46	-41	135	19 05	-41	136	311
23 49	-41	132	23 08	-40	132	22 28	-41	133	21 47	-41	134	21 06	-41	135	20 25	-42	136	19 43	-41	136	312
24 30	-41	132	23 49	-41	133	23 08	-42	134	22 26	-41	135	21 45	-42	135	21 03	-42	136	20 21	-42	137	313
25 10	-41	133	24 29	-42	134	23 47	-42	135	23 05	-42	135	22 23	-42	136	21 41	-43	137	20 58	-43	138	314
25 50	-42	134	25 08	-42	134	24 26	-43	135	23 43	-42	136	23 01	-43	137	22 18	-43	138	21 35	-43	138	315
26 29	-42	134	25 47	-43	135	25 04	-43	136	24 21	-43	137	23 38	-43	137	22 55	-44	138	22 11	-44	139	316
27 08	-43	135	26 25	-43	136	25 42	-44	137	24 58	-43	137	24 15	-44	138	23 31	-44	139	22 47	-45	140	317
27 47	-44	136	27 03	-44	137	26 19	-44	137	25 35	-44	138	24 51	-44	139	24 07	-45	140	23 22	-45	140	318
28 24	-44	137	27 40	-44	137	26 56	-44	138	26 12	-45	139	25 27	-45	140	24 42	-45	140	23 57	-46	141	319
29 02	-45	137	28 17	-45	138	27 32	-45	139	26 47	-45	140	26 02	-46	140	25 16	-45	141	24 31	-46	142	320
29 39	-46	138	28 53	-45	139	28 08	-46	140	27 22	-45	140	26 37	-46	141	25 51	-47	142	25 04	-46	143	321
30 15	-46	139	29 29	-46	140	28 43	-46	140	27 57	-46	141	27 11	-47	142	26 24	-47	143	25 37	-47	143	322
30 50	-46	140	30 04	-46	141	29 18	-47	141	28 31	-47	142	27 44	-47	143	26 57	-47	143	26 10	-48	144	323
31 26	-47	141	30 39	-47	141	29 52	-47	142	29 05	-48	143	28 18	-48	144	27 29	-47	144	26 42	-48	145	324
32 00	-47	141	31 13	-48	142	30 25	-48	143	29 37	-48	144	28 49	-48	144	28 01	-48	145	27 13	-49	146	325
32 34	-48	142	31 46	-48	143	30 58	-48	144	30 10	-49	144	29 21	-49	145	28 32	-49	146	27 43	-49	146	326
33 07	-48	143	32 19	-49	144	31 30	-49	145	30 41	-49	145	29 52	-49	146	29 03	-50	147	28 13	-49	147	327
33 39	-49	144	32 50	-49	145	32 01	-49	145	31 12	-50	146	30 22	-49	147	29 33	-50	147	28 43	-50	148	328
34 11	-49	145	33 22	-50	146	32 32	-50	146	31 42	-50	147	30 52	-50	148	30 02	-51	148	29 11	-50	149	329
34 42	-50	146	33 52	-50	147	33 02	-50	147	32 12	-51	148	31 21	-51	149	30 30	-51	149	29 39	-51	150	330
35 13	-51	147	34 22	-51	148	33 31	-51	148	32 40	-51	149	31 49	-51	149	30 58	-52	150	30 06	-51	151	331
35 42	-51	148	34 51	-51	148	34 00	-52	149	33 08	-51	150	32 17	-52	150	31 25	-52	151	30 33	-52	152	332
36 11	-52	149	35 19	-51	149	34 28	-52	150	33 36	-53	151	32 43	-52	151	31 51	-52	152	30 59	-53	152	333
36 39	-52	150	35 47	-52	150	34 55	-52	151	34 02	-53	152	33 09	-52	152	32 17	-53	153	31 24	-53	153	334
37 06	-53	151	36 13	-52	151	35 21	-53	152	34 28	-53	153	33 35	-54	153	32 41	-53	154	31 48	-54	154	335
37 32	-53	152	36 39	-53	152	35 46	-53	153	34 53	-54	154	33 59	-54	154	33 05	-54	155	32 11	-54	155	336
37 58	-54	153	37 04	-54	153	36 10	-53	154	35 17	-54	155	34 23	-54	155	33 28	-54	156	32 34	-54	156	337
38 22	-54	154	37 28	-54	154	36 34	-54	155	35 40	-54	156	34 45	-54	156	33 51	-55	157	32 56	-55	157	338
38 46	-55	155	37 51	-54	156	36 57	-55	156	36 02	-55	157	35 07	-55	157	34 12	-55	158	33 17	-55	158	339
39 09	-55	156	38 14	-55	157	37 19	-56	157	36 23	-55	158	35 28	-55	158	34 33	-56	158	33 37	-56	159	340
39 30	-55	157	38 35	-56	158	37 39	-55	158	36 44	-56	159	35 48	-56	159	34 52	-56	159	33 56	-56	160	341
39 51	-56	158	38 55	-56	159	37 59	-56	159	37 03	-56	160	36 07	-56	160	35 11	-56	160	34 15	-57	161	342
40 11	-56	159	39 15	-57	160	38 18	-56	160	37 22	-57	161	36 25	-57	161	35 29	-57	162	34 32	-57	162	343
40 30	-57	161	39 33	-57	161	38 36	-56	161	37 40	-57	162	36 43	-57	162	35 46	-57	163	34 49	-58	163	344
40 48	-57	162	39 51	-58	162	38 53	-57	162	37 56	-57	163	36 59	-57	163	36 02	-58	164	35 04	-57	164	345
41 04	-57	163	40 07	-58	163	39 09	-57	164	38 12	-58	164	37 14	-58	164	36 17	-58	165	35 19	-58	165	346
41 20	-58	164	40 22	-58	164	39 24	-57	165	38 27	-58	165	37 29	-58	165	36 31	-58	166	35 33	-58	166	347
41 35	-58	165	40 37	-59	166	39 38	-58	166	38 40	-58	166	37 42	-58	166	36 44	-59	167	35 45	-58	167	348
41 48	-58	166	40 50	-59	167	39 51	-58	167	38 53	-59	167	37 54	-58	167	36 56	-59	168	35 57	-59	168	349
42 00	-58	168	41 02	-59	168	40 03	-59	168	39 04	-59	168	38 06	-59	169	37 07	-59	169	36 08	-59	169	350
42 12	-59	169	41 13	-59	169	40 14	-59	169	39 15	-59	170	38 16	-59	170	37 17	-59	170	36 18	-59	170	351
42 22	-59	170	41 23	-60	170	40 23	-59	171	39 24	-59	171	38 25	-59	171	37 26	-59	171	36 27	-60	171	352
42 31	-60	171	41 31	-59	171	40 32	-59	172	39 33	-59	172	38 33	-59	172	37 34	-59	172	36 34	-59	172	353
42 38	-59	172	41 39	-60	173	40 39	-60	173	39 40	-60	173	38 40	-59	173	37 41	-60	173	36 41	-59	173	354
42 45	-60	174	41 45	-59	174	40 46	-60	174	39 46	-60	174	38 46	-60	174	37 47	-60	174	36 47	-60	174	355
42 50	-59	175	41 51	-60	175	40 51	-60	175	39 51	-60	175	38 51	-60	175	37 51	-59	176	36 52	-60	176	356
42 55	-60	176	41 55	-60	176	40 55	-60	176	39 55	-60	176	38 55	-60	177	37 55	-60	177	36 55	-60	177	357
42 58	-60	177	41 58	-60	178	40 58	-60	178	39 58	-60	178	38 58	-60	178	37 58	-60	178	36 58	-60	178	358
42 59	-60	179	41 59	-60	179	40 59	-60	179	39 59	-60	179	38 59	-60	179	37 59	-60	179	36 59	-60	179	359
43 00	-60	180	42 00	-60	180	41 00	-60	180	40 00	-60	180	39 00	-60	180	38 00	-60	180	37 00	-60	180	360
23°			24°			25°			26°			27°			28°			29°			

LAT 24°

DECLINATION (15° – 29°)
CONTRARY NAME TO LATITUDE

LAT 24°

TABLE 5.–Correction to Tabulated Altitude for Minutes of Declination

d /	1	2	3	4	5	6	7	8	9	10	11	12	13	14	15	16	17	18	19	20	21	22	23	24	25	26	27	28	29	30
0	0	0	0	0	0	0	0	0	0	0	0	0	0	0	0	0	0	0	0	0	0	0	0	0	0	0	0	0	0	0
1	0	0	0	0	0	0	0	0	0	0	0	0	0	0	0	0	0	0	0	0	0	0	0	0	0	0	0	0	0	0
2	0	0	0	0	0	0	0	0	0	0	0	0	0	0	0	1	1	1	1	1	1	1	1	1	1	1	1	1	1	1
3	0	0	0	0	0	0	0	0	0	0	1	1	1	1	1	1	1	1	1	1	1	1	1	1	1	1	1	1	1	2
4	0	0	0	0	0	0	0	1	1	1	1	1	1	1	1	1	1	1	1	1	1	1	2	2	2	2	2	2	2	2
5	0	0	0	0	0	0	1	1	1	1	1	1	1	1	1	1	1	2	2	2	2	2	2	2	2	2	2	2	2	3
6	0	0	0	0	0	1	1	1	1	1	1	1	1	1	1	2	2	2	2	2	2	2	2	2	2	2	2	3	3	3
7	0	0	0	0	1	1	1	1	1	1	1	1	2	2	2	2	2	2	2	2	2	3	3	3	3	3	3	3	3	4
8	0	0	0	1	1	1	1	1	1	1	1	2	2	2	2	2	2	2	3	3	3	3	3	3	3	3	4	4	4	4
9	0	0	0	1	1	1	1	1	1	2	2	2	2	2	2	2	3	3	3	3	3	3	3	4	4	4	4	4	4	4
10	0	0	0	1	1	1	1	1	2	2	2	2	2	2	3	3	3	3	3	3	4	4	4	4	4	4	5	5	5	5
11	0	0	1	1	1	1	1	1	2	2	2	2	2	3	3	3	3	4	3	4	4	4	4	4	5	5	5	5	5	6
12	0	0	1	1	1	1	1	2	2	2	2	2	3	3	3	3	3	4	4	4	4	4	5	5	5	5	5	6	6	6
13	0	0	1	1	1	1	2	2	2	2	2	3	3	3	3	3	4	4	4	4	5	5	5	5	5	6	6	6	6	6
14	0	0	1	1	1	1	2	2	2	2	3	3	3	3	4	4	4	4	4	5	5	5	5	6	6	6	6	7	7	7
15	0	0	1	1	1	2	2	2	2	2	3	3	3	4	4	4	4	4	5	5	5	6	6	6	6	7	7	7	7	8
16	0	1	1	1	1	2	2	2	2	3	3	3	3	4	4	4	5	5	5	5	6	6	6	6	7	7	7	7	8	8
17	0	1	1	1	1	2	2	2	3	3	3	3	4	4	4	5	5	5	5	6	6	6	7	7	7	7	8	8	8	8
18	0	1	1	1	2	2	2	2	3	3	3	4	4	4	4	5	5	5	6	6	6	7	7	7	8	8	8	8	9	9
19	0	1	1	1	2	2	2	3	3	3	3	4	4	4	5	5	5	6	6	6	7	7	7	8	8	8	9	9	9	10
20	0	1	1	1	2	2	2	3	3	3	4	4	4	5	5	5	6	6	6	7	7	7	8	8	8	9	9	9	10	10
21	0	1	1	1	2	2	3	3	3	4	4	4	5	5	5	6	6	6	7	7	7	8	8	8	9	9	9	10	10	10
22	0	1	1	1	2	2	3	3	3	4	4	4	5	5	6	6	6	7	7	7	8	8	8	9	9	10	10	10	11	11
23	0	1	1	2	2	2	3	3	3	4	4	5	5	5	6	6	7	7	7	8	8	8	9	9	10	10	10	11	11	12
24	0	1	1	2	2	2	3	3	4	4	4	5	5	6	6	6	7	7	8	8	8	9	9	10	10	10	11	11	12	12
25	0	1	1	2	2	2	3	3	4	4	5	5	6	6	6	7	7	8	8	8	9	9	10	10	10	11	11	12	12	12
26	0	1	1	2	2	3	3	4	4	4	5	5	6	6	6	7	8	8	8	9	9	10	10	11	11	11	12	12	13	13
27	0	1	1	2	2	3	3	4	4	4	5	5	6	6	7	7	8	8	9	9	9	10	10	11	11	12	12	13	13	14
28	0	1	1	2	2	3	3	4	4	5	5	6	6	7	7	7	8	8	9	9	10	10	11	11	12	12	13	13	14	14
29	0	1	1	2	2	3	3	4	4	5	5	6	6	7	7	8	8	9	9	10	10	11	11	12	12	13	13	14	14	14
30	0	1	2	2	2	3	4	4	4	5	6	6	7	7	8	8	8	9	10	10	10	11	12	12	13	13	14	14	14	15
31	1	1	2	2	3	3	4	4	5	5	6	6	7	7	8	8	9	9	10	10	11	11	12	12	13	13	14	14	15	16
32	1	1	2	2	3	3	4	4	5	5	6	6	7	7	8	9	9	10	10	11	11	12	12	13	13	14	14	15	15	16
33	1	1	2	2	3	3	4	4	5	6	6	7	7	8	8	9	9	10	10	11	12	12	13	13	14	14	15	15	16	16
34	1	1	2	2	3	3	4	5	5	6	6	7	7	8	8	9	10	10	11	11	12	12	13	14	14	15	15	16	16	17
35	1	1	2	2	3	4	4	5	5	6	6	7	8	8	9	9	10	10	11	12	12	13	13	14	15	15	16	16	17	18
36	1	1	2	2	3	4	4	5	5	6	7	7	8	8	9	10	10	11	11	12	13	13	14	14	15	16	16	17	17	18
37	1	1	2	2	3	4	4	5	6	6	7	7	8	9	9	10	10	11	12	12	13	14	14	15	15	16	17	17	18	18
38	1	1	2	3	3	4	4	5	6	6	7	8	8	9	10	10	11	11	12	13	13	14	15	15	16	16	17	18	18	19
39	1	1	2	3	3	4	5	5	6	6	7	8	8	9	10	10	11	12	12	13	14	14	15	16	16	17	18	18	19	20
40	1	1	2	3	3	4	5	5	6	7	7	8	9	9	10	11	11	12	13	13	14	15	15	16	17	17	18	19	19	20
41	1	1	2	3	3	4	5	5	6	7	8	8	9	10	10	11	12	12	13	14	14	15	16	16	17	18	18	19	20	20
42	1	1	2	3	4	4	5	6	6	7	8	8	9	10	10	11	12	13	13	14	15	15	16	17	18	18	19	20	20	21
43	1	1	2	3	4	4	5	6	6	7	8	9	10	10	11	11	12	13	14	14	15	16	16	17	18	19	19	20	21	22
44	1	1	2	3	4	4	5	6	7	7	8	9	10	10	11	12	12	13	14	15	15	16	17	18	18	19	20	21	21	22
45	1	2	2	3	4	4	5	6	7	8	8	9	10	10	11	12	13	13	14	15	16	16	17	18	19	20	20	21	22	22
46	1	2	2	3	4	5	5	6	7	8	8	9	10	11	12	12	13	14	15	15	16	17	18	18	19	20	21	21	22	23
47	1	2	2	3	4	5	5	6	7	8	9	9	10	11	12	13	13	14	15	16	16	17	18	19	20	20	21	22	23	24
48	1	2	2	3	4	5	6	6	7	8	9	10	10	11	12	13	14	14	15	16	17	18	18	19	20	21	22	22	23	24
49	1	2	2	3	4	5	6	7	7	8	9	10	11	11	12	13	14	15	16	16	17	18	19	20	20	21	22	23	24	24
50	1	2	2	3	4	5	6	7	8	8	9	10	11	12	12	13	14	15	16	17	18	18	19	20	21	22	22	23	24	25
51	1	2	3	3	4	5	6	7	8	8	9	10	11	12	13	14	14	15	16	17	18	19	20	20	21	22	23	24	25	26
52	1	2	3	3	4	5	6	7	8	9	10	10	11	12	13	14	15	16	16	17	18	19	20	21	22	23	23	24	25	26
53	1	2	3	4	4	5	6	7	8	9	10	11	11	12	13	14	15	16	17	18	19	20	21	22	22	23	24	25	26	26
54	1	2	3	4	4	5	6	7	8	9	10	11	12	13	14	14	15	16	17	18	19	20	21	22	22	23	24	25	26	27
55	1	2	3	4	5	6	7	7	8	9	10	11	12	13	14	15	16	16	17	18	19	20	21	22	23	24	25	26	27	28
56	1	2	3	4	5	6	7	7	8	9	10	11	12	13	14	15	16	17	18	19	20	21	21	22	23	24	25	26	27	28
57	1	2	3	4	5	6	7	8	9	10	10	11	12	13	14	15	16	17	18	19	20	21	22	23	24	25	26	27	28	28
58	1	2	3	4	5	6	7	8	9	10	11	12	13	14	14	15	16	17	18	19	20	21	22	23	24	25	26	27	28	29
59	1	2	3	4	5	6	7	8	9	10	11	12	13	14	15	16	17	18	19	20	21	22	23	24	25	26	27	28	29	30

TABLE 5.–Correction to Tabulated Altitude for Minutes of Declination (cont'd)

31	32	33	34	35	36	37	38	39	40	41	42	43	44	45	46	47	48	49	50	51	52	53	54	55	56	57	58	59	60	d '
0	0	0	0	0	0	0	0	0	0	0	0	0	0	0	0	0	0	0	0	0	0	0	0	0	0	0	0	0	0	0
1	1	1	1	1	1	1	1	1	1	1	1	1	1	1	1	1	1	1	1	1	1	1	1	1	1	1	1	1	1	1
1	1	1	1	1	1	1	1	1	1	1	1	1	1	2	2	2	2	2	2	2	2	2	2	2	2	2	2	2	2	2
2	2	2	2	2	2	2	2	2	2	2	2	2	2	2	2	2	2	2	2	3	3	3	3	3	3	3	3	3	3	3
2	2	2	2	2	2	2	3	3	3	3	3	3	3	3	3	3	3	3	3	3	3	4	4	4	4	4	4	4	4	4
3	3	3	3	3	3	3	3	3	3	3	4	4	4	4	4	4	4	4	4	4	4	4	4	5	5	5	5	5	5	5
3	3	3	3	4	4	4	4	4	4	4	4	4	4	4	5	5	5	5	5	5	5	5	5	6	6	6	6	6	6	6
4	4	4	4	4	4	4	4	5	5	5	5	5	5	5	5	5	6	6	6	6	6	6	6	6	7	7	7	7	7	7
4	4	4	5	5	5	5	5	5	5	5	6	6	6	6	6	6	6	7	7	7	7	7	7	7	7	8	8	8	8	8
5	5	5	5	5	5	6	6	6	6	6	6	6	7	7	7	7	7	7	8	8	8	8	8	8	8	9	9	9	9	9
5	5	6	6	6	6	6	6	6	7	7	7	7	7	8	8	8	8	8	8	8	9	9	9	9	9	10	10	10	10	10
6	6	6	6	6	7	7	7	7	7	8	8	8	8	8	8	9	9	9	9	9	10	10	10	10	10	10	11	11	11	11
6	6	7	7	7	7	7	8	8	8	8	8	9	9	9	9	9	10	10	10	10	10	11	11	11	11	11	12	12	12	12
7	7	7	7	8	8	8	8	8	9	9	9	9	10	10	10	10	10	11	11	11	11	11	12	12	12	12	13	13	13	13
7	7	8	8	8	8	9	9	9	9	10	10	10	10	10	11	11	11	11	12	12	12	12	13	13	13	13	14	14	14	14
8	8	8	8	9	9	9	10	10	10	10	10	11	11	11	12	12	12	12	12	13	13	13	14	14	14	14	14	15	15	15
8	9	9	9	9	10	10	10	10	11	11	11	11	12	12	12	13	13	13	13	14	14	14	14	15	15	15	15	16	16	16
9	9	9	10	10	10	10	11	11	11	12	12	12	12	13	13	13	14	14	14	14	15	15	15	16	16	16	16	17	17	17
9	10	10	10	10	11	11	11	12	12	12	13	13	13	14	14	14	14	15	15	15	16	16	16	16	17	17	17	18	18	18
10	10	10	11	11	11	12	12	12	13	13	13	14	14	14	15	15	15	16	16	16	16	17	17	17	18	18	18	19	19	19
10	11	11	11	12	12	12	13	13	13	14	14	14	15	15	15	16	16	16	17	17	17	18	18	18	19	19	19	20	20	20
11	11	12	12	12	13	13	13	14	14	14	15	15	15	16	16	16	17	17	18	18	18	19	19	19	20	20	20	21	21	21
11	12	12	12	13	13	14	14	14	15	15	15	16	16	16	17	17	18	18	18	19	19	19	20	20	21	21	21	22	22	22
12	12	13	13	13	14	14	15	15	15	16	16	16	17	17	18	18	18	19	19	20	20	20	21	21	21	22	22	23	23	23
12	13	13	14	14	14	15	15	16	16	16	17	17	18	18	18	19	19	20	20	20	21	21	22	22	22	23	23	24	24	24
13	13	14	14	15	15	15	16	16	17	17	18	18	18	19	19	20	20	20	21	21	22	22	22	23	23	24	24	25	25	25
13	14	14	15	15	16	16	16	17	17	18	18	19	19	20	20	20	21	21	22	22	23	23	23	24	24	25	25	26	26	26
14	14	15	15	16	16	17	17	18	18	18	19	19	20	20	21	21	22	22	22	23	23	24	24	25	25	26	26	27	27	27
14	15	15	16	16	17	17	18	18	19	19	20	20	21	21	21	22	22	23	23	24	24	25	25	26	26	27	27	28	28	28
15	15	16	16	17	17	18	18	19	19	20	20	21	21	22	22	23	23	24	24	25	25	26	26	27	27	28	28	29	29	29
16	16	16	17	18	18	18	19	20	20	20	21	22	22	22	23	24	24	24	25	26	26	26	27	28	28	28	29	30	30	30
16	17	17	18	18	19	19	20	20	21	21	22	22	23	23	24	24	25	25	26	26	27	27	28	28	29	29	30	30	31	31
17	17	18	18	19	19	20	20	21	21	22	22	23	23	24	25	25	26	26	27	27	28	28	29	29	30	30	31	31	32	32
17	18	18	19	19	20	20	21	21	22	23	23	24	24	25	25	26	26	27	28	28	29	29	30	30	31	31	32	32	33	33
18	18	19	19	20	20	21	22	22	23	23	24	24	25	26	26	27	27	28	28	29	29	30	31	31	32	32	33	33	34	34
18	19	19	20	20	21	22	22	23	23	24	24	25	26	26	27	27	28	29	29	30	30	31	32	32	33	33	34	34	35	35
19	19	20	20	21	22	22	23	23	24	25	25	26	26	27	28	28	29	29	30	31	31	32	32	33	34	34	35	35	36	36
19	20	20	21	22	22	23	23	24	25	25	26	27	27	28	28	29	30	30	31	31	32	33	33	34	35	35	36	36	37	37
20	20	21	22	22	23	23	24	25	25	26	27	27	28	28	29	30	30	31	32	32	33	34	34	35	35	36	37	37	38	38
20	21	21	22	23	23	24	25	25	26	27	27	28	29	29	30	31	31	32	32	33	34	34	35	36	36	37	38	38	39	39
21	21	22	23	23	24	25	25	26	27	27	28	29	29	30	31	31	32	33	33	34	35	35	36	37	37	38	39	39	40	40
21	22	23	23	24	25	25	26	27	27	28	29	29	30	31	31	32	33	33	34	35	36	36	37	38	38	39	40	40	41	41
22	22	23	24	24	25	26	27	27	28	29	29	30	31	32	32	33	34	34	35	36	36	37	38	38	39	40	41	41	42	42
22	23	24	24	25	26	27	27	28	29	29	30	31	32	32	33	34	34	35	36	37	37	38	39	39	40	41	42	42	43	43
23	23	24	25	26	26	27	28	29	29	30	31	32	32	33	34	34	35	36	37	37	38	39	40	40	41	42	43	43	44	44
23	24	25	26	26	27	28	28	29	30	31	32	32	33	34	34	35	36	37	38	38	39	40	40	41	42	43	44	44	45	45
24	25	25	26	27	28	28	29	30	31	31	32	33	34	34	35	36	37	38	38	39	40	41	41	42	43	44	44	45	46	46
24	25	26	27	27	28	29	30	31	31	32	33	34	34	35	36	37	38	38	39	40	41	42	42	43	44	45	45	46	47	47
25	26	26	27	28	29	30	30	31	32	33	34	34	35	36	37	38	38	39	40	41	42	42	43	44	45	46	46	47	48	48
25	26	27	28	29	29	30	31	32	33	33	34	35	36	37	38	38	39	40	41	42	42	43	44	45	46	47	47	48	49	49
26	27	28	28	29	30	31	32	32	33	34	35	36	37	38	38	39	40	41	42	42	43	44	45	46	47	48	48	49	50	50
26	27	28	29	30	31	31	32	33	34	35	36	37	37	38	39	40	41	42	42	43	44	45	46	47	48	48	49	50	51	51
27	28	29	29	30	31	32	33	34	35	36	36	37	38	39	40	41	42	42	43	44	45	46	47	48	49	49	50	51	52	52
27	28	29	30	31	32	33	34	34	35	36	37	38	39	40	41	42	42	43	44	45	46	47	48	49	49	50	51	52	53	53
28	29	30	31	32	32	33	34	35	36	37	38	39	40	40	41	42	43	44	45	46	47	48	49	50	50	51	52	53	54	54
28	29	30	31	32	33	34	35	36	37	38	38	39	40	41	42	43	44	45	46	47	48	49	50	50	51	52	53	54	55	55
29	30	31	32	33	34	35	35	36	37	38	39	40	41	42	43	44	45	46	47	48	49	49	50	51	52	53	54	55	56	56
29	30	31	32	33	34	35	36	37	38	39	40	41	42	43	44	45	46	47	48	48	49	50	51	52	53	54	55	56	57	57
30	31	32	33	34	35	36	37	38	39	40	41	42	43	44	44	45	46	47	48	49	50	51	52	53	54	55	56	57	58	58
30	31	32	33	34	35	36	37	38	39	40	41	42	43	44	45	46	47	48	49	50	51	52	53	54	55	56	57	58	59	59

APPENDIX E. SIGHT REDUCTION WORKSHEETS

The following seven pages contain sight reduction worksheets that you are free to reproduce for your personal use. They are nearly identical to the ones used in the text, but have larger spacing and print for your convenience. The first two worksheets are designed to give a simplified sight reduction of the most common sight—the sun shot. The first of this set is designed to be used with either H.O. 249 or H.O. 229. The next is designed to be used for direct calculation using a hand calculator.

The next two are universal worksheets designed to accommodate all of the navigation celestial bodies, giving reminder comments indicating which items refer to which bodies. Again, the first of these two accommodates either the H.O. 249 or H.O. 229 tables, and the second of the two is for calculator use.

The fifth worksheet is for using the noon sun shot to find both latitude and longitude. It can also be readily adapted to any other meridian sight using the appropriate GHA adjustments and altitude corrections.

The next worksheet is for working a group of stars using H.O. 249, Vol. I. The last worksheet is for lunar distance sights from the sun. It also can easily be adapted to stars and planets by making the appropriate changes in GHA determinations and altitude corrections.

Sun Worksheet for H.O. 229 or H.O. 249

Limb		H_S	
Date		*index*	_____
UT		*dip*	_____
		H_A	
DR Lat		*Alt*	_____
DR Lon		H_o	_____
AP Lat			
AP Lon			
		GHA	
		m s	
dec		GHA	
		AP Lon	_____
H_{TAB}		$360°$	_____
d	_____	LHA	_____ (E+, W–)
H_c	_____		
H_o	_____		
	Z	_____	
	Zn	_____	

Sun Worksheet for Calculators

Limb
Date
UT

H$_s$
index
dip _____
H$_A$
Alt
H$_o$

DR Lat
DR Lon
AP Lat
AP Lon   STO[1]

GHA
m s
GHA
Lon _____ *(E+, W–)*
LHA _____   STO[3]

dec
d _____
dec   STO[2]

$\text{Cos } A = (\sin[2] - \sin[1] \sin[3]) / (\cos[1] \cos[3])$

LHA GT 180°, **Zn** = A =
LHA LT 180°, **Zn** = 360° – A =

$\text{Sin } H_C = \sin[1] \sin[2] + \cos[1] \cos[2] \cos[3]$

STO[3]

H$_C$
H$_o$ _____

Universal Worksheet For H.O. 249 or H.O. 229

Body
Date
UT

H$_s$
index
dip
H$_A$
Alt
U/L
Temp, P
H$_o$ HP   *(Moon)*

DR Lat
DR Lon
AP Lat
AP Lon

GHA   *(Aries for stars)*
m s
v   *(Moon, planets)*
GHA
SHA   *(Of Star)*
GHA
AP Lon   *(E+, W–)*
360°
LHA

dec _____ *(Not stars or H.O. 249)*
d
dec

H$_{TAB}$
d   X   / 60' =
H$_C$
H$_o$

Z
Zn

Universal Worksheet for Calculators

Body

Date

UT

H_s _____

index _____

dip _____

H_A _____

Alt _____

HP _____ (Moon)

U/L _____

Temp, P _____

H_o _____

STO[1]

DR Lat

DR Lon

AP Lat

AP Lon

dec _____

d _____ (Not stars)

dec _____

STO[2]

GHA _____ (Aries for stars)

m s _____

v _____ (Moon, planets)

GHA _____

SHA _____ (Of Star)

GHA _____

LON _____ (E+, W−)

LHA _____

STO[3]

$\sin H_C = \sin[1] \sin[2] + \cos[1] \cos[2] \cos[3]$ **STO[3]**

H_C _____

H_o _____

$\cos A = (\sin[2] - \sin[1] \sin[3]) / (\cos[1] \cos[3])$

LHA GT 180°, **Zn** = A   =

LHA LT 180°, **Zn** = 360° − A   =

Worksheet for Sun Meridian Lat & Lon

Limb	Date	Meridian time

dec
coH
Lat ———— (– If body north)

H_s ————
index
dip ————
H_A
Alt
Temp, P
–H$_o$ ————
coH **89° 60'**

GHA
m s
GHA $\overline{359°\ 60'}$ (– if >180°)
(E lon)
Lon

Star Worksheet for H.O. 249, Vol. I					
Date		DR Position			AP Lat
Star					
UT					
1 May					
12^d 2000^h					
m s					
GHAγ					
AP Lon					
LHA γ					
H$_C$					
Zn					
H$_S$					
index					
dip					
H$_A$					
alt					
H$_O$					
intercept					

Sun Lunar Distance Worksheet

Date:	Estimated UT:	

$H_A =$ $h_A =$ $LD =$

$SD_{SUN} =$ $SD_{MOON} = SD_{TAB} + 0.26' \sin(h_A)$

            $SD_{MOON} =$ $+ 0.26' \sin(\quad) =$

$LD_{SD} = LD + SD_{SUN} + SD_{MOON} =$ STO[3]

Sun SD alt correction: **Moon SD alt correction:**

H_A h_A

LL SD _____   LL SD _____

H_{SD} STO[1] h_{SD} STO[2]

STO[3] = ([3] − sin [1] sin [2]) / (cos [1] cos [2])

Full sun alt correction: **Full moon alt correction:**

H_A h_A

alt _____   main

H_O STO[1]   LL _____

                                h_O STO[2]

$\cos LD_O = \sin [1] \sin [2] + \cos [1] \cos [2] \times [3]$; $LD_O =$

Compute LD for   UT:

Sun GHA   dec   STO[1]

Moon GHA _____   dec   STO[2]

Diff GHA   STO[3]

$\cos LD_1 = \sin [1] \sin [2] + \cos [1] \cos [2] \cos [3]$; $LD1 =$

Compute LD for   UT:

Sun GHA   dec   STO[1]

Moon GHA _____   dec   STO[2]

Diff GHA   STO[3]

$\cos LD2 = \sin [1] \sin [2] + \cos [1] \cos [2] \cos [3]$; $LD2 =$

Interpolate for UT:

$\Delta T = 60 (LD_O - LD1) / (LD2 - LD1) =$

$\Delta T =$ $UT =$

APPENDIX F. CONCEPTS IN PLANE TRIGONOMETRY

Trig functions can be defined by the ratios of two sides of a right triangle. The definitions of the most common three—the cosine, sine, and tangent—are shown in Figure F.1. Because it's a bit of a job to calculate these ratios from scratch, nowadays they are computed by digital calculators or listed in tables. Even though these functions are defined here in terms of a plane right triangle, they crop up in numerous other applications—from celestial navigation to quantum mechanics.

Things to Remember. To get a feel for the equations of celestial navigation, we just need to recognize a few things about these sine and cosine functions. As can be seen in Figure F.2, and as can also be verified with a hand calculator:

The cosine is an even function of A; it's symmetric about A = 0. That is, $\cos(-A) = +\cos(A)$. The sine is an odd function of A; it's antisymmetric about A = 0. That is, $\sin(-A) = -\sin(A)$. And a few special values are important to know: $\cos(0°) = 1$, $\cos(90°) = 0$, $\cos(180°) = -1$, and $\sin(0°) = 0$, $\sin(90°) = 1$, $\sin(180°) = 0$.

If $\sin A = X$, then A is called the inverse sine of X, written as $A = \arcsin X$, or $A = \sin^{-1} X$. On a calculator, the inverse of sine X is obtained by entering the number X, followed by pressing the INV button, and then SIN. As seen from the sine curve above, between 0° and 360° there are two angles that have the same sine. The same is true for the cosine: there are two angles that have the same cosine. This means that all of the trig equations in Appendix A that are expressed as trig functions on the left side of the equations have two solutions for the angles.

The two angles with the same sine are A and $B = (180° - A)$. The inverse sine on a calculator only returns angles from −90° to +90°. The two angles that have the same cosine are A and $B = (360° - A)$. The inverse cosine only returns angles from 0° to +180°.

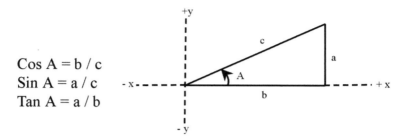

$$\text{Cos } A = b / c$$
$$\text{Sin } A = a / c$$
$$\text{Tan } A = a / b$$

Figure F.1 The definition of three common trig functions in terms of a right triangle's sides and the angle A.

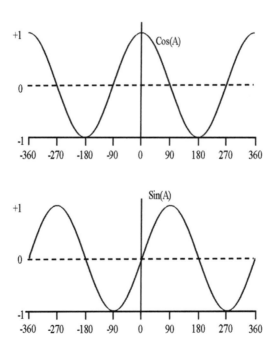

Figure F.2 Plots of cosine and sine versus the angle A, which is measured in degrees. The two curves are identical, except that the cosine leads the sine by 90°.

Appendix G. Sextant Arc Error Tables

The following tables are handy for checking sextant arc error. They give star-star arc distances adjusted for refraction by using the altitude of each star. You simply enter the table with the apparent altitudes (uncorrected for refraction) of each star, and extract the star-star distance that your sextant should read. The only correction needed is the sextant's index error.

The true unadjusted star-star distance is also given. The tabulated values of the refraction adjusted distances are the minutes above the whole degrees of that true distance. For example, entering the Bellatrix-Betelgeuse table with a star altitudes of 15° and 21°, we find 30.9´. So the sextant should read 7° 30.9´ after its index correction is made. Notice that the table is symmetric in the two star altitudes, as can also be seen from Equation 8.3.

Blank entries in the table are cases of geometry that have no solutions: either the difference in the coaltitudes is greater than the star-star distance, or the sum of the colatitudes is less than the star-star distance. These cases don't form the closed triangle used to calculate the altitude corrections (see Figure 8.2).

From inspection of the tables, it's apparent that the star-star distances are rather insensitive to the star altitudes; that the altitudes are only needed to the nearest whole degree; and that interpolation where needed, usually can be done mentally. Also a visible horizon is not needed because these altitudes can be directly computed from your known location and UT, or in some cases they can be found in H.O. 249, Volume I.

The star-star pairs have been selected to give arc distances across the 120° range of most sextants, and to cover a wide range of observer locations. Some consideration has been given to distributing the selected pairs throughout the year, but that was limited by the preceding two factors. The stars have also been selected for having low motion among themselves, called their *proper motion,* so that their star-star distances will not change significantly by 2025.

The main accuracy limitation is due to stellar aberration, which is a geometrical effect due to the component of the observer's velocity perpendicular to the light ray from the star. The direction of the light ray appears to shift forward in the direction of the observer's motion, just as the apparent wind does on a sailboat. The earth's most significant velocity is its orbital velocity about the sun. This orbital velocity of 29.8 km/sec compared to the 3×10^5 km/sec velocity of light, produces a maximum stellar aberration of 0.34´ of arc when the observer is traveling perpendicular to the line of sight to the star.

Since the angle between the observer's line-of-sight to the star and the earth's velocity depends on the earth's position in its orbit around the sun, the aberration depends on the time of year. Therefore, to make our tables independent of time, we have sacrificed correcting for aberration. (This is done by not using the earth-referenced coordinates in the Nautical Almanac, but by using so called *astrometric geocentric* coordinates for calculating the star-star distances.)

At any given time the apparent error of a given pair depends on how the star's individual aberrations combine in viewing their star-star distances. In some geometries the two aberrations partially cancel; in others they add, depending on the earth's velocity relative to the star directions. The maximum possible error is larger for larger star-star distances, finally reaching plus or minus 0.56' for Betelgeuse-Spica with their 113° star-star distance—and even then, only at very special viewing angles. In most cases the tabulated distances will be considerably better. Unless extreme accuracy is needed, these tables should be useful for checking your sextant's arc error.

On the other hand, for those wishing to push accuracy, this aberration problem can be directly solved by calculating your own refraction-corrected star-star distances for your observation time as discussed in Exercise 5.10.

Bellatrix – Betelgeuse
True Distance = 7° 31.8′

ALT	15	18	21	24	27	30	33	36	39	42	45	48	51	54	57	60	63	66	69	72	75	78	81	84	87
15	31.7	31.5	30.9																						
18	31.5	31.7	31.5	31.2																					
21	30.9	31.5	31.7	31.6	31.3																				
24		31.2	31.6	31.7	31.6	31.4																			
27			31.3	31.6	31.7	31.6	31.5																		
30				31.4	31.6	31.7	31.7	31.5																	
33					31.5	31.7	31.7	31.7	31.6																
36						31.5	31.7	31.7	31.7	31.6															
39							31.6	31.7	31.7	31.7	31.6														
42								31.6	31.7	31.7	31.7	31.6													
45									31.6	31.7	31.7	31.7	31.6												
48										31.6	31.7	31.7	31.7	31.7											
51											31.6	31.7	31.7	31.7	31.7										
54												31.7	31.7	31.7	31.7	31.7									
57													31.7	31.7	31.7	31.7	31.7								
60														31.7	31.7	31.7	31.7	31.7							
63															31.7	31.7	31.7	31.7	31.7						
66																31.7	31.7	31.7	31.7	31.7					
69																	31.7	31.7	31.7	31.7	31.7				
72																		31.7	31.7	31.7	31.7	31.7			
75																			31.7	31.7	31.7	31.7	31.7		
78																				31.7	31.7	31.7	31.7	31.7	
81																					31.7	31.7	31.7	31.7	31.7
84																						31.7	31.7	31.7	31.7
87																							31.7	31.7	31.7
ALT	15	18	21	24	27	30	33	36	39	42	45	48	51	54	57	60	63	66	69	72	75	78	81	84	87

Aldebaran – Bellatrix
True Distance = 15° 45.2'

ALT	15	18	21	24	27	30	33	36	39	42	45	48	51	54	57	60	63	66	69	72	75	78	81	84	87
15	44.9	44.8	44.5	44.2	43.8	43.3																			
18	44.8	44.9	44.8	44.7	44.4	44.1	43.7																		
21	44.5	44.8	44.9	44.9	44.9	44.5	44.3	44.0																	
24	44.2	44.7	44.9	44.9	44.8	44.6	44.4	44.2																	
27	43.8	44.4	44.7	44.9	44.9	44.8	44.7	44.5	44.4																
30	43.3	44.1	44.5	44.8	44.9	44.9	44.8	44.7	44.6	44.5															
33		43.7	44.3	44.6	44.8	44.9	44.9	44.8	44.7	44.6															
36			44.0	44.4	44.7	44.8	44.9	44.9	44.8	44.7	44.6														
39				44.2	44.5	44.7	44.8	44.9	44.9	44.9	44.8	44.7													
42					44.4	44.6	44.8	44.9	44.9	44.9	44.9	44.9	44.8	44.7											
45						44.5	44.7	44.8	44.9	44.9	44.9	44.9	44.9	44.8	44.8										
48							44.6	44.7	44.8	44.9	44.9	44.9	44.9	44.9	44.9	44.8	44.8								
51								44.6	44.8	44.9	44.9	44.9	44.9	44.9	44.9	44.9	44.9	44.8							
54									44.7	44.8	44.9	44.9	44.9	44.9	44.9	44.9	44.9	44.9	44.9	44.8					
57										44.7	44.8	44.9	44.9	44.9	44.9	44.9	44.9	44.9	44.9	44.9	44.9	44.9			
60											44.8	44.8	44.9	44.9	44.9	44.9	44.9	44.9	44.9	44.9	44.9	44.9	44.9	44.9	
63												44.8	44.8	44.9	44.9	44.9	44.9	44.9	44.9	44.9	44.9	44.9	44.9	44.9	44.9
66													44.8	44.8	44.9	44.9	44.9	44.9	44.9	44.9	44.9	44.9	44.9	44.9	44.9
69														44.8	44.9	44.9	44.9	44.9	44.9	44.9	44.9	44.9	44.9	44.9	44.9
72															44.9	44.9	44.9	44.9	44.9	44.9	44.9	44.9	44.9	44.9	44.9
75																44.9	44.9	44.9	44.9	44.9	44.9	44.9	44.9	44.9	44.9
78																	44.9	44.9	44.9	44.9	44.9	44.9	44.9	44.9	44.9
81																		44.9	44.9	44.9	44.9	44.9	44.9	44.9	
84																			44.9	44.9	44.9	44.9			
87																				44.9	44.9				
ALT	15	18	21	24	27	30	33	36	39	42	45	48	51	54	57	60	63	66	69	72	75	78	81	84	87

Aldebaran – Betelgeuse
True Distance = 21° 23.3'

ALT	15	18	21	24	27	30	33	36	39	42	45	48	51	54	57	60	63	66	69	72	75	78	81	84	87
15	22.9	22.9	22.7	22.4	22.1	21.8	21.4	21.1	21.5																
18	22.9	22.9	22.9	22.7	22.5	22.3	22.1	21.8	21.1	21.9															
21	22.7	22.9	22.9	22.9	22.8	22.6	22.5	22.3	22.1	21.9	22.1														
24	22.4	22.7	22.9	22.9	22.9	22.8	22.7	22.6	22.4	22.3	22.1	22.3													
27	22.1	22.5	22.8	22.9	22.9	22.9	22.8	22.8	22.6	22.5	22.3	22.4	22.4												
30	21.8	22.3	22.6	22.8	22.9	22.9	22.9	22.9	22.8	22.7	22.5	22.6	22.5	22.5											
33	21.4	22.1	22.5	22.7	22.8	22.9	22.9	22.9	22.9	22.8	22.7	22.7	22.6	22.5	22.6										
36	21.1	21.8	22.3	22.6	22.8	22.9	22.9	22.9	22.9	22.9	22.8	22.8	22.7	22.7	22.6	22.7									
39	21.5	21.1	22.1	22.4	22.6	22.8	22.9	22.9	22.9	22.9	22.9	22.8	22.8	22.8	22.7	22.7	22.7								
42		21.9	21.9	22.3	22.5	22.7	22.8	22.9	22.9	22.9	22.9	22.9	22.9	22.8	22.8	22.8	22.7	22.8							
45			22.1	22.1	22.3	22.5	22.7	22.8	22.9	22.9	22.9	22.9	22.9	22.9	22.8	22.8	22.8	22.8	22.8						
48				22.3	22.4	22.6	22.7	22.8	22.8	22.9	22.9	22.9	22.9	22.9	22.9	22.9	22.8	22.8	22.8	22.8					
51					22.4	22.5	22.6	22.7	22.8	22.9	22.9	22.9	22.9	22.9	22.9	22.9	22.9	22.9	22.9	22.9	22.8				
54						22.5	22.5	22.7	22.8	22.8	22.9	22.9	22.9	22.9	22.9	22.9	22.9	22.9	22.9	22.9	22.9	22.9			
57							22.6	22.6	22.7	22.8	22.8	22.9	22.9	22.9	22.9	22.9	22.9	22.9	22.9	22.9	22.9	22.9	22.9		
60								22.7	22.7	22.8	22.8	22.9	22.9	22.9	22.9	22.9	22.9	22.9	22.9	22.9	22.9	22.9	22.9	22.9	
63									22.7	22.7	22.8	22.8	22.9	22.9	22.9	22.9	22.9	22.9	22.9	22.9	22.9	22.9	22.9	22.9	22.9
66										22.8	22.8	22.8	22.9	22.9	22.9	22.9	22.9	22.9	22.9	22.9	22.9	22.9	22.9	22.9	22.9
69											22.8	22.8	22.9	22.9	22.9	22.9	22.9	22.9	22.9	22.9	22.9	22.9	22.9	22.9	22.9
72												22.8	22.9	22.9	22.9	22.9	22.9	22.9	22.9	22.9	22.9	22.9	22.9	22.9	22.9
75													22.8	22.9	22.9	22.9	22.9	22.9	22.9	22.9	22.9	22.9	22.9	22.9	22.9
78														22.9	22.9	22.9	22.9	22.9	22.9	22.9	22.9	22.9	22.9	22.9	22.9
81															22.9	22.9	22.9	22.9	22.9	22.9	22.9	22.9	22.9	22.9	22.9
84																22.9	22.9	22.9	22.9	22.9	22.9	22.9	22.9	22.9	22.9
87																	22.9	22.9	22.9	22.9	22.9	22.9	22.9	22.9	22.9
ALT	15	18	21	24	27	30	33	36	39	42	45	48	51	54	57	60	63	66	69	72	75	78	81	84	87

Zubenelgenubi – Antares
True Distance = 25° 8.3′

ALT	15	18	21	24	27	30	33	36	39	42	45	48	51	54	57	60	63	66	69	72	75	78	81	84	87
15	7.8	7.8	7.6	7.4	7.1	6.8	6.5	6.2	5.9																
18	7.8	7.8	7.8	7.7	7.5	7.3	7.1	6.9	6.6	6.4															
21	7.6	7.8	7.8	7.8	7.7	7.6	7.4	7.3	7.1	6.9	6.7														
24	7.4	7.7	7.8	7.8	7.8	7.7	7.6	7.5	7.4	7.2	7.1	7.0													
27	7.1	7.5	7.7	7.8	7.8	7.8	7.8	7.7	7.6	7.5	7.4	7.3	7.1												
30	6.8	7.3	7.6	7.8	7.8	7.8	7.8	7.8	7.7	7.6	7.5	7.5	7.4	7.3											
33	6.5	7.1	7.4	7.6	7.8	7.8	7.8	7.8	7.8	7.7	7.7	7.6	7.5	7.5	7.4										
36	6.2	6.9	7.3	7.5	7.7	7.8	7.8	7.8	7.8	7.8	7.7	7.7	7.6	7.6	7.5	7.5									
39	5.9	6.6	7.1	7.4	7.6	7.7	7.8	7.8	7.8	7.8	7.8	7.7	7.7	7.7	7.6	7.6	7.5								
42		6.4	6.9	7.2	7.5	7.6	7.7	7.8	7.8	7.8	7.8	7.8	7.8	7.7	7.7	7.6	7.6	7.6							
45			6.7	7.1	7.4	7.5	7.7	7.7	7.8	7.8	7.8	7.8	7.8	7.8	7.7	7.7	7.7	7.6	7.6						
48				7.0	7.3	7.5	7.6	7.7	7.7	7.8	7.8	7.8	7.8	7.8	7.8	7.7	7.7	7.7	7.7	7.7					
51					7.1	7.4	7.5	7.6	7.7	7.8	7.8	7.8	7.8	7.8	7.8	7.8	7.8	7.8	7.8	7.7	7.7				
54						7.3	7.5	7.6	7.7	7.7	7.8	7.8	7.8	7.8	7.8	7.8	7.8	7.8	7.8	7.8	7.8	7.7			
57							7.4	7.5	7.6	7.7	7.7	7.8	7.8	7.8	7.8	7.8	7.8	7.8	7.8	7.8	7.8	7.8	7.8		
60								7.5	7.6	7.6	7.7	7.7	7.8	7.8	7.8	7.8	7.8	7.8	7.8	7.8	7.8	7.8	7.8	7.8	
63									7.5	7.6	7.7	7.7	7.8	7.8	7.8	7.8	7.8	7.8	7.8	7.8	7.8	7.8	7.8	7.8	7.8
66										7.6	7.6	7.7	7.8	7.8	7.8	7.8	7.8	7.8	7.8	7.8	7.8	7.8	7.8	7.8	7.8
69											7.6	7.7	7.8	7.8	7.8	7.8	7.8	7.8	7.8	7.8	7.8	7.8	7.8	7.8	7.8
72												7.7	7.7	7.8	7.8	7.8	7.8	7.8	7.8	7.8	7.8	7.8	7.8	7.8	7.8
75													7.7	7.8	7.8	7.8	7.8	7.8	7.8	7.8	7.8	7.8	7.8	7.8	7.8
78														7.7	7.8	7.8	7.8	7.8	7.8	7.8	7.8	7.8	7.8	7.8	7.8
81															7.8	7.8	7.8	7.8	7.8	7.8	7.8	7.8	7.8	7.8	7.8
84																7.8	7.8	7.8	7.8	7.8	7.8	7.8	7.8	7.8	7.8
87																	7.8	7.8	7.8	7.8	7.8	7.8	7.8	7.8	7.8
ALT	15	18	21	24	27	30	33	36	39	42	45	48	51	54	57	60	63	66	69	72	75	78	81	84	87

Antares – Nunki
True Distance = 32° 33.6'

ALT	15	18	21	24	27	30	33	36	39	42	45	48	51	54	57	60	63	66	69	72	75	78	81	84	87
15	33.0	33.0	32.8	32.6	32.4	32.2	32.0	31.7	31.5	31.3	31.0														
18	33.0	33.0	33.0	32.9	32.7	32.6	32.4	32.2	32.1	31.9	31.7	31.5													
21	32.8	33.0	33.0	33.0	32.9	32.8	32.7	32.6	32.4	32.3	32.1	32.0	31.9												
24	32.6	32.9	33.0	33.0	33.0	32.9	32.8	32.7	32.7	32.5	32.4	32.3	32.2	32.1											
27	32.4	32.7	32.9	33.0	33.0	33.0	32.9	32.8	32.8	32.7	32.6	32.5	32.4	32.3	32.3										
30	32.2	32.6	32.8	32.9	33.0	33.0	33.0	32.9	32.9	32.8	32.8	32.6	32.6	32.5	32.5	32.4									
33	32.0	32.4	32.7	32.8	33.0	33.0	33.0	33.0	33.0	32.9	32.8	32.7	32.7	32.6	32.7	32.6	32.5								
36	31.7	32.2	32.6	32.8	32.9	33.0	33.0	33.0	33.0	33.0	32.9	32.8	32.8	32.7	32.8	32.7	32.6	32.6							
39	31.5	32.1	32.4	32.7	32.9	33.0	33.0	33.0	33.0	33.0	33.0	32.9	32.9	32.8	32.8	32.8	32.7	32.7	32.7						
42	31.3	31.9	32.3	32.5	32.7	32.8	32.9	33.0	33.0	33.0	33.0	33.0	33.0	32.9	32.9	32.9	32.8	32.8	32.8	32.8					
45	31.0	31.7	32.1	32.4	32.6	32.8	32.9	33.0	33.0	33.0	33.0	33.0	33.0	33.0	32.9	32.9	32.9	32.9	32.9	32.9	32.9				
48		31.5	32.0	32.3	32.5	32.7	32.8	32.8	32.9	33.0	33.0	33.0	33.0	33.0	33.0	33.0	33.0	33.0	32.9	32.9	32.9	32.9			
51			31.9	32.2	32.4	32.6	32.7	32.8	32.9	32.9	33.0	33.0	33.0	33.0	33.0	33.0	33.0	33.0	33.0	33.0	32.9	32.9	32.9		
54				32.1	32.3	32.5	32.6	32.7	32.8	32.9	33.0	33.0	33.0	33.0	33.0	33.0	33.0	33.0	33.0	33.0	33.0	33.0	32.9	32.9	
57					32.3	32.5	32.7	32.8	32.8	32.9	33.0	33.0	33.0	33.0	33.0	33.0	33.0	33.0	33.0	33.0	33.0	33.0	33.0	33.0	32.9
60						32.4	32.6	32.7	32.8	32.9	33.0	33.0	33.0	33.0	33.0	33.0	33.0	33.0	33.0	33.0	33.0	33.0	33.0	33.0	33.0
63							32.5	32.6	32.8	32.9	33.0	33.0	33.0	33.0	33.0	33.0	33.0	33.0	33.0	33.0	33.0	33.0	33.0	33.0	33.0
66								32.6	32.7	32.8	32.9	33.0	33.0	33.0	33.0	33.0	33.0	33.0	33.0	33.0	33.0	33.0	33.0	33.0	33.0
69									32.7	32.8	32.9	32.9	33.0	33.0	33.0	33.0	33.0	33.0	33.0	33.0	33.0	33.0	33.0	33.0	33.0
72										32.8	32.8	32.9	32.9	33.0	33.0	33.0	33.0	33.0	33.0	33.0	33.0	33.0	33.0	33.0	33.0
75											32.8	32.9	32.9	33.0	33.0	33.0	33.0	33.0	33.0	33.0	33.0	33.0	33.0	33.0	33.0
78												32.9	32.9	33.0	33.0	33.0	33.0	33.0	33.0	33.0	33.0	33.0	33.0	33.0	33.0
81													32.9	32.9	33.0	33.0	33.0	33.0	33.0	33.0	33.0	33.0	33.0	33.0	33.0
84														32.9	32.9	33.0	33.0	33.0	33.0	33.0	33.0	33.0	33.0	33.0	33.0
87															32.9	33.0	33.0	33.0	33.0	33.0	33.0	33.0	33.0	33.0	33.0
ALT	15	18	21	24	27	30	33	36	39	42	45	48	51	54	57	60	63	66	69	72	75	78	81	84	87

Antares - Spica
True Distance = 45° 54.3′

ALT	15	18	21	24	27	30	33	36	39	42	45	48	51	54	57	60	63	66	69	72	75	78	81	84	87
15	53.5	53.4	53.3	53.2	53.0	52.9	52.7	52.5	52.3	52.2	52.0	51.8	51.7	51.5	51.4	51.3									
18	53.4	53.5	53.4	53.4	53.3	53.0	52.9	52.8	52.6	52.5	52.4	52.2	52.1	52.0	51.9	51.9	51.8								
21	53.3	53.4	53.5	53.5	53.4	53.2	53.1	53.0	52.9	52.8	52.7	52.6	52.5	52.4	52.3	52.3	52.0	52.2							
24	53.2	53.4	53.5	53.5	53.4	53.3	53.3	53.4	53.1	53.0	52.9	52.8	52.7	52.6	52.6	52.6	52.5	52.5	52.5						
27	53.0	53.3	53.5	53.5	53.4	53.4	53.4	53.4	53.3	53.3	53.2	53.0	52.9	52.8	52.7	52.9	52.8	52.7	52.7	52.7					
30	52.9	53.2	53.3	53.4	53.5	53.5	53.4	53.4	53.4	53.3	53.2	53.1	53.0	52.9	52.9	52.9	53.0	52.9	52.9	52.9	52.8				
33	52.7	53.0	53.2	53.3	53.4	53.5	53.5	53.5	53.4	53.4	53.3	53.2	53.2	53.1	53.1	53.1	53.1	53.2	53.1	53.0	53.0	53.0			
36	52.5	52.9	53.1	53.4	53.4	53.5	53.5	53.5	53.5	53.5	53.4	53.4	53.3	53.3	53.3	53.2	53.2	53.2	53.2	53.2	53.2	53.1	53.1		
39	52.3	52.8	53.0	53.3	53.4	53.4	53.5	53.5	53.5	53.5	53.4	53.4	53.3	53.3	53.3	53.3	53.3	53.3	53.3	53.2	53.3	53.2	53.2	53.2	
42	52.2	52.6	52.9	53.1	53.3	53.4	53.4	53.5	53.5	53.5	53.5	53.4	53.4	53.4	53.4	53.4	53.3	53.3	53.3	53.3	53.3	53.3	53.2	53.2	53.2
45	52.0	52.5	52.8	53.0	53.2	53.3	53.4	53.4	53.5	53.5	53.5	53.4	53.4	53.4	53.4	53.4	53.4	53.4	53.4	53.3	53.3	53.3	53.3	53.3	53.3
48	51.8	52.4	52.7	53.0	53.1	53.3	53.4	53.4	53.4	53.5	53.5	53.5	53.5	53.5	53.5	53.4	53.4	53.4	53.4	53.4	53.4	53.4	53.4	53.3	53.3
51	51.7	52.2	52.6	52.9	53.1	53.2	53.3	53.4	53.4	53.4	53.5	53.5	53.5	53.5	53.5	53.5	53.5	53.4	53.4	53.4	53.4	53.4	53.4	53.4	53.3
54	51.5	52.1	52.5	52.8	53.0	53.1	53.3	53.4	53.4	53.4	53.4	53.5	53.5	53.5	53.5	53.5	53.4	53.4	53.4	53.4	53.4	53.4	53.4	53.4	53.4
57	51.4	52.0	52.4	52.7	52.9	53.1	53.2	53.3	53.4	53.4	53.4	53.4	53.5	53.5	53.5	53.5	53.5	53.4	53.4	53.4	53.4	53.4			
60	51.3	51.9	52.3	52.6	52.8	53.0	53.1	53.2	53.3	53.4	53.4	53.4	53.4	53.4	53.5	53.5	53.5	53.5	53.5	53.4					
63		51.8	52.3	52.6	52.8	52.9	53.1	53.1	53.2	53.3	53.3	53.4	53.4	53.4	53.4	53.4	53.4	53.4	53.5	53.5					
66			52.2	52.5	52.9	52.9	53.0	53.1	53.2	53.3	53.3	53.3	53.3	53.4	53.4	53.4	53.4	53.5	53.5	53.5	53.5				
69				52.5	52.7	52.9	53.0	53.1	53.2	53.2	53.3	53.3	53.4	53.4	53.4	53.4	53.5	53.5	53.5	53.5	53.5				
72				52.7	52.8	52.9	53.0	53.1	53.2	53.2	53.3	53.3	53.4	53.4	53.4	53.4									
75				52.7	52.8	53.0	53.1	53.1	53.2	53.3	53.3	53.4	53.4	53.4	53.4										
78						53.0	53.1	53.2	53.2	53.3	53.3	53.4													
81							53.0	53.1	53.2	53.2	53.2	53.3	53.4												
84									53.2	53.2	53.3														
87										53.2	53.3														

| ALT | 15 | 18 | 21 | 24 | 27 | 30 | 33 | 36 | 39 | 42 | 45 | 48 | 51 | 54 | 57 | 60 | 63 | 66 | 69 | 72 | 75 | 78 | 81 | 84 | 87 |

Bellatrix – Hamal
True Distance = 50° 29.2'

ALT	15	18	21	24	27	30	33	36	39	42	45	48	51	54	57	60	63	66	69	72	75	78	81	84	87
15	28.2	28.2	28.1	28.0	27.8	27.7	27.5	27.3	27.2	27.0	26.9	26.7	26.6	26.4	26.3	26.2	26.1								
18	28.2	28.2	28.2	28.1	28.0	27.9	27.8	27.7	27.6	27.4	27.3	27.2	27.1	27.0	26.9	26.8	26.7	26.6							
21	28.1	28.2	28.2	28.2	28.1	28.1	28.0	27.9	27.8	27.7	27.6	27.5	27.4	27.3	27.2	27.1	27.0	27.0	27.0						
24	28.0	28.1	28.2	28.2	28.2	28.2	28.1	28.0	27.9	27.9	27.8	27.7	27.6	27.5	27.4	27.3	27.3	27.2	27.2	27.2					
27	27.8	28.0	28.1	28.2	28.2	28.2	28.2	28.1	28.0	27.9	27.8	27.7	27.7	27.6	27.5	27.5	27.5	27.6	27.5	27.5	27.5				
30	27.7	27.9	28.1	28.2	28.2	28.2	28.2	28.2	28.1	28.0	27.9	27.8	27.8	27.7	27.7	27.7	27.6	27.8	27.7	27.7	27.8	27.6			
33	27.5	27.8	28.0	28.1	28.2	28.2	28.2	28.2	28.2	28.1	28.1	27.9	27.8	27.8	27.8	27.7	27.6	27.9	27.8	27.9	27.9	27.8	27.7		
36	27.3	27.7	27.9	28.1	28.2	28.2	28.2	28.2	28.2	28.2	28.1	28.0	28.0	27.9	27.9	27.8	27.7	28.0	27.9	28.0	28.0	27.9	27.9	27.9	
39	27.2	27.6	27.8	28.0	28.1	28.2	28.2	28.2	28.2	28.2	28.2	28.1	28.1	28.0	28.0	27.9	27.9	27.9	28.0	28.1	28.1	28.0	28.0	27.9	27.9
42	27.0	27.4	27.7	27.9	28.1	28.2	28.2	28.2	28.2	28.2	28.2	28.1	28.1	28.1	28.0	28.0	28.0	27.9	27.9	28.1	28.1	28.0	28.0	28.0	27.9
45	26.9	27.3	27.6	27.8	28.0	28.1	28.2	28.2	28.2	28.2	28.2	28.2	28.1	28.1	28.1	28.0	28.0	28.0	28.0	28.1	28.2	28.1	28.1	28.0	28.0
48	26.7	27.2	27.5	27.7	27.9	28.0	28.1	28.2	28.2	28.2	28.2	28.2	28.2	28.2	28.1	28.1	28.1	28.1	28.1	28.1	28.2	28.1	28.1	28.1	
51	26.6	27.1	27.4	27.7	27.8	28.0	28.1	28.1	28.2	28.2	28.2	28.2	28.2	28.2	28.2	28.1	28.1	28.1	28.1	28.1	28.2	28.1	28.1		
54	26.4	27.0	27.3	27.6	27.8	28.0	28.1	28.1	28.2	28.2	28.2	28.2	28.2	28.2	28.2	28.2	28.2	28.2	28.2	28.2	28.2	28.1			
57	26.3	26.9	27.2	27.5	27.7	27.9	28.0	28.1	28.1	28.2	28.2	28.2	28.2	28.2	28.2	28.2	28.2	28.2	28.2	28.2	28.1				
60	26.2	26.8	27.2	27.5	27.7	27.9	28.0	28.1	28.1	28.2	28.2	28.2	28.2	28.2	28.2	28.2	28.2	28.2	28.2	28.2					
63	26.1	26.7	27.1	27.4	27.6	27.8	28.0	28.1	28.1	28.2	28.2	28.2	28.2	28.2	28.2	28.2	28.2	28.2	28.2	28.2					
66		26.6	27.0	27.3	27.6	27.8	27.9	28.0	28.1	28.1	28.2	28.2	28.2	28.2	28.2	28.2	28.2								
69			27.0	27.3	27.5	27.7	27.8	27.9	28.0	28.0	28.1	28.1	28.1	28.2	28.2	28.2	28.2	28.2							
72				27.2	27.5	27.7	27.9	28.0	28.1	28.1	28.1	28.2	28.2	28.2	28.2	28.2	28.2								
75					27.5	27.8	27.9	28.0	28.1	28.1	28.2	28.2	28.2	28.2	28.1										
78						27.6	27.8	27.9	28.0	28.0	28.1	28.1	28.1	28.1											
81							27.7	27.9	28.0	28.0	28.1	28.1	28.1												
84								27.9	27.9	28.0	28.0	28.1													
87									27.9	27.9	28.0														

| ALT | 15 | 18 | 21 | 24 | 27 | 30 | 33 | 36 | 39 | 42 | 45 | 48 | 51 | 54 | 57 | 60 | 63 | 66 | 69 | 72 | 75 | 78 | 81 | 84 | 87 |

Betelgeuse – Regulus
True Distance = 62° 26.6′

ALT	15	18	21	24	27	30	33	36	39	42	45	48	51	54	57	60	63	66	69	72	75	78	81	84	87
15	25.4	25.4	25.3	25.2	25.0	24.9	24.8	24.6	24.5	24.3	24.2	24.1	23.9	23.8	23.7	23.6	23.5	23.4	23.3	23.3	23.2				
18	25.4	25.4	25.4	25.3	25.2	25.1	25.0	24.9	24.8	24.6	24.5	24.4	24.3	24.2	24.2	24.1	24.0	24.0	23.9	23.9	23.8	23.8			
21	25.3	25.4	25.4	25.4	25.3	25.3	25.2	25.1	25.0	24.9	24.8	24.7	24.6	24.6	24.5	24.4	24.3	24.3	24.2	24.2	24.1	24.1	24.1		
24	25.2	25.3	25.4	25.4	25.4	25.4	25.3	25.3	25.2	25.2	25.1	25.0	25.0	24.9	24.8	24.8	24.7	24.6	24.6	24.5	24.5	24.5	24.4	24.4	
27	25.0	25.2	25.3	25.4	25.4	25.4	25.4	25.4	25.3	25.3	25.2	25.2	25.1	25.0	25.0	24.9	24.9	24.8	24.8	24.8	24.7	24.7	24.7	24.7	24.7
30	24.9	25.1	25.2	25.3	25.4	25.4	25.4	25.4	25.3	25.3	25.3	25.2	25.2	25.1	25.1	25.0	25.0	25.0	24.9	24.9	24.9	24.9	24.8	24.8	24.8
33	24.8	25.0	25.2	25.3	25.4	25.4	25.4	25.4	25.4	25.3	25.3	25.3	25.3	25.2	25.2	25.1	25.1	25.0	25.0	25.0	25.0	25.0	25.0	25.0	
36	24.6	24.9	25.1	25.2	25.3	25.4	25.4	25.4	25.4	25.4	25.3	25.3	25.3	25.3	25.2	25.2	25.2	25.2	25.2	25.2	25.2	25.2	25.2		
39	24.5	24.8	25.0	25.2	25.3	25.3	25.4	25.4	25.4	25.4	25.3	25.3	25.3	25.3	25.3	25.2	25.2	25.2	25.2	25.2	25.2	25.2			
42	24.3	24.7	24.9	25.1	25.2	25.3	25.3	25.4	25.4	25.4	25.4	25.3	25.3	25.3	25.3	25.3	25.2	25.2	25.2	25.2	25.2				
45	24.2	24.6	24.9	25.0	25.2	25.2	25.3	25.4	25.4	25.4	25.4	25.4	25.3	25.3	25.3	25.3	25.3	25.3	25.3	25.3					
48	24.1	24.5	24.8	25.0	25.1	25.2	25.3	25.3	25.4	25.4	25.4	25.4	25.4	25.4	25.4	25.4	25.3	25.3	25.3						
51	23.9	24.4	24.7	24.9	25.1	25.2	25.2	25.3	25.3	25.4	25.4	25.4	25.4	25.4	25.4	25.4	25.4	25.4							
54	23.8	24.3	24.6	24.8	25.0	25.1	25.2	25.3	25.3	25.3	25.4	25.4	25.4	25.4	25.4	25.4	25.4								
57	23.7	24.2	24.5	24.8	25.0	25.1	25.2	25.2	25.3	25.3	25.3	25.4	25.4	25.4	25.4	25.4									
60	23.6	24.1	24.5	24.7	24.9	25.0	25.1	25.2	25.2	25.3	25.3	25.3	25.4	25.4	25.4										
63	23.5	24.0	24.4	24.7	24.9	25.0	25.1	25.2	25.2	25.3	25.3	25.3	25.4	25.4											
66	23.4	24.0	24.3	24.6	24.8	25.0	25.1	25.2	25.2	25.3	25.3	25.3	25.4												
69	23.3	23.9	24.3	24.6	24.8	24.9	25.0	25.1	25.2	25.2	25.3	25.3													
72	23.3	23.8	24.2	24.5	24.7	24.9	25.0	25.1	25.2	25.2	25.3														
75	23.2	23.8	24.2	24.5	24.7	24.9	25.0	25.1	25.1	25.2															
78		23.8	24.2	24.5	24.7	24.9	25.0	25.1	25.2																
81			24.1	24.5	24.8	25.0	25.1	25.2																	
84				24.4	24.7	24.8	25.0																		
87					24.7	24.8																			
ALT	15	18	21	24	27	30	33	36	39	42	45	48	51	54	57	60	63	66	69	72	75	78	81	84	87

Rigel – Regulus
True Distance = 75° 45.2′

ALT	15	18	21	24	27	30	33	36	39	42	45	48	51	54	57	60	63	66	69	72	75	78	81	84	87
15	43.7	43.6	43.5	43.4	43.3	43.2	43.1	42.9	42.8	42.7	42.5	42.4	42.3	42.2	42.1	42.0	41.9	41.8	41.8	41.7	41.6	41.6	41.6	41.5	41.5
18	43.6	43.6	43.6	43.6	43.5	43.4	43.3	43.2	43.1	43.0	42.9	42.8	42.7	42.6	42.5	42.5	42.4	42.3	42.3	42.2	42.2	42.1	42.1	42.1	
21	43.5	43.6	43.6	43.6	43.6	43.5	43.5	43.4	43.3	43.2	43.1	43.1	43.0	43.0	42.9	42.8	42.7	42.7	42.6	42.6	42.6	42.5	42.5		
24	43.4	43.6	43.6	43.6	43.6	43.6	43.5	43.5	43.4	43.4	43.3	43.2	43.2	43.1	43.1	43.0	43.0	42.9	42.9	42.8	42.8	42.8			
27	43.3	43.5	43.6	43.6	43.6	43.6	43.6	43.6	43.5	43.5	43.4	43.4	43.3	43.3	43.2	43.2	43.1	43.1	43.1	43.0	43.0				
30	43.2	43.4	43.5	43.6	43.6	43.6	43.6	43.6	43.6	43.6	43.6	43.5	43.5	43.4	43.4	43.3	43.3	43.2	43.2	43.2					
33	43.1	43.3	43.5	43.5	43.6	43.6	43.6	43.6	43.6	43.6	43.6	43.6	43.5	43.5	43.4	43.4	43.3	43.3	43.3						
36	42.9	43.2	43.4	43.5	43.6	43.6	43.6	43.6	43.6	43.6	43.6	43.6	43.5	43.5	43.5	43.5	43.4	43.4							
39	42.8	43.1	43.3	43.4	43.5	43.6	43.6	43.6	43.6	43.6	43.6	43.6	43.6	43.6	43.5	43.5	43.5								
42	42.7	43.0	43.2	43.4	43.5	43.6	43.6	43.6	43.6	43.6	43.6	43.6	43.6	43.6	43.6	43.6									
45	42.5	42.9	43.1	43.3	43.5	43.6	43.6	43.6	43.6	43.6	43.6	43.6	43.6	43.6	43.6										
48	42.4	42.8	43.1	43.2	43.4	43.5	43.6	43.6	43.6	43.6	43.6	43.6	43.6	43.6											
51	42.3	42.7	43.0	43.2	43.4	43.5	43.5	43.6	43.6	43.6	43.6	43.6	43.6												
54	42.2	42.6	42.9	43.1	43.3	43.4	43.5	43.6	43.6	43.6	43.6	43.6													
57	42.1	42.5	42.9	43.1	43.2	43.4	43.5	43.5	43.6	43.6	43.6														
60	42.0	42.5	42.8	43.0	43.2	43.3	43.4	43.5	43.5	43.6															
63	41.9	42.4	42.7	43.0	43.1	43.3	43.4	43.4	43.5																
66	41.8	42.3	42.7	42.9	43.1	43.2	43.3	43.4																	
69	41.8	42.3	42.6	42.9	43.1	43.2	43.3																		
72	41.7	42.2	42.6	42.9	43.0	43.2																			
75	41.6	42.2	42.6	42.8	43.0																				
78	41.6	42.1	42.6	42.8																					
81	41.6	42.1	42.5																						
84	41.5	42.1																							
87	41.5																								
ALT	15	18	21	24	27	30	33	36	39	42	45	48	51	54	57	60	63	66	69	72	75	78	81	84	87

Alpheratz – Betelgeuse
True Distance = 83° 32.0′

ALT	15	18	21	24	27	30	33	36	39	42	45	48	51	54	57	60	63	66	69	72	75	78	81	84	87
15	30.3	30.2	30.1	30.0	29.9	29.8	29.7	29.5	29.4	29.3	29.2	29.1	28.9	28.8	28.7	28.6	28.5	28.5	28.4	28.3	28.3	28.2	28.2		
18	30.2	30.2	30.2	30.2	30.1	30.0	29.9	29.8	29.7	29.6	29.5	29.4	29.3	29.2	29.2	29.1	29.0	29.0	28.9	28.9	28.8	28.8			
21	30.1	30.2	30.2	30.2	30.2	30.1	30.1	30.0	29.9	29.8	29.8	29.7	29.6	29.5	29.5	29.4	29.3	29.3	29.3	29.2	29.2				
24	30.0	30.2	30.2	30.2	30.2	30.2	30.2	30.1	30.0	29.9	29.9	29.8	29.7	29.7	29.6	29.6	29.6	29.5	29.5	29.5					
27	29.9	30.1	30.2	30.2	30.2	30.2	30.2	30.2	30.1	30.1	30.0	30.0	29.9	29.8	29.8	29.8	29.7	29.7	29.7						
30	29.8	30.0	30.1	30.2	30.2	30.2	30.2	30.2	30.2	30.1	30.1	30.0	30.0	29.9	29.9	29.9	29.8	29.8							
33	29.7	29.9	30.1	30.1	30.2	30.2	30.2	30.2	30.2	30.2	30.1	30.1	30.0	30.0	30.0	30.0	30.0								
36	29.5	29.8	30.0	30.1	30.2	30.2	30.2	30.2	30.2	30.2	30.2	30.1	30.1	30.1	30.1	30.1									
39	29.4	29.7	29.9	30.1	30.1	30.2	30.2	30.2	30.2	30.2	30.2	30.2	30.1	30.1	30.1										
42	29.3	29.6	29.8	30.0	30.1	30.2	30.2	30.2	30.2	30.2	30.2	30.2	30.2	30.2											
45	29.2	29.5	29.8	30.0	30.1	30.2	30.2	30.2	30.2	30.2	30.2	30.2	30.2												
48	29.1	29.4	29.7	29.9	30.1	30.1	30.2	30.2	30.2	30.2	30.2	30.2													
51	28.9	29.3	29.6	29.8	30.0	30.1	30.1	30.2	30.2	30.2	30.2														
54	28.8	29.2	29.5	29.7	29.9	30.0	30.1	30.1	30.2	30.2															
57	28.7	29.2	29.5	29.7	29.8	29.9	30.0	30.1	30.1																
60	28.6	29.1	29.4	29.6	29.8	29.9	30.0	30.1																	
63	28.5	29.0	29.3	29.6	29.8	29.9	30.1																		
66	28.5	29.0	29.3	29.5	29.7	30.0																			
69	28.4	28.9	29.3	29.5	29.8																				
72	28.3	28.9	29.2	29.5																					
75	28.3	28.8	29.2																						
78	28.2	28.8																							
81	28.2																								
84																									
87																									
ALT	15	18	21	24	27	30	33	36	39	42	45	48	51	54	57	60	63	66	69	72	75	78	81	84	87

Antares – Markab
True Distance = 104° 26.9′

ALT	15	18	21	24	27	30	33	36	39	42	45	48	51	54	57	60	63	66	69	72	75	78	81	84	87
15	24.4	24.4	24.3	24.2	24.1	24.0	23.8	23.7	23.6	23.4	23.3	23.2	23.1	23.0	22.9	22.8									
18	24.4	24.4	24.4	24.3	24.2	24.2	24.1	24.0	23.9	23.8	23.7	23.6	23.5	23.4	23.3										
21	24.3	24.4	24.4	24.4	24.3	24.3	24.2	24.1	24.1	24.0	23.9	23.8	23.7	23.7											
24	24.2	24.3	24.4	24.4	24.4	24.4	24.3	24.3	24.2	24.1	24.0	24.0	23.9												
27	24.1	24.2	24.3	24.4	24.4	24.4	24.4	24.3	24.3	24.2	24.1	24.1													
30	24.0	24.2	24.3	24.4	24.4	24.4	24.4	24.4	24.3	24.3	24.3														
33	23.8	24.1	24.2	24.3	24.4	24.4	24.4	24.4	24.4	24.3															
36	23.7	24.0	24.1	24.2	24.3	24.4	24.4	24.4	24.4																
39	23.6	23.9	24.1	24.2	24.3	24.4	24.4	24.4																	
42	23.4	23.8	24.0	24.1	24.2	24.3	24.3																		
45	23.3	23.7	23.9	24.1	24.2	24.3																			
48	23.2	23.6	23.8	24.0	24.1																				
51	23.1	23.5	23.7	23.9																					
54	23.0	23.4	23.7																						
57	22.9	23.3																							
60	22.8																								
63																									
66																									
69																									
72																									
75																									
78																									
81																									
84																									
87																									
ALT	15	18	21	24	27	30	33	36	39	42	45	48	51	54	57	60	63	66	69	72	75	78	81	84	87

Betelgeuse – Spica
True Distance = 113° 24.7'

ALT	15	18	21	24	27	30	33	36	39	42	45	48	51	54	57	60	63	66	69	72	75	78	81	84	87
15	21.8	21.7	21.6	21.5	21.4	21.3	21.1	21.0	20.9	20.7	20.6	20.5	20.3												
18	21.7	21.8	21.7	21.7	21.7	21.6	21.4	21.3	21.2	21.1	21.0	20.9													
21	21.6	21.7	21.7	21.7	21.7	21.6	21.5	21.4	21.3	21.2															
24	21.5	21.7	21.7	21.7	21.7	21.6	21.6	21.5	21.5																
27	21.4	21.6	21.7	21.7	21.7	21.7	21.6	21.6																	
30	21.3	21.5	21.6	21.7	21.7	21.7	21.7																		
33	21.1	21.4	21.5	21.6	21.7	21.7																			
36	21.0	21.3	21.5	21.6	21.7																				
39	20.9	21.2	21.4	21.5	21.6																				
42	20.7	21.1	21.3	21.5																					
45	20.6	21.0	21.2																						
48	20.5	20.9																							
51	20.3																								
54																									
57																									
60																									
63																									
66																									
69																									
72																									
75																									
78																									
81																									
84																									
87																									
ALT	15	18	21	24	27	30	33	36	39	42	45	48	51	54	57	60	63	66	69	72	75	78	81	84	87

APPENDIX H. DIP SHORT OF HORIZON

The table below gives the dip correction short of the natural sea horizon in minutes of arc for distances d in nautical miles, and for the height of the eye h in feet. The corrections are calculated from Equation 9.2, $Dip_s = 0.415767 \times d + 0.565786 \times h/d$. Notice that for each given height, the dip correction becomes constant when the distance reaches $d = 1.169\sqrt{h}$. At that distance the true horizon is visible, and the correction becomes equal to the standard correction given in the almanac, $0.971\sqrt{h}$.

Height

Dist	8	9	10	11	12	13	14	15
0.25	18.2	20.5	22.7	25	27.3	29.5	31.8	34.1
0.5	9.3	10.4	11.5	12.6	13.8	14.9	16	17.2
0.75	6.3	7.1	7.9	8.6	9.4	10.1	10.9	11.6
1	4.9	5.5	6.1	6.6	7.2	7.8	8.3	8.9
1.25	4.2	4.6	5.1	5.5	6	6.4	6.9	7.3
1.5	3.7	4	4.4	4.8	5.2	5.5	5.9	6.3
1.75	3.3	3.7	4	4.3	4.6	4.9	5.3	5.6
2	3.1	3.4	3.7	4	4.2	4.5	4.8	5.1
2.25	3	3.2	3.5	3.7	4	4.2	4.5	4.7
2.5	2.9	3.1	3.3	3.6	3.8	4	4.2	4.5
2.75	2.8	3	3.2	3.4	3.6	3.9	4.1	4.3
3	2.8	3	3.2	3.4	3.5	3.7	3.9	4.1
3.25	2.8	3	3.1	3.3	3.5	3.7	3.8	4
3.5	2.8	3	3.1	3.3	3.4	3.6	3.8	3.9
3.75	2.8	3	3.1	3.3	3.4	3.6	3.7	3.9
4	2.8	3	3.1	3.3	3.4	3.6	3.7	3.8

Appendix I. Sunrise/Sunset Azimuth Tables

The following table is constructed using our standard altitude equation with an altitude of –36.6′, which represents the zero altitude of the sun's center, corrected –33.8′ for refraction, plus a height-of-eye correction of – 2.8′ corresponding to 8.5 feet. (The effects of greater eye height would be negligible in practical cases.)

The table can be used for both the sun's upper and lower limbs with negligible error, except at polar latitudes. For example, at latitude N65° on the summer solstice, the sun will change its azimuth by as much as 4° as its disk moves from its center (the tabulated value) to one of its limbs. Furthermore, we can easily visualize that for sufficiently high altitudes and declinations the sun will never set, making the sun's azimuth sweep out 360° while never setting.

Sunrise/Sunset Azimuth from tabulated angle Z

North Latitudes	South Latitudes
Sunrise Zn = Z	Sunrise Zn = 180 – Z
Sunset Zn = 360 – Z	Sunset Zn = 180 + Z

DECLINATION SAME NAME AS LATITUDE

LAT	0	1	2	3	4	5	6	7	8	9	10	11	12	13	14	15	16	17	18	19	20	21	22	23	24	LAT
0	90	89	88	87	86	85	84	83	82	81	80	79	78	77	76	75	74	73	72	71	70	69	68	67	66	0
5	90	89	88	87	86	85	84	83	82	81	80	79	78	77	76	75	74	73	72	71	70	69	68	67	66	5
10	90	89	88	87	86	85	84	83	82	81	80	79	78	77	76	75	74	73	72	71	70	69	68	67	65	10
15	90	89	88	87	86	85	84	83	82	81	79	78	77	76	75	74	73	72	71	70	69	68	67	66	65	15
20	90	89	88	87	86	84	83	82	81	80	79	78	77	76	75	74	73	72	71	69	68	67	66	65	64	20
25	90	89	88	86	85	84	83	82	81	80	79	78	76	75	74	73	72	71	70	69	68	66	65	64	63	25
30	90	88	87	86	85	84	83	82	80	79	78	77	76	75	73	72	71	70	69	68	66	65	64	63	62	30
35	90	88	87	86	85	83	82	81	80	79	77	76	75	74	72	71	70	69	67	66	65	64	62	61	60	35
40	89	88	87	86	84	83	82	80	79	78	76	75	74	72	71	70	68	67	66	64	63	62	60	59	57	40
45	89	88	87	85	84	82	81	79	78	77	75	74	72	71	69	68	66	65	63	62	60	59	57	56	54	45
50	89	88	86	85	83	81	80	78	77	75	74	72	70	69	67	65	64	62	60	59	57	55	53	52	50	50
55	89	87	86	84	82	80	79	77	75	73	71	70	68	66	64	62	60	58	56	54	52	50	48	46	44	55
60	89	87	85	83	81	79	77	75	73	71	69	66	64	62	60	58	55	53	50	48	45	43	40	37	34	60
65	89	86	84	82	79	77	74	72	69	67	64	62	59	56	53	51	48	44	41	38	34	29	25	19	10	65
70	88	85	82	79	77	73	70	67	64	61	58	54	50	47	43	38	33	28	21	11						70
75	88	84	80	76	72	68	64	59	55	50	45	39	33	25	13											75
80	87	81	75	69	62	56	49	40	30	16																80

302

Sunrise/Sunset Azimuth from tabulated angle Z

North Latitudes	South Latitudes
Sunrise Zn = Z	Sunrise Zn = 180 − Z
Sunset Zn = 360 − Z	Sunset Zn = 180 + Z

DECLINATION CONTRARY NAME TO LATITUDE

LAT	0	1	2	3	4	5	6	7	8	9	10	11	12	13	14	15	16	17	18	19	20	21	22	23	24
0	90	91	92	93	94	95	96	97	98	99	100	101	102	103	104	105	106	107	108	109	110	111	112	113	114
5	90	91	92	93	94	95	96	97	98	99	100	101	102	103	104	105	106	107	108	109	110	111	112	113	114
10	90	91	92	93	94	95	96	97	98	99	100	101	102	103	104	105	106	107	108	109	110	111	112	113	114
15	90	91	92	93	94	95	96	97	98	99	100	101	102	103	104	105	106	107	108	109	110	111	112	114	115
20	90	91	92	93	94	95	96	97	98	99	100	101	102	103	104	105	106	107	108	109	110	111	112	114	115
25	90	91	92	93	94	95	96	97	98	99	100	101	102	103	104	105	106	107	109	110	111	112	113	114	116
30	90	91	92	93	94	95	97	98	99	100	101	102	104	105	106	107	108	109	111	112	113	114	115	116	118
35	90	91	92	93	94	96	97	98	99	101	102	103	104	106	107	108	109	111	112	113	114	115	117	118	119
40	89	91	92	93	95	96	97	99	100	101	103	104	105	107	108	109	111	112	113	115	116	118	119	120	121
45	89	91	92	94	95	96	98	99	100	102	103	105	107	108	109	111	112	114	115	117	118	120	121	123	124
50	89	91	92	94	96	97	99	100	102	103	105	107	108	110	111	113	115	116	118	120	121	123	125	127	128
55	89	91	93	94	96	98	100	101	103	105	107	109	110	112	114	116	118	120	122	124	126	128	130	132	134
60	89	91	92	94	96	98	100	101	103	105	107	109	111	113	116	118	120	122	124	126	128	130	132	134	143
65	89	91	93	96	98	101	103	106	108	110	113	115	118	121	123	127	132	135	138	142	146	150	154	160	
70	88	92	94	97	100	103	106	109	112	115	119	122	125	129	133	137	141	146	151	157					
75	88	92	95	99	103	107	111	116	120	124	129	134	140	146	154										
80	87	92	98	104	110	116	123	130	138	147															
LAT																									

1300   Shipmaster guides, called portolanos, began to appear in the Mediterranean, giving directions of rhumb lines, distances, and crude sketches of ports and coastal features.

1375   The development of nautical charts was a long and slow process, perhaps punctuated by the beautiful *Atlas Catalan* made in 1375 by the Jew Abraham Cresques of Majorca. Apparently this atlas still exists today. The advent of the mariner's compass is unclear. But Cresques had been referred to as "master of maps and magnetic compasses," so the mariner's compass must have appeared sometime in the fourteenth century. The Jews and Muslims were the intellectual powerhouse of Spain until the fall of Granada, in 1492, to the Catholic monarchs, Ferdinand and Isabella, who persecuted or expelled all the Jews and Muslims who wouldn't convert to Christianity.

1460   The concept of latitude and longitude dates back to Eratosthenes, in 150 B.C. But in the old world, latitude was of no great importance because of the narrowness of the Mediterranean. However, it became a significant concern when the Portuguese began their exploration down the coast of Africa. The first instruments to measure latitude were called quadrants and were graduated directly with the names of ports, not in degrees. They obtained their latitude directly by measuring the altitude of Polaris. During this period Polaris was some 3½° off the pole, so they simply calibrated their measurements with Polaris in the same location relative to the ship's meridian by using certain "guard" stars.

1474   Abraham Zacuto published one of the earliest tables of the sun's declination in a form useful to mariners, called *Almanach Perpetuum*.

1485   In 1481 the Portuguese started exploring south of the equator, rendering Polaris useless. With Polaris below the horizon in equatorial latitudes, another technique was needed. One approach was to use the sun on the meridian, the famous noon shot of marine lore. To use these noon shots of the sun, its declination must be tabulated, since it changes by the hour. An Englishman called Robert of Montpellier made the first sun declination tables in 1292–1295, but they did not become available to seamen until about 1485, when the noon sun sight made its debut.

1505   The same concept of the meridian sight, used on the noon sun shot, was applied to the Southern Cross, a dramatic constellation in the Southern hemisphere. Two stars of the cross, Acrux and Gracrux, almost lie on the same meridian (SHA = 173° 16.2′ and 172° 7.7′ respectively) so they measured the Altitude of Acrux (dec = S63° 7.6′ now) when Gracrux was directly above Acrux. Their ship's latitude was thus the declination plus the co-altitude (observing our sign conventions for latitude and declination). Furthermore, since Acrux's declination was a constant addition to all Acrux sights, they simply marked their instrument's arcs directly with the names of ports.

1514   Johann Werner proposed the cross-staff (sometimes call Jacob's staff) for marine use. But historians believe the cross-staff was invented by the Chaldean astronomers around 400 B.C. From ancient times, all kinds of gadgets were used to measure angles.

1533   John Aborough, master of the *Michael of Barnstaple*, mentioned the use of compasses onboard ship.

1598   King Philip III of Spain offered an award for the discovery of longitude.

1656   Benjamin Hubbard wrote the first American text on navigation, *Orthodoxal Navigation*.

1714   Longitude Act. British Parliament offered awards for providing a practical solution to finding longitude at sea. Three awards were offered, with amounts depending on the procedure's accuracy: £20,000 (millions of dollars in today's U.S. currency) for an error in longitude less than 30′, £15,000 for 40′ uncertainty, and £10,000 for 60′.

1734   Hadley designed an improved version of his octant, which is the basis of all modern sextants. My eighteenth-century Hadley-type octant is made out of something like ebony or lignum vitae with an ivory arc and vernier. Brass is used for the index arm and mirror fittings. The vernier can be read to one minute of arc. Even today, it seems to be accurate to within one minute, making it perfectly adequate for marine navigation after some 260 years!

1736   John Harrison's new clock, called H-1, performed well on a trial voyage to Lisbon aboard the *Centurion*.

1740   The *Centurion* sailed for the South Pole under Commodore George Anson without Harrison's new clock, the beginning of a longitudinal tail of woe. In March of 1741 a 58-day storm just west of Cape Horn delayed Anson's fleet. Scurvy killed six to ten men a day, and Anson lost five out of six ships in his fleet. On May 24 Anson arrived at the latitude of Juan Fernandez Island. Because he didn't know his longitude, he didn't know to go east or west! First he went four days west, then two days east. Then he hit the impenetrable, mountainous Chilean coast, so he had to turn west again. On June 9th he reached Juan Fernandez. He lost 80 lives while zigzagging for two weeks because he didn't know his longitude. This disaster emphasized the need for finding a solution to the longitude problem.

1759   Harrison finished H-4. H1 saw sea trials to Lisbon, Portugal. H2 never went to sea, and after about 20 years in the making, H3 went to sea trials in 1759.

1761   H-4 went to Jamaica on sea trials with Harrison's son, William. The much smaller H-4 lost only five seconds in two months!

1766   British astronomer Nevil Maskelyne published the first *Nautical Almanac* (for the year 1767). It's been published every year since.

1773   John Harrison received his last payment from Parliament of £8250. Even though the cumulative amount he received was about equal to the original £20,000 prize money, it was merely viewed as payments for his contributions and was never actually recognized as the longitude prize.

1774   Parliament passed a revised longitude act with more restrictive conditions.

1794   Captain Thomas Truxton wrote the first textbook published in America: *Remarks, Instructions, and Examples Relating to the Latitude and Longitude; also the Variation of the Compass, Etc.*

1802   Nathaniel Bowditch published his famous *New American Practical Navigator*, a revision of a text originally written by John Hamilton Moore and revised by still others.

1828   Parliament finally repealed the longitude act, and the longitude board disbanded.

1837   Sumner discovered his LOP, and published a pamphlet on it six years later. His method computes two different longitudes from two different assumed latitudes. Then he draws a straight line between these two points to form the LOP.

1855   The first American almanac, called the *American Ephemeris and Nautical Almanac*, was published by the U.S. Depot of Charts and Instruments.

1875   French Captain Marq de Saint Hilaire published the method we use today, calculating altitude and azimuth from one DR position.

1917   After the development of the marine chronometer, many tables for getting longitude from time sights started appearing around 1770. But the first altitude-azimuth tables for use in the St. Hilaire intercept method were made by John E. Davis and published in London in 1917.

1924   A radio direction finder (RDF) was placed aboard the ship *Olympics*.

1928   The U.S. Navy Hydrographic Office published H.0. 208, J. Y. Driesonstok's short tables, *Navigation Tables for Mariners and Aviators*.

1930   While a student at the Naval Academy in Annapolis, Arthur A. Ageton invented the short tables of logarithms for sight reduction.   These were published by the United States Hydrographic Office as H.O. 211.   Many related short tables were developed afterwards.

1936   With the advent of the first digital computers, The U. S. Hydrographic Office published the first precomputed sight reduction tables, H.O. 214, *Tables of Computed Altitude and Azimuth*. These nine volumes tabulated results to 0.1´ for whole degrees of latitude and hour angle, and for each half degree of declination.

1937   RDF came into widespread use to give radio bearing from the ship. Radar went to sea on the U.S.S. *Leary*.

1944   Many hyperbolic radio systems were developed after the war: Consol, Omega, Decca, and Loran, to name a few.

1947   After WWII, precomputed sight reduction tables for air navigation were developed for air navigation. Called H.O. 249, Volume I, was published in 1947. Later the more precise H.O. 229 was produced for marine navigation.

1950   Inertial guidance systems were developed by the military and later put into commercial use. Basically they use highly sensitive and stabilized pendulous gyros to measure accelerations that are continuously twice integrated to give distance and direction from the starting point. Hence these systems are independent of all outside signals.

1967   First commercial use of satellite navigation.

1980   Satellite navigation in the form of the GPS (Global Positioning System) came into widespread use by the general public. It gives range-range fixes from known satellite positions in earth orbits.

2005   You can now have a GPS receiver in your watch or buy a handheld one for as low as $129. But many navigators continue to learn and use celestial navigation, not only for GPS backup, but perhaps even more so, for the joy and satisfaction of guiding their vessels over the open oceans independently of external aids.

Appendix K. Annotated Bibliography

Celestial Navigation:

Bauer, Bruce, *The Sextant Handbook*, International Marine / McGraw-Hill, Camden, Maine, 1992. This is an excellent comprehensive book on sextants.

Blewitt, Mary, *Celestial Navigation for Yachtsmen*, International Marine, 1964. Blewitt's little book is a reader-friendly bare-bones treatment for the beginner. It's based on sight reduction by precomputed tables, mainly H.O. 249.

Bowditch, Nathaniel, *The American Practical Navigator*, National Imagery and Mapping Agency, 2002. With its roots dating back to 1794, this classic has been updated by so many authors and editors that it has lost some of its verve and appeal to readers of celestial navigation. Its comprehensive cover of modern navigation squeezes celestial navigation into a small part of the total volume. It uses H.O. 229 for sight reductions, but includes no excerpts of sight reduction tables for use with its examples. The book contains a large number of tables, including the log-trig tables used before the age of computers. It also has a large glossary of navigation terms.

Cunliffe, Tom, *Celestial Navigation*, Fernhurst Books, 1989. Cunliffe's book is similar to Blewitt's in content, presenting the standard H.O. 249 sight reduction using minimal concepts.

Cutler, Thomas J., *Dutton's Nautical Navigation*, 15th Edition, Naval Institute Press, 2004. This is another up-to-date, comprehensive, revised classic, similar to Bowditch. It treats the use of H.O. 229, H.O. 249 , and the Ageton short-table method; plus, it gives readers some insight to the Navy's STELLA celestial navigation computer program.

Grey, Leonard, *100 Problems in Celestial Navigation*, Paradise Cay Publications and Celestaire, Inc., 1999. This is a fine compilation of armchair celestial navigation problems that can be worked without actually taking sights. The exercises are organized into 19 vicarious worldwide cruises aboard a 37-foot ketch. You can work the sights using the excerpts provided from the *Nautical Almanac* and from H.O. 249, or by any other methods we've discussed. There is an emphasis on star shots, plotting fixes, and on realism, including sighting and timing errors that can occur in actual practice.

Meeus, Jean, *Astronomical Algorithms*, Willmann-Bell, 2000. This is not a book on how to do celestial navigation. Rather, among other things, this book gives the mathematical algorithms for computing the positions of all the navigational celestial bodies, useful for those interested in computing their own almanac data.

Morris, W. J., *The Nautical Sextant*, Paradise Cay & Celestaire (2010). The details of sextants—their makes and models, construction, repairs, and history—make this book invaluable for adjusting, repairing, and restoring these fine, enduring instruments.

Sight Reduction Tables:

Bayless, Allen C., *Compact Sight Reduction Tables (modified H.O. 211, Ageton's Table)*, Cornell Maritime Press, 1980.

Bennett, George G., *The Complete On-Board Celestial Navigator*, International Marine, 2003. Bennett offers a customized compact celestial navigation book that includes both a five-year almanac and specialized sight-reduction short tables. All data and calculations are to the whole minute of arc. As in all short-table methods, special rules are used for properly combining tabular values; these are somewhat complex, particularly for the azimuth.

Davies, Thomas D., *Concise Tables for Sight Reduction*, Cornell Maritime Press, 1984.

Davies, Thomas D., *Sight Reduction Tables for the Sun, Moon, and Planets: Assumed Altitude Method of Celestial Navigation*, Cornell Maritime Press, 1982.

NIMA Pub. No. 249 (previously H.O. 249), *Sight Reduction Tables for Air Navigation*, in three volumes. Volume I is for seven selected stars, Volume II for latitudes 0-40°, and Volume III for latitudes 39°-89°. Volumes II and III cover declinations 0°-29°, which is all that is needed for the sun, moon, and planets. Volume I comes with a CD-ROM. The air navigation tables are only tabulated to one minute of arc, while NIMA Pub 229 tabulates to one-tenth of a minute. Currently in stock at the Government Printing Office, but they have no plans to continue printing them. Her Majesty's *Nautical Almanac* Office publishes the same tables under the title *Rapid Sight Reduction Tables for Air Navigation* AP3270/NP303, Volumes I, II, and III.

H.O. 208 and H.O. 211 are out-of-print sight reduction short tables that you might be able to find on the used market.

NIMA Pub. No. 229 (previously H.O. 229), *Sight Reduction Tables for Marine Navigation*, in six volumes, each for 15° of latitude. Includes a CD-ROM of the tables for use on Macintoshes or PCs. Some, but not all, of these volumes are available from the Government Printing Office. Marine suppliers also provide both H.O. 229 and H.O. 249 at 90 percent of the original size. These versions are published by Celestaire, and at a lower price than the Government Printing Office.

Pepperday, Mike, *Celestial Navigation with the S Table: A Complete Sight Reduction Method for All Bodies in Nine Pages*, Paradise Cay Publications, Inc., 1992.

Schlereth, Hewith, *Sight Reduction Tables for Small Boat Navigation: Latitudes 0°-58°, Declination 0°-29°*, Seven Seas Press, 1983.

Websites:

A web search on celestial navigation will turn up hundreds of thousands of hits, including government agencies, chat rooms, blogs, marine suppliers, and publishers. Many of these sites are ephemeral, with changing web addresses, topics, and organization, including many of the ones listed below. If you can't find what you want, an internet search should help.

The National Geospatial-Intelligence Agency's website has one of the more interesting websites for navigators. It contains many free downloadable Adobe PDF files of interest to navigators, such as Bowditch, H.O. 229, H.O. 249, and others. It even has a celestial navigation calculator that you can use to solve the navigation triangle. Pilot charts of the world's oceans are divided into five ocean groups; each group has 12 charts, one for each month of the year. The web address is http://www.nga.mil/NGAPortal/MSI.portal (observe case).

The Astronomical Applications Department of the U.S. Naval Observatory (USNO) has a nice website at http://www.usno.navy.mil/USNO. It also has a celestial navigation calculator that gives H_o and Zn for an entered AP and UT. This calculator returns the altitude and zenith of all navigational bodies that are above the horizon at the specified AP and UT, regardless of whether their observation is practical (due to a lighted sky). Search on "celestial navigation data" to find this calculator and other relevant CN topics. In addition, this website contains many other interesting items on astronomy and celestial navigation, such as the star chart on the back cover of this book.

The National Institute of Standards and Technology has a website at http://tf.nist.gov/timefreq. It contains detailed information on their services, such as the format of their time-standard broadcasts, and their phone numbers for obtaining UT. You can also obtain the correct time from their animated clock at http://nist.time.gov/timezone.cgi?Central/d/-6/java.

Her Majesty's Nautical Almanac Office, a division of the UK Hydrographic Office, has a website at http://www.hmnao.com/nao with a large number of items interesting to CN navigators. Services similar to those on the USNO website include publications such as the

UK sight reduction tables (NP 303/AP 3270, equivalent to H.O. 249, and NP 401, equivalent to H.O. 229), several almanacs (including the UK nautical almanac), and even a sight reduction program that runs on a PC.

With many boats now carrying a laptop onboard, the website at http://www.navigation-spreadsheets.com has a real buy. More than 25 Excel spreadsheets are available at a nominal price.

At a website called NavList, hundreds of celestial navigation enthusiasts discuss a wide variety of topics related to celestial navigation and navigation in general, from history to navigation instruments of all kinds. You can search through an archive of over 25,000 posts for topics and images of interest to you. The address is http://fer3.com/NavList.

The Free Software Foundation (at www.fsf.org) offers a great program called "Stellarium." You can download it free at http://stellarium.org. This is a virtual planetarium, showing the location, as well as other information, on over a million astronomical objects, including stars down to the tenth magnitude. It's a great star chart for learning the night sky. Additionally, a stellar attraction for celestial navigators is that it reads out the altitude and azimuth of any object you point at, according to the time and location of your choice. This allows you to check your calculated and observed altitudes and azimuths independently. With this installed on a computer, you need only a sextant to start practicing celestial navigation—but only as a precursor to learning sight reductions.

History of Navigation:

Bowditch, Nathaniel, *The American Practical Navigator,* U.S. Navy Hydrographic Office, 1958 and 1962. These are identical editions, except that the 1962 edition contains corrections from the 1958 version. They contain a wealth of information for those interested in the history of celestial navigation.

Cotter, Charles, H., *A History of Nautical Astronomy*, Hollis and Carter, 1968.

Harding, Lewis A., *A Brief History of the Art of Navigation*, Willima-Frederick Press, 1952.

Leckey, Squire, T. S., *"Wrinkles" in Practical Navigation*, George Philips and Son, 1881. This is an amazingly good book; its eighteenth edition was published in 1917.

May, W. E., *A History of Marine Navigation*, W. W. Norton & Company, 1973.

Sobel, Dava, *Longitude*, Walker & Company, 1995. This short little book has made a mini splash in the book world with some nice reviews. It's mainly about the British longitude prize of 1714 and John Harrison's quest for making a chronometer that would provide GMT sufficiently accurate to fix longitude at sea to within 30 minutes of arc. It's an interesting, well-written story.

Taylor, E. G. R., *The Haven-Finding Art*, Abelard-Schuman, 1957.

Vanvaerenbergh, M. and Ifland, P., *Line of Position Navigation*, Unlimited Publishing LLC, 2003. This book contains a complete reprint of Captain Sumner's 1843 publication and a translation of St. Hilaire's 1873-75 articles, making it highly useful for anyone interested in the thinking of the fathers of the "new celestial navigation" (i.e., by lines of position). The authors provide detailed notes on the original publications that fill in potential gaps for the modern reader.

ABBREVIATIONS USED IN THE TEXT

A	azimuth angle used in direct computation
AP	assumed position (a geographical reference point)
codec	co-declination (also cd)
coH	co-altitude (also coalt)
coL	co-latitude
d	declination, declination increment
Dec	declination
DR	dead reckon
DSD	double second difference
EP	estimated position
FOV	field of view
GHA	Greenwich hour angle
GMT	Greenwich mean time
GP	geographical position (of celestial body)
GPS	global positioning system
GT	greater than
H	altitude (general, not specific)
H_A	apparent altitude
H_C	calculated altitude
H_O	observed altitude
HP	horizontal parallax
H_S	sextant altitude
H_{TAB}	tabulated altitude
kn	knot, knots (nautical miles per hour)
L	latitude (also Lat)
LD	lunar distance (in general)
LD_O	fully corrected lunar distance
LD_{SD}	semidiameter-corrected lunar distance
LAN	local apparent noon

Abbreviations Used in the Text

LHA	local hour angle
LL	lower limb
LMT	local mean time
Lon	longitude (sometimes L_1, etc.)
LonD	longitude difference
LOP	line of position
LT	less than
nm	nautical miles
PA	parallax
PLOP	point on the LOP
RBA	relative bearing angle
RFIX	running fix
SD	semidiameter
SHA	sidereal hour angle
UL	upper limb
UT	universal time
t	meridian angle
Z	azimuth angle used in tables
Zn	azimuth from true north
ZT	zone time

INDEX

INDEX

A (cont'd)

Atlas Catalan 304
augmentation 63, 120
azimuth 18, 19, 26, 196–198, 200–202, 206, 210–212, 219, 238
azimuth angle 18, 19, 26, 44
azimuth equation 48, 49, 197, 201–202, 238
azimuth rules 48, 196, 198

B

backlash 140
back sight 211
bearing angle 21, 112, 114, 230
Beaufort scale 186
Big Dipper 85
Bowditch, Nathaniel 30, 107, 108, 186, 188, 192, 212, 307, 310, 313, 314

C

calculated altitude 26
calculators 47–51, 191–194, 240–244
Cassiopeia 85–89
Celestaire, Inc. 33, 127, 190, 310, 311, 312
charts
    gnomonic (great circle) 305
    Mercator 28, 162, 175, 223, 230, 233
    pilot 184
    planet 73, 249
    star 60, 74, 75, inside back cover
Chichester, Francis 171
CHU 176
co-altitude 6–8
cocked hat 157–159
co-declination 16–18
co-latitude 16–18
collimation (see *sextant adjustments*)

INDEX

P (cont'd)

R

S

U (cont'd)

U.S. National Geospatial-Intelligence Agency (NGA) 184, 190
U.S. National Institute of Standards and Technology (NIST) 176, 313
U.S. Naval Observatory (USNO) 313

V

variation (see *magnetic*)
v-correction 61, 65, 216, 253
Venus 34, 59, 61, 65, 77, 78, 90, 156, 207
vertical circle 112, 113, 114, 226, 229
visible horizon 143, 239, 300

W

watch, error rate 176
whole horizon mirror (see *sextant*)
WWV 176
WWVH 176

XYZ

zenith 6, 74, 75, 113, 114
zone meridian 177

Other Books That May Be of Interest

2011 *Nautical Almanac*
100 Problems in Celestial Navigation
Celestial Navigation With the S Table
Emergency Navigation Card
Starfinder Book
The Nautical Sextant

These and many other books are available at
www.paracay.com and www.celestaire.com.